D0919241

Republicans, Negroes, and Progressives in the South, 1912–1916

Republicans, Negroes, and Progressives in the South, 1912–1916

Paul D. Casdorph

The University of Alabama Press
University, Alabama

Library of Congress Cataloging in Publication Data

Casdorph, Paul D.

Republicans, Negroes, and Progressives in the South, 1912-1916

Bibliography: p.
Includes index.
1. Southern States—Politics and government—1865–1950. 2. Republican Party—History.
3. Southern States—Race relations. 4. Progressivism (United States politics) I. Title.
F215.C267 324.2736'0975 80-15398
ISBN 0-8173-0048-1

Contents

Tables

For Barker

Preface

The central concern for all political parties in the American South following the Civil War has been the so-called Negro question. In the eleven
former Confederate states the Republicans more than any other political
group have been forced in their deliberations to grapple with the rightful
place of the Negro. Although the GOP occupied a minority status in a sea
of Democrats throughout the South in the decades following 1900, the
party was nonetheless influenced by Bourbon moves to bring about black
disfranchisement. As Democratic politicians in one state after another
barred the Negro from the polling booth, Republican organizations in all
of them divided into lily-white and black-and-tan factions. Many Republicans sought "respectability" by making their party all white in the aftermath of disfranchisement, while other GOP groups in the South continued
their traditional affiliations with the Negro after 1900. When Theodore
Roosevelt launched his famous Bull Moose crusade to challenge William
Howard Taft for the presidency and worked to build a viable white
opposition party in the region, it was inevitable that southern Republicans
would divide into warring camps. The Republican schism in the old
Confederacy was complicated by the lily-white–Negro struggle already
under way among southern Republicans for control of jobs handed out by
Republican administrations in Washington. An important outcome of the
titanic confrontation between the Roosevelt and Taft loyalists which this
book seeks to clarify is that both camps made it nearly impossible for the
Negro to continue his associations with the GOP after 1912. Though the
mass exodus of southern Negroes to the Democratic party did not come
until 1932, their departure was hastened by the conservative-progressive
fight for control of the GOP.

This monograph is a study of the disastrous schism in the Republican
party during 1912–1916 as manifested in the states of Alabama, Arkansas,
Florida, Georgia, Louisiana, Mississippi, North and South Carolina, Tennessee, Texas, and Virginia. It is not intended to be a study of Theodore
Roosevelt's Bull Moose campaign in the old Confederacy, but an account
of how the eleven GOP organizations in the South reacted to disruption of
the national party. Yet from the moment in late 1911 when Roosevelt
began to act like a contender for the 1912 Republican nomination, the
party in every southern state divided into contesting Roosevelt and Taft
factions. I spent countless hours poring over southern newspapers to map
out the 1912, 1914, and 1916 campaigns from the Republican-Bull Moose
point of view. Once the main outlines of the southern campaigns were
established from the oftentimes frustrating search through newspapers for
the merest notice of minority party activity, I augmented the study with
materials from various national and state manuscript collections and from
biographical data gleaned from libraries all over the South.

The fight among southern Republicans had a decided impact upon the 1912 nomination, and it caused both sides more anxiety than the party wars in any other section of the country. The mighty politicking by southern Republican leaders for control of the machines that sent delegations to national GOP conventions took place virtually unnoticed by the huge Democratic majorities in the South. Thus a major effort has been made to identify those white and Negro politicians and laymen in the South active in the Republican party during the period. Although their combined activities did much to determine who would be the Republican presidential nominee in 1912 and 1916, many of them had a stronger commitment to the federal patronage than to anything as abstract as national party principles. Republican presidents in this era of fledgling civil service reform gave federal jobs to the party faithful throughout the South before the election of Woodrow Wilson, and party leaders were eager to support the winning candidate in any Republican fight. The Roosevelt-Taft drive to secure control of the southern party was mostly an effort by local GOP functionaries to gauge the winner in advance. And because Democrats got control of the patronage-dispensing apparatus after 1913, the Progressive drive to build a white opposition party in the region was doomed to failure from the outset. Any nucleus for a new party was destroyed, when, like the Negroes, the renegade Republicans who followed the Bull Moose standard realized they could expect no favors when federal positions were handed out by future Democratic and Republican administrations.

My greatest debt of gratitude for help in compiling the manuscript must go to the innumerable librarians across the country who responded to my calls for materials. The sharp eye of a colleague, Ida F. Kramer of West Virginia State College, detected several faults in the early drafts, and for her scrutiny I am deeply grateful. Robert F. Maddox of Marshall University took time from his own writing to read the entire study and to offer more than a few suggestions for its improvement. The late Holman Hamilton, a great teacher and past president of the Southern Historical Association, listened attentively and offered sound advice on several matters. John Gable, executive director of the Theodore Roosevelt Association, likewise offered insights that proved helpful. Elizabeth Scobell, Marilyn Bushey, Ruthine Gee, Ron Wiley, and Michelle Koplove of the West Virginia State College Library helped in many ways by sending requests for library loans and by looking the other way when I needed special library privileges. Sue Forest and Sylvia Newman of the West Virginia College of Graduate Studies likewise responded cheerfully to my calls for library loans. Jesse Smith and Ann Shockley graciously opened the J. C. Napier Papers to me on a beautiful Saturday morning at the Fisk University Library in Nashville. Allen W. Jones, archivist at Auburn University, and Milo B. Howard, Jr., director of the Alabama State Department of Archives and History, acted promptly to make the last stages of the research much easier. And I wish to acknowledge in a special way the invaluable assistance of Lois Lunsford, former director of the Victoria College Library, who went beyond the "extra mile" in helping with the first phases of my work.

My father and mother, Newell D. Casdorph and Virginia Miller Casdorph, furnished more support, moral and otherwise, than any son has a right to expect. Finally, my work would have been infinitely more difficult without the devotion of my wife, Patricia Barker Casdorph, who helped in countless ways and who always provided an atmosphere that made my task easier.

PAUL D. CASDORPH
Charleston, West Virginia

Chapter 1

The Setting

Three weeks before Theodore Roosevelt was nominated for the presidency by the Progressive party after his humiliating rejection by the 1912 Republican National Convention, he wrote to his friend John M. Parker, New Orleans cotton broker and future governor of Louisiana: "I want to make as strong a fight as I know how in this business. Really if I could carry one of the eleven ex-Confederate states, I feel as though I could die happy." The South figured prominently not only in the memorable campaign that followed but also in the disastrous preconvention struggle for the nomination when Roosevelt and his chief rival, William Howard Taft, tore the GOP asunder in their quest for convention delegates. The two Republican giants made the entire region a battleground in 1912, and though Roosevelt and the Progressives fought mightily to build a white opposition party in the South, Thomas Woodrow Wilson and the Democrats carried all eleven states.[1]

Because southern politicians have been eager to preserve and strengthen the special interests of their region, attempts to win the American South have played a major role in presidential contests from the beginnings of the republic. Before 1865 their principal aim was the retention of chattel slavery, or, as it became known, "the peculiar institution," and after Appomattox their emphasis shifted to creation and maintenance of a social structure based upon white supremacy and a rigid separation of the races. The Democratic party, meeting little meaningful challenge from Republicans, Greenbackers, Populists, or Fusionists, became the sole vehicle for expressing this peculiarly southern view after 1876 when an alien Reconstruction terminated. Even so, as the new century approached, the ineffectiveness of the Republican party south of the Mason-Dixon Line prompted many southern politicos including John M. Parker to work at building a viable alternative party in the South—a party that would be attractive to "responsible whites" unwilling to join the GOP because of the lingering stigma of "Black Republicanism." Although many of these reformers joined the Bull Moose crusade in 1912 along with disgruntled Republicans seeking a new lease on their states' federal patronage, no real challenge was mounted against the Democratic colossus across the old Confederacy.

The Republicans did not threaten the Bourbon Democrats after Reconstruction because the "party of Lincoln" had become indelibly stamped on the southern mind as pro-Negro. Indeed, for a southern white to question the supremacy of the Democratic party was tantamount to being branded as "a renegade to race, to God, and to Southern womanhood." In the

South, only Tennessee had a Republican governor in 1912, Ben W. Hooper, elected on a Fusionist ticket with prohibition Democrats two years before; two members of Congress, Richard W. Austin and Sam R. Sells, from districts in the mountains of east Tennessee; and a single member of the Senate, the wealthy Chattanooga plow manufacturer, Newell Sanders, who had been appointed by Hooper following the death of Robert Love Taylor. A few Republicans served in state legislatures and held minor offices across the South. And the "fighting ninth" district of Virginia was represented in Congress by C. Bascom Slemp until he resigned to become personal secretary to President Calvin Coolidge. With these exceptions, the South remained a Democratic fiefdom, although a Republican organization of sorts was maintained in each southern state controlled primarily by Negroes and federal officeholders appointed by a nearly unbroken chain of Republican administrations after the Civil War.[2]

When the GOP divided itself nationally and in the South during 1912 into snarling Roosevelt and Taft factions, the 252 national convention delegates[3] from the eleven ex-Confederate states understandably played a key role in the preconvention maneuvering of both groups. Similarly, during the campaign proper, both Republican and Bull Moose candidates vied for the traditional sources of party strength: Negroes, who made up the bulk of party voters in the region and who were often recipients of courteous attention from northern party leaders at the approach of each national convention; southern federal officeholders, who were mostly white and who controlled many southern state organizations in league with Negro bosses after 1876; lily-white factions that had become increasingly powerful following disfranchisement and wanted the GOP to have a broader voter appeal in the South; and a handful of progressive-minded Democrats, opposed to the Bourbon-imposed status quo, who sought to break up the region's one-party politics. When the votes were counted, however, in this as other presidential canvasses, neither Roosevelt nor Taft had garnered a single electoral vote in the South; Wilson and the Democrats carried all but 46 of the total 1,051 southern counties.[4]

The historic schism within the ranks of Republicanism commenced when the close friendship and camaraderie that had bound President William Howard Taft and Theodore Roosevelt disintegrated quickly in the months following the Rough Rider's return from Africa and Europe. Although the broad outlines of that heroic yet tragic quarrel are well known, the dissolution of political ties between the president and former president was more than the severing of a personal bond. It produced, as all students of American politics know, a profound impact upon both major parties throughout the first half of the twentieth century. While the nation watched with disbelief, the two giants of the Grand Old Party succeeded in dividing Republicans North and South into hostile camps during the eighteen-month interval from June 1910 until January 1912, when Roosevelt resolved to make another bid for the White House.

Although an admiring public gave him a rousing welcome following his fifteen-month sojourn abroad, Roosevelt's homecoming was soon marred when he found his hand-picked successor wrestling with an ever-widening division among Republicans over the contending forces of progressivism and conservatism. And Taft was seemingly powerless to check the flow of events threatening to rip the party apart. When the former president became convinced that Taft was siding with conservatives and not adhering to the policies of his administration, he readily put himself forward as the champion of progressives everywhere. Roosevelt lost no time in beginning to act and talk like an active presidential candidate at the same time Taft was obliged to tell Archie Butt, his military adviser and confidant, that he and TR had come to a parting of the ways.

Long before the troubles of 1912, both Roosevelt and Taft had been disappointed in dealing with the South and particularly with the legitimate role of the Negro in the southern wing of the GOP. Each had faced an intolerable situation as president, seeking to placate the traditional if somewhat tenuous northern Republican commitment to Negro rights by appointing limited numbers of blacks to federal office in the South, while at the same time fending off vociferous charges of being a debased administration that subjugated Anglo-Saxons. Theodore Roosevelt had found himself most embroiled in what Willard B. Gatewood aptly termed "the art of controversy" in his relations with the South. He enjoyed boasting of close ties with the region because of his mother's Georgia birth and the distinguished service rendered by his Bulloch uncles in the Confederate army, but he also demonstrated an amazing ineptitude when attempting to cope with southern problems. Roosevelt was openly contemptuous of southern Democrats throughout his presidency, especially those in the United States Senate. Yet, shortly after entering the White House, he named a former governor of Alabama, Thomas G. Jones, to a federal judgeship on the advice of Dr. Booker T. Washington, who became his chief southern adviser on appointments and party strategy. But these conciliatory gestures were short-lived because of his own blundering and insensibility to southern mores. Ironically, instead of helping the Negro, Roosevelt actually contributed to the Negro's discomfort in an age of disfranchisement.[5]

The Rough Rider had been in the White House a scant four weeks when he extended his famous dinner invitation to Booker T. Washington in October 1901, thereby starting his troubles with the South. When Roosevelt realized that Washington was visiting in the capital with Whitefield McKinlay—a Negro officeholder from South Carolina who was later collector of customs at Georgetown in the District of Columbia and a member of the Taft camp during 1912—the meeting was arranged to court the nation's best-known Negro. TR had learned from Mark Hanna before 1904 the necessity of securing control of southern GOP organizations (these factions had guaranteed his vice-presidential nomination four years earlier) and he no doubt believed the counsel and support of Washington would be a valuable asset. But whatever his motives, the White House dinner with a Negro unleashed a barrage from southern politicians and newspaper editors. "Not since Lincoln had a President been so bitterly abused in the South," writes Dewey Grantham. One contemporary paper called the tête à tête "foolish" and warned that Roosevelt had "destroyed the kindly, warm regard and personal affection which had been growing up in the south." Although Washington maintained a discreet silence, the outburst plainly perplexed Roosevelt, who wrote in 1915 that the affair had been "misinterpreted by the white men of the South and by the black men of the South; and in the North it had no effect, good or bad."[6]

Roosevelt further infuriated the Bourbon South without offering real succor to Negroes by his actions in 1902–1903 concerning the black postmistress at Indianola, Mississippi. Mrs. Minnie Cox had been named postmistress of the Mississippi delta town with its significant Negro population by Benjamin Harrison and reappointed by William McKinley; by all accounts, she conducted her post office in a creditable manner and consistently received favorable reports from postal inspectors. Her position became untenable, however, when a group of whites attempted to capitalize on TR's efforts to reorganize the Republican party in other southern states by his recognition of lily-white groups and started a campaign for her removal. When physical threats were employed, Mrs. Cox resigned and moved with her husband to Birmingham, Alabama. Roosevelt faced an immediate crisis. He steadfastly refused to appoint a replacement for her and ordered postal services transferred to a neighboring town, thus subjecting himself to more abuse by southern Democrats. Although James K. Vardaman, editor of the Greenville *Commonwealth* and future U.S. senator from Mississippi, branded him a "political boll weevil pregnant with evil" and censured his "low down dirty and contemptible conduct . . . regarding the Indianola Post Office," Roosevelt answered his critics with a statement on "equal rights and the selection of public officials regardless of color." When Mrs. Cox refused to resume her duties, TR ultimately named a new postmaster and reopened the office, but his recognition of the need to reward Negroes in the southern GOP with office earned him the sneers of southern whites.[7]

While the Indianola affair was before the country, Roosevelt entangled himself in another controversy involving a southern Negro: Dr. William D. Crum, a prominent South Carolina physician, whom he appointed to the prestigious position of collector for the port of Charleston. The appointment, which was first sent to the Senate in December 1902, was an integral part of TR's bid for reelection in 1904. Crum, who was GOP committeeman for the district around Charleston and a delegate to every Republican national convention since 1884, had first attracted national attention when Harrison designated him postmaster at Charleston. White opposition to the appointment became so intense that Crum asked the president to find another nominee, and his close association with Harrison—whom he had supported at the 1884 National Convention—made him persona non grata in administration circles during the McKinley-Hanna years. Therefore, as Roosevelt sought to undo the southern machines put together by Hanna, Crum obviously became an asset. Similar appointments had been made in other parts of the South without fanfare, but the naming of a Negro to high federal office in the "Cradle of the Confederacy" soon resulted in a cause célèbre for southern senators, who began a campaign to block the nomination. A considerable controversy developed when the Senate withheld final confirmation until January 1905, although the president kept Crum in office by issuing temporary appointments. Roosevelt won the South Carolina delegation in the 1904 National Convention, but the problems with Crum produced some uneasy moments as the Negroes grew restive over the GOP-controlled Senate's slowness at overcoming southern objections to the confirmation.[8]

If the Crum affair pointed out the problem of keeping Republican ties with the Negro while attempting to attract Southern whites, the episode culminating in the discharge of black troops following a shooting spree at Brownsville, Texas, in 1906 caused national GOP leaders even greater anguish. An unknown number of troops from three companies of the Twenty-fifth U.S. Infantry stationed at Fort Brown on the Rio Grande supposedly shot up the town on the night of August 31, following a period of strife with local townspeople. Though eyewitnesses claimed to have seen black troopers firing in the melee, which resulted in the death of a bartender and the wounding of two others, not one soldier was ever tried, let alone convicted, in any court, civil or military. Their guilt or innocence remains a matter of conjecture. Yet several army documents did indict the men, and when none would speak out, Roosevelt ordered 160 of them cashiered from the service on the pretext that the army could not harbor criminals. Even though most southern whites applauded TR's swift action, the incident did not end with Roosevelt's second administration but had a far-reaching impact upon the GOP and its relation to Negroes, North and South. Taft, as secretary of war, found himself in the uncomfortable position of having to execute the discharges when Roosevelt left on an inspection tour of the Panama Canal, thereby incurring considerable Negro hostility himself; as late as 1912, Taft invited one of the discharged soldiers to travel about the country with him in an effort to win black votes.[9]

Roosevelt's response to these episodes as well as his lackadaisical attitude toward lynchings in the South should not be interpreted as an anti-Negro bias or even political expediency, but simply as impetuousness and hasty action. He did appoint blacks to office in a number of southern states, including Alabama and Georgia, where he retained Negro patronage referees, and he relied upon the advice of Booker T. Washington when considering southern appointments until he left the White House. Moreover, Roosevelt was able to gain enough Republican organizations in the South to capture the 1904 nomination—although the untimely death of Mark Hanna in February 1904 did not hinder his chances—and he was able to manipulate these same groups in 1908 to secure the nomination for Taft. Negro Republicans in the South had not fared as well from 1901 to 1909 as they might have, but Roosevelt had stood by Mrs. Cox and Dr. Crum. Though he leaned toward the budding lily-white movement, blacks remained with him in 1904 rather than support the Democratic party, then in the process of enacting disfranchising statutes in every southern state and still the party of Coleman L. Blease, Benjamin R. Tillman, and James K. Vardaman.[10]

After Taft became Roosevelt's favorite for the 1908 Republican nomination, most southern GOP organizations were more than anxious to support him even though Taft's attitude toward blacks—at least in terms of tangible benefits—was more negative than the colonel's. As the search for delegates was taking place, Taft was chagrined and repulsed at the mad rush for favor. The Republicans under Roosevelt may have been anything but pro-Negro and pro-South, yet southern members of the party, black and white, hungry for federal jobs, were willing to compromise principle for the economic benefits and social standing that came with administration approval. Taft's repugnance at this quadrennial thirst for preference caused him to reopen an issue that had plagued the party since 1860 regarding the number of delegates from the South to Republican national conventions. Although the South's electoral vote regularly went to the Democrats, each southern state sent sizable delegations to every GOP convention—and these delegations often cast the deciding vote for the party nominee and were usually for sale to the highest bidder. Thus aroused, the would-be president alienated much of the southern GOP during the 1908 preconvention campaign by declaring the region "a section of rotten boroughs . . . and that it would delight me if no southern state were permitted to have a vote in the National Convention except in proportion to its Republican vote."[11]

Southern influence was strong enough to vote down a proposal in the 1908 National Convention that would have significantly reduced the size of delegations from the region. The 240 delegates from the eleven ex-Confederate states chosen by an at-large and congressional district formula would have been cut to 84 under the new plan. R. H. Angell, a delegate from Virginia, pleaded for justice in the convention debates: "We ask that you do not treat us as the Democrats have treated us. By this action you would ratify what the Democrats have done in our state, and I ask you not to do it." Interestingly, his comparison of delegate curtailment to the disfranchisement movement was sufficient to block adoption of the measure by a vote of 471 to 506; all 240 southern delegates predictably voted against it. Thus the national GOP not only spurned a proposal by its next presidential candidate to limit the South's participation in its national conventions, but in doing so it agreed to continue having Negroes share in party deliberations and to keep paying lip service to southern Republicanism.[12]

Yet the southern delegates voted for Taft; he received 702 ballots and the nomination on the first roll call. In spite of strong sentiment for Roosevelt and a lengthy demonstration on the convention floor for a third-term nomination that was squelched by Senator Henry Cabot Lodge, Taft emerged as the clear choice of the party. Eight southern states—Alabama, Arkansas, Florida, Louisiana, Mississippi, North Carolina, Tennessee, and Texas—voted solidly for him, while the remaining three—Georgia, South Carolina, and Virginia—cast a scattered sixteen votes for Ohio Senator Joseph B. Foraker, Vice-President Charles W. Fairbanks, and Charles Evans Hughes of New York. Foraker, who got eleven of the sixteen southern ballots not cast for Taft, had recently been a thorn in the side of Roosevelt over the Brownsville affair, and his championing of Negro rights while demanding Senate investigation of the discharges no doubt accounted for his southern votes. In the November election, however, Taft received 321 electoral votes to 162 for William Jennings Bryan, although the Democrats swept the South. Although Bryan got the electoral vote of the region with 1,025,432 popular ballots to 505,428 for his Republican opponent, Taft managed to carry 153 counties in nine of the eleven states. They were located primarily in the Appalachian highlands of Virginia, Tennessee, Georgia, North Carolina, the German counties of central Texas and not in the Confederate South. Although he carried thirty-one more counties than Roosevelt had in 1904, it was nonetheless obvious that the Republicans under Taft could expect no favors from the Bourbons.[13]

Blacks, who still constituted the backbone of the southern party, voted for Taft in 1908, but the old coalitions were deteriorating rapidly, and, contrary to long tradition, no Negro was asked to make a seconding address in the national convention because of an expanding lily-whiteism in the South. Taft had been a careful observer of the furor surrounding the Crum affair and other southern appointments by his predecessor. He was convinced that Roosevelt's policies had contributed nothing to the Negro's well-being, and as president-elect he resolved to appoint no blacks to office "where the race feeling was strong." A small concession was made by assigning Negroes to office in the North and recognizing blacks with federal jobs in the Washington bureaucracies; later, he wrote that the "greatest hope the Negro has, because he lives chiefly in the south, is the friendship and sympathy of the white men with whom he lives in the community." Taft clearly abandoned the southern black early in his administration and, in doing so, notes Paolo Coletta, "he failed to see or follow the humanitar-

ian mission associated with the Republican party, with the result that
Negroes both North and South began to drift toward the Democratic
party."[14]

He set out on a thirteen-thousand-mile tour of the country after the
inauguration that gave the South its first exposure to the genial president.
Although Taft had bound himself to a no-win southern policy and es-
chewed the company of Negroes whenever possible, he was cordially
welcomed and received by most southerners throughout the journey. From
Winona, Minnesota, where he carelessly incurred the wrath of midwestern
Progressives by proclaiming the recently enacted Payne-Aldrich Tariff
"the best bill the Republican party ever passed," his speechmaking excur-
sion continued into Utah and California before entering Texas and the
South. En route from El Paso and a brief meeting with Mexican President
Porfirio Díaz, Taft told a trackside gathering at Del Rio, Texas, that his
junket was nonpartisan and that he was "going abroad trying to get
information as to the condition of the country and the needs of the
people." After a visit to Fort Sam Houston in San Antonio, which had
been under his direction while he was secretary of war, he traveled to his
brother's mammoth cattle ranch near Corpus Christi, where "he rode a
cow pony to a roundup of 1,300 head of cattle." On his way east, however,
the chief executive took time out to address the all-Negro student body at
Prairie View College in east Texas and condescendingly praised the state of
Texas for providing them with "a useful education."[15]

Taft chose to reaffirm his commitment to conservation when he arrived
in St. Louis on October 25 to join a flotilla of paddle-wheel steamers on a
four-day outing down the Mississippi, sponsored by the Lakes-to-the-Gulf
Waterway Association, an organization whose "pet project" was the
creation of a permanent channel from the Illinois River to the Gulf of
Mexico. At a gala banquet on the eve of the trip attended by Vice-
President James S. Sherman, Speaker of the House Joseph J. Cannon, and
Governors Charles S. Deenen of Illinois and Herbert S. Hadley of Missouri, the group's president, W. K. Kavanaugh, declared: "This personally
conducted journey of President Taft is being made to call [the nation's
attention] to the commercial necessities and possibilities of deepening the
river." Taft got in the spirit of things by voicing support for waterway
improvement and the meeting erupted in a storm of applause when he told
them it "was only part of a still greater movement inaugurated by Theodore Roosevelt and properly called by him the conservation of our natural
resources." Roosevelt's name, Taft was learning, could still bring forth
considerable enthusiasm, even in the South. The president was reportedly
tired when he arrived in New Orleans after brief stopovers in Memphis,
Helena, Arkansas, and Vicksburg; at New Orleans he spoke out for an
upgraded system of river navigation: "The waterways of this country must
be eventually used to carry the bulk of heavy merchandise."[16]

Taft stopped at Tulane University, where a chorus of four hundred students serenaded him with "Dixie" before he left on an automobile jaunt through the French Quarter with Alcee Fortier, noted Louisiana historian, who lectured him on local history. Then he traveled eastward into the deep South. At Jackson, Mississippi, he addressed large crowds at the state fair on November 1 and reiterated his view on the rightful place of the Negro in southern life. While speaking on the topic of "Agriculture and Farming," he called for a better method of educating farm laborers: "I am glad your large Negro population is well adapted to the cultivation of provident methods." He speculated that Negroes "may grow to be good citizens and useful to the community by acquiring land, as they have acquired it in the past, and become strong farmers and useful citizens to the entire state."[17]

The presidential entourage then moved through Alabama and Georgia to Savannah and Richmond, where Taft delivered a major address outlining his recommendations to the forthcoming Sixty-first Congress. It was a Progressive message in the Rooseveltian tradition, calling for conservation of national resources, increased acreage for national preserves, more money for water and soil conservation, additional laws for enforcing the antitrust statutes, greater power for the Interstate Commerce Commission, and formation of a postal savings bank; in closing, he called for government funding for a proposed memorial to Robert E. Lee. In this last speech before returning to the White House, Taft took time to remind his "immense audience" that after eight months in office he had faithfully carried out his practice of "showing respect for the South by appointing men to federal offices in the South whose appointments would commend themselves in the community where they live."[18]

Taft's blatant abandonment of the Negro left this segment of the southern GOP in an awkward position. With the Democrats denouncing Negroes and demanding their elimination from politics, blacks had little choice but to bite the bullet and remain in the Republican party. The Negro had married himself to the GOP after Appomattox and, although there had been great expectations in the beginning, it soon became obvious that national and regional GOP leaders would take his loyalty for granted. "By the 1880's," wrote Leslie H. Fishel, Jr., "separation had become difficult if not impossible, divorce out of the question, and those Negroes and whites with the most to gain from a continuance of the union kept reminding the colored man of his obligation to a party whose appeal was illusory, and whose most attractive quality was a memory." From 1896, when the Republicans controlled the presidency and both houses of Congress, until 1910, the party did nothing to fulfill its old promises; the McKinley, Roosevelt, and Taft administrations simply ignored enforcement of the Fifteenth Amendment, allowing the black franchise to remain at the mercy of the Bourbons but knowing perfectly well that the allegiances of the past would ensure the Negro's continued support of Republicanism. In the 1912 campaign, both Roosevelt and Taft were more than willing to play upon the inability of Negroes to find succor elsewhere.[19]

Yet definite advantages accrued to the Negro from his affiliation with the party. Many southern blacks felt an emotional reinforcement from association with the party of Lincoln; a few lucky ones were rewarded with meaningful positions as delegates to national conventions and as functionaries in state GOP organizations; and the federal service afforded some jobs even though both Roosevelt and Taft played down Negro appointments. In Mississippi the party boss, Lonzo B. Moseley, regularly arranged for Negroes to be selected as jurors in the federal courts in return for party service. Only in states where the lily-white faction controlled the party machinery were Negroes totally denied appointments. Norris Wright Cuney dominated the party in Texas until his death in 1896 and was collector of customs at Galveston, one of the best paying federal jobs in the South; Perry Howard of Mississippi was a leader in the state GOP and an assistant attorney general of the United States. Besides Booker T. Washington, who held no federal job but nonetheless derived great prestige from his association with TR, other Negroes held positions of influence in the party after 1900, including Joseph E. Lee, collector of customs at Jacksonville, Florida; Walter L. Cohen of Louisiana, recorder of deeds in the U.S. Land Office at New Orleans; Judson W. Lyons, who became register of the Treasury after the death of Blanche Kelso Bruce in 1898; Whitefield McKinlay, friend of Dr. Washington and collector of customs in the District of Columbia after 1910; and Henry Lincoln Johnson of Georgia, recorder of deeds in Washington, D.C. Finally, southern blacks took pride that two members of their race, Hiram Revels and Blanche K. Bruce, had served as Republicans in the United States Senate and that twenty others had represented the party between 1870 and 1901 in the House of Representatives.[20]

The officeholding faction of the southern GOP found themselves at the mercy of Roosevelt and Taft even more than the Negroes. Although presidents since Washington had attempted to control the dispensing of patronage, they were obliged to recognize the realities of politics and to consult with interested congressmen when making appointments. Because few southern Republicans sat in Congress after 1900, both Roosevelt and Taft could ignore congressional courtesy in all but a handful of districts when selecting such officials as postmasters, federal district attorneys, revenue collectors, customs officials, and federal marshals. That these appointees were totally dependent upon the administration for continuance in office in return for party loyalty during the early twentieth century was a foregone conclusion. The unique relationship between the southern officeholder and Republican administrations was underscored dramatically when Webster Flanagan made his famous "What are we up here for?" speech at the 1880 National Convention during a debate over inserting a pro-civil-service plank in the platform. Flanagan, a Texan who held a variety of federal appointments from 1870 until 1913, stated the dilemma of southern Republicans clearly when he asked why they served as convention delegates if not to be rewarded with jobs at home.[21]

Although Negroes received a few appointments, the officeholders were primarily white and made up a distinct faction within southern republicanism. The mere hint of patronage removal was enough to send terror into their hearts and helped Roosevelt in his unmerciful manipulation of the group to overthrow the organizations put together by Mark Hanna when he sought the 1904 nomination. Taft permitted the same pressures to be applied in 1908, and as soon as he was in office he withdrew congressional courtesy from a number of insurgents opposed to his policies; his stand on Negro appointments hardly needs reemphasis. Each southern state had a referee, who was usually state chairman or national committeeman, to oversee appointments and to report deviations in party loyalty to the White House. The referee also closely supervised the composition of delegations to GOP national conventions when they were chosen at district and state conventions and usually saw to it that they were top-heavy with officeholders. In 1912, when the classic misuse of the patronage was employed to secure the renomination of Taft, the twenty-man Mississippi delegation included twelve officeholders, while the Louisiana delegation of the same number had nine federal employees; the Georgia delegation had twenty officeholders out of twenty-eight delegates, including a recorder of deeds at Washington, D.C., one collector of internal revenue and his deputy, a former keeper of the Federal stores, eighteen postmasters or their close relatives, one United States marshal, and one U.S. commissioner. Other southern states had similar ratios, and all of them took great care to support the winning candidate for the party nomination.[22]

Lily-white groups, which first came into being during the 1880s as whites began to feel that continued Negro involvement with the party would hamper its growth, constituted a third component of southern Republicanism on the eve of the 1912 campaign. The drive to exclude blacks from the party in the South met with varying degrees of success in different states; a countering push that proved unsuccessful was launched by Negroes to have the movement squelched by sympathetic GOP leaders in the North. The deep-seated desire of Republican presidents after 1865 to win approval of the southern "white masses" created a favorable climate in which lily-whiteism could flourish. The name apparently originated at an 1888 Republican state convention in Texas when a group of whites attempted to put Negroes out of the meeting; Norris Wright Cuney, the Texas Negro leader, promptly labeled the insurgents lily-whites, and the term soon was applied to the Republican party in the entire South. Over time, various tactics were devised to drive the Negro out. After passage of Jim Crow laws across the South, the most favored plan besides packing GOP conventions with whites was simply to hold party functions in segregated facilities in order to deny admittance to Negroes.[23]

The first all-white Republican convention in North Carolina was held in 1902, when Jeter C. Pritchard, the lone Republican from the South in the United States Senate, became convinced that after disfranchisement in his state Negro support was no longer necessary for reelection. Thinking that Theodore Roosevelt favored the movement, he went to Alabama to confer with Democrats, eager to join the GOP except for the race issue. When a number of Alabama Republicans jumped on the bandwagon, holding a state convention with no blacks present, Negro leaders such as Booker T. Washington and Walter L. Cohen of Louisiana appealed to other Republican senators to repudiate both Pritchard and lily-whiteism. In Texas, the first Republican convention with whites only met in 1892, although Cecil A. Lyon, a close friend of TR from their Rough Rider days together, did not get complete control of the state party until 1902, when he was made state chairman. Lily-whites under Pearl Wight in Louisiana gained control of the patronage during Roosevelt's first administration, but Mississippi had no lily-white movement until the 1920s. In 1912, most of the lily-whites supported Roosevelt because Taft had relied increasingly upon the office-holders for his renomination effort in the South.[24]

A fourth group in the South, which contained a broad assortment of dissidents, including numerous Progressives who felt the region suffered because of its one-party politics, normally supported the party on some issues. Never large and composed mostly of antimachine Democrats and intellectuals such as John M. Parker and William Garrott Brown of North Carolina, this catchall grouping afforded little help in 1912 to Roosevelt or Taft. After flirting with TR and the Bull Moosers, most of them returned to the Democratic fold, voting for Wilson and his brand of progressivism.

Parker, a Mississippian by birth but a resident of New Orleans from 1871, entered politics after a successful business and civic career, during which he served as president of the New Orleans Board of Trade (1893), the New Orleans Cotton Exchange (1897–1898), and the Southern Commercial Congress (1908–1911). In 1910 he joined in formation of the Good Government League, a reform Democratic group opposed to the "Old Regulars" in Louisiana politics, which secured the election in 1912 of Judge Luther E. Hall as governor. Thereafter, Parker, who had known Roosevelt since the Spanish-American War, left the Democratic party in July 1912 to join the Bull Moose crusade and became his chief lieutenant in the South. He was able to capitalize upon discontent among Louisiana sugar planters over Democratic tariff policies to build one of the few Progressive party organizations in the country that could win elections. Parker gained considerable national attention from his consistent advice against Negroes assuming an active role in the new party and from his respectable but unsuccessful 1916 race for governor in Louisiana. Although he was nominated a few weeks later by the Progressive National Convention for the vice-presidency, he rejoined the Democrats when Roosevelt abandoned the Bull Moose cause. Following the nomination of Charles Evans Hughes by the Republicans, Parker campaigned alone for a few weeks before telling his followers to vote for Wilson. After serving as food administrator for Louisiana during World War I, he returned to reform politics within the Democratic party and subsequently won election as governor in 1920 following a vigorous campaign in which he charged the "Old Regulars" with "responsibility for corruption, gambling, and vice."[25]

William G. Brown, on the other hand, represented the view that a large part of the southern population leaned toward the Republicans and could overthrow the region's disastrous one party domination. Born in 1868 at the height of Reconstruction, Brown, the son of an Alabama banker, was educated at Howard College in his native state before receiving two degrees from Harvard in 1891 and 1892. He remained at Cambridge until 1902 as director of the university archives and as a lecturer in American history and earned a reputation as an intellectual and political commentator. Failing health, however, caused him to retire to the South, where he earned his living as a journalist for a number of national magazines including *Harper's Weekly*.

Settling at an Asheville, North Carolina, tubercular sanatarium, where he died in 1913 at age forty-five, he sought to employ his writing skills to build a strong Republican party in the South. Brown thought the southern branch of the GOP was corrupt and contained too many hangers-on greedy for federal jobs; he advocated that the way to beat Democrats was for southern Republicans to give up their policy of catering to the federal officeholders and their control of delegates to GOP conventions. Although overtures were made to Taft and other national leaders to implement his suggestions, it was obvious that Roosevelt's entry into the 1912 race forced Taft into courting the very southern delegates Brown had been condemning. He continued to urge a viable southern party during early 1912, but disenchantment with Taft and utter dislike for Roosevelt caused him to support Wilson in November, especially after he realized that his election would end the South's political isolation.[26]

In spite of all its disparate parts, southern Republicanism not only managed to weather the storms created by the Progressive movement in national politics, but it also elected thirteen men to Congress in the twelve-year period preceding the 1912 campaign. The South returned approximately one hundred members to each Congress in the decade after 1900, although never more than six in any one session were Republicans and all of those were from Virginia, North Carolina, and Tennessee. The Fifth-sixth Congress chosen in 1898 had eight GOP members from the South, including Richard A. Wise of Virginia, one time private in Jeb Stuart's cavalry, a physician, and former member of the state legislature;

Robert Bradley Hawley of Texas, who represented the district around Galveston for two terms and was chairman of the powerful House Committee on Military Affairs during the Spanish-American War; and Truman H. Aldrich of Alabama, a kinsman of Rhode Island Senator Nelson A. Aldrich and an influential coal and steel magnate. Three of the remaining five, including one Negro, were from North Carolina and two from the Appalachian counties of east Tennessee.[27]

A combined gerrymandering after the 1900 census and the loss of voting power by blacks through disfranchisement led to a reduction in the number of congressional Republicans from the South. Aldrich and Hawley, who had received help from the Populists, were defeated for reelection in 1900 when that source of electoral strength dried up after the turn of the century. Two North Carolinians, Edmund S. Blackburn and James M. Moody, as well as two Tennesseans, Henry R. Gibson and Walter P. Brownlow, were the only southern Republicans elected to the Fifty-seventh Congress. Blackburn and Moody were defeated in 1902 so that only Gibson and Brownlow from Tennessee along with Campbell Slemp of Virginia's ninth district served in the Fifty-eighth Congress; Blackburn won reelection in 1904 to join Slemp, Brownlow, and Nathan Hale of Tennessee, who replaced Gibson. In 1906, however, the total dropped to three with only Brownlow, Hale, and Gibson serving in the Sixtieth Congress. A revitalized lily-white movement in North Carolina elected three Republicans in 1908 on the coattails of Taft: John M. Morehead, who became state chairman and Taft's man in the state during the 1912 canvass; Charles H. Cowles, grandson of Governor W. W. Holden and longtime member of the North Carolina legislature; and John G. Grant, former sheriff of Henderson County and a state legislator. Their election with that of Brownlow, Richard W. Austin, a former United States marshal who had defeated Hale in the Tennessee primary, and Slemp made a total of six southern Republicans in the Sixty-first Congress. Morehead, Cowles, and Grant were plowed under in the landslide of 1910 that buried Republicans all over the country and produced the first Democratic Congress since Cleveland's second administration. In the South, only Austin, Sam R. Sells, who was elected to Brownlow's seat after his death in July 1910, and C. Bascom Slemp, son of Campbell Slemp, survived the debacle.[28]

More southern Republicans undoubtedly would have been returned to office except for the full impact of disfranchisement that swept the region after 1890–1892 as a result of GOP failure to accept the Force Bill sponsored by Henry Cabot Lodge of Massachusetts to protect the Negro ballot. Defeat of the bill, according to Stanley P. Hirshson, dramatized "a marked and sharp decline in the nature and degree of Republican interest in the Negro," and not until a generation later would the party pursue "an aggressive southern policy." The shift in national GOP strategy and a series of court cases upholding the first attempts at disfranchisement in Mississippi gave the Bourbons a clear field at crippling the black man as a viable political force, thereby effectively eliminating the Republican party from southern politics. The southern commitment to barring the Negro from the polling place was reinforced by "fusion" efforts between Populists and Republicans during the 1890s, when an attempt had been made to forge a new political coalition among the "lower orders," both black and white, who did not share the world view of the Democrats. Frightened by the Populist challenge and unrestrained by fears of retaliation from Washington, the Democrats quickly hobbled the traditional bulk of Republican strength in one southern state after another with such devices as the poll tax, grandfather clauses, all white primaries, and the literacy test.[29]

A genuine paradox, however, developed from the influence upon the South of the Progressive movement with its thrust toward a more widely based democracy at a time when the disfranchising impulse was rampant. Most scholars agree that the reform era associated with the movement in American political life extended from 1901, when Theodore Roosevelt, who came to typify the entire Progressive period, entered the White House, until 1917 and the country's involvement in World War I. A broad array of individuals and groups both political and humanitarian joined forces under the Progressive banner to work for a new order in American life. A major goal of the entire group was the regulation of business and economic affairs for the common welfare and rejection of the burgeoning social Darwinism of the late nineteenth century. Most southern states accordingly established railroad commisions to control public transportation and the extraction of natural resources during the period. They were able to secure other concrete reforms prior to 1920, including a modern banking system, a Postal Savings Bank, the direct election of United States senators, commissions to regulate transportation, adoption of an income tax amendment, woman's suffrage, and improvements in city and state government.[30]

Although some agrarian reforms were accomplished prior to 1900 in the South resulting from agitation by Greenback, Granger, Populist, and related farmer organizations, the region did not join in the drive for general political change until the new century. Progressivism in the South did not come about until "whites found peace and security of sorts in the elimination of black voters and the formal segregation of the races." Then, continues Jack Temple Kirby, "turning from this racial settlement, which they regarded as a great reform, they sought to improve their institutions and achieve 'progress' on a wide front." It was accomplished by a new kind of southern politician who gained prominence after the decline of Bourbon influence in what has been termed "the revolt of the rednecks." And, though the new politician was usually a demagogue and a race-baiter, many brought a measure of Progressive improvement to the South after it became clear that white Democrats could engage in factional struggles without the Negro being used as a "pawn" by opposing groups.[31]

Indeed, the whites-only aspect of Progressivism in the South presented the Republican party with some difficult choices, and the argument can be advanced that the party's failure to adopt a unified approach formed the basis for the southern GOP's division after 1900 into warring lily-white and black-and-tan factions. The lily-whites immediately recognized the advantages of disfranchisement and worked to drive the Negro from Republican ranks in an effort to make the party more presentable in southern eyes. At the same time, however, blacks took an understandable offense at both the Jim Crowism that accompanied Progressivism and the lily-white attack and started looking for their own salvation. Eventually, they went outside the Grand Old Party. This cleavage was very evident during the 1912 campaign, when the lily-whites alligned themselves behind the Progressive Roosevelt while the Negroes tended to support Taft.

The GOP congressmen from the South, although from three states, consistently voted against the Progressive wing of the party throughout the 1909–1917 period. All six, Morehead, Grant, Cowles, Brownlow, Austin, and Slemp, joined with six border state Republicans in opposition to Progressive legislation proposed by western and northern Insurgents during the Sixty-first Congress. Even the three North Carolinians put in office with lily-white support in 1908 rejected the Insurgent Republicans who yoked themselves with the Democrats during this Congress to enact several reform measures. The fights between regular Republicans and the Insurgent-Democrat combination found the southern GOP members staying loyal to the White House for both practical patronage and philosophical reasons. Furthermore, the three who survived the off-year election in 1910, Sells, Austin, and Slemp, energetically supported Taft in 1912. That the Insurgent-Progressives could expect no help from the southern Republicans, who presumably spoke for the party rank and file in the South, is illustrated by their voting records during three notable clashes in 1909–1910: the fight over national conservation policies, the drive aimed at curtailing the powers of Joseph G. Cannon as Speaker of the House of Representatives, and the move for downward revision of the tariff.[32]

The congressional insurgents made conservation a national issue after January 1910, when Taft deviated from the policies of his predecessor in their eyes by firing Gifford Pinchot as chief forester of the United States. Following 1872, when Congress authorized creation of Yellowstone National Park, the acreage set aside for parks and forest preserves had increased steadily until the total stood at nearly 200 million acres at the time Pinchot was dismissed. A number of historical sites and national monuments had been established under a 1906 act, and by 1911 an additional 84,000 acres had been placed under government control for that purpose. Theodore Roosevelt, with the devoted assistance of Pinchot, who had been appointed chief of the Bureau of Forestry in the Department of Agriculture by President McKinley, had withdrawn much of this land through his vigorous conservation policies and had worked for consolidation of the various government agencies overseeing the public lands. The former president wrote in his autobiography published in 1916 that his leadership in preserving the nation's resources had been his foremost contribution to domestic policy. For Taft, however, the concept of conservation had "become vague, well-nigh meaningless," although he supported Roosevelt's policies after he entered the White House, including speeches made on his 1909 trip through the South.[33]

But the South had not profited from Roosevelt's land withdrawals even though the southern GOP congressmen supported Taft's discharge of Pinchot and subsequent reversal of TR's freewheeling conservation tactics. Representatives from the South had been present at the 1908 White House Conference on Conservation, many of whom supported Roosevelt in 1912, and formation of the Inland Waterways Commission in 1907 had encouraged the states to join in long-range planning for water resource development. Yet only three national forests and no parks had been established by the beginning of the 1912 presidential campaign in two southern states: in Florida, the Ocala National Forest near Pensacola was authorized in 1908 with 647,970 acres; and the Arkansas and Ozark National Forests, both in Arkansas, were created in 1907 and 1908 with 1,262,390 and 963,500 acres, respectively. The South therefore had a mere 2,873,860 acres of a total 163,412,043 that had been set aside for 159 national forests in the continental United States. In addition, an insignificant acreage was controlled by the War Department as battleground parks and military cemeteries of the Revolutionary and Civil War periods.[34]

Even so, few southerners of either party seemingly took notice when Taft refused to reappoint Roosevelt's secretary of the interior, James R. Garfield, replacing him with Richard A. Ballinger, a former mayor of Seattle and a staunch conservative. Later, however, the entire nation watched aghast as Ballinger and the new administration permitted public lands in Alaska to be leased for private exploitation by the massive Guggenheim-Morgan interests, thereby contravening the earlier policies of Pinchot and Roosevelt. When Pinchot and Louis R. Glavis of the Public Land Office yelled foul play, conservation suddenly became a partisan issue and Insurgent Republicans joined with House Democrats in demanding a full investigation of all Bureau of Forestry practices. Their direct appeal to sympathetic Progressives in Congress understandably left Taft little choice but to dismiss both men even at the risk of precipitating a conservative-Insurgent confrontation. When a bill creating an investigating committee passed the House on January 20, 1910, with strong administration backing, all six GOP members from the South except Morehead, who was absent, supported the measure. The southern Republicans also voted with party regulars in a futile move to defeat an amendment to the bill by Insurgents and Democrats mandating that members of the committee be elected by the full House. Because the original bill had called for Speaker of the House Joseph G. Cannon, who was friendly to Taft and Ballinger, to designate the committee, adoption of the amendment was a decided victory for the Progressives. Yet southern Republican opposition to it reemphasized not only the conservative nature of the party in the South but also its inclination to support the administration whenever possible.[35]

The vote against Cannon and the regulars on the conservation question was part of a running battle being waged by House Insurgents to check the awesome powers of the Speaker; in the two or three elections prior to 1909 the issue had become known as Cannonism. "Uncle Joe" Cannon, who had represented an Illinois district almost continuously since 1872 and had been Speaker since 1903, ruled the lower chamber with an iron fist. Although liked personally by the most ardent Progressives, he used his extraordinary power as presiding officer to ward off any serious effort by Insurgent Republicans and Democrats to have their legislation enacted. Nor did House regulars, including the six southern Republicans, object to his unhesitating use of prerogatives such as controlling appointments to the all-powerful Rules Committee that determined the routine procedural order of the House, appointing only pro-administration members to key committees, personally selecting all committee chairmen, and selectively recognizing from the chair who could or could not have the privilege of the floor.[36]

The Progressive-administration dispute over Cannon came to a head during the Sixty-first Congress on March 19, 1910, when George W. Norris of Nebraska, an Insurgent who had been in Congress since 1903, spearheaded an attack against him. On a strictly procedural question and by first-rate parliamentary maneuvering, Norris was able to muster sufficient Progressive and Democratic votes to force passage of a resolution creating a new Rules Committee and barring the Speaker from membership on it, but 156 regulars including all but two of the southern Republicans (Brownlow of Tennessee, who had left the House because of an illness that would take his life within four months, and Slemp of Virginia, who was absent) voted to sustain Cannon and the administration. The "defrocking" of Cannon was thus accomplished without southern GOP support. "The Duke of Danville" immediately offered to resign as Speaker, and a Democrat, Albert Sidney Burleson of Texas, who would later become postmaster general under Woodrow Wilson, introduced a second resolution to throw him from the chair. But the fight had been primarily against the system rather than the genial Uncle Joe so that the partisan Democratic move to oust him was beaten back by the same Insurgents who had opposed him in the rules fight. Although southern Republicans predictably voted to keep him as presiding officer, one scholar of the period, Russell B. Nye, has observed, "The fact remained that the House struck a blow at Taft and the Republican machine. To the people Cannon represented boss rule and his defeat was a progressive victory."[37]

Earlier five of the six southerners sided with the administration when Taft called a special session of the Sixty-first Congress during the summer of 1909 to consider a revision of the tariff. A general movement led by Progressives and congressional Insurgents of both parties after 1900 had been leading toward a readjustment of the schedules to fit changed conditions with downward revision, although the GOP had made the protection of American industry an article of faith since the Civil War. The tariff had not been rewritten since McKinley's time, when the highly protective Dingley law of 1897 was drafted, so that Insurgent clamoring for reform had caused recurrent dissension within Republican ranks for more than a decade. Roosevelt had shied away from all tampering with the tariff during 1901–1909 because of a well-documented ignorance concerning economic matters, but growing demands for change forced a plank in the 1908 national party platform declaring "unequivocally for a revision of the tariff by a special session of Congress immediately following the inauguration of the next President." Taft accordingly interpreted this as a party mandate for downward revision throughout the campaign and in his inaugural address. Although Insurgents fought hard for a scaling down of tariff rates during the 1909 special session, the Payne-Aldrich bill finally passed into law was a product of endless deals and logrolling encounters between congressmen of every political stripe. The regulars generally supported protection, but every district had its own special interests, and F. W. Taussig, the acknowledged authority on U.S. tariff history, later wrote that "the act of 1909 brought no essential change in our tariff system; . . . the act finally enacted brought no real breach in the tariff wall, and no downward revision of any serious consequence."[38]

The regular-Progressive fight over passage of the Payne-Aldrich Tariff melted away in the House when the Insurgents voted for its passage, but not until they had made repeated attacks upon the schedules affecting their own constituencies. Moreover, after debates over the law began to reflect competition within the marketplace, the normally solid support of the southern Republicans for the administration was broken because they, too, represented special economic interests. The new tariff contained duties on four thousand items, and the raising or lowering of any one often influenced the economies of whole states and regions, including those in the South. Thus, Richard W. Austin of the second Tennessee district became the solitary southern Republican and indeed the only non-Democrat in the House to oppose the tariff because the duty on iron ore was lowered, threatening closure of several mines in east Tennessee. The *Congressional Record* indicates that he spoke out loudly during the debates, accusing

"Jim Hill of the Great Northern Railroad" of wanting to haul more Canadian ore into the country and "trust leaders in the East" of seeking "to open up and operate recently acquired ore lands in Cuba" at the expense of his district. But Walter P. Brownlow, his fellow congressman from Tennessee, made an impassioned speech on the floor defending both Taft and the new tariff, arguing that it would benefit the South and ultimately make the region an equal economic partner with the North. The remaining southern Republicans apparently agreed with Brownlow and, drawn by a fierce loyalty to the administration, voted for the bill to demonstrate anew the conservative flavor of southern Republicanism.[39]

But the reemergence of Theodore Roosevelt as a national political figure following his return from abroad in July 1910 soon upset the close bond between conservatives and the southern GOP. The former president sent out shock waves among all Republicans with his speech at Osawatomie, Kansas, two months later when he unflinchingly embraced the Progressive cause.

His doctrine of New Nationalism, which he spelled out for the first time, gave dissident party members in the South and elsewhere a rallying standard other than the administration's. The Kansas address, delivered at a dedication ceremony commemorating the exploits of John Brown, contained a veritable manifesto of Progressive demands: a strong military, regulation of corporations and penalties for offending business leaders, stronger conservation measures, a "Square Deal" for every citizen, a national tariff commission to streamline the tariff-making process, a national income tax, and a reorganized judiciary, among other reforms. Throughout the West and Midwest where the Insurgent impulse was strongest Roosevelt was received as a conquering hero, but conservative Republicans in other parts of the country, especially in the East and South, viewed his hurling the Progressive gauntlet with alarm.[40]

Nonetheless, Roosevelt embarked upon a lengthy speaking tour that took him into the South, where he seized every opportunity to expound his doctrine of putting "national need before sectional and personal advantage." After speaking in several Virginia towns, he defended the New Nationalism before a large crowd in Knoxville on October 7, telling them "that it was not revolutionary, but rather was designed to put a stop to things which might bring on a revolutionary movement if unchecked." Earlier, he told a Bristol, Virginia, audience that "bossism was the negation of democracy" because the political caciques were often in league with the monetary interests. The next day in Atlanta, Roosevelt again spoke about the New Nationalism although he said nothing about its relationship to southern politics. He clearly considered it a national issue and not a regional one. At the Arkansas State Fair in Hot Springs on October 10, however, he asserted that "the kind of legislation which was necessary 130 years ago is no longer sufficient to meet present needs." He also renewed his assault upon the possessors of wealth and demanded the elimination of privilege: "The mass of wealth such as some of our citizens possess is of such size that it is unsafe to leave the average citizen at his mercy. The New Nationalism doesn't mean anarchy and it doesn't mean socialism, and I don't attack the honest man of wealth when I attack the dishonest man; rather I stand up for the honest man." His message was clear: he demanded nothing short of a complete restructuring of national priorities. Roosevelt's brand of Progressivism was a far cry from the feeble call for improved conservation methods and elimination of the Negro from politics made by Taft during his trip through the South eleven months earlier.[41]

Although Roosevelt became increasingly critical of Taft and the administration after the Osawatomie speech, the real break did not develop until October 1911, when Attorney General George W. Wickersham initiated an antitrust suit against the United States Steel Corporation. Prosecution of the massive conglomerate for violation of the Sherman Antitrust laws centered around an allegation that, while president, TR had been misled into approving the purchase by U.S. Steel of the nearly defunct Tennessee Coal and Iron Company. The official suggestion that Roosevelt had been duped was more than the old campaigner could tolerate and he openly tore into Taft, criticizing the entire administration attempt at trustbusting. He further blistered the president for wanting to break up corporations for no reason other than size and with no thought of actual wrongdoing or violation of statute. This, he said, was wrong and contrary to both the Progressive spirit and the New Nationalism. His stance attracted many wavering Republicans and provided the final falling out with Taft.[42]

In the meantime, Roosevelt made a second thrust into the South during March 1911 as part of another whirlwind national speaking tour. "Just what is the subject of Col. Roosevelt's making a six thousand mile swing around the circle," editorialized the New Orleans *Picayune*, concluding that he was "making the tour preliminary to the next presidential campaign just to see how the land lies." Throughout the southern part of the trip, he regularly consulted with local GOP leaders, many of them out of favor with the administration, and often invited them to share the limelight. Two of his staunchest southern supporters in 1912, John M. Parker and Cecil A. Lyon of Texas, accompanied Roosevelt over a good portion of their states, and there is little doubt that he was already sounding them out regarding GOP support for another presidential bid.[43]

Roosevelt downgraded use of the phrase "New Nationalism" during his southern speeches, although he continued stressing the regulation of big business and related issues. While addressing the Southern Commercial Congress in Atlanta on March 9 on "The South's Obligation in Statesmanship and Business Endeavor," he called for "strict regulation of all industrial combinations" through "responsible legislation" and urged the

South to reap the full benefits of her abundant natural resources. Taft, who spoke to the assemblage one day later, entreated the "young men of the New South to take up the political issues of the day from a broad and liberal standpoint, and to eliminate from their consideration all narrow partisanship and sectionalism." The president withdrew to the Augusta Country Club for a golf outing as TR sped across the South delivering speeches in Alabama, Mississippi, Louisiana, and Texas. Throughout, he sounded the theme of civic responsibility and the citizen's duty to ensure good government; in New Orleans, where Roosevelt addressed a large audience on civic righteousness, the desirability of large families, and "honesty in business and in all dealings among men," he refused to say one word about politics or his own plans for the future. In Houston, Texas, however, where he addressed an estimated forty thousand persons, the Rough Rider chose to answer the persistent questioning by reporters about his reasons for the southern trip: "He had long made up his mind," reported the Dallas *Morning News,* "that after coming back from Africa and Europe, where he enjoyed everything from lions to kings, he wanted to have a chance to go around the country, and, if possible, to say 'howdy' and 'thank you.' For, he observed, any man who had been President of the American people remains forever their debtor."[44]

Although Roosevelt maintained a public aloofness regarding another presidential candidacy, his correspondence and talks with party leaders nationally and in the South reflect an unmistakable willingness to reenter the White House. And his increased activity throughout the remaining months of 1911 caused considerable soul-searching among the normally conservative Republicans in the South. The administration could no longer count on the unqualified support of the southern party with TR talking and acting like a viable candidate. Negroes, lily-whites, dreamy-eyed visionaries, federal officeholders, antiadministration men, administration henchmen, and Republicans of every persuasion would be forced to take sides as the Roosevelt-Taft imbroglio intensified with the approach of 1912.

Chapter 2

"My Hat Is in the Ring": The Upper South

In retrospect there appears little doubt that Theodore Roosevelt had resolved by early January—or perhaps even before the first of the year—to contest Taft for the presidency in November 1912. Even though his actual declaration of candidacy did not come until February 22, both Roosevelt and Taft were laying the groundwork for a preconvention campaign across the South by the first of January. Both realized that the eleven ex-Confederate states would figure heavily in the eventual outcome. While Roosevelt and his agents were courting and cajoling southern Republican leaders well before the country knew of his candidacy, Will Taft and the standpatters were doing the same. The president was efficiently and methodically corraling favorable delegations from the region to the forthcoming Republican National Convention.

As the Progressive elements in the party turned to Wisconsin Senator Robert M. La Follette and, finally, to Theodore Roosevelt, the beleaguered Taft had little alternative but to go to the conservative old guard—to such men as Nelson Aldrich of Rhode Island and entrenched federal officeholders in the South whose "rotten boroughs" could be manipulated from Washington. Roosevelt's Osawatomie speech, with its call for a New Nationalism and sweeping social realignments, had alarmed the president, driving him further in the direction of standpat elements within the GOP. Taft, whom TR had once considered a safe Progressive, wrote to an old friend as the 1912 campaign opened that he represented "a safer and saner view of our government and constitution than does Theodore Roosevelt, and whether beaten or not I mean to labor in the vineyard for these principles."[1]

Following Roosevelt's return in 1910, Taft had increasingly surrounded himself with conservative advisers and confidants, who by their very natures could hardly be expected to fathom the spirit and mind of Progressivism. The president led conservative Republicans to defeat in 1912 precisely because he and his comrades subscribed to a view of the Constitution that was out of step with the mainstream of American thought in the first decades of the new century. George W. Norris, an astute political observer who was elected to the Senate in 1912, later wrote that the president was a Progressive at heart but surrendered to the conservatives who beset him in the White House. On election eve, however, Taft, according to his biographer, thought the "party had naturally divided itself" between the conservative East and the agrarian West over the tariff question.[2]

As the Republican division spread to every state organization, including those in the South, party leaders were suddenly confronted with a genuine dilemma. Most GOP chiefs were practical politicians, not progressive or conservative ideologues. For many of them, particularly those in the South, where Republican voter strength was minimal, the question was simply who would win: Roosevelt or Taft. Although most southern Republican leaders no doubt leaned to the Taft position, more than a few were attracted to the dynamic nature of Roosevelt and felt that he had a real chance to recapture the presidency. Also, many Republicans in the South outside the pale of administration influence saw the Roosevelt candidacy as an opportunity to wrest control of the party machinery in their states from the entrenched organizations.[3]

The rapid, wildfire splitting of Republicans compounded the task of presenting the candidacy of both men to the country because neither could afford to alienate any sizable portion of the party. Yet, throughout January, Theodore Roosevelt received numerous public figures at his home in Oyster Bay, and he increasingly talked and acted like a candidate. Such men as Senators Joseph M. Dixon of Montana and William E. Borah of Idaho, George W. Perkins, publisher Frank Munsey, Gifford Pinchot, former Secretary of the Interior James R. Garfield, Frank Knox, and others began to work within the party to advance his candidacy.

Roosevelt personally commenced at the same time a plan of asking for support from GOP leaders in several southern and border states, including Governor William E. Glasscock of West Virginia, Julian Harris of Georgia, Pearl Wight and John M. Parker of Louisiana, Judge J. W. Pritchard and Richmond Pearson of North Carolina, and Governor Herbert S. Hadley of Missouri. With the exception of Glasscock, who later opted for Taft in order to remain loyal to the regular party, each of these early confidants was instrumental in enticing substantial party strength away from the president in his state and in lining up Republican support for the Rough Rider during the preconvention campaign. Afterward most of them joined TR in formation of the Progressive party.[4]

Meanwhile, several personal emissaries were sent by Roosevelt and his growing band of advisers into the South to persuade other Republican chiefs that he was the logical choice for the nomination. Among them were a shadowy party hack named Ormsby McHarg and Sloan Simpson, postmaster at Dallas and son of the wealthy Texan John M. Simpson, who had carried the Republican banner for governor in 1908 against Thomas M. Campbell. William W. Cocks, who had represented Roosevelt's home district around Oyster Bay in Congress until the Democratic avalanche of 1910, was sent into Texas and adjoining states during the early campaign, and the wealthy New York financier George W. Perkins, who would later bankroll much of the Progressive or Bull Moose party, was also busy writing articles and making speeches—one of them in Baltimore—in behalf of Roosevelt.[5]

Ormsby McHarg was the chief Roosevelt agent in the South during the initial phases of the campaign and made repeated trips into Alabama, Florida, Georgia, North Carolina, and Louisiana drumming up support for another TR candidacy. He speedily developed the plan of holding often spurious state conventions in the region to name rival Roosevelt delegations to the national convention in order to contest the regularly chosen ones who would normally be expected to be in the Taft camp. McHarg had been elected to the North Dakota legislature in 1899, "which elected a United States Senator who [in turn] opened the door to national politics to him." McHarg had been in charge of organizing the South for Taft in 1908. With the blessing of Roosevelt following that election, he was appointed assistant secretary of labor and commerce in 1909, a post he held for about eighteen months. Although McHarg worked for Roosevelt in 1912, several explanations have been advanced to account for his apparently sudden dislike of Taft. Victor Rosewater of Kansas believed McHarg had taken the job as assistant to Secretary Charles Nagel on a temporary basis but that "he did not expect to retain his position and that his antagonism to the President was not due to his separation from the federal payroll."[6]

As the proselytizing activity by McHarg and others for Roosevelt was getting under way nationally and in the South, Taft told a group of reporters that he fully expected TR to declare for the presidency but that he was "in the contest to the death." Before the end of January, The New York *Times* said, a "frantic" and chagrined president sent Henry Cabot Lodge and TR's son-in-law, Congressman Nicholas Longworth of Ohio, to Sagamore Hill in an effort to ascertain if Roosevelt was indeed a bona fide candidate only to learn "that when the proper time arrived the Colonel would declare himself." Even though Roosevelt would not or could not declare for the Republican nomination, Taft realized that the southern wing of the party would play a major if not decisive role in the eventual outcome; and, throughout January and February, the president, too, was in communication with Republicans in the South both personally and through his secretary, Charles D. Hilles.[7]

The southern GOP leaders flocking to the Roosevelt standard generally represented the lily-white faction of the party, causing Taft to reassess his previous disregard for the Negro. Taft conferred with several groups of black Republicans from a number of southern states in the early phases of the campaign in search of the best method of countering the Roosevelt-McHarg strategy. Likewise, Booker T. Washington and his personal secretary at Tuskegee, Emmett J. Scott, who became a special assistant to the secretary of war in Wilson's administration, kept Taft fully informed of

Roosevelt's activity among Negroes both in Alabama and across the lower South.[8]

Taft entrusted his preconvention campaign to Hilles and Congressman William B. McKinley of Illinois, both of whom played a major part in securing delegations from the South committed to the president. McKinley, who made several jaunts into the South on behalf of Taft in 1912, worked hand-in-glove with the president during the campaign as chairman of the Republican Congressional Campaign Committee; he lost his four-term seat in the House in 1912, although he was later returned to Congress and in 1920 was elected to the Senate. The Taft organization took a determined, almost hard-nosed approach to the southern wing of the party from the beginning of 1912. Hilles and McKinley developed the policy of calling early GOP conventions in the South, where there were no presidential preference primaries and therefore control of the party machinery would assure control of delegates.[9]

Hilles managed the day by day details of the campaign with Republican leaders throughout the South as well as in the remainder of the country; by a combination of tactful persuasion and unbridled threats to use the federal patronage for the sole advantage of Taft, he whipped one southern organization after another into line for the president. He had become Taft's personal secretary in April 1911, following a checkered career that included the superintendency of a boys' industrial home in Ohio and a short stint as assistant secretary of the treasury. During the 1912 campaign, he was made chairman of the Republican National Committee, a post he held until the 1916 candidacy of Charles Evans Hughes; Hilles remained on the National Committee until 1938 and managed a part of Coolidge's 1924 election campaign against John W. Davis. His masterful direction of the southern strategy in 1912, as reflected in his personal letters now in the Yale University Library, did much to win the renomination of Taft and to thwart Roosevelt's efforts in the eleven ex-Confederate states.[10]

Although the major contenders in 1912 were Taft and Roosevelt, Wisconsin Senator Robert M. La Follette conducted a vigorous campaign for the nomination until his mental and physical collapse on February 2. In January 1911, when the National Progressive Republican League had been formed with an announced platform of "restoring the republican party to the people," La Follette was not only a leader of the movement but certainly the foremost leader of the Progressive element within the party. This coalescing of the reform wing of Republicanism was centered mostly in the Midwest and found little party support in the East and South. When La Follette opened his formal campaign for the nomination in July 1911, Roosevelt was maintaining a coy silence following his Osawatomie speech and was so far from being an announced candidate that the Wisconsin senator was the leading Progressive challenger to the renomination of Taft during late 1911.[11]

La Follette's campaign organization, at least on paper, assumed national proportions, including activity within several state Republican organizations in the South, but his appeal among southern Republicans was decidedly limited, because of Taft's tight rein over the patronage. A majority of Republicans in the South were temperamentally and philosophically opposed to a La Follette candidacy, and Roosevelt, too, was soon to learn the effectiveness with which an incumbent president can control federal officeholders as a weapon for renomination. In Texas, Tom Daley, a regular Republican who had lived for thirty years in the district around Texarkana, reported to the administration that although La Follette had some support in the state he thought the district could be carried for Taft easily in the local convention. And in North Carolina, former Congressman John M. Morehead wrote repeatedly to Taft's campaign managers downgrading La Follette sentiment in the Tar Heel State as insignificant.[12]

The La Follette boom stopped abruptly on February 2, however, when he momentarily lost his balance while addressing the prestigious Periodical Publisher's Association in Philadelphia. Following several speakers, including the Democratic hopeful, Woodrow Wilson, La Follette rose to the platform late in the evening; already fatigued and disturbed over news that a beloved daughter would undergo surgery the next morning, he "lost his temper repeatedly—shook his fist—at listeners who had started to walk out too tired to listen longer, was abusive, ugly in manner. Stopped many times to shout at men walking out." Although La Follette never withdrew from the race, his personal secretary John Hannan told Congressman Henry A. Cooper of Wisconsin, who also attended the meeting, "this is terrible—he is making a d——d fool of himself. This ends him for the Presidency." The Wisconsin statesman did not receive a single vote from the South after his name was placed before the Republican National Convention in June.[13]

News of the La Follette debacle spread over the country with startling quickness. Progressive Republicans—including his former champions Gilson Gardner and Gifford Pinchot—could now swing unreservedly to Roosevelt. Even though La Follette himself "never authorized either the withdrawal of his candidacy or a transfer of his support to Roosevelt," the colonel clearly benefited from his demise as a viable candidate. When asked by reporters the next day about La Follette's breakdown, Roosevelt had said, "too bad, I'm sorry." And when queried further about the effect of La Follette's removal as Republican front runner on the Progressive crusade, the Rough Rider remarked that the Progressive movement "is greater than any one man in it."[14]

Roosevelt and Taft partisans had been proceeding in their quest for national convention delegates as though La Follette had never been in the race. The La Follette candidacy was not seen by either as a serious threat, especially in the South, where each was attempting to gain support. And when Roosevelt made his fateful announcement on February 22 in Columbus, Ohio, that "my hat is in the ring," only two southern states— Florida and Georgia—had held Republican conventions. Neither gave the least notice to La Follette, although Roosevelt and Taft activity of varying intensity was well under way throughout the region.[15]

In the upper South, Virginia Republicans promptly resolved themselves into opposing factions with State Chairman C. Bascom Slemp, who had represented the ninth congressional district since 1907, early emerging as the Taft leader. Slemp's district, composed of twelve counties in the mountains of extreme southwestern Virginia where antebellum plantations had been scarce and the Negro a rarity, had long been a Republican bastion because the electorate had no inbred hostility toward the GOP. The ninth furnished most of the state's Republican strength and was well known for its "wild and woolly" politics as well as its tight machine organization. James A. Walker, last commander of the famed Stonewall Brigade and lieutenant governor of Virginia before switching to the Republican party in 1893, represented the district in Congress for two terms in the 1890s. The violent nature of politics in the ninth surfaced in 1899, when Walker, a noted firebrand, who had been defeated for re-election the year before by Judge William F. Rhea of Bristol, was wounded twice in an exchange of gunfire while taking a deposition from one of Rhea's attorneys for use in contesting the election.[16]

Campbell Slemp, the father of C. Bascom Slemp and a wealthy coal and timber operator in eastern Kentucky and southwestern Virginia, captured the district in 1902 from the Democrat Rhea. The elder Slemp, who had been the unsuccessful Republican candidate for lieutenant governor in 1899, held the seat until his death in 1907, when he was succeeded by his son. C. Bascom Slemp remained in Congress for the next sixteen years and during much of that time was the lone Republican in the House from the South in addition to being party boss and lily-white leader in the state. He refused to stand for reelection in 1922 when he became personal secretary to Calvin Coolidge because of his familiarity with southern Republican politics.[17]

Even though Slemp had been working for Taft since the previous summer, the ninth district GOP Executive Committee was summoned into session at Bristol on January 15, 1912, to adopt a resolution praising the administration and Slemp's record in Congress. The pro-Taft document was finally accepted during a stormy session with only one dissenting vote, but not before a vocal opposition by a budding Roosevelt faction had been sounded. Alanson T. Lincoln, who operated a furniture manufacturing company and was a former state legislator, led the resistance to Slemp's hold on the district and state GOP organizations, although others would later come forward to lead the formal Roosevelt movement in the state.[18]

As state chairman, Slemp worked closely in his handling of party matters with Alvah H. Martin, Virginia member of the Republican National Committee since 1908 and a Norfolk bank president. Martin remained on the committee until 1920 and the Harding campaign, but he worked for Taft during the 1912 canvass. An opposing faction in the Republican organization was led by Royal Cabell of Richmond, who was leader of the patronage-holding group. Cabell, a lawyer and graduate of both Princeton and Richmond College, had been postmaster at Richmond under Roosevelt and was named collector of internal revenue in 1909 by Taft, a post he held until 1913 when removed by Wilson. Although Cabell differed with the Slemp-Martin management of the party—primarily because Slemp exercised congressional courtesy over Virginia appointments—he did not side with the Roosevelt dissidents but remained loyal to Taft and was ultimately named a delegate-at-large to the 1912 Republican National Convention.[19]

President Taft, attempting to deal with a growing Roosevelt momentum, called Martin and Cabell to Washington in early January to tell them he was displeased with Republican factional fights in Virginia. He wanted the squabbling stopped before the state convention on March 12 in Roanoke, even though Slemp, who was unable to attend the conference because of an illness in his family, telegraphed the White House in advance that "we have enough votes instructed and agreed upon to positively elect Martin National Committeeman and control the state convention." At the meeting Taft was informed by Martin that Cabell "had attempted to ruin the party for the sake of factional advantage to accrue to him and those behind him." In response, the president and Hilles placed the Virginia campaign in the hands of Slemp and Martin at the same time Cabell was seeking to reassure Taft of his loyalty to the administration.[20]

Although the Republicans under Slemp and Alvah Martin held a tight rein in southwestern Virginia, where members of the party were regularly elected to legislative and local offices, the remainder of the Old Dominion was dominated by "The Ring" or conservative Democrats under the leadership of U.S. Senator Thomas S. Martin, Congressman Hal Flood, and Claude Augustus Swanson, a former governor who had been in the U.S. Senate since 1911. Thomas S. Martin, who controlled the conservative machine in Virginia during twenty-four years in the Senate, had first won election in 1893, when he bested Fitzhugh Lee—Civil War general and nephew of Robert E. Lee—in a stiff fight for the seat formerly held by Eppa Hunton. Martin and his organization consistently opposed any serious reform attempts by the Progressive Democrats until after World War I.[21]

The election of Andrew J. Montague as governor in 1901 offered the first meaningful threat to conservative domination of the state, when he defeated the Republican candidate, Colonel J. Hampton Hoge, by a vote of 116,683 to 81,366. Although charging the Democrats with corruption and inefficiency in a spirited campaign, the lily-white Republicans did not do well in this final election before Negro disfranchisement in Virginia. Montague, who became a leader in the drive for educational reform throughout the South, ran on a platform calling for better public schools, party primaries, improved roads, and related Progressive issues; as governor, however, he met with only limited success because of opposition from Bourbon majorities in the legislature.[22]

Montague's term was highlighted by a constitutional convention in 1902 that resulted in the nearly total disfranchisement of the Virginia Negro through adoption of a capitation tax as a voting prerequisite. The State already had a literacy test or an understanding clause aimed at the Negro, but black voting was virtually eliminated by the poll tax provision in the new constitution. Although twelve Republicans and no Negroes sat in the convention, the Virginia GOP opposed exclusion because such a policy was obviously harmful to the party, whereas Democrats—both Bourbon and Progressive, including Governor Montague—favored the plan. Blacks were later driven from active participation in Republican councils by the lily-white faction because that group thought the nonvoting Negro a liability in its drive for political respectability.[23]

Constitutional disfranchisement in Virginia had an immediate impact upon both major parties by sharply reducing the eligible electorate. The 1900 presidential tally for Bryan had been 146,079 to 115,769 for McKinley, but the totals dropped further in 1904 to 80,649 for Alton B. Parker and 48,180 for Theodore Roosevelt. When the Roosevelt organization was put in gear four years later in behalf of Taft, the Republican candidate received 52,568 votes to Bryan's 82,936. During the 1905 gubernatorial canvass, L. L. Lewis, the Republican nominee, attempted to disassociate himself and the party from its traditional Negro allegiances in the campaign against Claude A. Swanson, emphasizing anew the decline in black voting strength. Upon his election, Swanson, a former congressman and faithful cog in the Martin machine, who had been a staunch advocate of disfranchisement, shortly reversed the fledgling Progressive trend among Virginia Democrats initiated by his predecessor, Montague.[24]

The easily accomplished reestablishment of Bourbon rule through a reduced electorate obviously worked to the advantage of Martin and The Ring because the voters could be more readily managed by a well-organized machine. At the start of the 1912 presidential campaign, moreover, The Ring, which supported Wilson for the Democratic nomination, remained in solid control of the state. William H. Mann, a longtime leader in the movement for statewide prohibition, had been elected governor in 1910 with machine backing to succeed Swanson, who went to the Senate the same year and later became secretary of the navy under Franklin D.

Roosevelt. In 1912, however, Mann and the Democratic organization—like their counterparts throughout the South—completely ignored the hopelessly outnumbered Republicans and their schism into Roosevelt and Taft camps.[25]

The split among Virginia Republicans burst into the open when the various district conventions began meeting to select delegates for the March 13 convening of the regularly scheduled state convention in Roanoke. George L. Hart, secretary of the GOP State Executive Committee, sent out word for party regulars to work for a resolution endorsing Taft in each convention as a means of getting delegates to the Roanoke meeting who would be favorable to the president; Hart later informed Hilles that "our friends are leaving no stone unturned to make control of State and District matters secure." A majority of Republicans in Virginia were undoubtedly for Taft in the initial phases of the campaign, although several district gatherings got out of hand when the issue of endorsing the president arose. A few districts named rival delegations, and at the third district meeting in Richmond, reported one newspaper, there were "exciting times . . . with some scuffling and fighting taking place."[26]

Slemp, Martin, Hart, and the regular or officeholding wing of the party were thus able to secure a substantial majority of the state convention delegates for Taft by prompt and decisive action. And Taft's cause in the state was helped substantially when Slemp made an open appeal for Negro support in the campaign. Roosevelt did not appear to have a well-functioning organization in Virginia prior to the all-important state gathering, although he was not without followers. Six days after the Rough Rider tossed his hat into the ring at Columbus, Thomas Lee Moore, for several years U.S. attorney for the western district of Virginia, announced his formal support. Moore, who guided Roosevelt's fortunes in the state during the campaign and later became the Virginia member of the Progressive National Committee, had been elected commonwealth's attorney for Montgomery County in 1895 and was one of twelve Republicans in the 1901 Constitutional Convention before being appointed U.S. attorney in 1902 by Roosevelt.[27]

In neighboring North Carolina, the party likewise divided along fast developing regional and national lines. Roosevelt personally took a hand in the Old North State early in the campaign when he wrote to ask Judge Jeter C. Pritchard of Asheville to visit New York to discuss the political situation in North Carolina and the South. As a result of the meeting, Pritchard, a close ally of National Committeeman Edward C. Duncan and a longtime party worker, supported TR in 1912. In the 1890s, when Fusionist politics between Populists and Republicans dominated the state, Pritchard was elected to the U.S. Senate along with Marion Butler, a Populist, who was now active in the Republican party. He was defeated for reelection, however, in 1902 by a Democrat-controlled legislature, although Roosevelt subsequently named him judge of the fourth district, U.S. Court of Appeals in western North Carolina, a post he retained until his death in 1921.[28]

The man destined to rally the emerging Roosevelt forces in the state was not Pritchard, but former Congressman Richmond Pearson, who was also a federal appointee of the former president's. He directed Roosevelt's fortunes in North Carolina during the campaign, first within the regular party organization and afterward as national committeeman for the Progressive or Bull Moose party. A Princeton graduate who had been named U.S. consul at Vervier and Liege, Belgium, by Ulysses S. Grant, Pearson served briefly as a Democratic member of the North Carolina legislature, 1884–1886, before being elected to three terms in the House of Representatives as a Republican during the Fusionist era. Following his defeat for reelection in 1900, Roosevelt appointed him to several diplomatic posts. Pearson tendered his resignation from the foreign service when Taft took office in 1909. Many observers at the time felt that Taft's ready acceptance of his resignation caused his militant opposition to the president that surfaced by January 1910. Except for directing the 1912 Roosevelt canvass, Pearson lived in quiet retirement until his death in 1923.[29]

State Chairman John Motley Morehead, Pearson's rival in party affairs, took control of Taft's forces in the state. Like Roosevelt, the president had intervened personally in North Carolina when Morehead was named state chairman in 1910 with the hope that under his direction the Republican party could become a viable opposition force to the Democrats. But the rising swell of insurgency after 1910, the ineptitude of Taft in dealing with the South, and the Roosevelt volcano combined to render his rebuilding efforts useless; TR, after all, would poll more votes in the state than Taft. Morehead was a graduate of the University of North Carolina, a buyer and dealer in tobacco, and a woolen mill executive at Spray when elected to his single term in the House. He did not stand for reelection in 1910, but continued to work for Taft throughout the period, regularly keeping the White House informed about developments in the state. The state chairman was hostile to Roosevelt in 1912 and worked increasingly for Taft's renomination and election. Morehead survived the 1912 disaster by staying loyal to the regular Republican organization and, unlike his counterparts in other southern states, remained state chairman until 1916 when he became national committeeman for North Carolina.[30]

Morehead presided over perhaps the best Republican organization in the South, although the North Carolina party, like those in Virginia and Tennessee, had a definite sectional basis. Republican strength in the state was confined primarily to the western mountainous regions, where plantations and slave labor in the antebellum era were largely unknown and accordingly there was no appreciable antipathy to the Negro. In 1908, the North Carolina party reached a temporary high-water mark by electing three members of Congress, including Morehead, and giving Taft an unusually high GOP vote. But an amendment to the state constitution in 1901 severely restricting the black franchise had seriously weakened state-wide Republican strength. Following the administration of the Republican-Fusionist Governor Daniel L. Russell at the turn of the century, the party elected only four representatives to Congress before 1920.[31]

President Taft developed a more than passing interest in North Carolina in 1912—although the Democrats had remained in solid control of the state following elimination of the Negro as a viable political force—and called its Republican leaders to Washington early in the campaign to discuss the best plan for holding the state for the administration. There was more than a little maneuvering and in-fighting among the North Carolinians, and the presidential blessing eventually went to Morehead. Seemingly because of their previous association with Theodore Roosevelt, both Richmond Pearson and Marion Butler, who were in the capital city at the time, were not received with favor by the president. National Committeeman Duncan, an opponent of Morehead's in state party affairs, arrived in Washington for the January 17 confab only to be denied an audience at the White House because of his family connections with Judge Pritchard.[32]

Duncan, who fought Morehead tooth and nail during the campaign, played a role in North Carolina Republican circles not unlike that of Royal Cabell in Virginia. Duncan had managed the Taft campaign in 1908 and was a great friend of Postmaster General Frank H. Hitchcock, which gave him control of the state's patronage, contrary to the wishes of Morehead, who had wanted to exercise congressional courtesy over appointments. For several years he was collector of the port at Beaufort, and he served two terms in the state legislature during the Fusionist era and as collector of internal revenue for North Carolina, which tightened his grip over federal officeholders in the state. As founder and president of Merchants National Bank in Raleigh, Duncan had the time and personal resources to engage in political activities. During the 1912 canvass, however, he did not go over to the Roosevelt banner but opposed Taft's new-found champion, Morehead, from within the regular organization. Although Richmond Pearson wrested the national committeemanship from him at the May 15 Republican State Convention, Duncan was put back on the committee by Taft and Hilles when Pearson was expelled for joining the Bull Moosers.[33]

Taft intervened personally in the Morehead-Duncan struggle when Hilles, no doubt at the president's urging, placed the administration's confidence in Morehead to handle North Carolina matters. Still, the state chairman complained about Taft's policy of making federal appointments only in cases of actual vacancy. Morehead wrote to Hilles on February 8 in an attempt to downgrade his adversary: "The Pritchard-Duncan combination is spreading the word that the state organization obtains very few nominations from the White House and they do not permit these to pass the Senate." Furthermore, Taft himself evidenced a concern over party loyalty in the state when he asked Attorney General Wickersham on February 5 to investigate a report that the U.S. Circuit Court clerk at Asheville, who was a brother-in-law of Judge Pritchard, was "opposed to my renomination."[34]

In an attempt to manipulate the patronage to his own advantage, the president called a group of Southern Negro Republicans, including White-field McKinlay, to the White House on January 31, about two weeks following his earlier conference with Morehead and his lieutenants. Henry Lincoln Johnson, the Negro GOP chief from Georgia, and others present complained to Taft that his agents were exceeding his instructions in barring Negroes from all federal appointments in the region. The black leaders were told that this policy would be reversed immediately, and, apparently in an effort to court their vote, the president "voiced his abhorrence of Lynchings and of those that deny Negroes the right of suffrage." Taft made halfhearted gestures at placating the Negroes throughout the campaign, especially in Louisiana, Texas, and Alabama, but his change of mind came only after it became clear that Roosevelt was leaning toward an all-white opposition party in the South.[35]

Although Congressman Robert N. Page told reporters that the fight among North Carolina Republicans was of no consequence because they "are as much concerned as ever with their occupation of eating from the pie counter and [that] there was little prospect of a stampede to the Roosevelt bandwagon," Taft and the administration thought otherwise. In the hope of calming the rift between Duncan and Morehead, the president on February 19 withdrew all Senate nominations for federal appointments in the state made since the first of the year. Both men had made recommendations for appointment of eight postmasters and two customs collectors, but Taft decided to withhold all further patronage slots until after the state convention that was scheduled to assemble on May 15. The Raleigh *News and Observer* speculated that the appointments would not be forthcoming until Morehead had demonstrated his ability to whip the state into line for Taft.[36]

After the administration's chastisement of Duncan, former Senator Marion Butler—now aligned with the Morehead faction—started an unsuccessful drive to gain his seat on the national committee. Butler had first entered North Carolina politics as a Democratic member of the state senate in 1890, but shortly shifted to the Populist organization, becoming president of the state Farmer's Alliance in 1892 and president of the National Farmer's Alliance and Industrial Union two years later. He became chief architect of fusion agreements with the Republicans in North Carolina, which resulted in his election to the United States Senate in 1894 after a GOP-Populist combination gained control of the legislature. Judge Pritchard was sent to the Senate upon the death of Zebulon B. Vance, although Butler opposed the Republican Pritchard in state politics and was unable to work with him in Washington. Butler edited the well-known *Caucasian,* which he used to espouse his political views, from 1888 until his death in 1938; he was defeated for reelection in 1901 by a Democratic-controlled legislature, but he continued as chairman of the Populist National Executive Committee until 1904, when he joined the Republicans.[37]

Meanwhile, Roosevelt's strength in North Carolina was mushrooming with each passing day as Morehead struggled to keep the party on an even keel for Taft. At a meeting of the State Executive Committee on February 28 in Raleigh to fix the date for the upcoming state convention, the seriousness of the division became evident when Morehead managed to get through a resolution endorsing the president by the narrowest of margins but failed to obtain a document calling for his renomination. Thomas Settle, another congressman during the Fusionist era, although never a Roosevelt supporter, offered a resolution condemning the administration. In an attempt to court the various factions, Morehead hosted a magnificent dinner party after the committee meeting for over seven hundred guests representing all shades of Republican sentiment. He stipulated that there should be no serious political talk at the gala affair, but the Raleigh *News and Observer* reported: "There was not a little talk that indicated the feelings of Mr. Morehead's guests, and . . . assuming noise as a touch stone Roosevelt's adherents outnumbered those of Mr. Taft greatly."[38]

The success of the Roosevelt bandwagon was primarily the work of Richmond Pearson and his co-workers who had organized Roosevelt for President Clubs across the state during January and February. Pearson had been in touch with the colonel from the first days of the campaign and had made trips to both New York and Oyster Bay for personal conferences. The importance of North Carolina to the Roosevelt camp was plain enough when Governor Chase S. Osborn of Michigan issued a call for a national conference of Republican governors favorable to the Rough Rider to meet in Chicago and issue a formal declaration urging Roosevelt to be a candidate. Six governors and various selected political leaders, including Pearson, attended the meeting. Upon his return to North Carolina, Pearson told reporters: "Republicans all over the country are holding Mr. Taft responsible for the divided condition of the party everywhere . . . There is no question as to the allegation that Mr. Taft has ruined himself in the South." This attitude pervaded the Roosevelt organization and prompted Medill McCormick of Chicago to write one North Carolina Republican asking for a report on conditions in the state and telling him, "The situation is simple. Colonel Roosevelt can and will be nominated if those who believe in his nomination organize immediately."[39]

In Tennessee, however, the Republican organization was dominated by regulars committed to the administration, which made it difficult for Roosevelt to make headway in the first months of the campaign even though the state had a formidable GOP base. A fiercely loyal brand of Republicanism in the mountainous counties of east Tennessee had been a threat to Democratic domination of the state since 1865. When Abraham Lincoln wanted to dispel the GOP's sectional image during the election of 1864, he had reached into the area to make Andrew Johnson his running mate against George B. McClellan. The region had been firmly in the Republican fold since 1900, and during the first decades of the century it regularly elected two congressmen. Significantly, the east Tennessee congressional districts bordered those in southwestern Virginia and western North Carolina, which also sent Republicans to Washington during the period. The southern Appalachians were thus an island of GOP strength in an otherwise Democratic domain. Verton Queener writes that in 1906 Scott County, which was "slightly" more Republican than most east Tennessee counties, had "only about 150 Democrats; there were several districts where a Democrat [was] as much a curiosity as a circus."[40]

Among the long list of Republican leaders produced by east Tennessee was Ben Wade Hooper of Cooke County, formerly an officer in the Spanish-American War and a lawyer of wide reputation, who has been described as an able and honest campaigner as well as a moderate in politics. Hooper, the only Republican governor in the South during 1912, had been elected in 1910 when the Democrats split over the twin issues of prohibition and the official conduct of Governor Malcolm R. Patterson. Bootlegging and an outrageous flouting of the state's liquor laws were openly condoned and even encouraged during Patterson's administration, causing "Independent" Democrats and sizable numbers of Republicans to cast about for a mutually agreeable dry candidate to replace the errant governor.[41]

The fatal rupture among Tennessee Democrats started when Patterson, a wet, was vigorously opposed in the 1908 primary by Edward C. Carmack, a fervent prohibitionist and the brilliant if somewhat caustic editor of the Memphis *Commercial Appeal.* Although defeated for his party's nomination, Carmack assumed the editorship of the influential Nashville *Tennessean,* where he continued his espousal of prohibitionist views laced with vitriolic attacks upon Patterson. One such outburst against Colonel Duncan Cooper, a personal and political friend of the governor, provoked a pistol fight in the streets of Nashville in which Carmack was slain by Cooper and his son, Robin Cooper. Both father and son were convicted of first-degree murder by a Nashville jury, causing an already agitated political atmosphere to become red hot because many Tennesseans were convinced that the governor had a hand in the affair. The son's conviction was overturned on appeal to the state supreme court, but when Patterson granted the senior Cooper a full pardon, the wrath of the state's dry element exploded.[42]

When Patterson announced for a third term a few days after granting Cooper's reprieve, the anti-Patterson faction of the party, now calling themselves "Independent" Democrats, held a convention in Nashville to consider a course of action for the upcoming 1910 elections. The Republicans, sensing a golden opportunity, held their state convention in August 1910 and proceeded to adopt a prohibitionist platform and to select Hooper as their gubernatorial nominee. He was subsequently endorsed by the Independents. Even though, as the furor mounted, Patterson withdrew in favor of Robert L. Taylor, a former governor and then U.S. senator, the Independents did not return to the fold but continued in their steadfast support of Hooper. In the spirited campaign that followed, he was able to beat Taylor by a vote of 134,000 to 122,000 and thereby became the first Republican in the South to win statewide elective office in this century. Hooper was elected to a second term in 1912 with the support of dissident Democrats, but met stiff opposition from organization Democrats and Bull Moosers as well as the personal hostility of Theodore Roosevelt.[43]

Although Hooper was subjected to great pressures by the Roosevelt and Taft camps in 1912 before he finally resolved to cast his lot with the administration, the first indication of trouble within the Tennessee party surfaced at a conference of GOP leaders in Nashville on January 10. Hooper was present at the gathering that had been called to resolve a growing factionalism in the state and to seek a plan for securing an undivided delegation to the national convention. Three of the fourteen present—Hooper, State Treasurer G. Tom Taylor, who would become Roosevelt's chief agent in the state, and State Senator John C. Houk—had recently returned from a White House conference with Taft, and though Hooper stoutly denied the allegations, various newspapers speculated that the gathering was convened to stamp out a budding Roosevelt movement in Tennessee.[44]

Ten days later, State Chairman Newell Sanders presided over a meeting of the State Executive Committee, where he scotched the so-called Brownlow wing of the party that identified with the Roosevelt campaign. Sanders, a wealthy Chattanooga plow manufacturer and graduate of Indiana University before moving to Tennessee in 1897, was a personal friend of Hooper and manager of Taft's renomination effort in the state; he had been active in Republican politics since the 1890s, and when Senator Taylor died in March 1912 during the presidential canvass, Hooper appointed him to Taylor's unexpired term. Under an agreement handed down by Taft and his national managers in 1912, Sanders was given complete charge of all Tennessee affairs outside of R. W. Austin's second congressional district. Represented in the House by Austin since 1909, this east Tennessee district was a Republican stronghold, and Taft would not allow Sanders as state chairman to meddle with Austin's claims to congressional courtesy in patronage or campaign matters.[45]

When the State Executive Committee met on January 20, the anti-Sanders or Brownlow wing of the party—named for the late Congressman Walter P. Brownlow—attempted to block adoption of a pro-Taft resolution. This group, whom Hooper characterized in his autobiography as "discredited political hacks," was spearheaded by John C. Houk, G. Tom Taylor, and Harry B. Anderson, who attempted to ram through a resolution committing the state organization to a primary for selecting delegates to the Republican National Convention. Party primaries were of course a vital part of the Progressive cause, and when the proposal was dismissed by the Sanders-dominated committee, The Knoxville *Journal and Tribune* commented: "It would be death to the knife with a determined attempt to send a Tennessee delegation to the national convention committed to Theodore Roosevelt." Houk, a state senator and former congressman, afterward became Roosevelt's campaign manager in Tennessee, while Anderson, a lawyer and after 1926 a federal judge, later presided over the convention that formally organized the Progressive party in the state.[46]

Hooper, whose political future depended upon the support of Independent Democrats, wanted desperately to divorce his own reelection efforts from national politics and from early January took a position of noninterference with selection of delegates to the national convention. Therefore, the State Executive Committee, at the urging of Hooper and with the apparent acquiescence of Sanders, adopted a plan for holding two state conventions in 1912. The governor told the meeting that he personally favored a party primary for naming delegates, but since this method was contrary to the wishes of the committee he wanted the two-convention scheme. The approved plan provided that a convention for the nomination of state officers would meet two months prior to the one for picking national convention delegates. Hooper told the committee further that if there were to be a struggle over naming Roosevelt or Taft delegates, it might better come after the state ticket had been selected. After he had withdrawn, the committee voted resolutions demanding the election of both Taft and Hooper.[47]

State Treasurer G. Tom Taylor spoke for disgruntled Republicans in the state when he indicated that the convention for naming delegates to Chicago had been set at a late date so "the officeholders and their following could see which way the national convention cat was going to jump." Hooper and Sanders, according to the Roosevelt supporters, were not sincere in their support of Taft "unless they see that Roosevelt has no chance; that if Roosevelt grows formidable they will be equally ready to swing to him." Taylor, a prominent businessman from Union City, had been a follower of Walter P. Brownlow and was thus in the anti-Sanders camp, although he had been active in Tennessee Republican politics since 1896, when he was one of McKinley's managers in the state. When Hooper had taken over the party in 1910, Taylor was named state treasurer and insurance commissioner by a combination of regular Democrats and anti-Sanders Republicans. Already at odds with Sanders and the GOP organization, Taylor early identified himself with the Roosevelt movement and eventually became leader of the state's Bull Moosers.[48]

Meanwhile, Roosevelt hit upon the idea of having several Republican governors across the country issue a declaration calling upon him to seek the presidency as a means of getting his candidacy before the nation. Hooper was thus put in the position of having to say yes or no to the national Roosevelt campaign. John Franklin Fort, a former governor of New Jersey, wrote to Hooper confidentially and to William E. Glasscock of West Virginia on January 19, as well as to several Republican governors in the North, asking if he could express a preference for the colonel; and the New York *Times* repeatedly telegraphed the Tennessee governor asking if he would declare for Roosevelt. Whether by plan or happenstance, Hooper was also bombarded with letters and telegrams pleading that he come out for the Rough Rider and disassociate himself entirely from Sanders and the Taft campaign.[49]

Hooper responded in late January to Fort's invitation, reiterating his previous stand of "trying to prevent the mixing of state and national politics that will make a mess of both." Politics in Tennessee, he said, had suffered in the past from being "tied to national kites," and he intended therefore not to "lead any movement in the interest of any national candidate for the presidential nomination." Shortly before a formal call to Roosevelt was formulated by Glasscock, Joseph M. Carey of Wyoming, Walter R. Stubbs of Kansas, Chester H. Aldrich of Nebraska, Robert P. Bass of New Hampshire, Osborn of Michigan, and Hadley of Missouri, Fort informed Hooper that Roosevelt knew about his position and hoped that he might change his mind in the future.[50]

Eleven days after the call from the governors, on February 22, Roosevelt made his statement in Columbus, where he had been addressing the Ohio Constitutional Convention, that "his hat was in the ring." The battle lines for 1912 had been drawn tightly on February 12, when Taft gave his famous speech before a Lincoln Day dinner in New York attacking "Progressives" in the Republican party as "political emotionalists or neurotics, who have lost that sense of proportion, that clear and candid consideration of their own weaknesses, as a whole, and that clear perception of the necessity of checks upon hasty political action." From mid-February forward there could be no sidestepping the contest—Republican leaders in all sections of the nation would be required to declare themselves, as Governor Hooper soon learned.[51]

Congressman R. W. Austin informed Hooper from Washington on February 15 that "political rumors" regarding the governor had reached the ears of Taft. Hooper replied that certain "politicians had been trying to poison the mind of the President against him" and advised Austin that the "whole trouble" stemmed from the state committee calling two state conventions at his urging. Nonetheless, he told Taft's national campaign manager, William B. McKinley, a few days later that the president was "personally popular in Tennessee . . . the state organization is loyally supporting [him] and from present indications he will get the vote of Tennessee in the national convention." But his attempt to mend fences did not satisfy the administration. Assistant Attorney General James A. Fowler was sent to try to cajole Hooper into making a public statement supporting Taft.[52]

Not to be outdone by Roosevelt, Taft and his managers arranged for nine Republican governors to pledge support for the president on February 26 about two weeks after the colonel's call. Hilles applied pressure through Fowler, who was still in the state, and Sanders to have Hooper issue a favorable statement. According to the New York *Times*, he did an about-face and telegraphed national Taft headquarters that the president "is personally popular in Tennessee and his administration commands general public confidence"; thus he joined Governors Adolph O. Eberhart of Minnesota, Beryl F. Carroll of Iowa, M. E. Hay of Washington, Phillips L. Goldsborough of Maryland, John K. Tener of Pennsylvania, William Spray of Utah, Simeon S. Pennewill of Delaware, and Aram J. Pothier of Rhode Island "in going on record in favor of the President's renomination."[53]

William J. Oliver, at this time a party regular but later Bull Moose national committeeman for Tennessee, immediately reacted to Hooper's declaration by sending an urgent note on February 29 informing him that a majority of the state's Republicans were for Roosevelt, especially in east Tennessee, where the "federal officeholders cannot control the voters." Oliver, a wealthy railroad contractor and equipment manufacturer from Knoxville, then requested permission to write Roosevelt that Hooper's policy "is going to be hands off" during the campaign. The governor responded the same day, telegraphing Oliver that he "was correct"; as head of the Republican party in Tennessee, Hooper said, "he did not want to take sides in the fight for convention delegates," therewith lending verbal support to a Taft candidacy but remaining resolute in his desire to stay out of a searing party fight over the actual naming of delegates to the Republican National Convention.[54]

Oliver, who had been a member of the first Highway Commission appointed in 1909, received a degree of notoriety during World War I, when he was charged with sabotage and conspiracy to defraud the government in the manufacture of defective artillery shells. Although he was exonerated after a lengthy court battle, the war episode ruined his business, his fortune, and his health. Oliver became head of a Roosevelt for President Club organized in Knoxville with well over four hundred members in March 1912 and was soon joined by Judge Hugh B. Lindsay in directing TR's statewide campaign. Lindsay, a well-known lawyer from east Tennessee and a workhorse in the GOP, however, like many Republican leaders across the country, intended to remain in the Roosevelt camp only until the outcome of the presidential nominating convention became known. He did not follow Oliver into the Progressive party after the renomination of Taft, but remained firmly planted in the GOP. As early as 1887, Lindsay had been elected to the state legislature as a Republican, and he was the party's candidate for governor in 1918 and for the U.S. Senate in 1922.[55]

The Republican schism that developed in Tennessee following Roosevelt's decision to run in 1912 paralleled the party fracturing throughout the country. Indeed, neither GOP contender had the slightest hope of winning electoral votes in the upper South, although the combined delegate strength from Virginia, North Carolina, and Tennessee in the national convention made it imperative that each win in the preconvention fights. Furthermore, the nature of the party in this part of the old Confederacy with its elected officeholders and their vested interests in maintaining a viable party organization intensified the intraparty struggle. Roosevelt ran second behind Wilson in North Carolina and Virginia, while Taft beat TR in Tennessee in November, but the area's elected Republicans remained solid for the Old Guard. Not only Hooper but the GOP congressmen from Tennessee and Virginia as well refused to support Roosevelt or to join the Progressive party after its formation.

Chapter 3

"My Hat Is in the Ring": The Lower South

The Republican base in the upper South, where a sizable GOP vote composed primarily of white voters located in Appalachian enclaves could be counted upon by either Roosevelt or Taft regardless of which faction controlled the state organization, was nonexistent in most states of the lower South. The party was at a particularly low ebb in South Carolina, where Taft garnered a mere 3,963 votes out of a total 66,397 cast in the 1908 election and where he and Roosevelt combined received less than 2,000 tallies in 1912. Yet the state organization, made up mostly of Negroes under the tight grip of the federal officeholders and totally committed to whichever administration was currently in power, was opposed by a dissident faction of lily-whites who wanted control of the state's patronage. This latter group eventually formed the nucleus of a small Roosevelt movement when its leaders failed to be recognized by Taft and Hilles at the 1912 National Convention.[1]

Prior to disfranchisement—which occurred in 1896 with ratification of a new state constitution—the Republican vote in South Carolina had been sufficient to elect an occasional legislator or congressman. Pitchfork Ben Tillman, however, who defeated the aristocratic Wade Hampton for the governorship in 1890 and remained for a dozen years thereafter as the undisputed political boss of the state, was able to eliminate the Negro from participation in state politics through the most rank and demagogic appeals to white supremacy. When Tillman became governor in 1891, a Negro Republican, Thomas E. Miller, represented the state in the House of Representatives, but the 1895 Constitutional Convention, which was controlled by the white supremacists, adopted the usual poll tax and literacy determinants to Negro voting. The work of the convention was more than effective—the resultant decline in Negro registration and a strengthened determination to maintain a one-party state caused the Republican vote to drop from 21,733 in 1892 to 3,963 when Taft ran for president in 1908.[2]

As the 1912 GOP campaign opened, two men, John G. Capers and Joseph W. Tolbert, vied for control of the minuscule South Carolina party, which had been nearly forgotten by national leaders until both Roosevelt and Taft realized the value of the state's delegation to the national convention. Capers had been appointed Republican chieftain by Roosevelt prior to 1904 as part of his drive to build his own organizations in the

South. His father was Ellison Capers, who had been a brigadier general in the Confederate army, Episcopal bishop of South Carolina, and afterward chancellor of the University of the South at Sewanee, Tennessee. Although a Democrat until the nomination of Bryan, when he joined the Republican party, John G. Capers was appointed collector of internal revenue and later U.S. attorney by Roosevelt. He also served on the Republican National Committee until 1912. Though he supported the Rough Rider that year, he remained loyal to Taft after the president's renomination and did not bolt the party for the Bull Moose cause.[3]

Although Capers remained as national committeeman, his connections with TR caused Taft to place the administration's confidence in Tolbert, who had been state chairman since 1900. Nor had the president reappointed Capers to federal office after 1909. Tolbert, a planter at Ninety-six, South Carolina, and known as "tieless Joe" because he never wore a tie in manhood, was summoned to the White House along with Charleston Postmaster Wilmot L. Harris in early 1912 and given command of party affairs in the state. Upon his return, a meeting of the State Executive Committee was called by the officeholding faction now headed by Tolbert, Harris, and U.S. Attorney J. Duncan Adams, which adopted resolutions "reading John G. Capers out of the position of national committeeman and effecting a strong organization for the present administration." The officeholders also expressed confidence in Taft and indicated that Capers would not be a member of the regular delegation to Chicago nor would he be recognized as head of any independent group of Republicans purporting to represent South Carolina.[4]

Recognizing his repudiation by Taft and Hilles, Capers, who maintained a law practice in Washington, embarked upon a letter-writing campaign urging South Carolina Republicans to reject Tolbert as party boss. Capers reminded the press and the administration that he was still the legitimate national committeeman and that L. W. C. Blalock of Newberry, a former collector of internal revenue, was the sitting state chairman and not Tolbert. "Our organization," he informed Taft, "is called 'lily white' because we protest against the Republican party in the state being all black." Tolbert's faction, according to Capers, was nearly an all-black group—twenty-two of its twenty-five-member State Executive Committee were Negroes, and of the forty-three counties in the state, forty-two had Negro county chairmen. Capers then asked: "Are the colored men in the state who really represented devoted interest in the Republican party in the nation-at-large going to allow themselves to be led in solid phalanx in this way for the sole purpose of carrying on their shoulders a few white officeholders headed for the pie counter."[5]

Nonetheless, the officeholders continued in their steadfast support of the president; Charleston Postmaster Harris wrote to Hilles four days after Roosevelt's Columbus declaration that it would create confusion in the state convention on February 29, but "it has had the effect of drawing the true friends of the President closer to him and making them more determined than ever that he be nominated." J. Duncan Adams also wrote to Hilles expressing concern because Roosevelt's announcement came so close to the meeting of the state convention but saying the Tolbert followers were "going to do our very best." He suggested further that the administration send "a good speaker and one that will be willing to come to our convention and make a rousing speech." It would help, he reasoned, to secure a solid delegation for Taft in the state gathering.[6]

Republicans in Florida and Georgia had already held state conventions before the meeting of the Taft wing of the South Carolina party on February 29 in Columbia. Although Tolbert and his adherents had expected difficulty in the meeting, there was no demonstration for the colonel, and a solid at-large delegation to Chicago was chosen for Taft. The somewhat docile convention put out a statement claiming to represent the only "regular" organization in the state and recommending that Tolbert replace Capers as national committeeman at the national convention. Tolbert and Adams, along with two Negroes, J. R. Levy and W. T. Andrews, were named as delegates to Chicago; the district delegates were to be chosen later at local conventions. Capers did not attend the gathering, but gave out a statement in Washington that his "executive committee" would call a second convention later in the year to determine a course of action.[7]

Conditions were similar in Georgia, where the state organization, which was also small and dominated by the black-and-tan faction, held a state convention on February 14 to choose a delegation to the Chicago convention well before Roosevelt tossed his hat into the ring. Even though a Taft at-large delegation was selected before the colonel's forces had an opportunity to organize, the former president had been in touch with Republican activities in Georgia since early January through Julian Le Rose Harris, editor of the widely circulated *Uncle Remis Magazine*. A son of the noted folklorist and essayist Joel Chandler Harris, founder of the magazine, Harris had printed a number of editorials favorable to Roosevelt, and although he played a peripheral role in southern Republican affairs, TR regularly conferred with him throughout 1912. Furthermore, Harris used his journal to advocate a greater justice for the Negro; and Roosevelt addressed his famous letter to him later in the year stating that there was no place in the Progressive party for the southern black.[8]

The Georgia party in 1912 was composed predominantly of Negroes, which no doubt contributed to Roosevelt's poor showing in the state. Following adoption of the all-white primary and its mandatory use in all counties after 1898 by the Democratic State Executive Committee, the GOP became primarily a black organization as white Republicans increasingly registered as Democrats in order to participate in the primaries. When Roosevelt took over the presidency in 1901, he followed a policy of appointing Negroes instead of white Republicans to positions within the party if not to federal office, and, although total disfranchisement did not come until 1908, the black-and-tans dominated the party in Georgia after the turn of the century. Perhaps an accurate picture of the party was painted by Ben J. Davis, long time editor of the Atlanta *Independent*, national leader of the Negro Odd Fellows, and GOP national committee-man for the state during the 1920s, when he wrote that out of 365 delegates attending the 1912 state conclave more than 150 were Caucasian, "the largest representation of white men who ever visited a Republican convention in Georgia."[9]

Although the Bourbon Democrats—led by the Confederate triumvirate of John B. Gordon, Joseph E. Brown, and Alfred E. Colquitt—dominated Georgia politics from the end of Reconstruction until the small farmers became politically active in the early 1890s, neither the Negro nor the Republican party was driven totally from the state's political scene. In the hard-fought primary of 1906, however, Hoke Smith won the gubernatorial nomination over Clark Howell on a progressive platform calling for various reforms, including stricter railroad regulation, but affording the Negro little hope of social justice. "The time had arrived," Smith argued, "to put the Negro out of politics and to end the disgraceful spectacle of the wholesale buying and selling of Negro votes and having the Negroes the umpire in every dispute among white factions." Two years later, at his urging, an amendment was added to the state constitution that drove the black man from Georgia politics through implementation of a grandfather clause and a provision requiring that a person own five hundred dollars in real property before qualifying to vote.[10]

Disfranchisement received the support of many Georgia politicians, including the Populist leader Thomas E. Watson, who after first opposing the plan came to recognize that fear of Negro political participation was harmful to Populist hopes for victory in the South. Watson, who served as a Populist member of Congress in the 1890s, the party vice-presidential nominee with James B. Weaver in 1896, and the 1904 presidential candidate, came to feel, according to C. Vann Woodward, that "once the 'bugaboo of negro domination' was removed . . . every white man would act according to his own conscience and judgment in deciding how he should vote." He came to this view after money had been used by the Democrats to buy Negro votes against his unsuccessful bid for reelection to the House; and in 1912 he employed his *Watson's Jeffersonian Weekly* to support Roosevelt and the Bull Moosers after the colonel decided against Negro involvement in the new party. The 1908 constitutional revisions limiting Negro voting produced an immediate decline in Republican strength so that Taft received a mere 6,172 votes out of a total 121,070 cast in 1912, and Charles Evans Hughes in 1916 got but 11,294 out of a total vote of 159,710.[11]

The party itself in Georgia was reduced to a mere shell of an organization with sharply divided factions contending for control of the patronage-dispensing apparatus. When the first district convention met at Savannah on February 12, 1912, to select delegates to both state and national conventions, no Roosevelt sentiment surfaced, but a bitter fight took place among the officeholding factions. Interestingly, both groups endorsed Taft for renomination, but Henry S. Jackson, collector of internal revenue at Atlanta and national committeeman after 1912, sought control of the gathering in his bid to wrest the state machine from Henry S. Blun, postmaster at Savannah. Jackson, who was national committeeman until his death in 1927, held sway over Georgia Republican politics during the Taft, Wilson, Harding, and Coolidge administrations. An executive of the Southern Railroad before his recognition as Taft's agent in the state, Jackson was a son of Howell Edmunds Jackson, Democratic member of the U.S. Senate from Tennessee, 1881–1886, and a justice of the United States Supreme Court until his death in 1895.[12]

Even though the father remained a lifelong Democrat and was appointed to the high court by Grover Cleveland upon the death of L. Q. C. Lamar, the son readily embraced the Republican party. Jackson's rival for mastery of the party in Georgia was Blun, national committeeman, 1908–1912, and postmaster at Savannah since 1902. Blun was a banker of considerable wealth, president of the influential National Association of Postmasters, which gave him national political clout, and a longtime officer in the Georgia National Guard. He was forced from his position as national committeeman in 1912 primarily through the efforts of Ben J. Davis, who used both his newspaper and his position as head of the Negro Odd Fellows, which had twenty-five thousand members in Georgia alone, to tout Jackson as leader of the Negro-dominated GOP in the state.[13]

Jackson worked diligently—and was praised accordingly among Negro politicians by Davis—to bring whites into active participation in Republican activities in order to give the party a degree of "respectability." He was aided by Henry Lincoln Johnson, Negro recorder of deeds in Washington, in a drive to take the reins from Blun and State Chairman Walter H. Johnson in 1912 and to get a solid Taft delegation to Chicago. Henry L. Johnson, described by Cornelius Troup as one of the most "influential politicians in the last quarter of the nineteenth century and the first quarter of the twentieth," was educated at Atlanta University and the University of Michigan Law School before entering Georgia Republican politics. At the 1908 National Convention, he was responsible for having the first pro-Negro stance inserted into a national party platform. Johnson enjoyed

long leadership among black Republicans not only in Georgia but throughout the South before and after his appointment as recorder in 1909 by
Taft.[14]

Both Jackson and Henry Lincoln Johnson were busy informing the
White House about developments in the state for weeks prior to the state
convention. Although the meeting took place in Atlanta well before
Roosevelt and his followers could organize a bandwagon, Johnson told
Hilles on February 2: "The situation in Georgia is perfect. There is no
opposition that can possibly affect the clear and undisputed title to a single
one of our delegates." Jackson, whom Taft would soon have occasion to
distrust, also reported to the presidential secretary: "You may have seen
some of the articles in the newspapers as to the Roosevelt movement here,
but this amounts to nothing." The colonel's support in Georgia, according
to Jackson, was "composed of about five or six negro men headed by
former collector [H. A.] Rucker, and not one of them is registered;
therefore not a one of them could vote . . . or even hold a mass meeting
without violating the law."[15]

When State Chairman Walter H. Johnson called the meeting to order,
Ben J. Davis's Atlanta *Independent* reported that "if there was one
Roosevelt man [present], he failed to mention Teddy's name or offer any
opposition to the Taft program." The "unanimous and harmonious"
gathering quickly chose four delegates-at-large to Chicago and instructed
them to vote "first, last, and all the time" for Taft's renomination. Walter
H. Johnson, a native of Muscogee County and son of James Johnson, a
Unionist congressman in the 1850s and a Reconstruction governor of the
state, opened the convention by reviewing his twenty-five years of service
to the party in Georgia and thanking those who had labored with him. He
was not only a perennial delegate to GOP national conventions, but, like
most southern Republican leaders with long service to the party, he was
also the recipient of numerous federal appointments, including postmaster
at Columbus, collector of internal revenue, and United States marshal.
Henry S. Blun and Johnson remained loyal to the national Republican
organization but together formed the core of opposition to Jackson–Henry
L. Johnson domination of the party during the 1912 campaign; they
refused, however, to become identified with the Roosevelt campaign when
it developed a few months later.[16]

In Florida, the Republican party was also small and controlled by
Negroes, but unlike the situation in Georgia, a full-blown Roosevelt
movement was under way when the GOP state convention met on February 6 in Palatka. The Florida convention, which was the first to meet
anywhere in the nation, was purposely called early by state leaders working
hand-in-glove with Hilles and Postmaster General Hitchcock before the
anticipated Roosevelt candidacy could become established. Moreover, it

set the pattern for other GOP gatherings in the region during 1912, when division and rancor between the backers of Roosevelt and Taft led to a rump convention and the naming of a rival delegation to Chicago.[17]

Ormsby McHarg's trip across the lower South during January in behalf of Roosevelt feeling out disgruntled Republicans no doubt prompted the administration to seek an early convention in Florida. There is some question whether he actually conferred with Florida Republicans prior to the Palatka gathering, although he was in neighboring Alabama in mid-January talking with Judge Oscar R. Hundley and Joseph O. Thompson of that state. Some months after the February 6 state convention, McHarg reportedly "entered the State of Florida not at the request of any Florida Republicans but at the instigation of certain interests in the North and with him he brought a considerable amount of money for the purpose of organizing an opposition to the Regular Reorganized Republican Party." Whether acting on its own initiative or in league with McHarg, however, a Roosevelt mass meeting in Escambia County met on January 26 and elected delegates instructed to vote for Roosevelt at the upcoming state gathering after the regularly called county convention had failed to do so; and when these and similar delegates were not recognized at Palatka, a rival Roosevelt state convention was called into session.[18]

Although Roosevelt and Taft combined polled less than 14,000 votes in Florida in 1912, each man eagerly sought the state's twelve delegates, the least number from any southern state to the Republican National Convention. The state's GOP vote had been seriously crippled since 1885–1889, however; Roosevelt had polled a mere 8,314 votes in 1904 and Taft failed to do much better in 1908, with 10,654 tallies or about 21 percent of the presidential vote. The decline in Republican strength was tied directly to black disfranchisement and the reestablishment of Democratic superiority through constitutional revision. As late as 1880, Negroes outnumbered whites in nine Florida counties that contained one-half of the state's population; though the Bourbons had been in power since 1877, they had made no move to exclude the Negro and the Republicans as a threat to one-party domination of the state. Significantly, the Constitutional Convention of 1885 did not insert a poll tax provision when it rewrote the state's governing document but granted authority to the legislature to enact such a tax, not to exceed one dollar per year, with the proceeds to be devoted to education. Negro control of local black-belt politics was completely scotched, however, by provisions empowering the governor to appoint county commissioners and mandating the bonding of all county officers.[19]

The 1889 legislature used the limiting clauses in the constitution to enact a poll tax and, in addition, passed a multiple-ballot-box law similar to that of South Carolina which, according to H. D. Price, "struck the Negro, and the Republican party in Florida, at their weakest points." Additional restrictive legislation followed, such as substitution of a complicated Australian ballot for the cumbersome multiple-ballot scheme and implementation of the all-white primary. By 1901–1902 the Republican party as a vote-getting organization had nearly collapsed in the state. The elimination of a GOP–Negro threat resulted in the election of a reform governor, Napoleon Bonaparte Broward, in 1904 and the beginnings of a rudimentary Progressive movement in Florida that extended through his two successors. The removal of Negroes from the polling place gave white Democrats the opportunity to enact reform legislation without fear that opposing factions could use blacks as political pawns. Not until the election of Sidney J. Catts, a backwoods Baptist preacher from Alabama, in 1916, was the Bourbon-Progressive alliance created by Broward in the aftermath of disfranchisement overturned.[20]

White Progressives in Florida, like those in Georgia and the rest of the South, however, had no intention of extending their electoral reforms to include the Negro or the Republican party so that when the Palatka meeting came to order in February 1912, it represented few bona fide voters. Yet Joseph E. Lee, secretary of the State Executive Committee and a staunch administration man, attempted to control the gathering by carefully excluding Roosevelt men chosen in Escambia and other counties. A Negro, Lee had long been a force in Florida and the lower South after his appointment to the "fattest federal job" in the state—collector of customs at Jacksonville—by McKinley. Both Roosevelt and Taft had kept him on as collector, but in 1912 he not only presided over the state convention but also joined forces with Henry S. Chubb, who held the dual posts of state chairman and national committeeman, in securing Florida for the president.[21]

Although Lee had spearheaded a fight against the lily-whites for nearly two decades, Chubb informed the White House when the state conclave assembled that the "personnel of the delegates was largely white men and the colored delegates were responsible, reputable men to a large degree." Henry S. Chubb managed the party in Florida from 1899 when he was named state chairman until his death in 1918. He had been born in Wisconsin and educated in Vermont before arriving in Florida in 1879 at age twenty-one. After locating at Winter Park, where he became general manager for an organization that operated five hundred acres of orange groves, he studied the orange industry and became an expert on its practical aspects. Long active in Republican politics, he was appointed by McKinley as receiver of the U.S. Land Office at Gainesville, a post he retained until well into the Wilson administration, and he was named national committeeman in 1911, replacing James N. Coombs, with the blessing of Taft.[22]

The state convention immediately split into rival factions when the Taft-dominated Executive Committee refused to seat Roosevelt adherents sent by mass meetings in Columbia, Escambia, and Hillsborough counties, although they seemingly held valid credentials. Chubb and Lee, however, consistently took the position throughout the campaign that a division had not occurred because the Roosevelt delegates had not been legitimately picked at the local conventions and therefore their expulsion had no effect. After the departure of the Roosevelt delegates to form a separate caucus, the Taft followers named a slate of delegates to Chicago and a state ticket to oppose the Democrats in November while "a brass band played popular airs."[23]

William R. O'Neal, who was tapped as the party's gubernatorial nominee, was a native of Belpre, Ohio. He came to Orlando in 1885 and became active in a variety of insurance, publishing, and banking interests; he was also a founder of Rollins College and served as its acting president on five different occasions. O'Neal worked closely with Chubb and the Taft campaign in 1912; he served as GOP national committeeman after Chubb's death and ran unsuccessfully for both the U.S. House and Senate before his own death in 1946.[24]

The Roosevelt rump convention, which met the same day in Palatka, also chose a slate of delegates to the forthcoming national convention, though all of them were later abandoned by the national Roosevelt campaign. Meanwhile, Chubb kept up a propaganda barrage by repeatedly telling the press: "There was absolutely less than six delegates who left the hall out of the total number constituting the convention during its session." Yet several Florida newspapers thought the insurgents were more numerous than the Taft loyalists. Chubb further informed the White House: "When the convention was nearly over, four delegates left the hall. There was no split or bolt except the retiring of these three or four delegates."[25]

Roosevelt, who was visiting in Miami at the time of the Palatka gathering, was apprised of its deliberations, but apparently was confused about his advocates in the state. Ten days following the convention, Frank Knox, who was in daily contact with the Rough Rider, wrote on behalf of Roosevelt to John H. Dickinson of Palatka, who was presumably one of the three or four bolters: "Your telegram relating to the endorsement of Colonel Roosevelt is very interesting and gratifying. This committee would be pleased to have you write fully and completely of the circumstances surrounding the Florida convention." Some weeks later, McHarg came to the state representing the national campaign committee to initiate a genuine Roosevelt movement under the direction of H. L. Anderson, a Jacksonville attorney.[26]

In Alabama, in marked contrast to the fumbling efforts in South Carolina, Georgia, and Florida, a fully developed Roosevelt boom was present from the opening of the campaign. Joseph Oswalt Thompson, an old-line Republican and former postmaster at Tuskegee (where his father had been mayor), announced for Roosevelt on January 9 and served with

Judge Oscar R. Hundley of Huntsville as the Rough Rider's chief agent in Alabama. Roosevelt had appointed Thompson his referee at the urging of Booker T. Washington after 1901, which meant that he was the "official dispenser of patronage for the state,"[27] when the former president was attempting to create his own GOP organizations in the South. A native of the state and graduate of Alabama Military Institute, Thompson was a wealthy cotton planter with landholdings in several counties and a perennial federal officeholder. He was no longer referee after 1909, but held the dual posts of GOP state chairman and collector of internal revenue under Taft.[28]

Thompson lost his job as state chairman through administration interference at a state convention in August 1911 and was replaced by Pope M. Long of Cordova, a Taft stalwart. Nonetheless, he worked with Hundley during the 1912 campaign for Roosevelt, although both men ultimately left the GOP and cast their lots with the Progressive party when it was organized. McHarg, apparently wishing to capitalize upon discontent within the Alabama party, approached Thompson and Hundley in early January, asking them to form a Roosevelt movement in the state. Hundley, another Alabama native and graduate of the Vanderbilt Law School, was a longtime railroad attorney and from 1886 to 1897 a member of the state legislature. An influential and respected member of the Alabama bar, he was appointed judge of the state's Northern Judicial District in 1903 by Roosevelt, although he had not joined the Republican party until 1896 when Bryan's nomination for the presidency forced him to leave the Democrats because of conscience.[29]

When the State Executive Committee met in Birmingham on January 11, 1912, to set the date for the Republican State Convention, it was apparent that the pro-Taft element was in complete control and in no mood to accept a challenge from the Rooseveltites. At best, the party leadership under National Committeeman Prelate D. Barker and Pope M. Long represented a skeletal electorate as a result of the 1901 state constitution that barred Negroes from active political participation because of the now famous grandfather clause. After 1900, the Republicans were able simply to maintain ranks by engaging in occasional skirmishes with the Democrats and by appointments to federal offices in the state from Republican presidents. In a few hill counties, they controlled local offices and usually sent one or two representatives to the legislature.[30]

Although Booker T. Washington and the black community fought attempts to limit the ballot, disfranchisement came about through the urging of Governor William F. Sanford and the Bourbons, who used the familiar argument that elimination of Negro political corruption and vote fraud would permit the state to move forward. With the recent Populist challenge—which had considerable Negro participation—firmly in mind, the 1901 Constitutional Convention put together a document that required a poll tax and the ability to read and write any part of the federal Constitution in the English language. A grandfather clause was included to protect illiterate white voters, but the impact upon black voting had the same disastrous effect as in neighboring states; the 55,561 tallies cast for McKinley in 1900 dropped to 25,561 for Taft in 1908. Moreover, as a direct result of disfranchisement, a more cohesive Democratic party initiated a fledgling Progressive movement under Governor Braxton Bragg Comer, 1907–1911, when such measures as railroad legislation, child labor laws, and forest conservation were enacted into law.[31]

At the January meeting of the Republican State Committee, the battle lines between the warring party factions became tightly drawn. One newspaper reported that "the waters had been well-oiled, and all possibility of a storm eliminated as a result of prearrangement" by the Taft faction. Not only was Taft's administration praised and endorsed in the most glowing terms along with Barker and Long's handling of the Alabama party, but representatives of the Roosevelt element were even denied permission to plead the colonel's case before the committee. The state convention was set for March 7 in Birmingham, and to the disgust of the TR men, the delegates to be chosen there were pledged in advance by the committee to support the president in the national convention.[32]

Barker and Long were called to the White House in early February along with other Republican caciques from the South in a further attempt to scotch the swelling Roosevelt movement. National Committeeman Barker was entrusted with the campaign in Alabama, and he corresponded regularly during 1912 with GOP leaders in other parts of the country in Taft's behalf. Although he was a native of Connecticut and had moved to the state in 1857, Barker remained a force in both Alabama and national councils from 1865 until his death. After serving in the Confederate army during the Civil war, he joined the Republican party, and in 1871 President Grant appointed him collector of internal revenue for the second Alabama district; under Hayes he served as collector for the entire state. Barker of course lost out during Cleveland's first administration, but in 1890 Harrison named him postmaster at Mobile, a position he retained under McKinley, Roosevelt, and Taft. He stayed loyal to the regular organization in 1912, as did many GOP chieftains, North and South, who fought off the Roosevelt threat, which, had it been successful, would have ruined their hold on the patronage.[33]

Roosevelt's backers in the state attempted to discredit the regular organization. Judge Hundley told newspapermen on January 12 that State Chairman Long had packed the state committee with federal officeholders beholden to the president for retention of their jobs. According to Hundley, more than half the committee that had just declared for Taft held "commissions either under President Taft or by appointment of Taft's appointees, and among the number holding such commissions will be found one or more, who are deputy marshals under Mr. Long." The continued drive for Roosevelt by Thompson and Hundley embodied among other organizational techniques the apparent free use of campaign badges, which prompted Long to write the White House that, though "everything looks rosy," Taft badges were "badly needed as a counter measure."[34]

Shortly after McHarg's foray into Alabama in support of Roosevelt, an organizational meeting in Birmingham of "progressive republicans" under the direction of Dr. Louis Edelman issued a call for all Republicans to "make a fight for the election of national convention delegates who will work for the nomination of a man of progressive ideas for the Presidency." Presumably that man was Theodore Roosevelt, and the Progressive movement within the state GOP, which according to Edelman had been under way since 1910, advocated a platform demanding the direct election of senators, direct primaries for president and vice-president, direct election of delegates to national conventions with the opportunity for voters to express a choice for the top spots on the national ticket, amendment of the state constitution to provide for the initiative, referendum, and recall, and a realistic corrupt practices act. Clearly, this platform paralleled the declarations made by Roosevelt at Osawatomie and on countless hustings since his return from abroad.[35]

Joseph O. Thompson's association with this and other schemes favorable to Roosevelt's nomination led the administration to oust him as keeper of the federal building in Birmingham. Birmingham Postmaster Truman H. Aldrich, who with Barker and Long had conferred at the White House during early February and who would carry the party's gubernatorial banner in 1912, was chosen by Taft to replace the recalcitrant Thompson. A native of New York, Aldrich had moved to Selma in 1870 after receiving a mining engineering degree from Rensselaer Polytechnic Institute. He engaged in banking before taking up coal mining in the state and in 1892 became general manager of the massive Tennessee Coal, Iron, and Railroad Company; Aldrich was also a serious student of geology and published widely in that field. A lifelong Republican and former congressman, he was named postmaster by Taft and held the job until Wilson appointed him to the War Industries Board during World War I.[36]

With Thompson thus eliminated from any position of influence, the Taft element sought to consolidate its grip on the party machinery at the district meetings in late February that would name delegates to the March 6 state convention. In meeting after meeting the Taft people won complete control, endorsing both the administration in Washington and Barker's handling of affairs in Alabama. Several districts even adopted resolutions "deploring" Roosevelt's candidacy, and the meeting at Montgomery declared against a third term for any presidential candidate. State Chairman Long promptly informed Hilles that Taft delegates had been elected in all nine districts and that he was "taking no chances" prior to the Birmingham convention. And Barker, in Charleston, South Carolina, on administration business, told the *Evening Post* that "the nomination of Theodore Roosevelt would be the greatest stroke of luck that has ever befallen the Democrats" and that in his opinion the former president would "never get the support of the conservative Republicans of this country."[37]

Meanwhile, Thompson and Hundley devised their own plan, with the full support of Roosevelt, for getting up a delegation to the national convention to contest the one for Taft certain to be named at the state conclave. First, Thompson told reporters he "had not the slightest doubt that Col. Roosevelt would be nominated . . . and overwhelmingly elected" in the aftermath of his Columbus declaration. At the same time, a call was issued to all Republicans who could support the colonel to meet in Birmingham on March 16, about two weeks after the regular state convention, "for the purpose of discussing ways and means to accomplish" his nomination. The call also expressed Roosevelt's disapproval of the recent district conventions and requested an inquiry into the "irregular methods being adopted and used to thwart the will of the people and looking to securing legal delegations to the next national convention from this state."[38]

In adjacent Mississippi, where Taft had gotten only 4,315 votes in 1908, the party was in such poor shape that neither presidential aspirant demonstrated interest in the state's twenty delegates to Chicago during the first part of the campaign. Both the Negro and the Republican party vote had been reduced sharply by the much touted "second Mississippi plan" created in 1890 through a rewriting of the state constitution. Eight years later, when the U.S. Supreme Court upheld the restrictive features of the new document in *Williams v. Mississippi*, its citizenship, "understanding," and poll tax provisions as prerequisites for voting made it a model for disfranchisement across the lower South. Moreover, the plan had no grandfather clause to protect illiterate white voters so that all segments of the electorate were affected, although the Negro was hardest hit by its limiting clauses.[39]

The overriding issue in the 1890 Constitutional Convention had been disfranchisement of the Negroes, more because they were political pawns than because of their race. Again, the cry of black voting corruption and fraud was used as a means of ensuring both white supremacy and Democratic party ascendancy. The convention was dominated totally by Democrats; only one Republican, Isaiah T. Montgomery, founder of the all-black community at Mound Bayou, sat among its 134 members. Another Negro, F. M. B. Cook, was shot and killed in Jasper County for campaigning as a convention delegate. Such tactics led the able southern scholar, Albert D. Kirwan, to assert: "From 1890 the legal Negro voter, and consequently the Republican party, has been a negligible factor in state-wide elections. The Republican party, which had polled 52,000 votes for Hayes in 1876 and more than 43,000 for Blaine as late as 1884, cast less than 1,500 for Harrison in 1892. In no election thereafter until 1920 did the party poll as many as 6,000 votes."[40]

The diminutive party in Mississippi was used exclusively for the renomination of Taft in 1912 by Lonzo B. Moseley, whom one national magazine characterized as controlling the state's Republican organization in league with certain Negroes. He had been national committeeman and referee since 1904 and a federal officeholder since 1890, when Benjamin Harrison appointed him deputy U.S. marshal. Moseley reportedly whipped "his organization into line by sending twenty delegates to Chicago and by making the Negroes professional jurors in the Federal Court." In 1912, he was not only national committeeman but also leader of the State Executive Committee, and as such he was chief dispenser of the state's patronage. *Colliers Magazine* further reported that "for more than a generation he dominated the 900,000 Negroes of the State. The total Republican vote of the state is 4,500. And of these 4,000 are Negroes." In addition to his other jobs, Moseley held three federal posts simultaneously at the time of the 1912 race: clerk of the U.S. District Court, federal jury commissioner, and United States commissioner.[41]

Although Moseley had complete charge of the regular party machinery before and during the all-important Republican State Convention at Jackson on March 28, a dissident group of Negroes outside the patronage clique attempted to identify themselves with the budding Roosevelt movement beforehand. Led by Dr. Sidney Dillon Redmond, a prominent physician-lawyer, this faction sought in vain for recognition from the colonel only to be cruelly rejected both during the preconvention drive for delegates and after formation of the Bull Moose party; thus Taft won Mississippi by default. Redmond, forty-one years of age in 1912, was a graduate of Rust College at Holly Springs, Mississippi, and the Illinois Medical College; he later attended the Howard University Law School and was admitted to the Mississippi bar. Throughout his life, Redmond was active in Republican circles but was not a member of the officeholding faction. He regularly attended state and national conventions, however, and was a founder of the American Trust and Savings Bank in Jackson. Redmond's wife was a daughter of Hiram Revels, United States senator from Mississippi during Reconstruction.[42]

The Negro Republicans who followed Redmond finally bolted the regular GOP and voted for Wilson, although another group of anti-Moseley blacks remained in the party and fought without success for Roosevelt. Perry W. Howard, Redmond's half-brother, carried on a correspondence with the Roosevelt campaign during the summer of 1912, remained in the regular organization, and was ultimately seated in the national convention as a Roosevelt delegate. This Negro leader, who later became national committeeman after the Bull Moose bolt had been spent, was active in Republican activities until his death in 1961. Howard attended both Rust College and Fisk University before receiving a law degree from DePauw University in 1905; he practiced law in Mississippi before going to Washington during the Harding administration as an assistant attorney general under Harry M. Daugherty.[43]

Mississippi Democrats understandably ignored the squabbles between Moseley, Howard, and Redmond for control of the state's bantam-sized Republican organization, which was primarily a Negro party and one that was badly divided. The three-sided contest among Woodrow Wilson, Champ Clark, and Oscar Underwood for delegates to the Democratic National Convention in fact engendered little interest among the state's white voters, although Underwood won the May 7 preferential primary by a slight margin. And at the party's national conclave in Baltimore the Mississippians voted forty-five times as a unit for Underwood before joining Alabama, Florida, and Georgia on the next ballot in voting for the Progressive Wilson. This latent switch from a conservative candidate to join her sister states in the lower South did not include, however, an embracing of Theodore Roosevelt and his brand of Progressivism although it, too, demanded creation of an all-white party in the South.[44]

When Roosevelt determined later in the campaign to bar Negroes from the Progressive party, he turned to a lifelong Democrat, Benjamin F. Fridge of Ellisville, to lead his fortunes in the state. Fridge, who subsequently became Bull Moose national committeeman, was a prominent banker and lumberman as well as a veteran of the Spanish-American War. His son Arthur, also a Democrat, was adjutant general of the Mississippi National Guard in 1912, although he took no part in the Roosevelt movement. Fridge had known the colonel for several years prior to the campaign, was a close friend of the Louisianian, John M. Parker, and had been associated with his drive to create a white opposition party in the South.[45]

Unlike Mississippi, where Taft's forces dominated the GOP organization throughout the preconvention campaign, in Louisiana an intense Roosevelt bandwagon under the direction of Pearl Wight of New Orleans was developing several weeks before the colonel's Columbus declaration. Although John M. Parker, who had been Roosevelt's host during his 1911 visit to New Orleans and who subsequently became his chief lieutenant in the South, was in close touch with Oyster Bay from early January 1912, he did not actively join the campaign until August, following TR's break with the Republican party. Roosevelt, however, depended upon Wight from the start to handle his affairs in the Pelican State, including an invitation to visit Sagamore Hill, and consulted with him throughout 1912. Wight, who was referee and national committeeman, had been leader of the lily-white

Republicans since the turn of the century—the group that became the nucleus of Roosevelt's sizable support in Louisiana.[46]

A native of Maine, Wight had first arrived in New Orleans by way of Pennsylvania at age twenty-two during the height of Reconstruction. He immediately launched upon a business career as head of Woodward, Wight, and Company, dealers in hardware, machinery, and mill supplies for the maritime trade, which he directed until 1909 when he sold out to his employees. He also dabbled in Republican politics while amassing a fortune in the South American fruit trade, shipbuilding, railroading, and banking. Along with Parker he was organizer of numerous cotton and commercial expositions in the lower South; Wight was long active in New Orleans and southern civic affairs. As a New Englander, he understandably affiliated with the pint-sized GOP in Louisiana and in 1905 became national committeeman and referee for Roosevelt after spearheading a drive to make the Republican party a lily-white club following disfranchisement.[47]

When the Negro was barred from the polling booth by constitutional mandate in Louisiana as in other southern states, a lily-white drive was started to make the GOP "respectable" by eliminating him from the party. Thus, the lily-whites' admiration for Roosevelt dated from 1902, when as president he commenced a policy of recognizing "the better elements of Republicans." Wight, as leader of this faction, continued as referee under Taft, to the growing dissatisfaction of the Negroes, so that a party schism was ready-made when the 1912 presidential campaign developed. Wight, who had first received political recognition from TR, had an understandable desire to lead the lily-whites back into the Roosevelt camp, which prompted the colonel to dispatch his trusted aide Frank Knox on a mission to the Louisianian early in the campaign to solicit and make certain of his support.[48]

At best, however, there were few Republicans in Louisiana to be led under either presidential banner because the 1898 constitution had effectively disfranchised the state's Negro voters as well as many illiterate white ones. This "white supremacy constitution" contained a grandfather clause that exempted males 21 years of age or older whose father or grandfather could vote before January 1, 1867, from educational and property tests to register. Otherwise, a literacy test was required which most Negroes in the state could not pass, and the impact upon the Republican party was as instantaneous and drastic as similar constitutional rewritings in other parts of Dixie. McKinley received 18,000 votes in 1896, but his vote dropped to 14,000 in 1900, a decline of 22 percent; Roosevelt got 5,205 tallies in 1904, although in 1908 Taft did some better with nearly 9,000. At the time the 1898 constitution was drafted, over 130,000 Negroes were on the registration books, but by early 1900, only 5,320 were still registered, yet Negroes counted for approximately half the state's population. The lily-white Republicans had an obvious numerical advantage in the state GOP as the number of qualified Negro voters continued to plummet until 1910, when only 730 were on the rolls. As late as 1940, only 879 blacks were qualified to vote in the state.[49]

The intensity of Populist insurgency in Louisiana as well as the court decision in *Plessy v. Ferguson,* upholding the separate but equal doctrine, had goaded the Bourbons to work for disfranchisement when that group became convinced a combined Negro–illiterate white vote could conceivably wrest control of the state from them. Under the leadership of Governor Foster J. Murphy, an amendment to the 1879 constitution was submitted to the voters in 1896 to bring about disfranchisement. The proposal failed to be ratified, although a lopsidedly Bourbon legislature, elected at the same time, imposed a series of restrictive balloting laws upon the state's illiterate voters. A new voter registration law barred at least 90 percent of Louisiana Negroes from voting, as well as many Populists and Republicans. With the non-Democratic vote thus reduced, a constitutional convention was summoned into session during 1898 for the purpose of limiting the state's voters to include only those who were literate, property-owners and their sons, and those who had been eligible to vote in 1867 and their descendants. The work of this convention and the 1913 constitution that followed meant that not until the latter half of the twentieth century would the Republican party be a viable force in Louisiana politics.[50]

The tiny Louisiana GOP found itself divided into three distinct parts when in 1912 Roosevelt and Taft began their quest for national convention delegates: the Negroes or black-and-tan faction, the lily-whites, and the numerous politicos in the Customs House at New Orleans. An unusually complicated party structure was compounded by the huge number of sugar planters in Louisiana who flocked to the Republican standard in 1912 and later to the Bull Moose party because of dissatisfaction with Democratic tariff policies that placed sugar on the free list.

Many of the sugar growers who drifted into the GOP, led by William J. Behan, although formerly Democrats, joined Wight and the lily-whites for the 1912 canvass; others followed the lead of Jules Godchaux, who reportedly had an understanding with Hilles that if reelected Taft would oppose free sugar. Behan, who was chairman of the Republican State Executive Committee in 1912, early sided with the Rooseveltites and worked with Wight to secure a TR delegation to Chicago. A rich sugar planter, he left the Democrats during Cleveland's administration as a result of the party's effort to put sugar on the free list and affiliated with the Republicans because of their protection and sound money policies. Behan had served as an officer in the Confederate army with Robert E. Lee throughout the Virginia and Maryland campaigns and was present at

Appomattox; later he entered Louisiana Democratic politics and served both as mayor of New Orleans and as a member of the state legislature. This political activity gave him clout not only with the planters but among the state's white voters generally.[51]

Another advocate of Roosevelt and lily-whiteism was Edward J. Thilborger of New Orleans, secretary of the Republican State Executive Committee since 1910. He was not directly associated with the planter faction, but was a lawyer and longtime member of the GOP and served as referee in bankruptcy of the U.S. Circuit Court at New Orleans from 1919 until Franklin D. Roosevelt was elected president in 1933. Thilborger not only worked with Wight and Behan for the Rough Rider within the regular organization in the first weeks of the campaign, but he was a chief organizer of the Progressive party in Louisiana and secretary of the Bull Moose State Central Committee from 1912 until 1916. In 1912 he also held the proxy of Wight on the Republican National Committee at the meeting in Chicago that led to the birth of the Progressive party.[52]

The lily-whites—recognized since 1908 as the legitimate Republican organization in Louisiana—displayed enough muscle in the party primary held on January 24, 1912, to nominate a state ticket and to elect several members of the State Executive Committee. Although the black-and-tan faction put up a hot fight, the lily-whites named their man, Hugh S. Suthon, as the gubernatorial nominee and grabbed a majority of the seats on the state and congressional committees. Several Negroes were named to the state committee, including J. Madison Vance, correspondent and confidant of Booker T. Washington, and Walter L. Cohen, also an ally of Washington's as well as leader of the black-and-tans. The lily-white vote would have been more top-heavy, reported the New Orleans *Picayune,* except "nine-tenths of the Lily Whites had registered as Democrats, so that they could participate in the Michael-Hall contest" for the Democratic nomination. A mere 967 votes were cast during the Republican primary in sixteen of the seventeen wards in the city of New Orleans and St. Bernard and Plaquemine's parishes, yet these were enough to hand the lily-whites a handsome victory.[53]

Walter L. Cohen, along with Victor Liosel, the acknowledged chief of Negro Republicans in Louisiana, immediately blasted the primary results to the press, charging that the lily-whites had used crooked tactics and even voted dead men at the polls, the same arguments used by whites to disfranchise Negroes in most southern states. Cohen was registrar of deeds in the U.S. Land Office at New Orleans until the post was abolished in 1911. Schooled in politics by former Governor P. B. S. Pinchback, he sided with Taft in 1912 and was seated as a delegate at the Chicago convention. Later he was confirmed as comptroller of customs despite strong senatorial opposition and held the post under Harding, Coolidge, and Hoover. Cohen worked hand-in-glove with Liosel, then U.S. marshal for Louisiana, to secure the Negro vote for Taft. Born of French parentage, Liosel, whose father had served in the Napoleonic campaigns, was a major planter in St. James Parish and was long associated with the GOP as federal officeholder and captain of the Negro faction.[54]

The old-line politicos in the Customs House at New Orleans constituted yet another Republican band vying for position and anxious to retain their grip on the patronage as the 1912 campaign intensified. This sizable group of federal officeholders formed a faction distinct from the Wight and Liosel-Cohen wings of the party and was solidly in the Taft camp from the outset because of its total dependence on the administration for jobs. Frank B. Williams, traditional leader of this clique and former referee, lost influence with Hilles early in the year, causing the president to hand over management of the Louisiana party to Clarence S. Herbert, collector of customs at New Orleans. As the Roosevelt boom gained momentum and Wight was removed as referee, (although he retained his place on the national committee), Herbert took over and later headed a pro-Taft delegation to Chicago following a White House-dictated compromise between the "customs house gang" and the Negroes.[55]

When Wight and the lily-whites were written off by the administration as irredeemably pro-Roosevelt, Herbert was given a clear field as Taft's manager for the remainder of the campaign. A native of Plaquemine, a descendant of original Acadian migrants, and a graduate of the Tulane Law School, Herbert had been appointed collector of internal revenue by Taft in 1911; he had been in the treasury service since 1903. At the 1912 Republican National Convention he was named national committeeman to replace Wight as a result of his close association with Hilles and the president. Interestingly, his brother Alvin E. Herbert was elected Louisiana secretary of state in 1912 on the Democratic ticket.[56]

The elevation of Herbert and the compromise imposed from Washington between the Negroes and the "customs house gang" created animosities within the Louisiana party that were not resolved until a meeting of the State Executive Committee in early March. Liosel, representing the black-and-tans and firm for Taft, was named state chairman in place of Frank B. Williams, who was forced out when three agents were sent into the state by Hilles and the national committee to perfect the Taft organization. As a result, Thilborger, who was still secretary of the State Executive Committee, resigned to join Wight and the Rooseveltites formally. These actions may have brought a degree of harmony to the elements backing Taft, but the Taft organization's forcing out of Williams and Thilborger and ignoring of Wight and the lily-whites led to the summoning of rival conventions in the state and the dispatch of three separate delegations to Chicago, each purporting to represent Louisiana in the national convention.[57]

Compared to the complicated factionalism that permeated Republicanism in Louisiana during 1912, the preconvention struggle in Texas was a simple tug-of-war between Roosevelt and Taft supporters for control of the state GOP organization. The pattern of events in Texas was fixed when Taft and Hilles recognized well before Roosevelt became an announced candidate that Cecil A. Lyon—state chairman since 1900, national committeeman since 1904, and personal friend of the Rough Rider—would be an obstacle to getting a pro-administration delegation from the Lone Star State. Therefore, a decision was made in early February to entrust the president's reelection drive to a prominent Houston businessman and sometime New Englander, Henry F. MacGregor, following a meeting at the White House at which Hilles urged him to lead the Taft campaign.[58]

Although announcement that MacGregor was assuming command of Taft's forces in Texas reportedly evoked a "chuckle" from Roosevelt and was ridiculed by National Committeeman Lyon, he waged an effective campaign for the president. MacGregor, who held the whip over the federal officeholders and controlled the allegiance of the Negroes, had been born in New Hampshire and moved to the Gulf Coast in the 1880s. Throughout his career in Texas, where he amassed a fortune operating streetcar lines in Galveston and Houston, MacGregor spent lengthy intervals in his home state. His extensive business interests included real estate, oil properties, banking, and, following 1912, a joint venture with Texas Governor Will Hobby in publishing the influential Houston *Post*. He generally took a secondary role in Republican activities until coming forward to lead the administration forces.[59]

Immediately upon his return from Washington, MacGregor undertook a fence-mending journey around the state seeking to line up support for Taft. He even sought an accommodation with Lyon for joint control of the party but was unequivocally rebuffed by that Roosevelt stalwart. In his search for loyal convention delegates, the new Taft general did, however, enlist the support of Hillsboro Postmaster Harry Beck and William H. Atwell, U.S. attorney at Dallas. Beck had been former National Committeeman E. H. R. Green's first lieutenant among the Negroes during the first years of the century before Lyon gained complete control after 1904 under the aegis of Roosevelt. Atwell had been appointed federal attorney by McKinley and was thus not directly affiliated with the colonel; he remained loyal to the GOP throughout 1912 and was subsequently rewarded with a federal judgeship by Warren G. Harding in 1922. He was also the party's 1922 gubernatorial nominee against Pat Neff.[60]

Although MacGregor shortly replaced Lyon as national committeeman and referee, he was seeking in 1912 to manipulate a party that had no possibility of winning at the polls. Texas Republicans, like their counterparts across the South, had fallen to a role of token opposition following disfranchisement; they had not elected a governor since Reconstruction nor a member of Congress since the 1890s. Although McKinley had polled 131,000 votes in 1900, the Republican tally fell drastically in the aftermath of two voting laws adopted in 1903 and 1905 so that Roosevelt got a mere 50,565 votes out of 232,919 cast in 1904 and Taft did little better four years later with 68,506 out of a total vote of 297,904. Yet several pockets of Republican strength existed in the state, primarily in the German counties of central Texas that had consistently returned GOP members to the legislature since the Civil War; in a handful of counties with large Negro populations in east Texas and along the Gulf Coast south of Houston; and, regrettably, in two or three counties along the Rio Grande where unscrupulous politicians often exploited the native Mexican population.[61]

Political parties in the state had enjoyed a free hand until the Terrell Election Laws imposed stringent regulations upon them. Although a white primary law was not enacted until 1923, the earlier statutes required a poll tax, a signed pledge of party loyalty, and a mandatory primary for any political organization receiving more than one hundred thousand votes in a previous election; they not only barred masses of Negroes from voting but ended the threat of their fusion with Populist and other protest movements as had happened in the 1880s and 1890s. Furthermore, because large numbers of poor whites and Mexican-Americans were also kept from the polling booth, the Democrats remained in perpetual control of the state because only they had the requisite numbers and resources to meet the primary and other requirements of the laws.[62]

The nearly nonexistent Republican vote did not alter the reality that Roosevelt could ill afford to have the forty-man Texas delegation to Chicago—by far the largest from the South—go to Taft by default. Roosevelt predictably appointed as his chief agent National Committeeman Cecil A. Lyon, a solid supporter from the first days of the campaign. A native of Georgia, but a Texan since childhood and a graduate of Austin College and the Pennsylvania Military College, Lyon had extensive business interests in the state and was a longtime commander of an infantry regiment in the Texas National Guard. He was not only leader of the lily-white faction but had been Roosevelt's host during the former president's much publicized visit to Texas in 1905, when the Rough Rider had spent most of his time hunting wolves and rattlesnakes near the Texas-Oklahoma border with Quanah Parker, the fabled Indian chieftain. In October 1912, Lyon pulled a murderous pearl-handled pistol from his coat on a sidewalk in Milwaukee to keep the curious at bay following Roosevelt's wounding by a lunatic during the campaign.[63]

Even before Roosevelt officially tossed his hat in the ring, two emissaries had been sent into Texas to gain Lyon's support: Frank Knox, who also talked with Wight in Louisiana, conferred with the Texan on his swing across the country in the colonel's behalf in mid-February, and former Congressman William W. Cocks of New York arrived in San Antonio a few days later. Shortly afterward, Lyon announced that he would work for an uninstructed delegation to Chicago as the best method of heading off Taft, and he sent out word that those he had appointed to the federal service while he was referee should not endanger their jobs by joining in the fray for Roosevelt. This plea came on the heels of a new Hilles-MacGregor policy of "terrorizing" the officeholders for Taft.[64]

Lyon's hold on the party not only received a sharp rap when he was removed as referee, but Hilles and MacGregor picked up a formidable ally when Colonel John M. Simpson, the Republican nominee for governor four years earlier, came out for the president. Simpson, whose son Sloan was postmaster at Dallas, was a Tennessee native and veteran of the Confederate army but had come to Texas after the Civil War and built a fortune in ranching and banking. He was a former Democrat who could not stomach the "Bryanization" of his party, and he enjoyed considerable clout with conservative Republicans and Democrats as leader of the powerful Texas Cattle Raiser's Association. Nor could Lyon count on the black-and-tan faction, which was irretrievably in the Taft corner throughout the campaign. Emmett Scott, personal secretary to Booker T. Washington, accurately voiced the attitude of the Negroes when he informed the White House from Tuskegee: "The most flagrant representative of 'Lily Whiteism' in the South is the man, Cecil Lyon of Texas, and the colored people of the United States have his name engraved on their memories as the most consistent representative of this odious type of republicanism."[65]

Even the Democrats—who for the most part ignored the Roosevelt-Taft tilt—joined in downgrading Lyon. The San Antonio *Express* reported that Senator Joseph W. Bailey of Texas condemned Roosevelt's "third term ambitions" during a Washington speech in which he jokingly invited Taft to join the Democratic party "in case of failure at Chicago." Furthermore, La Follette's supporters came out with a strongly worded statement criticizing Roosevelt's candidacy following the Wisconsin senator's unfortunate collapse. Their organization, the Progressive League of Texas, tore into Lyon, urging that his control of the Texas GOP be terminated immediately. But the Texan continued to make headway in his efforts to secure the state for Roosevelt and to enjoy the total confidence of the former president himself. Lyon was shortly named to a seven-man national campaign committee—the "Roosevelt general staff"—and placed in charge of the Southwest.[66]

Undeterred by mounting criticisms, Lyon traveled to San Antonio and Houston for personal chats with regional GOP leaders, where he also found that sentiment for Roosevelt predominated among the party rank and file. He publicly operated on the premise that the Texas Republican organization was almost wholly for Roosevelt, with the exception of the officeholders who were being pressured by Hilles and MacGregor, as he sought to convene the State Executive Committee for a March 5 meeting in

Fort Worth. Lyon did not expect support from Texas Negroes in his crusade to maneuver the committee into a favorable stance for the Rough Rider.[67]

Webster Flanagan, collector of internal revenue at Austin and still remembered for his "What are we up here for?" speech, informed the White House in early February that Lyon was seeking to call the state committee into session and warned Hilles it was "being done under cover" so that Taft's people would not have time to organize. A son of J. W. Flanagan, United States senator from Texas during Reconstruction and a perpetual officeholder from the 1870s until the inauguration of Woodrow Wilson (except during Cleveland's administration), he had every reason to be leery of Lyon's hold on the state GOP and the intensity of Roosevelt's support in the state. Although no longer referee, Lyon still held the dual posts of national committeeman and state chairman and was in a position to outgeneral the Taft people—Flanagan among them—when the committee met. By a vote of twenty-seven to one, the Lyon-dominated committee endorsed Roosevelt for the nomination at Chicago.[68]

In Arkansas, the regular party machinery, which was under the heavy hand of National Committeeman Powell Clayton and State Chairman Harmon L. Remmel, was solidly behind the president throughout January and February and simply would not tolerate a Roosevelt challenge. Even so, the colonel had enthusiastic supporters during the early foment over his candidacy who set out in a futile effort to get the state's eighteen votes in the national convention for him. Although in the South only South Carolina with twelve votes had a lesser voice in the Chicago conclave, the state's delegation was nonetheless a desirable plum for Roosevelt. But unlike Lyon's brilliant effort in neighboring Texas, the Rooseveltites hit a stone wall of resistance from Republican stalwarts whose support of Taft never wavered.

Clayton remained the driving force in Arkansas GOP politics from his election as governor during Reconstruction and his subsequent tenure in the U.S. Senate until his death in 1914 at age eighty-one. The Pennsylvania native, who had served as ambassador to Mexico under McKinley and Roosevelt, not only managed the official party but delivered votes that strengthened his influence in national circles. The party under his tutelage in 1908 gave 37 percent of the state's vote and nine counties to Taft and came close to electing a congressman from the third district in northern Arkansas. Roosevelt recognized Clayton's power when he complained in early March to Durand Whipple of Little Rock, vice-chairman of the State Executive Committee, about "the difficulty of making any headway against the machine in Arkansas." The man from Oyster Bay concluded that his only hope in the state was "to convince Clayton and Remmel that Roosevelt is going to win."[69]

Although Clayton made his home in Washington and was suffering from an illness that would take his life within two years, he enjoyed the complete confidence of Taft and Hilles during the president's drive for renomination and reelection. Roosevelt was correct that the national committeeman, who was not only referee but along with Remmel a controlling force among the Negroes, would be anxious to support the winning presidential aspirant in order to maintain his hold over the patronage and the party organization after the campaign. Yet neither Clayton nor Remmel, who was a New York native and prominent lumberman in the state, gave any thought to supporting the Rough Rider in 1912. After serving a single term in the legislature during the 1880s, he was the party nominee for governor in 1894 against James P. Clarke and in 1896 against Daniel W. Jones, when he polled an unprecedented 48 percent of the vote. In close association with Clayton, Remmel led a faction of the party known as the "Regulars" in addition to serving as collector of internal revenue, a federal post he held over a twenty-five-year period under four presidents before his death in 1924.[70]

Although an occasional Republican won election to the legislature or to local office after the turn of the century, the party officiated over by Clayton and Remmel in 1912 had little hope of victory in a statewide race because of a disfranchising process that had started in 1889 and ended with implementation of the disastrous white primary law of 1897. Thus, the Arkansas Republican party found itself in a situation similar to sister organizations across the South that had been bridled by a Bourbon majority hell-bent upon retaining white supremacy through control of a one-party society. When Governor Jeff Davis stated during his third inaugural address in 1905 that Arkansas had come to a parting of the ways with the Negro, he was also saying that the Republican party in the state had been both eclipsed and emasculated as a threatening organization.[71]

Disfranchisement in Arkansas came after the 1888 election, when a Populist group known as the Agricultural Wheel, in league with the state GOP, walked away with 46 percent of the vote and elected two congressmen. The alarmed Democrats reacted by attempting to pass a secret ballot law designed by James P. Clarke, who, after becoming governor, appointed H. L. Remmel to the State Board of Charities. Although the measure passed the state senate, it failed in the house, blocked by Republicans and Populists. An election law enacted in 1891 and an amendment to the state constitution the following year, however, produced the desired results and enabled the Democrats to control elections, with little opposition from Republicans or Populists. When Populist organizing activity increased and the Republicans opened night schools to help Negroes cope with the new and complicated election statutes, the Bourbons responded with the final instrument of disfranchisement, the all-white primary.[72]

Arkansas was obviously influenced by the effectiveness of the nearby Mississippi plan. But the state at no time adopted the harsher methods employed in other parts of the South to thwart Negro voting, such as property requirements, grandfather clauses, and literacy tests. Many Negroes could still vote after 1897, as evidenced by their successful participation in the defeat of a 1912 constitutional amendment proposing an educational requirement for voting. Yet the overwhelming majority of Negroes as well as many poor whites were systematically excluded from the franchise, thus destroying the vote-getting potential of the GOP. A sharp decline in voter turnout was experienced in several counties with large concentrations of Negroes after 1892 when as much as one-half of the electorate stayed away from the polls. Jeff Davis dominated Arkansas politics as governor and U.S. senator until his death in 1913 through an undisguised appeal to racism. When he was first elected to the governorship in 1900, he beat Remmel, his Republican opponent, by a two-to-one margin and thereby set the state's voting pattern until the second half of the century.[73]

Even though Roosevelt recognized the difficulty of carrying the state with its crippled Republican vote and of making inroads against Clayton's powerful opposition, a miniature bandwagon was gotten up in his behalf during February and March. The early Roosevelt thrust under the direction of two disgruntled Republicans, Harry K. Cochran and Little Rock attorney James A. Comer, both of whom were outside the patronage sphere commanded by Clayton and Remmel, was successful in organizing Roosevelt clubs in a number of locations, including Zinc, Magazine, and Little Rock. Cochran, reputedly ardently for Roosevelt, conducted a poll among Arkansas Republicans, asking whom they preferred for president and gleefully announced on February 20 that he had received 851 replies to his inquiry: Roosevelt 691, Taft 160. Two weeks later, however, as the Roosevelt forces were attempting to paint a rosy picture for their man, the influential *Arkansas Gazette* reported that after "a careful investigation" in Boone County, it found that, though state Senator Fayette Christian was strong for the colonel, unfortunately his following was small and most Republicans in the county and state were for Taft; furthermore, Newton County, "the strongest republican county in Arkansas," favored the president by a heavy majority.[74]

State Chairman Remmel, undaunted by the small-scale Roosevelt activity, issued a call on February 27 summoning the Republican State Committee into session one month later to handle routine party matters, including setting the date for the crucial state convention. When word leaked out that Clayton and Remmel were drafting a pro-Taft resolution for the committee's approval, Cochran and the Roosevelt Club at Little Rock started making plans for a Roosevelt demonstration to coincide with the arrival of the committeemen. Cochran, who died the following year, had been born at Staunton, Virginia, in 1852, arrived in Arkansas in 1881 as a representative of the Waters-Pierce Oil Company, and later operated a successful grain supply business in Little Rock. A lifelong Republican and a friend of Theodore Roosevelt, Cochran along with Comer led a group to Chicago for a conference with the colonel's national strategists in early March and upon his return to Little Rock grandly announced that a movement to secure the Arkansas delegation to the Republican National Convention would be "pushed vigorously." With the official Roosevelt mantle upon him, Cochran told reporters that a number of prominent Republicans would be brought into the state during the campaign and that after a thorough assessment of the situation, "Gov. Powell Clayton did not have the delegation in his vest pocket."[75]

James A. Comer, the Little Rock lawyer who made the trek to Chicago with Cochran and later became state chairman of the Bull Moose in Arkansas, had been born in Edwardsville, Illinois, reared in St. Louis, and educated at Valparaiso University before coming to the state in the 1890s. Admitted to the Arkansas bar in 1897, he practiced law until his death in 1935, a good part of the time in partnership with Powell Clayton, Jr. Although he was a Republican prior to 1912 and prominent in the Progressive party before its collapse in 1916, Comer put his organizing talents to work in the 1920s to become Grand Dragon for Arkansas in the revived Ku Klux Klan; later he was founder of the Women of the Ku Klux Klan, a national auxiliary order. But in the first weeks of 1912, the efforts of Comer and Cochran to block the headlong drive of the regular organization to gather up the state for Taft did not get off the ground. When the State Committee met on March 26, the "Roosevelt demonstration" was not able to keep Clayton and Remmel from getting a vote blocking adoption of resolutions proposed by the National Roosevelt League for a Presidential preferential primary. The committee not only rejected the very bedrock of the Progressive campaign but added insult to injury by calling for the reelection of Taft, leaving little doubt that the administration was in complete control as the 1912 campaign opened.[76]

Chapter 4

Primaries and Conventions

Every Republican organization in the eleven former Confederate states had undergone a fracturing of some degree by the beginning of March as a result of the Roosevelt challenge. With the possible exception of Texas, North Carolina, and Tennessee, where the colonel found strong support among party regulars, Taft appeared to have the southern machines—called by some, rotten boroughs—in his "vest pocket." In two states, Florida and Georgia, state Republican conventions met prior to Roosevelt's Columbus declaration, and both had chosen Taft delegations to the national convention before a meaningful opposition could organize itself. South Carolina held its state conclave seven days later; it was a Taft show with little or no visible opposition. Yet in each southern state there was some measure of support for the Rough Rider's candidacy so that before the Chicago convention state gatherings were summoned in all but two southern states to put on a demonstration for Roosevelt and to name a rival delegation favoring his nomination.

Nowhere in the South were statewide Republican primaries held to designate national convention delegates; thus state conventions were the only vehicles for venting party strife. Although the cry of "let the people rule" and the holding of direct presidential primaries were mainstays of Progressive polemics in 1912, there was surely no real demand for them in the South by dissident Republicans who flocked to Roosevelt's banner in search of federal jobs. Practically every district and state convention across the region saw a fight as both Roosevelt and Taft devotees sought to manipulate the result in favor of their man. GOP organizations in Alabama, Tennessee, Virginia, and Mississippi held their conventions during March, and none of them, nor indeed many Republicans in any part of Dixie, voiced much concern over the fight raging in other sections of the country to select delegates by primary elections.

Although most southern states had some form of primary legislation on the books when the Roosevelt-Taft fray opened, the laws were usually written in a manner that excluded Republicans and other minority parties. A few states, including Florida and Alabama, held Democratic primaries during 1912, and in Texas one was proposed but scuttled by the State Executive Committee that was dominated by the followers of Wilson. The outrageous tactics employed in southern GOP conventions embarrassed Republicans nationally. Preferential primaries in the North and West played a prominent role in presidential politics for the first time in 1912. The major primaries contested by Roosevelt and Taft in North Dakota, Wisconsin, Illinois, Pennsylvania, Oregon, Nebraska, Massachusetts,

Maryland, California, New Jersey, New York, Ohio, and South Dakota were for the most part ignored by Republicans in the South, who were busy with their own battles.[1]

Roosevelt had urged acceptance of the primary in his Osawatomie speech, along with ringing appeals for the initiative, referendum, and recall as vital ingredients of his New Nationalism. And he continued to laud use of primaries, as did many of his Progressive adherents, in speeches around the country, including those in the South, during his 1911 tour of Georgia, Alabama, Mississippi, Louisiana, and Texas. He reiterated his position before the Ohio Constitutional Convention when he opened the 1912 campaign. Shortly after Montana Senator Joseph M. Dixon, who was a North Carolinian by birth and rearing with extensive contacts among southern Republicans, was made Roosevelt's national campaign manager, he hurled the now famous challenge at William B. McKinley in March for the holding of a presidential primary in every state. Taft's manager not only refused to consider the idea, but said he and the administration were satisfied with the present plan of obtaining convention delegates. Taft himself spoke out for the Old Guard on March 7 in Toledo, when he denounced the total New Nationalism doctrine, heaping particular scorn upon primaries and the recall of judicial decisions.[2]

Victor Rosewater, chairman of the Republican National Committee, who played a prominent role in the events of 1912, felt Roosevelt came to believe that the primary for nominating presidential and vice-presidential candidates had no appeal with grass-roots America, which explained his giving up the issue as the campaign progressed. Nonetheless, many party stalwarts who otherwise would have been in his camp were driven into the Taft camp because they thought he favored primaries. Other Progressives, however, including the Pinchot brothers and former Indiana Senator Albert J. Beveridge, embraced the idea. Gifford Pinchot stated the position of his wing of the party clearly when he declared on March 1 in Danville, Illinois, that "progressives believe in the rule of the people and Mr. Taft does not." This, he said, "was the major issue of the campaign." Some Republicans, such as George W. Perkins, former associate of J. P. Morgan, and newspaper tycoon Frank Munsey, who together financed much of the Rough Rider's 1912 campaign, accepted the entire platform. Perkins, who helped organize such industrial giants as International Harvester, the Northern Securities Company, and United States Steel, even contributed $15,000 of his personal funds to assist Roosevelt in his abortive drive to win the New York primary.[3]

As the national debate was boiling over whether "the people shall rule or not," the GOP in Alabama prepared for the first state convention of consequence in the South following the Columbus declaration. Before the gathering, however, Joseph O. Thompson, acknowledged Roosevelt leader in the state, joined the Progressive bandwagon, demanding that the State Executive Committee authorize a primary in Alabama to resolve the

Roosevelt-Taft conflict and to settle the issue of whether he or U.S. Marshal Pope M. Long was the rightful state chairman. The intensity of the Alabama fight attracted considerable attention in the national press, although Taft's forces under the command of Long and Prelate D. Barker not only scoffed at the primary idea but managed to capture a majority of the district conventions when they met in early March to select delegates to the state gathering in Birmingham. They did so by using every political weapon at their disposal, including threats against recalcitrant officehold-ers, with the full sanction of the White House.[4]

When the four-hundred-member convention assembled on March 7, several pro-Taft resolutions were adopted by the nearly unanimous body before an all-Taft delegation-at-large headed by Oscar D. Street was named to join those previously tapped in the district conventions. A state ticket and presidential electors were also named before resolutions were rammed through offering "strong condemnation to the third term idea, the initiative, referendum, recall, (and) ex-President Roosevelt's Columbus speech." Every mention of Taft's name met with hearty applause, and before adjournment, Long, who was reconfirmed as state chairman, em-phatically rejected holding a Republican primary in Alabama. Although Judge Hundley and Thompson continued the fight for Roosevelt, pressed for a primary, and eventually convened a rival state convention, the Taft group now held the upper hand. Following his rejection as state chairman, Thompson told a reporter that he had not attended the Birmingham conclave because as a lawyer he never tried a case before a packed jury and he did not intend to follow the practice as a politician.[5]

Meanwhile, in South Carolina, where a Roosevelt movement per se did not materialize in the days leading up to Chicago, the fight within the GOP was confined to a halfhearted challenge for control by John G. Capers following the February 29 state convention in Charleston. Although the opposing faction led by State Chairman Joe Tolbert had White House support and managed to capture all but one of the district conventions during March, Capers and Blalock—both of whom Taft called "congenital liars"—summoned the remnants of the lily-white Executive Committee into session on March 4 and announced plans for a rival state gathering to be held in May. When Capers and his group declared loyalty to Taft and the Old Guard, the Charleston *Evening Post* responded that "only micro-scopic inspection would disclose a germ of political principle in either faction." The intraparty strife, said the Democratic paper, was a "sordid and ill-smelling struggle between the 'ins' eager to stay 'in' and the 'outs' ready to resort to Rooseveltism or any other 'ism' through which access to the pie-counter might possibly be had."[6]

Several delegations chosen at the district conventions began to waver in their devotion to the president and to voice a preference for Roosevelt as the national convention approached, which brought forth claims and counterclaims by both state and national leaders. Senator Dixon released a statement on April 20 claiming that two of the Negro delegates-at-large intended to vote for the colonel although they had been instructed to vote for Taft at the state convention. McKinley retorted that at least two of those mentioned by Dixon were known not to be delegates at all and that one Negro, C. M. English, a Charleston funeral director, had been discredited at his district gathering. Although Dr. J. R. Levy, a Negro physician at Florence and a delegate to Chicago, estimated that 95 percent of the state's Negroes were for Roosevelt, Thomas L. Grant, a delegate-at-large, told reporters that sixteen of the state's eighteen votes would be cast for Taft at Chicago. The controversy came to a head when Capers and Blalock, who had resolved to stay within the regular party, decided not to hold a lily-white convention for fear that it would be dominated by the Roosevelt men. South Carolina thus remained under the complete charge of Taft during the preconvention campaign.[7]

Events were much different, however, in North Carolina, where a Roosevelt tidal wave swept the state before the May 15 state convention. A miniconvention under the sponsorship of Richmond Pearson—now a member of the Roosevelt National Campaign Committee—met on March 8 to organize for the colonel. About seventy-five Republicans, reported the Richmond *Virginian,* from all sections of the state "and particularly from the western and piedmont counties" mapped out a strategy for getting the state's twenty-four national convention delegates. Although Pearson enjoyed the confidence of Roosevelt, who repeatedly urged him to "keep harmony among our people," Zeb Vance Walser of Lexington was called to Oyster Bay on March 17 and given charge of the campaign in the state because Pearson's time was given over to the national campaign. Walser, a native of Davidson County and lifelong Republican who had served as a state legislator and attorney general, did much to win the state for Roosevelt in the May 15 convention. Later, at Chicago, Walser defiantly led the North Carolinians from the convention auditorium when Roosevelt was denied the Republican nomination.[8]

Chairman Morehead and the administration were seemingly powerless to check the Roosevelt onslaught, although they exerted great efforts to do so. In a move to calm the continuing rift between Morehead and Duncan, both men were called to the White House on March 16, where they agreed to cease hostilities until the presidential campaign ended. Previously, Taft had demanded that Morehead justify why the moratorium on federal appointments in the state should be lifted. The whip was cracked even harder when Hilles, reacting to press reports that Morehead was seeking accommodation with the burgeoning Roosevelt forces, told the state chairman "to have this mischievousness contradicted." Ironically, the county conventions that met throughout April and May went overwhelmingly for Roosevelt at the same time Morehead was directed to give out declarations that there could be no compromise with the Roosevelt people. Yet the total ineffectiveness of Taft's campaign was dramatized on May 1 when the Raleigh *News and Observer* reported that forty-two of the state's one hundred counties had held Republican conventions and not one delegate had been instructed for the president.[9]

The first of Tennessee's two state conventions met on March 12 in Chattanooga to name a state ticket amid a highly charged party fight with Governor Hooper still trying to separate his own reelection from national politics. Matters were complicated when the county and district conventions that met to choose and instruct Hooper delegates also insisted on drafting pro-Taft resolutions. Newell Sanders, state chairman and Taft's manager in the state, stated ten days before the convention "that of ninety-six counties in Tennessee, seventy-eight have been heard from and seventy-five of these had endorsed" the president. "Mr. Taft," Sanders announced, "will get the vote of Tennessee" in the national convention. Although Hooper would have wished otherwise, his intimate association with Sanders, whom he appointed to the Senate on April 8, caused national Roosevelt leaders to resolve that "it would be folly not to fight [Hooper] all along the line."[10]

As Roosevelt himself was writing encouragement to William J. Oliver of Knoxville, his chief agent in Tennessee, a number of pro-Roosevelt rallies were organized prior to the March 12 gathering with an eye to winning at the next convention in mid-May, when delegates to Chicago would be chosen. A meeting at Knoxville, in the heart of east Tennessee Republicanism, on March 2 resulted in the formation of a Roosevelt for President Club by four hundred clamoring enthusiasts, although the "first decided stand in Tennessee for Theodore Roosevelt," exclaimed the Knoxville *Journal and Tribune,* occurred when the Bradley and Marion county conventions instructed their delegates to support the former president in both state gatherings. Yet Roosevelt was obviously the underdog, prompting Oliver—who had been named president of the Knoxville group—to implore Hooper—the state's most popular Republican: "If you don't help us, please don't help the bear." The governor, anxious about his own reelection, reiterated his intent of keeping a "hands off policy," but replied, "I know you fellows are to fight about the delegates to the national convention, but I want you to fight fair and let the majority rule."[11]

At the time, however, Hooper may not have been completely neutral, and he confided in his autobiography that the TR men in Tennessee "cared nothing for Roosevelt's candidacy and in no sense were 'progressive,' but merely political saboteurs." The Republican regulars were wary of the so-called "anti-administration men," and when Judge H. B. Lindsay delivered a blistering address in support of Roosevelt, Congressman Austin, a friend of Hooper's and a party stalwart, apprised Hilles of the speech, which he considered a calculated insult to President Taft. He also sought to have Lindsay's brother removed as postmaster at Coal Creek, which was hardly conducting a fair contest.[12]

Although Taft and the regular organization under Sanders were in complete control and had ruled the district conventions, true to the wishes of Hooper the Chattanooga assemblage devoted no time whatever to the raging Roosevelt-Taft conflict. Hooper was quickly named the party's gubernatorial candidate, and H. N. Cate was nominated by acclamation for a vacancy on the state Court of Appeals following adoption of a lengthy platform calling for statewide prohibition. Opposition to liquor had been the anvil upon which the governor forged his winning combination in 1910 from Republicans and Independent Democrats, and the Roosevelt adherents were in no mood to throttle that program. Both Hooper and Cate, a prohibition Democrat, were nominated by a unanimous convention after one speaker declared that, before Hooper, "we had sixty-seven saloons in Chattanooga and sixty-five democratic headquarters; if you've got 350 saloons in Nashville you've got 345 democratic headquarters." In March 1912, Tennessee Republicans of all persuasions were for Hooper and against demon rum. Presidential politics would have to wait until their governor was safely nominated for a second go at the executive mansion in Nashville.[13]

In Virginia, where the state convention met in Roanoke on March 13, one day after the Chattanooga conclave, the party organization brought into line by National Committeeman Alvah H. Martin and George L. Hart, secretary of the State Executive Committee, had managed to capture nearly all of the district conventions for Taft. But the uncertainties of the Roosevelt maelstrom caused Martin to lead a group of district leaders to Washington on March 1 for a meeting with Hilles concerning the challenge surely to arise at Roanoke. A peculiar situation had developed when the Negroes—barred from high party councils by a lily-white leadership—began to voice support for Roosevelt as a means of regaining lost power. Yet, John Mitchell, Jr., editor of the widely read Richmond *Planet,* a Negro newspaper, editorialized that neither Republican hopeful had anything to offer the black man. Martin, who was directing the campaign alone while Congressman Slemp kept a death vigil over a favored brother in Louisville, Kentucky, returned from Washington with the strategy of countering the influence of the pro-Roosevelt Negroes by holding the district conventions in places that denied them admittance under the infamous Jim Crow laws; one such gathering in the Odd Fellows Hall at Norfolk had not a single Negro present. Furthermore, when Hart met with a Republican group threatening to call a statewide meeting for Roosevelt, the secretary told them that they had started too late because by March 2 he had "already certified enough delegates instructed for Mr. Taft to guarantee the result." And when the Roosevelt state leaders asked for a list of the reputed Taft delegates, Hart was thrown into a tizzy but told

Hilles he put them off by saying he had no power to comply with the request without authorization from the state and district executive committees.[14]

Unabashed by Taft victories in the district conventions, a few Rooseveltites pressed for holding a party primary prior to the state convention as a way of resolving the delegate issue. Slemp, who had returned to the state, stated that no primary would be held in Virginia because he lacked authority to authorize such action. Slemp, who was state chairman, further warned the dissenters, "That the delegates will be instructed for Taft is a foregone conclusion." But as the convention came to order, Dr. J. M. Daugherty, a Scott County physician, started a vigorous floor fight against instructing the delegates to Chicago for the president. A Richmond newspaper reported that he proclaimed Roosevelt's cause "amid deafening cheers [and] talked himself so hoarse that his words became unintelligible." J. L. Graves, postmaster at Wytheville, graduate of the University of Virginia Law School, and former commonwealth's attorney, who was an ally of Slemp in ninth district politics, marshaled a drive for a resolution to instruct, which finally carried by a vote of 702 to 64. It was a crushing blow to the colonel's prospects in the Old Dominion. With the delegation to the national convention settled upon, the body adjourned by calling for a referendum on prohibition, thereby conveniently sidestepping the all-important liquor question, then the paramount issue in Virginia politics.[15]

The first weeks in March were a period of intense presidential politicking all over the nation. While Wilson, fast emerging as the front runner for the Democratic nomination, toured the country, gaining a great popular following, the Republicans became ever more enmeshed in their mighty struggle to nominate one man who would further democratize the nation and another who would, if given the opportunity, moor it more firmly upon the foundations of an antiquated conservatism. Governor Hooper's assessment that Tennessee Republicans backing Roosevelt were merely "anti-organization men" was no doubt true for the bulk of Roosevelt's southern supporters. Paradoxically, the Rooseveltian drive for a New Nationalism with its pleas for a greater responsiveness to the popular weal brought with it violent and bloody confrontations over the selection of national convention delegates in nearly every state where the convention system prevailed. Perhaps it was in Oklahoma, a state considered by many to be part of the South in sentiment, that the most combative of the GOP conventions took place. At one point, a Roosevelt delegate toting a revolver menacingly approached the pro-Taft presiding officer. In the ensuing donnybrook, one man died of a heart attack and three others were injured by fist fights before Roosevelt won the state's ten delegates-at-large. In state after state, fights and pressure tactics of every description were used in the search for Roosevelt delegates to Chicago.[16]

The struggle in Alabama started immediately after adjournment of the state convention, when Joseph O. Thompson and Judge Hundley began a private campaign to convince a majority of the State Executive Committee that Thompson was still state chairman and that Pope M. Long had not been legitimately named his successor at Birmingham. Although Ormsby McHarg later arrived in the state to urge the calling of a second convention, Roosevelt personally encouraged Thompson and Hundley to proceed in his behalf and to secure a favorable delegation to Chicago by whatever means necessary. "If I had a few more like you," he told Hundley, "the southern delegations to the convention would not be what they bid fair to be." In response, a conference of Roosevelt men, characterized by Long as "sore-heads devoid of influence," was convened on March 15 to undo Long and Barker's earlier work for Taft. Numbering about one hundred members, this gathering recognized Thompson as head of the party in Alabama and resolved to make a fight for the delegates-at-large and for district delegates in the ninth district around Birmingham. Thompson was handed a mandate to hold a second state convention, and the assembly urged him to seek a party primary as the best means of gauging the true sentiment of the state's Republicans.[17]

Ridicule was employed by the regulars to play down the Thompson-as-chairman ploy, and Long even produced a letter Thompson had written acknowledging him as chairman. According to Long, Thompson had turned over the party stationery to him following the Birmingham convention. The Old Guard leadership further claimed that several members of the "old" Executive Committee reputedly headed by Thompson had already declared for Taft and that "he was hog tied" before he got Roosevelt's balloon off the ground. Other committee members bragged that they had not attended the Roosevelt meeting or sent in their proxies because they did not recognize Thompson as chairman and therefore no communication from him was official. Still Thompson sent out the call for a convention, claiming his actions were supported by 90 percent of the Alabama GOP, the state convention notwithstanding. And though T. H. Aldrich and other Taft leaders vehemently denied the allegations, word spread that federal employees following Thompson's lead were to be axed by the administration. Government examiners at Birmingham recommended that fifteen to twenty employees of the local post office be dismissed for supporting Roosevelt, which caused McHarg to lash out at the Taft leadership when he arrived at the home of Judge Hundley in mid-April. These "political frame-ups," he said, would hinder "the people of America who are clamoring for Mr. Roosevelt." McHarg also threw down the gauntlet while praising the efforts of Thompson and Hundley, declaring: "Alabama was in good shape and the solid southern delegations which Mr. Taft is banking on heavily will be found shattered when the convention seats delegates."[18]

Meanwhile, national attention fastened on North Dakota, where the first state primary would give all Republican candidates, including La Follette, who was yet maintaining the façade of a campaign, an opportunity to demonstrate their vote-getting appeal. Although Roosevelt did not campaign in the state, he recognized the March 19 primary's importance when he told Frank Knox: "It would be unfortunate if we do not carry North Dakota because the East will construe it not as a defeat for Taft but as a defeat for me." And when La Follette unexpectedly exhibited strength, Roosevelt realized the possibility of defeat because of his affiliation with conservative GOP elements in the state and instructed Dixon to ready a press statement playing up the vote as "anti-administration" and as a victory for Progressivism. Astoundingly, La Follette did win a stunning victory, defeating Roosevelt by a vote of 34,123 to 23,669 and unquestionably hurting the Rough Rider's campaign. The pitifully meager 1,876 votes polled by Taft offered little consolation to southern Roosevelt leaders, who were insisting that a Republican majority supported their candidate as justification for calling rival state conventions in his behalf.[19]

Even in Mississippi, where pro-Taft Negroes dominated the party, an effort was made to drum up support for Roosevelt prior to the March 28 state convention in Jackson. Senator Dixon apparently sought to work out a scheme with Dr. Redmond and another Negro, J. W. Hair of Jackson, to have blacks defeat resolutions favorable to the administration in the district conventions. But Booker T. Washington, the archenemy of lily-whiteism, became concerned lest many of them might go over to the Roosevelt movement.[20]

Washington had been asked by the Board of Trustees at Tuskegee to stay out of the 1912 campaign, which prompted his trusted secretary, Emmett J. Scott, to write Washington's friend and associate at Mound Bayou, Mississippi, Charles Banks, lamenting: "I wish I knew some way to write to the Roosevelt managers in the matter of Redmond's circular, but there is no one to whom I can write." It was a far cry from 1904 and 1908, when Washington and the Rough Rider had worked together in the South. And it was becoming increasingly clear that the Roosevelt candidacy offered nothing to the southern Negro. Even Redmond was thrown to the wolves at Chicago. A small concession was gained from the Negro point of view, however, when Banks, president of the Mississippi chapter of the National Negro Business League and national vice-president of the organization, hammered out an agreement with Moseley, national committeeman and Taft referee in the state, whereby each district convention would send one white and one black delegate to the state conclave.[21]

When the convention came to order, Redmond and the Negroes loyal to him immediately challenged the pro-Taft group led by Moseley, and tempers became heated. "While pistols may not actually have been drawn," one newspaper reported, "there were numbers of delegates who let it be known they were prepared to draw if the occasion required it." But, as one might expect, the regulars, or the faction faithful to Moseley, enjoyed the full weight of the administration and soon had the body organized to their advantage.[22]

Outnumbered and unprepared for a bloody encounter, Redmond and his people withdrew from the assembly hall to hold a rump convention where they named a full slate of delegates to the national gathering pledged for Roosevelt. This was primarily a Negro delegation that was never recognized by the GOP National Committee. Meanwhile, the regular convention, which ignored its errant brothers, endorsed Taft's administration and the handling of Mississippi Republican affairs by Moseley before naming a delegation-at-large committed to the president. Upon adjournment, Moseley, who would shortly be an honored guest at the White House, triumphantly telegraphed Hilles: "Out of 20 delegates who will go to Chicago, to the big convention, 19 are instructed to vote for Taft, last and all the time, and they have expectations of swinging the twentieth into line before the showdown."[23]

Nationally, the campaign reached fever pitch intensity in the days following the Mississippi convention, when Roosevelt, smarting from setbacks in the South and in New York, where the Republican machine rigged the primary to his disadvantage, began to lash out at Taft with a vengeance. Because of an exceedingly complex balloting system—the tally sheets in some districts were nearly fourteen feet in length—and the nonarrival of ballots in several city precincts, Roosevelt received a mere 15,262 tallies in the New York primary, which he promptly labeled "a political farce." Following the discouraging news now coming in quick succession from North Dakota, Virginia, Mississippi, and Colorado, where the state convention instructed for Taft after a particularly stiff fight, Roosevelt told the Old Guard in Chicago on March 27 that the will of the people had been undermined and warned that he might lead a third-party movement if not treated fairly by the GOP. After Taft told the Philadelphia Chamber of Commerce three days later that better days were coming for America, the primary in Wisconsin resulted in yet another setback for Roosevelt. His name had not been entered in the April 2 primary although he did receive a healthy 47,514 write-in votes so that La Follette won his home state with a whopping 133,354 tallies. The Wisconsin senator, however, was stopped cold for the remainder of the campaign. The president polled a scant 628 votes in the state, and, in an effort to offset the disappointing result, Hilles gave out a statement on election night indicating that fifty-three members of the Republican National Committee were for Taft. Yet, his previous defeats notwithstanding, Roosevelt's fortunes took a turn for the better and changed the entire flavor of the campaign when he won the important Illinois primary on April 9 by a thumping 139,000 margin over the hapless Taft.[24]

Back in the South, the Liosel-Herbert faction of the Louisiana GOP held its state convention on April 8, one day after the Illinois primary. Although Roosevelt was counted out at this meeting, his friends had been busy in the state following the March 9 session of the State Executive Committee in which the Taft campaign staff had been perfected and several pro-

Roosevelt committeemen forced out. Frank B. Williams and Pearl Wight, neither of whom had attended the confab after being ousted by Taft and Hilles, served immediate notice that a competing state convention would be held on May 2 in Alexandria. Wight in the meantime got up a new state committee loaded with lily-whites and Roosevelt men, saying the state organization was made up almost entirely of officeholders who did not speak for a majority of Louisiana Republicans. Moreover, Clarence S. Herbert, Taft's man in the state, started to fight back, using the threat of patronage removal and accusing Williams of being in the Roosevelt tent, although the former referee had repeatedly voiced his loyalty to the president; Herbert issued a stern warning as well for all Republicans "to stay away from the convention in Alexandria."[25]

An unsettling argument developed among Taft leaders when Liosel, who had been named state chairman to replace Williams, disagreed with former Governor Henry C. Warmouth over the party's position on the sugar question prior to the April 9 state convention. The growing dissatisfaction among Louisiana sugar producers with national Democratic policy including sugar on the free list when the Democratic-controlled House of Representatives considered tariff legislation led Warmouth, one of the foremost sugar planters in the world, to advocate that the GOP endorse Independent Democrats for Congress if they supported protection for the crop. Certainly candidates sponsored by Independent Democrats and Republicans would have greater voter appeal in the solid South, but Liosel would have nothing to do with the scheme and insisted that "only died-in-the-wool republicans" receive the party nod for Congress. Republican failure to capitalize on discontent among the planters was one reason why large numbers of Democrats in southern Louisiana aided in the election of Whitmell Pugh Martin to Congress in 1914 on the Bull Moose ticket.[26]

Another troublesome row surfaced in the state convention when the Taft leadership barred several Negro delegates even as spectators before selecting an all-white delegation-at-large to the national convention and instructing for the president. The New Orleans *Picayune* noted that Liosel and Herbert were "always in command and carried it unanimously for Taft." The blatant ejection of the Negroes was an attempt to lure lily-whites away from Wight and the burgeoning Roosevelt movement, even though Hilles had assured Booker T. Washington that Louisiana and Texas Negroes would be treated fairly by the administration. Later, blacks under the leadership of Walter Cohen, who had broken with Liosel, and J. Madison Vance—both of whom enjoyed the confidence of the aging schoolmaster at Tuskegee—organized a convention in late April to designate yet another delegation to Chicago. In the meantime, however, the general election for governor and other state offices on April 16 found the Republicans, white and black, coming off badly at the polls. Significantly, Liosel, Herbert, and Victor Romain wrote a joint letter to Hilles on March 20 urging that administration influence be exerted to postpone a hearing in the Senate Finance Committee dealing with free sugar until after the election. "Our people are greatly aroused," the missive said, and delay "may help us considerably to elect two Republican congressmen in November." Even so, the Republican gubernatorial candidate, Hugh S. Suthon, polled a disappointing 1,961 votes in the statewide election against Judge Luther E. Hall. Failure of the party to receive 10 percent of the total vote cast meant that under Louisiana law the Republican party in the state lost its right to exist as a viable political entity.[27]

At the same time Taft was using the awesome power of the administration to carry the southern conventions as well as those in Connecticut and Delaware, where a delegation headed by Senator Henry A. du Pont was instructed for him, Roosevelt won bigger than ever in several large state primaries where he was able to make a direct voter appeal. He carried Pennsylvania on April 13 by more than 60,000 votes over Taft to gain sixty-seven of the state's seventy-six national convention delegates and crush the formidable machine of Boies Penrose which had backed the president. Then he won in Oregon on April 19, where Taft was even trounced by La Follette, who did limited campaigning, and in Nebraska on April 21 Roosevelt's tally was considerably greater than the Taft–La Follette vote combined. While on his way north to campaign personally for the April 30 primary in Massachusetts, Taft grabbed the offensive by stepping up his attacks on Roosevelt, whom he accused of attempting to destroy the Republican party. Although the presidential tug-of-war was swept to the back pages when news arrived that the steamship *Titanic* had gone down in the North Atlantic with great loss of life, Taft managed to poll more votes in Massachusetts than Roosevelt amid continued wrangling by both men. Still, Roosevelt got twenty-eight of the state's forty-six delegates, including the eight-man delegation-at-large. He called off the vendetta long enough to suggest that these delegates should vote for Taft because he had received the statewide vote. Most political observers agreed with Roosevelt that Taft's failure to win over the entire state, even with support from the powerhouse of an organization headed by Senator Murray Crane, meant his chances of reentering the White House had dropped to virtually zero.[28]

While on the hustings, both men made quick jaunts into the South during late April. After his speechmaking in Massachusetts, Taft traveled through South Carolina and Georgia with his wife and daughter as well as southern GOP dignitaries before returning to the White House. The trip was billed as nonpolitical even though he celebrated St. Patrick's Day in Savannah by telling the Hibernian Society meeting there how much the Irish had contributed to American life. The president also told his audience that he was pleased with the result in Massachusetts. Roosevelt, on the other hand, returning from his campaign in Illinois and Nebraska, made an extensive speaking whirl through Arkansas and North Carolina to line up support in the upcoming state conventions in both states. He spoke repeatedly of his determination to break the solid South and even declared his support for the grandfather clause in a bid for Democratic votes on April 23 in Goldsboro, North Carolina.[29]

Meanwhile, as Taft was relaxing briefly with his family at the Georgia seaside and TR was returning north to Oyster Bay, Pearl Wight and Frank B. Williams summoned the nonofficeholding faction of the Louisiana GOP into the much touted convention at Alexandria. Immediately after Williams, still calling himself state chairman, convened the all-white gathering on May 2, a vicious fight erupted over the selection of Jules Godchaux, a wealthy planter supporting Taft because he thought him for free sugar if reelected, and Major William J. Behan, one of the state's most outspoken Roosevelt men, as temporary chairman. When it became obvious that the impasse could not be resolved because the temporary chairman would rule on disputed delegates to the meeting, both factions amicably agreed not only to split into separate conventions but to take turns at using the assembly hall.[30]

The Taft people took over first, quickly named a delegation to Chicago, passed resolutions praising the administration, and recognized Williams as state chairman instead of Liosel, who enjoyed the backing of Hilles and the president as well as the state's Negroes. Williams was picked to head the pro-Taft delegation to the national convention after he delivered a blistering appeal for the convention "to stand firm for the lily-white Republican party in the state." Yet the protestations of support for Taft by this wing, however feeble they might have seemed, demonstrated its allegiance to regular Republicanism, thus permitting its members to escape the onus of irregularity, a sure road to suicide in future party councils.[31]

The remaining lily-whites who occupied the auditorium later in the afternoon unabashedly organized themselves into a Roosevelt convention, thereby irretrievably breaking with the administration-dominated national committee. Led by Wight, Behan, and Thilborger, this forum, which had been spurred into action by a visit from McHarg to the state two weeks previously, named a pro-Roosevelt delegation to Chicago without hesitation and then adopted the usual laudatory resolutions. Before adjourning, they pledged themselves to accept Williams as state chairman rather than choosing a new State Committee committed specifically to Roosevelt. Its deliberations ended, said the New Orleans *Picayune,* amid an intense enthusiasm and with " 'three cheers for Teddy' echoing through the hall."[32]

Across the Mississippi River in Arkansas, however, two distinct conventions were held at Little Rock on May 7, when the Roosevelt men formed their own conclave after refusing to recognize the regular meeting called by the Clayton-Remmel organization. Roosevelt's forces had become active following their rout at the March 26 meeting of the State Executive

Committee in order to gain control of the upcoming county conventions. While McHarg was busily encouraging leaders in adjacent states to call separate conventions, William H. Mason of New York, another personal representative of TR, arrived in early April for a round of conferences that resulted among other things in opening a permanent Roosevelt headquarters at Little Rock that did much to publicize the colonel's candidacy among the state's Republicans. Also, the former president's rapid-paced tour of Arkansas coincident with the county meetings had attracted enthusiastic crowds and added fuel to his drive to break Taft's mastery over the regular organization. Harry K. Cochran and James A. Comer, who were still in charge of the Roosevelt campaign, managed to get a handful of the county delegates, but events in the important Pulaski County gathering at Little Rock on April 25—when a rowdy fist fight broke out between the opposing factions and culminated in the holding of dual conventions—presaged what would happen at the state assemblage one week later.[33]

Understandably, the repeated setbacks at the hands of the Taft-dominated machine caused Roosevelt's backers not only to hold a separate convention on May 7—a date prescribed by Arkansas law for minority party conventions—but also to select a complete Republican State Committee and organization for the colonel. Comer was named state chairman to repace Remmel, and, after picking a delegation to Chicago, the convocation nominated a slate of candidates for the November elections headed by A. S. Fowler of Little Rock for governor. A resolution capitalizing on Roosevelt's rhetoric about primaries and Taft's control over the southern machines was passed, stipulating that "the term of office of any member of the state central committee or any office thereof shall automatically cease whenever he becomes an applicant for appointive office." The Roosevelt men also tore into Clayton and Remmel, charging that they had used the Republican party in Arkansas "for the sole purpose of distributing federal patronage" rather than working to build up the party as a vote-getting organization. Furthermore, the platform adopted not only demanded a presidential primary, but also appealed for Negro support by urging a change in state election statutes "to secure to every qualified voter the right to cast his vote and to have the same counted." Although Roosevelt had declared himself for the grandfather clause when he spoke in North Carolina, his followers in Arkansas found themselves trapped in the crossfire between the shift in national campaign tactics and a pending vote in November on an amendment to the state constitution authorizing such a measure in the state. In an effort to capture the Negroes, who surely constituted the bulk of Republican strength and who were working hard to head off the constitutional change, Roosevelt's sympathizers put a plank into their platform opposing this form of disfranchisement.[34]

At the convention of the regular faction, which the *Arkansas Gazette* reported as having the greater attendance, policemen were on hand to quash any demonstration for Roosevelt. They were not needed, however, because the "anti-administration men" were elsewhere. The convention was both uneventful and unanimous in its demonstrations for Taft. This group, too, nominated a complete slate for state office, tapping Judge Andrew I. Roland of Malvern as the gubernatorial nominee to oppose Fowler and Joseph Taylor Robinson, who had won the state Democratic primary on March 27. Roland, a native of Grant County and a lawyer, was not only the party nominee two years earlier but he had been judge of Hot Springs County since 1904 when first elected by a combined Republican-Democratic vote; he would again be the party candidate for governor in the 1913 special election to replace Robinson, who was elected to the Senate before serving out his term. Before adjournment, the regulars picked a list of presidential electors and adopted a brief platform favoring Taft, all under the firm tutelage of Chairman Remmel.[35]

In Alabama, Roosevelt's disciples had been following the counsel of McHarg as well as getting charged up for their rival state convention on May 11 in Birmingham. They had steadily lambasted the Taft-dominated state committee since the March 15 organizational meeting for TR, and Judge Hundley, who had been campaigning in New Hampshire for the colonel, soon joined the Roosevelt chorus by telling reporters during a stopover in Washington that the March 7 GOP State Convention had selected delegates to the national convention prematurely and unfairly. Hundley answered a recent assertion by Taft that the federal patronage was "being used less in his campaign than in any previous contest" by suggesting the president have his people call a primary in Alabama, "where there is ample provision for a fair expression of the will of the party." T. H. Aldrich, the Birmingham postmaster, who was also in Washington, assured the press that all delegates to Chicago from the state had been regularly and properly chosen. "The number of delegates holding federal office," he said, was "smaller than ever before in the history of the party."[36]

In their continuing search for legitimacy, the backers of Roosevelt in Alabama held county conventions throughout the state on May 4 in which uniform resolutions were adopted endorsing Roosevelt for the Republican nomination and recognizing Thompson as state chairman instead of Long. The two hundred or so delegates named at these gatherings formed the larger convention at Birmingham, where "a mere mention of Roosevelt's name provoked continuous applause." Called to order by Thompson, this forum heard a rousing address by Judge Hundley in which Taft was "flayed" and then quickly selected twelve delegates-at-large to Chicago with one-half vote each. Surprisingly, Thompson announced that he intended to step down as chairman although he would remain active in the campaign. Several Taft delegates to the national convention chosen at the regular GOP conclave, reported the Birmingham *Age-Herald,* looked on from the gallery when the three-hour convocation concluded by writing a platform in favor of Roosevelt and his policies. Although Roosevelt's friends announced from the podium that only four of the approximately two hundred delegates present were officeholders, it was nonetheless apparent that Taft's hold on the state organization with its threat of patronage removal was a powerful deterrent that kept many otherwise friendly Republicans from the meeting.[37]

But Taft and the Alabama GOP leadership were becoming increasingly alienated from the state's massive black population. Though the Montgomery *Colored Alabamian* joined the Richmond *Planet* in denouncing both TR and Taft "as enemies of our people," the Negro paper singled out Taft for special scorn. In several editorials during the preconvention fights it consistently reminded readers that Taft was "a Negro hater" because of his earlier comments that he would "appoint Negroes to office in no locality where the white people are opposed to them." And the *Colored Alabamian* joined other Negro papers in pounding Taft's relation to the Brownsville debacle: "The serious minded everywhere will remember and never forget that it was Mr. Taft who recommended that the brave colored soldiers be discharged from the United States Army without a trial and 'without honor.' " Yet Thompson and the Roosevelt movement in Alabama could take little solace from its anti-Taft bias. "Many Negroes throughout the United States," the Montgomery paper editorialized, "who can vote are fighting over the question as to whether they should support President Taft or ex-President Roosevelt. Both . . . should be repudiated by Negro voters everywhere. There is no difference between them."[38]

At the same time Roosevelt and his cohorts were holding questionable conventions in many southern states as well as creating an unacceptable political climate for most southern Negroes, he again demonstrated his national appeal by walking away with the important Maryland and California primaries. In Maryland, a border state with traits in common with the cotton South, Roosevelt won the May 6 contest over Taft by the narrow margin of 29,647 to 26,618. The result hinged on the voting in a single county—Howard, just west of Baltimore—where he won by sixty-six votes to capture the state's sixteen national convention delegates; a handful of votes in the other direction would have given Taft a majority of the delegates to the state convention and a victory in the only primary south of Mason and Dixon's line. Eight days later, on May 14, he carried California over Taft by the lopsided vote of 138,563 to 69,345. This triumph not only assured him of the state's delegation to Chicago but also pushed Governor Hiram Johnson to the forefront as a possible running mate. And, although Progressivism had a firm hold on the California electorate—La Follette received 45,000 tallies in the Republican voting—Champ Clark of Missouri defeated Woodrow Wilson in the Democratic balloting.[39]

In North Carolina, the only southern state where Roosevelt's agents had a real possibility of getting a favorable delegation without resorting to political shenanigans and rival conclaves, the Roosevelt bandwagon continued to make headway prior to the May 15 get-together in Raleigh. Taft's refusal to reconsider his ban on federal appointments in the state until differences between his managers, John M. Morehead and Edward C. Duncan, had been resolved made it nearly impossible for the president to pick up support among party regulars. Morehead maintained that the entire issue was "a mountain of political flub-dubbery constructed out of a mole hill," but one of Dixon's correspondents ecstatically told the TR manager: "President Taft's action in withdrawing the nominations of ten collectors and postmasters is being severely criticized and is contributing to his undoing in North Carolina." Beyond a doubt, the flap over appointments made it easier for Roosevelt to seize the initiative in the state. He won by substantial majorities in the district and county conventions; in New Hanover County, where a GOP primary was held, he got all twenty delegates to the Raleigh convention, thus demonstrating his hold on the party rank and file. The victory engineered by Pearson and Walser was so complete that when the state assemblage came into session, the Charlotte *Daily Observer* reported: "A Roosevelt tidal wave had swept the state from Murphy to Manteo and the convention presented almost a solid front for the former President." The issue was never in question. The Old North State belonged to the colonel.[40]

The North Carolina convention was an unquestioned victory for Roosevelt, and, although Morehead, who was still state chairman and Taft's man, called the meeting to order, he was quickly replaced as presiding officer by Zeb Walser. Marion Butler, the old Populist and onetime U.S. senator, now allied with Morehead, was overwhelmingly defeated in his effort to become national committeeman. The coveted spot was given to Richmond Pearson, long a member of the Roosevelt team. Then, surprisingly, Morehead was reelected state chairman over Colonel Virgil E. Lusk of Asheville, the candidate of the pro-Roosevelt faction, by the uncomfortably close margin of 545 to 535. "The Morehead-Butler crowd," said the Charlotte *Daily Observer,* "had lost on every question that had come to a vote and when Butler himself went down before the Roosevelt rough riding, they stood by the doomed ship and made one last attempt to save the captain." Although Morehead was kept on as chairman, Walser brought the conventioneers to red hot pitch by saying that "Roosevelt on his recent visit to North Carolina, had told him that North Carolina was not trying to get on the bandwagon, because the Tar Heel State had been for him since there was no wagon." Amid the hoopla, a delegation to Chicago led by Pearson and Walser was instructed for Roosevelt and a favorable platform was adopted before a resolution was passed condemning Taft for withdrawing the federal appointments as "ill-advised, indefensible, subversive to good government and good morals, and in violation of the statutes governing the civil service." Yet, accepting the inevitable, the Taft forces did not organize a counterconvention as the TR people had been doing in other southern states.[41]

Conditions were different across the mountains in Tennessee, where the second GOP convention met on the same day and instructed for Taft despite an anticipated bolt by the Roosevelt phalanx. Although a Roosevelt headquarters had been opened at the Hermitage Hotel in Nashville shortly after the nominating convention for Governor Hooper in March, William J. Oliver, Roosevelt's manager in the state, was less than successful at gaining support for his man in the district conventions that met prior to the May 15 convention. Many of the local gatherings, which resulted in splits and often violent confrontations, were victories for Taft; in all of them the heavy influence of Hooper and Sanders could be seen seeking party harmony and support for the president. Unable to make headway against the entrenched regulars, Oliver, who was frustrated with the State Committee, charged Hooper with working to assist officeholders favoring Taft and stated that a separate convention would be called if Roosevelt was not treated fairly by the Republican organization. Further threatening Hooper, the Roosevelt chieftain hinted that a rival GOP candidate for governor might be put in the field if a delegation without representation for the colonel was sent to Chicago.[47]

Taft appeared to have the state neatly bottled up before the second conclave, but the Tennessee campaign was disrupted when Newell Sanders arrived in Washington to take his Senate seat and began conferring with Taft on federal appointments at the expense of the two Republican congressmen from east Tennessee. R. W. Austin complained to the White House that "Sanders seems determined to have his way, even if it means driving influential support from the President." The Taft-dominated State Committee, however, had complete control of the Tennessee organization and scored a major victory by designating John H. Early of Chattanooga as temporary chairman of the state gathering. This meant, reported the Charlotte *Daily Observer,* that "enough Taft delegates [would] be seated to give the Taft forces control of the convention." Meanwhile, Senator Dixon and the national Roosevelt campaign—hoping to counter the drift toward Taft—put out a press release claiming that their man could already count on 725 pledged delegates, whereas the president and La Follette had only 158 between them, and, one day before the convention, called upon Tennessee Republicans to join North Carolina and Minnesota in opting for the Rough Rider.[43]

Oliver and state Senator John Houk addressed the convention amid a great deal of confusion. Both lauded Roosevelt and denounced the State Committee's actions as unfair. Although the Roosevelt men fought long and hard, resorting to parliamentary maneuvering in a futile attempt to block organization of the body, the assembly was in no mood for compromise as it hurriedly named a Taft delegation-at-large headed by Sanders to the national convention. The Roosevelt men threw in the sponge, deciding not to hold a rump convention after friends of Governor Hooper urged a policy of conciliation and harmony in the interest of the state campaign. The olive branch, however, did not extend to the platform, which was a Taft document throughout; it not only specifically instructed the Tennessee delegation to vote for the president at Chicago, but, according to the Atlanta *Journal,* slapped at Roosevelt by denouncing the "initiative, referendum, and recall of judges and judicial decisions and protesting against any amendment to the Sherman Anti-Trust law, except to make its enforcement more certain and effective." Unlike North Carolina, Taft and the Old Guard had won total victory in Tennessee.[44]

Roosevelt's faction in Georgia held a state convention of their own in Atlanta on May 17. The regular GOP convention in February had met when Roosevelt's candidacy was at the speculative stage, and, of course, chose a slate of national convention delegates pledged to Taft. In the weeks that followed, however, the Roosevelt group, led by J. St. Julian Yates and Atlanta attorney William J. Tilson, launched a two-pronged attack on the Taft-controlled State Committee in an effort to have the previous assembly overturned. At the national level, letters were written to key Republicans in the state warning them: "If the Southern delegations go to Mr. Taft, and if Mr. Roosevelt and his friends get control of the National Convention, then the South will be punished by the Roosevelt people." Furthermore, the ubiquitous McHarg made a thrust into the state, reported the Atlanta *Independent,* "in an attempt to wipe out the Taft slate to the national presidential convention in Chicago and to substitute therefore a full Roosevelt delegation." Apparently, he worked with both disgruntled Negroes and lily-whites who wanted to organize a Roosevelt boom and to discredit the Taft machine. Henry S. Jackson, collector of internal revenue and Taft's manager, issued a denial that the Taft delegates had been chosen irregularly or that coercion had been used to have the convention called early.[45]

Tilson, who headed the early Roosevelt campaign, joined the anti-Taft clamor by denouncing the February conclave as illegal. He said it was convened "on a hurry up call from Washington sixty days before a convention could be held" under Georgia law. Therefore, the Taft delegates already named, according to his reasoning, were not entitled to seats at Chicago and a second convention was necessary to overcome the stigma of illegality. In much the same vein, Yates, president of the Roosevelt Progressive Republican Clubs of Georgia and afterward Bull Moose national committeeman, charged that federal officers were being used to keep Roosevelt's devotees from meetings for the former president. Then, seemingly unbothered by the pressures of the national campaign, Yates announced that a state convention would meet on May 17 as well as district gatherings the next day "to send a full contesting delegation to the national convention." Moreover, while he and Tilson were making preparations for the rival assembly, Roosevelt, who liked to think he had considerable support in the state because of his mother's relations, urged his Georgia lieutenants to play up his having received "a scattering vote . . . in the democratic primary." He promised also to make "a hard hitting campaign in both Georgia and North Carolina."[46]

Delegates to the session organized by Tilson and Yates had been picked at Roosevelt get-togethers one week earlier in more than one hundred of Georgia's 146 counties. The meeting was called to order by Yates, although Judson Lyons, a Negro attorney from Augusta and treasury registrar during Roosevelt's administration, was promptly named temporary chairman. Negroes dominated the convention throughout, which was somewhat surprising in view of Roosevelt's repeated statements eschewing southern Negro support in 1912; the Atlanta *Journal* reported that out "of 122 delegates in attendance less than a dozen were white men." Nonetheless, Lyons gave a rousing speech "eulogizing Republican leaders in general and Roosevelt in particular . . . declaring that Roosevelt was unbeatable and would carry the Chicago convention." Although Georgia was entitled to four delegates-at-large to the national conclave, eight were appointed—four white and four Negro—with one-half vote each and instructed for the Rough Rider. The convention was merely a pep rally for Roosevelt, and before it broke up, Yates, who was not named to the delegation, told the dissidents to stand firm for the colonel, for if nominated, he would "hall up a respectable majority in Georgia next November and break the solid south."[47]

Outside the South, national attention focused on the May 21 primary in Ohio, regarded by most political observers as the fateful test for both candidates. Using a special train, Roosevelt traveled more than eighteen hundred miles across the state between May 15 and 20 flailing away at the president as "a fathead and puzzlewit," and, at Columbus on the seventeenth, he renewed his threat to bolt the party "if President Taft is nominated by the seating of fraudulent delegates" from the South and elsewhere at the national convention. Taft, on the other hand, fought mightily to save his own state from the Roosevelt offensive. Accompanied by such notables as Senator Theodore H. Burton, Secretary of State Philander C. Knox, Secretary of Commerce and Labor Charles Nagel, and several Ohio congressmen, the president set out from Marietta on May 12, giving sixty-three speeches as he crisscrossed the state. Mingo Sanders, a Negro former soldier drummed from the army after the infamous Brownsville incident, also escorted Taft's entourage in an effort to arouse the Negro vote against Roosevelt. Nor did the president himself pull many punches in his unsuccessful fight to win the Buckeye State as he tore into Roosevelt at every crossroads. In Steubenville, reported the Chicago *Tribune,* "Mr. Taft did not hesitate to enter into personalities, and throughout his address bristled with the terms 'demagogue,' 'dangerous egotist,' and 'flatterer.' "[48]

But as the two old campaigners grappled for primary victories in the North, electioneering in the South continued to center around Roosevelt and his agents, who called rival conventions among disgruntled Republicans wherever they could be found. In Virginia, for instance, they resorted to a Negro group under the leadership of Jesse M. Newcomb, a white lawyer from Newport News, who had been snubbed by the regular organization. The Negroes, smarting under their earlier rejection at the convention managed by Congressmen Slemp and Alvah H. Martin that had instructed for Taft, held an organizational meeting at Richmond on April 10 to discuss grievances and to declare for Roosevelt. Now headed by Newcomb and J. R. Pollard, a Negro attorney from Newport News and a revenue collector during Roosevelt's administration, the Negroes attacked the State Committee and the earlier state convention "as not representing a majority of the party in Virginia" and, thus justified in their actions, sent out a call for a new convention to meet on May 16.[49]

Although Slemp reassured the White House that Virginia was safe for the president and would stay with him "straight through," the black-and-tan leaders, who were in touch with Dixon and Roosevelt, drifted toward the colonel, according to the Richmond *Virginian,* "in hopes of getting the federal patronage." As the antiadministration agitation increased among Virginia blacks, John Mitchell, Jr., editor of the Richmond *Planet,* told his readers that neither GOP candidate had anything to offer the southern Negro. "President Taft," he editorialized, "has not treated us right and we know it. As for ex-President Roosevelt, it would be an insult to refer to his past record on the Negro question. It is too painful a subject at this time to comment further." When the May 16 "mass republican state convention" opened in Richmond, however, the lure of federal appointments was strong enough that J. Thomas Newsome, a second Negro attorney from Newport News, told the assemblage: "The time has come for the Negro to assert his rights, [and] if Roosevelt fails to get the Presidential nomination the best thing for us to do is to vote for the democratic nominee." The three hundred-odd delegates, two hundred of whom were Negroes, making up the convention quickly named a new Republican State Committee with J. M. Newcomb as chairman before naming and instructing a pro-Roosevelt delegation-at-large to Chicago. A platform was adopted that not only announced for the colonel but condemned the "lily whiteism" and "bossism" of the Slemp-Martin machine. Like similar black-and-tan groups across the lower South, these delegates were never recognized by the GOP National Committee and were eventually tossed aside by Roosevelt and the Bull Moosers. In the days before the nomination, however, when all possible help was needed, it was a different story.[50]

In Florida, where the pot had continued to boil following the "hurry up" convention of February 7 that terminated in a rump meeting and the selection of two delegations, the Roosevelt camp held a second conclave on May 18 in Jacksonville. Although a Roosevelt delegation had been designated in February, the colonel's friends sent out a call for a new convention after McHarg had entered the state from Georgia giving them $2,500 to build up an opposition movement to the Taft-controlled regular organization led by Henry S. Chubb. McHarg and the Florida Roosevelt-ites had become alarmed lest the handful of bolters from the earlier meeting might not be recognized at the national convention. All the while, Taft sought to retain control over the delegation already instructed for him by sending autographed photographs to each member and applying the threat of patronage removal. At the same time, H. L. Anderson of Jacksonville and McHarg were encouraging Florida Republicans to ignore the federal officeholders and to take matters into their own hands for Roosevelt.[51]

The May 18 meeting was a coming together of anti-Taft Republicans from over the state and itself became a split convention. The main body led by Anderson adopted a pro-Roosevelt platform that favored a party primary for Florida's nearly nonexistent GOP, nominated a state ticket headed by William C. Hodges for governor because the earlier O'Neal slate was unacceptable to the Roosevelt camp, and instructed a new delegation to the national convention. Meeting in the Jacksonville Odd Fellows Hall, the convention denounced the Palatka gathering that had declared for Taft as irregular. It also adopted resolutions censuring the president for "appointing a Democrat to a federal judgeship in Florida [and] for favoring the Catholic Church whenever he had a chance." Unlike Georgia, where both Negroes and lily-whites outside the administration's favor teamed up in a common front for Roosevelt, this body was a white man's show throughout with Anderson, who became Bull Moose national committeeman following TR's rejection of the southern Negro, in complete command. Those Negroes present bolted under the leadership of Charles H. Alston, a Negro attorney from Tampa, charging discrimination and named a second pro-Roosevelt delegation. Alston, a Raleigh, North Carolina, native and graduate of Shaw University, had been active in state Republican politics since 1894 when first admitted to the Florida bar. He reportedly participated in more than eleven thousand criminal cases, including rape and murder trials, not one of which ever resulted in the death penalty for his clients. At Chicago, however, when the GOP National Committee met to rule on disputed delegates prior to the convention, neither Alston's nor Anderson's delegates were seated.[52]

The rump conventions in Florida named the last delegates from the South to be chosen except in Texas, where party boss Cecil A. Lyon could not hold a convention until May 28 because of limitations imposed by the state's Terrell Election Law. In the interval, however, Roosevelt scored a major victory when he carried the May 21 primary in Ohio by a 32,000-vote margin over Taft and La Follette combined, even though he failed to get a majority of the state's delegation to the national convention. Taft managed to win thirty-two of the forty-two district delegates, and when the Ohio Republican State Convention met on June 3, his followers not only captured the new state GOP committee but also the delegation-at-large. Roosevelt immediately branded his undoing in the Buckeye State as "pure political brigandage" and declared it "was fresh and conclusive proof that Mr. Taft and his advisors care nothing for the will of the people." When "the people" did speak again in the New Jersey primary on May 28, the colonel received a decisive statewide majority, hauling in twenty-two of the state's twenty-eight delegates to Chicago. Both men had campaigned hard for the contest, and a near riot occurred in Atlantic City when the curious crowded to see Taft, but, as usual, it was the fiery Roosevelt who seized the voter's imagination. "The victories for Col. Roosevelt ranged from 2 to 1 to 4 to 1," said the New York *Times,* while "all of the majorities for Taft were small."[53]

Finally, the South Dakota primary on June 4—just two weeks before the big convention—resulted in another popular victory for Roosevelt when he ran roughshod over Taft and La Follette in a hotly contested three-cornered fight. The primary results, however, meant many things to many people. Roosevelt had certainly triumphed in the greatest number and marshaled a good plurality of the popular vote in the twelve states holding elections, thus supporting his argument that most Republicans favored him and his Progressive policies. Yet Taft could assert just as plausibly that Roosevelt polled little more than half the total votes cast and his victories were produced by Democrats seeking to embarrass the Republicans. But wherever he lived in 1912, the average voter in both parties unquestionably found the appeal of the primaries a welcome relief from the convention system of picking delegations to national conventions with all of its built-in evils.[54]

National attention soon fixed on the struggle in Texas, where Lyon was emphasizing Roosevelt's popularity among rank and file Republicans as he sought to hold the party in line before the May 28 convention in Fort Worth. In the weeks following the March 5 meeting of the State Executive Committee that had resulted in a victory for TR, both Lyon and MacGregor raised the ugly but familiar threat of patronage removal to influence the county and district gatherings. And as Dixon was sending formal congratulations to Lyon for delivering "body blows" to the Taft forces and for denouncing carpetbag influence among Texas Republicans, MacGregor ran a paid advertisement in several newspapers warning officeholders that, although Lyon was state chairman, their commissions had been signed by President Taft. They were also advised that Lyon was totally devoid of influence at the White House and that retribution would be swift for federal employees contributing funds to the Roosevelt-Lyon war chest.

Texas Negroes were totally in the administration fold because of Lyon's long leadership in the lily-white movement and, unlike their counterparts in other states, none joined in rump demonstrations for the Rough Rider. Although Lyon and other Roosevelt champions kept up a steady propaganda barrage claiming their man to be the chief contender for the state's forty-man delegation to Chicago, several influential Republicans bolted to the Taft campaign. Julius M. Oppenheimer, a leader of the German faction in central Texas and Bexar County (San Antonio) chairman, issued a statement saying that 95 percent of the Texas party was for Taft and that Roosevelt was supported primarily by federal officeholders who were afraid to voice any opinions. Lyon had been in command of the Texas party for more than twenty years but, without support in Washington and with powerful groups at home aligned against him, he could do little but start a movement for Roosevelt and hope that his group would be seated at Chicago.[55]

The situation in Texas was similar to that in Arkansas, where dual conventions were held on the same day, except that MacGregor and the Taft people in effect became the bolting group. Lyon's political know-how and the unsettling proceedings in the county and district conventions prompted MacGregor to hold a separate gathering without attempting to meet in the same hall with the Roosevelt faction. The regularly called or Lyon convention met in Fort Worth's Savoy Theatre as planned and quickly adopted resolutions favoring "the nomination of the people's friend, the peerless statesman, patriot, and leader, Theodore Roosevelt." Further resolutions praised Lyon and "his administration of the party's affairs in Texas . . . as our national committeeman and state chairman" as well as instructing the delegation to vote for Roosevelt "as long as his name is before the convention." An estimated four hundred participants attended the meeting; the Taft-MacGregor affair was smaller, with about three hundred in attendance. Both gatherings, however, were mere hurrah sessions for their respective candidates, and each predictably selected a slate of delegates to the national convention. The Roosevelt delegation-at-large was headed by Lyon, Edward C. Lasater, and Henry L. Borden, the latter two becoming the Bull Moose candidates for governor and attorney general, respectively, later in the year. Meanwhile, the Taft meeting formulated resolutions endorsing MacGregor for national committeeman to replace Lyon, calling the president "a wise, just, and honest administrator," and declaring its unswerving loyalty to the "National Republican Party." This convention put up a delegation headed by MacGregor and included such party stalwarts as William M. "Gooseneck" McDonald, a Negro long associated with the anti-lily-white forces, and Judge C. K. McDowell of Val Verde County in far west Texas. When the controversy was transferred to Chicago, the National Committee recognized the MacGregor group, even though Lyon still enjoyed an iron-fisted and legitimate control over the official party apparatus.[56]

The two gatherings at Fort Worth completed the convention process in the eleven ex-Confederate states and brought the number of delegations-at-large from the region to twenty-two. Although the state conclaves named only at-large delegations, they were by far the most prestigious personnel sent to the national body scheduled to open on June 18 because they represented the entire state and generally included major party leaders such as national committeemen, state chairmen, and influential officeholders. In addition, the states were permitted two delegates from each congressional district who were picked in district assemblies. Under the official call for the 1912 Republican National Convention the number of delegates-at-large was normally set at four—two for each United States senator—although provision was made for additional members if the state had congressmen-at-large. This arrangement gave the South fifty-four: Texas, eight; Alabama, Florida, and Louisiana, six each; Arkansas, Georgia, Mississippi, North Carolina, South Carolina, Tennessee, and Virginia, four each.

Furthermore, the celebrated "southern contests" resulted from the policy of McHarg and national Roosevelt campaign managers encouraging and abetting the manufacture of rival delegations across the South. Their challenge to Taft's organizations produced twice the number of authorized at-large delegations from the region, with only North Carolina, South Carolina, and Tennessee sending uncontested groups to Chicago. Alabama, Arkansas, Georgia, Mississippi, Virginia, and Texas sent two at-large delegations each, while Florida returned three and Louisiana, four, for a total of twenty-two delegations comprising 114 contestants for fifty-four seats. A good percentage of the ninety-nine congressional districts in the eleven states likewise sent rival delegations, which meant the National Committee and later the convention itself would be forced to spend a vast amount of time adjudicating disputed seats from all southern states. The contested southern delegations obviously held the key to the nomination, and a strong argument can be advanced that the manner of their resolution was the single most important factor determining whether Taft or Roosevelt would win the 1912 Republican nomination.

Chapter 5

Chicago, June 1912

In the ten-day interval between the Texas conventions and the start of GOP National Committee hearings on June 7 to resolve the disputed contests, both Roosevelt and Taft were concerned over temporary organization of the national convention. Since the temporary chairman would ultimately rule on seating the contesting delegations, it was crucial for Roosevelt to find a friendly candidate. When the Sub-Committee on Arrangements settled upon New York Senator Elihu Root for the job, TR's supporters commenced a fight to block his confirmation in the convention and to substitute their own man. Roosevelt eventually threw his support to Wisconsin Governor Francis E. McGovern and repeatedly blasted Root, whom he regarded as pro-Taft, throughout early June; he also expressed a preference for Minnesota Senator Moses E. Clapp and Governor Herbert S. Hadley of Missouri for the post at various times. Pearl Wight and Cecil A. Lyon, Roosevelt's two southern supporters on the National Committee, favored Hadley for the job.[1]

A more immediate problem for the presidential contenders centered around the fight to win the all-important disputed delegations in the upcoming committee sessions. While Hilles and Taft were meticulously preparing legal briefs for presentation to the national committeemen, TR, who was feeling as fit as the proverbial Bull Moose, left his battle to McHarg and Dixon. Although Roosevelt held a lengthy conference at Sagamore Hill on May 27 with Dixon and Medill McCormick of Illinois regarding his list of delegates, he refused to disclose strategy or numbers to questioning reporters. McCormick, reported the Richmond *Virginian,* "popped out of the door for a moment and modestly ventured the prediction that Roosevelt 'would canter in the nomination.' " Because of the need to capture as many delegates as possible, a controversy arose over tickets for the convention. When the National Committee refused to allocate 250 tickets directly to TR, Dixon charged Colonel Harry S. New, chairman of the Committee on Arrangements, with handing out convention passes solely for the benefit of Taft. Supposedly, the tickets were issued through the National Committee with no preference to any candidate, but the charges and countercharges during 1912 prompted Victor Rosewater to write later that when "scalpers priced serial tickets as high as $100, those left out were certain something was wrong in distribution."[2]

New released an official statement that challenges had been filed to 228 delegate seats prior to the start of hearings. The number was higher than the total anticipated by the president's managers, who attempted at the last hour to induce the La Follette workers to cooperate with them in the organization of the convention. The Roosevelt followers launched a campaign to ensure that the hearings be open and given the full benefit of publicity. Two hundred fifty-two seats out of a total 1,078 in the convention had been allocated to the South, and the National Committee ruled on 176 disputed delegates from the region or 69 percent of those from the eleven ex-Confederate states. Contests were presented from every southern state. In the end, 166 of the questioned seats were awarded to Taft and a mere 10 to Roosevelt. Many of the cases resolved by the committee and placed on the temporary roll, except for several contests abandoned by the Roosevelt camp, were reheard amid great confusion and heated debate in the convention proper. And, when the convention followed in refusing to seat the pro-Roosevelt delegates, charges of "theft," "stolen convention," and "fraudulent delegates" were hurled at the chair as the Roosevelt men rejected further participation in its deliberations.[3]

The committee decided to hear the contests in alphabetical order. Alabama came first on June 7, attracting considerable national attention as the first southern contest. Contested seats from the South made up more than half of the total filed, and although Taft had a comfortable majority on the committee so the outcome was a foregone conclusion, Roosevelt's lieutenants fought for every possible delegate. Alabama was entitled to twenty-four delegates, and the Roosevelt faction offered challenges to fourteen seats stemming from the TR activity led by Thompson, Judge Hundley, and McHarg. In the weeks following the Alabama state convention, however, Barker and Long were not only concerned with rival delegates from the state, but also with a rebellion among several Taft delegates who began expressing a desire to support Roosevelt in the national gathering. Any defections on the eve of the convention produced sensational headlines, but these delegates from the third and seventh districts, none of whom were among the officially contested group, caused a good deal of confusion at national Roosevelt headquarters. After the colonel, who was pleased to have their support, learned the identity of his new delegates, he told Judge Hundley on June 4: "Everything is going splendidly, and if the national committee will but give us a square deal upon the contests, I do not think there need be any doubt at all regarding the nomination."[4]

Taft's agents in Alabama, however, understandably had a different view of the revolt and initiated a countermove to downplay the defections. Yet all three of the announced bolters, Byron Trammell, postmaster at Dothan, and his fellow delegate from the third district, John B. Daugherty of Hartford, as well as C. D. Alverson of Pell City in the seventh, were ultimately seated by the National Committee. Oscar D. Street, a lawyer in charge of arguing the Alabama disputes for the president, wrote to Senator Charles Dick of Ohio, one of Taft's national managers, that he felt "disgusted and humiliated" at Alverson for going over to Roosevelt. "It is just such 'cattle,' " Street said, "who have brought disgrace to the whole body of southern republicans. I believe this man is bought and doubtless the same is true for the other two." A meeting of the Taft leaders was held at the Hillman Hotel in Birmingham on June 3 prior to leaving for Chicago to discuss what action should be taken on contests filed by the Roosevelt faction. But it was soon obvious that the Roosevelt thrust had not cooled the fighting spirit of the Taft delegates, who defiantly adopted a resolution damning the initiative, referendum, and recall and pledged themselves to support P. D. Barker as the National Committeeman for Alabama. "We do hereby extend to President Taft our united and unshaken loyalty," they resolved further, "and we will stand by him first, last, and all the time." At Chicago these same men adopted the unit rule for balloting in an attempt to offset the three dissenters, although Trammell told reporters he would "vote for Roosevelt if they chop my head off." Trammell added fuel to the fire by declaring that Roosevelt had entered the campaign at Columbus after the third district convention, and "the entrance of 'TR' in the race changed the entire Republican complexion and under such circumstances he had the right to support the Colonel if he wanted to."[5]

Meanwhile, the Alabama cases were heard by the National Committee, and every contested seat went to the Taft delegates. Roosevelt's followers among the committeemen voted with the Taft majority to throw out the delegation-at-large and those from the first, second, and fifth districts. It was part of the Roosevelt-Progressive strategy not to stand by any cases from the South or elsewhere that did not have genuine merit. Hundley and the national Roosevelt campaign decided, however, to fight for the ninth district delegates. Senator Dick and Street argued that the Taft delegates had been chosen properly by a regular organization that had been so recognized by the State Committee for the past four years and that the call for the district convention had been legally drafted. The Roosevelt claimants, on the other hand, maintained that the Taft men had bolted from a meeting of the ninth district Executive Committee, "leaving a majority to do business, and that as a result a call was issued and the election held which resulted in the sending of a regular Roosevelt delegation to Chicago." Therefore, the question before the National Committee was which convention sending delegates from the ninth had done so lawfully.[6]

Although the district appeared to be legitimately in the Roosevelt fold, a roll call vote gave the delegates to Taft by a thirty-eight to fifteen margin. In this first confrontation, the Chicago *Tribune* reported that Senators Boies Penrose of Pennsylvania and Murray Crane of Massachusetts of the Taft forces were "walking among their colleagues suggesting how they should vote." The Taft representatives from the sixth district were seated quickly by a voice vote when the Roosevelt challengers failed to appear. Both Judge Hundley and J. O. Thompson were among the rejected delegates as the National Committee seated the entire Alabama delegation headed by P. D. Barker and Pope M. Long. Moreover, it was the ninth district fight that provoked Roosevelt into branding the committee with "a moral, if not legal crime." "Again and again," he charged from Oyster Bay, "we have sent to the penitentiary election officials for deeds not one whit worse than what was done."[7]

Amid continued cries of "stolen delegates" and "fraudulent contests" by the Rooseveltites, the National Committee ruled on the Arkansas challenges during its first day of deliberations. Although contests were presented for the delegates-at-large and for six of the state's seven congressional districts, the committee ruled in every instance for the Taft claimants headed by Powell Clayton. J. A. Comer and McHarg argued for the would-be Roosevelt delegates, even though the at-large delegation was immediately thrown out on a roll call after it was determined that Comer's official brief contained objectionable language. And McHarg charged that Negroes had been barred from the first district convention at Paragould because the meeting was held in locations where they were not safe. Unabashed by Roosevelt's rejection of Negro participation in his cause, he stated that because the convention had been held where all Republicans were not welcome it was irregular and the Taft-instructed delegates had been improperly chosen. The vote, however, went against the Roosevelt supporters as it did in the second district where McHarg also contended that Negroes had been excluded. The Roosevelt delegates in both districts were rejected by a unanimous committee vote.[8]

Although the Arkansas cases were completed on June 8 along with the bitterly contested California disputes, a major effort was made to win in the state's fifth district, where conditions were similar to those in the Alabama ninth. Here it was argued that the Roosevelt men had a clear majority in the district gathering but were turned from the convention hall by an armed policeman. One of the disowned delegates, Winfield S. Holt of Little Rock, even produced photographs of the meeting place where the alleged exclusion had taken place. He charged also that in his own ward in Little Rock, National Committeeman Clayton had personally refused to allow suspected Roosevelt men to enter the convention auditorium. Before the National Committee again ruled in favor of the regular organization, Holt retorted that postmasters dominated Republican politics in Arkansas and had conspired to deny Roosevelt representation on the national convention delegation from the state. When National Committeeman Henry S. Chubb of Florida tauntingly asked if there was "any law which prevents a postmaster from voting in Arkansas," Holt replied: "No, but we object to their running the whole show." The contests in the remaining districts—third, fourth, and seventh—centered around the holding of dual conventions, with the National Committee quickly deciding for the Taft adherents in all instances.[9]

Although Roosevelt wrote to one of his boosters, C. T. Bloodworth of Corning, Arkansas, reiterating that "only strict justice be done and that I do not want any delegate for me not clearly entitled to his seat," it was clear that Powell Clayton and the regular organization had retained their hold on the state GOP. Even before the opening session of the Chicago convention, Clayton was informed from the White House that Taft was ignoring the Roosevelt challenge by promptly forwarding his recommendations for postmaster appointments to the Senate for confirmation. Meanwhile, the rejected Roosevelt delegates arrived home in Arkansas following their humiliation at Chicago. Winfield S. Holt, a former Little Rock postmaster and a Connecticut native, told the Memphis *Commercial Appeal* that he had "talked to many republicans from all parts of the country while in Chicago, and all were of the opinion that President Taft could not be reelected." Another longtime Republican, Ulysses S. Bratton, then postmaster at Little Rock and secretary of the State Executive Committee, joined the pro-Roosevelt chorus by declaring that TR would be nominated on the first ballot. Still not convinced of Clayton's hold on the Arkansas party and the power of Taft's steamroller, several Roosevelt delegates, including Holt, Comer, Harry K. Cochran, A. S. Fowler and Harry Trieber, returned to Chicago on a futile chase to have their claims recognized by the convention proper.[10]

Immediately after resolution of the Arkansas disputes on June 8, the National Committee turned to the complicated and muddied Florida contests. The entire state representation, consisting of six delegates-at-large and three districts for a total of twelve, was contested by three sets of claimants: the pro-Taft group chosen at the February state Republican convention, which was headed by National Committeeman Chubb, and two Roosevelt delegations, one of which was led by H. L. Anderson of Jacksonville. First came the at-large contests, with McHarg presenting the colonel's case and saying Anderson's group was "the regular Roosevelt delegation." His argument that there was "no Republican party in Florida" to explain the unusually large number of delegations from the state was used repeatedly in an effort to discredit the Chubb representatives. Joseph E. Lee, the Negro collector of customs from Jacksonville, who was arguing the president's position, scotched McHarg's reasoning by telling the committee that the Taft delegation had been picked at the Palatka convention "by a regular procedure." "We would be better off," Lee reminded him, "if men did not come into our state and try to mislead republicans by means of powers that should not be exercised throughout the republican party." Finally, Chubb, who was voting on his own case as Florida committeeman, called for a roll call vote on the delegates-at-large. "I want this committee," he said, "to come down hard on such damnedable contests as these" as a forty-four to zero ballot was rolled up for the Taft faction.[11]

Although Chubb conferred with Taft on June 1 regarding rumors that delegates pledged to Taft planned to defect to Roosevelt, he had given an earlier confidential report to Hilles assuring him that the Florida delegates had been "hand picked." Moreover, he told Hilles there was "not the slightest doubt that all of them will vote for Taft." Chubb's report indicated also that Lee, who had been appointed collector by McKinley and who was reportedly "one of the best known colored men in Florida," was steadfastly loyal to the president. Lee, a lawyer and college graduate worth $75,000 in 1912, had supported Taft during the Brownsville controversy, which caused the Florida legislature to pass a resolution demanding his removal. When this occurred, J. N. Stripling of Jacksonville, who had been passed over by McKinley and Roosevelt for the collectorship, traveled to Washington in an attempt to secure the post. Taft, however, had continued Lee in office, and now, reported Chubb, he is "happy that he will have an opportunity to show his appreciation." In a prepared statement for the committee hearings, Chubb and Lee charged that McHarg had worked with Stripling, a onetime U.S. attorney, to organize a Roosevelt movement in Florida after the regularly called GOP state convention in February. But, Chubb said, his convention had been legitimately summoned with the official call published in Jacksonville, Tampa, and Pensacola newspapers. He likewise informed Hilles before the hearings that a "death blow would be struck the Republican party in Florida" if Roosevelt should get control of the National Committee and seat the "McHarg delegates."[12]

Chubb's fears proved groundless, however, when the committee awarded the remaining delegates to Taft. In the first district contest, McHarg asserted that no Republican gatherings had been held to elect delegates "except the private conventions of federal officeholders." "It is ridiculous to talk of contests being filed and heard in Florida," he argued, as the committee seated both Taft delegates on a voice vote. The evidence offered by both sides proved "so flimsy" that Thomas Thornson, committeeman from North Dakota moved that no Florida representation be seated in the convention, but the motion was easily defeated by the Taft majority. Yet, reported the Chicago *Tribune,* contests in the second and third districts were settled for Taft "by a unanimous vote, without a roll call, after less than five minutes of argument."[13]

The committee brushed aside demands for adjournment after seven hours of continuous sessions and proceeded directly to the Georgia cases. Like Florida, the entire state was contested—four delegates-at-large and two each from twelve congressional districts for a total of twenty-eight. McHarg and Dean E. Ryman, an Atlanta attorney and Roosevelt supporter, argued for the insurgents, while Henry Lincoln Johnson, Negro lawyer, officeholder, and head of the Taft delegates, presented the president's side. No doubt sensing another defeat before the committee,

McHarg proposed that the entire delegation be "bunched in one presentation," but when Senator Dick objected, the contests were broken down with the at-large delegates considered first. Ryman used the argument that the district and state Republican conventions that chose the Taft delegates were invalid because of a peculiarity in the Georgia election laws requiring that a new registration list be made up every April. He determined, therefore, that "the Taft conventions were illegal because they were held without any regard to the lists" and that the Roosevelt forces had "organized under strict provisions of the law." The committee seated the Taft delegates-at-large after Johnson pointed out that the same voters who participated in the February state convention had voted for governor of the state the preceding January. "If these delegates were not lawfully elected," he continued, "then the election of the governor was illegal." All twenty-eight seats were eventually awarded to the Taft faction, even though Roosevelt's advocates continued to put up a halfhearted fight for the districts.[14]

Roosevelt felt that his best chance in Georgia lay in attempting to break the solidarity of Taft's delegation rather than in pressing the credentials of his own group named at the May convention in Atlanta. A week before the Roosevelt gathering he had written to Senator Dixon: "You might be able to obtain almost the whole delegation if you ask Clark Grier of Dublin, Georgia, to come to New York and see you personally. Do not have him come to Washington or meet with anyone but yourself." Grier, who remained a warhorse in the Georgia GOP for years and was Hoover's campaign manager in 1928, issued a statement on June 16, after the committee hearings, that he and four other delegates intended to switch from Taft to Roosevelt in the convention. Joining with Grier, whose wife was postmistress at Dublin, were John H. Boone, postmaster at Hazelhurst, J. E. Peterson of Fort Grimes, Clay County, and two Negroes, J. C. Styles of Dawson, Terrell County, and S. S. Mincey, a prominent turpentine producer at Alley, Georgia. The Grier statement was immediately refuted by Henry Jackson, Walter Johnson, and Henry S. Blun for the Taft camp, and all but Grier and Boone had retracted their part in the TR bolt before the convention's opening session.[15]

The brief blaze over the Georgians deserting to Roosevelt, one of whom was reportedly offered five hundred dollars to abandon Taft, caused considerable press speculation about southern Negroes in the convention. Although Henry L. Johnson told the White House on June 13 that "the colored delegates are loyal and firm," the fear persisted that some might go over to Roosevelt. The organization of numerous Roosevelt clubs open to white voters only in Georgia left little doubt that the Negro would be barred from party councils should TR win the nomination at Chicago. Yet innuendo that Georgia Negroes might be for sale caused them to be both resentful and defensive. Of the twenty-eight man delegation, only Grier and Boone persisted in their support for TR. But at a caucus of the group on June 17 a fight erupted as the latter was attempting to justify his actions. While Boone was speaking for Roosevelt, several of the Negro delegates became so "disorderly," reported the Charlotte *Daily Observer,* "that Boone lost his temper and called the disturbers 'a bunch of infernal scoundrels.' " The intervention of Walter L. Johnson prevented more serious trouble, however, when "the Negroes advanced on Boone who picked up a chair and lifted it menacingly in the air." All twelve Negroes stood by Taft, although "long green and gold coins were flaunted and hurled at them in tremendous quantities," said the Atlanta *Independent,* but "every colored delegate has stood the test and obeyed the mandates of their constituency."[16]

At the preconvention hearings, the first ten Georgia districts were heard in a group after McHarg successfully argued for their consolidation to save time. Senator Dick agreed to the plan after TR's people expressed a willingness to submit the twenty-odd delegates on the same basis as the at-large delegation. Again the committee acted promptly, seating only Taft men without argument or a roll call. Judson W. Lyons, a Negro lawyer from Atlanta and Roosevelt supporter, declared that the president's delegates in the eleventh district had been "hand picked and did not represent the voters of the district," although they were also recognized along with the Taft representatives from the twelfth. After winning the state for Taft, National Committeeman Jackson triumphantly notified the president: "Georgia delegates delighted with outcome of contest and with the success of the brief prepared by me and turned over to Lincoln Johnson." Yet a group of pro-Roosevelt Negroes headed by H. A. Rucker of Atlanta, a former collector of internal revenue, stayed in Chicago after being "steamrolled to a fare-you-well" along with a number of white delegates in an effort to win acceptance by the convention.[17]

After the marathon session of June 8, the National Committee did not turn its attention to the South until June 12, when the Louisiana cases were called. The Indiana disputes were resolved on Monday, June 10, and Kentucky came the following day, when the Roosevelt forces charged Senator William O. Bradley with importing voters from Ohio and West Virginia to ensure the result for Taft. Deviating from its alphabetical approach, the committee took up cases from California and Arizona before proceeding to the hotly contested Louisiana fight. Here three delegations presented credentials, each representing the entire state, although the committee predictably seated the pro-Taft group headed by Victor Liosel at the expense of the two Roosevelt delegations led by Frank B. Williams and Pearl Wight.

The situation was muddied by a "settlement" imposed upon the regular organization in February by the National Committee which had made Liosel state chairman. When the at-large contests were summoned, William Hayward of New York, secretary of the committee, related that he, Ralph Williams of Oregon, and E. C. Duncan of North Carolina, had brought the Louisiana factions together in a show of harmony prior to the April 9 Republican State Convention. According to Hayward, all segments of the Louisiana party had signed the document that recognized Liosel; he also claimed that the envoys sent into the state from Washington had completed the compromise on February 13 before Roosevelt became a candidate. Williams, however, who was present and who had been ousted as state chairman, denied ever designating a representative to sign the compact, although Hayward stoutly maintained that Hugh S. Suthon, gubernatorial candidate and leader of Williams's pro-Roosevelt delegation, had held his proxy at the February meeting. Pearl Wight, leader of the second TR group present, charged that the committeemen knew that Roosevelt would be a candidate for the Presidency before the settlement was drafted; the lily-white boss had refused to be a party to it. L. H. Pugh of Napoleonville, Louisiana, who put Williams's case before the committee, even agreed that the settlement had contributed to the proliferation of delegations from the state as he attempted to sway the result. It became so complicated that Borah of Idaho, reported the New York *Times,* "declared that he was unable to disentangle the three cornered fight." Following rejection of a proposal by Senator Dick to consolidate the at-large contests with all but one of the district disputes, the committee voted forty-eight to two for seating the Liosel at-large group.[18]

Although most Roosevelt members voted for Taft in the at-large hassle, McHarg and his cohorts decided to press several of the district suits. Wight, however, withdrew contests in the first, second, sixth, and seventh districts after losing the earlier struggle. The fifth district presented the only real fight, even though the committee took time to consider briefly the third and fourth Roosevelt challenges before giving both to Taft. In the fifth, a district convention was called to meet at Tulula, but a flood caused the gathering to be shifted to Vidalia, where two delegates to the national convention, W. T. Insley, postmaster at Delhi, and S. W. Green, were chosen and instructed for the president. But when Green refused to pledge himself to support Taft, C. S. Herbert, the administration boss in the state, "arbitrarily arranged for the election of F. H. Cook in his place." Frank B. Kellogg of Minnesota introduced a resolution to seat Green, but on a voice vote the decision went to Cook, making the twenty-man Louisiana delegation solid for Taft. The much-talked-about steamroller had moved into action.[19]

Amid continued charges of rascality and growing anger by the Roosevelt forces, the committee sped on to the Mississippi cases. The state's at-large contests were considered after settlement of the Michigan disputes and centered around events in the state convention at Jackson. Because the Roosevelt slate had filed first, the Taft delegates led by National Committeeman Lonzo B. Moseley appeared as the challengers. Like Georgia and Louisiana, the entire state was up for grabs, and in all three, reported the Chicago *Tribune,* "The evidence showed that officeholders were busy in behalf of the President, in spite of civil service laws and rules against pernicious political activity of men in office." In no state was this complaint more valid than in Mississippi. Before the Roosevelt men had left the Jackson gathering to form their own convention, M. J. Mulvihill, postmaster at Vicksburg, announced his intention of serving as temporary chairman and organizing the body for Taft. But when W. E. Mollison, a Negro for Roosevelt, made a motion to seat Daniel W. Gary, it was adopted by a three-to-one margin. Sensing victory, a second motion was hurriedly instituted to make Gary permanent chairman; this motion carried by an even larger vote. Then, as "Gary ascended the platform to take the gavel, M. H. Daly, United States Postmaster at Coldwater, pressed a pistol against Gary and threatened to kill him; he was surrounded by United States Marshals, Policemen, and others, and hauled and finally was thrown from the platform."[20]

Although Gary, Mollison, Dr. Redmond, and the Roosevelt boosters had withdrawn from the state convention under physical threat, the National Committee speedily seated the Moseley delegation. During the hearings, Mollison, who argued for the Roosevelt contestants, "convulsed the committee with his references to national committeeman Moseley as an 'associate of kings and princes, and a magnificent man ordinarily,' whom he had never seen 'in the wrong before.' " Also, the New York *Times* commented further, Gary, a Negro, addressed the committee and "made a statement which E. P. Jones, the Taft negro chairman declared was untrue." As they left the hearing room, Gary, "who towered six feet, started toward Jones. . . . There was an interchange of amenities outside, but no fisticuffs."[21]

Following the Mississippi at-large contests, an explosive situation developed over defection of several Negro delegates from Taft to Roosevelt. News that some had received cash from the Taft campaign hit the already electrified atmosphere in Chicago like a bombshell. W. A. Attawing of Greenville, Mississippi, had informed McHarg in April "that the delegates from this state are normally for the President, but still there is a strong undercurrent for the Colonel." He thought Roosevelt would be well advised to work through Charles Banks of Mound Bayou, the friend and confidant of Booker T. Washington. Banks had been advised by his mentor "to act any way your judgment and conscience dictates," but Roosevelt apparently decided to work through Dr. Redmond, who had been for him since February. In an effort to court the black Mississippians, Roosevelt wrote to Redmond on June 11 that he "would not like to definitely commit myself at present" although he wanted "some colored man to second my nomination." And he strongly hinted that Perry W. Howard, Redmond's half-brother, would be a suitable man for the task.[22]

Finally, after the National Committee had seated Banks as a district delegate, he issued a public letter addressed to Taft's national manager, William B. McKinley, telling him he was returning money he had received to pay the traveling costs of some of the Mississippi delegates. A copy of the missive, which renounced allegiance to Taft, was sent to Dixon, who of course exploited its contents to the fullest. Although Moseley made a hurried trip to Washington for a conference with Hilles and the president about the delegation and other Mississippi matters, the breakaway movement continued to gain momentum. Two days after the Banks letter, five members of the delegation, Banks, Gary, Howard, Wesley Cratyon, and W. P. Locker, all Negroes, sent a formal declaration to Roosevelt pledging to support him in the national body. "Some of us," the statement said, "were elected in conventions convened in early March where the delegates to the conventions had practically all been chosen just about the time you made public announcement that you would stand as a candidate." Furthermore, the dissenters said their instructions did not "represent in any degree the real feeling of the Republicans of Mississippi."[23]

Although the five had announced an intention to support TR following the committee hearings, their actions did not signal an exodus of Negroes from the Taft banner. Roosevelt's vacillation on the "Negro question" prompted a majority of blacks in the national convention to stay with the president even though many became disillusioned with Taft's weak appeal before the country. All of the Mississippi district contests already instructed for Taft were decided with minimum debate. Several fierce clashes, however, occurred between Francis J. Heney, a peppery Roosevelt follower from California, and the Taft managers as the hearings on the state proceeded. Heney, a former prosecuting attorney, became so loud and inflammatory during the arguments over the Mississippians that several unsuccessful bids were made to throw him from the deliberations. The eighth district around Jackson and embracing Warren, Yazoo, Madison, Hinds, and Rankin counties presented the only genuine contest; here Perry W. Howard, widely thought to be for the Rough Rider even before the Columbus declaration, was seated along with Wesley Crayton. They were recognized after an "agreement" had been achieved for party harmony in the state, but not before Borah of Idaho, a leading Progressive on the committee, denounced "the making of any agreement as an 'outrage and an insult.' "[24]

Before moving on the same afternoon, June 13, to the North Carolina cases, the committee resolved the disruptive Missouri fight in which the entire state was at issue. Although not one of the eleven ex-Confederate states, Missouri's border state status and the role of Governor Herbert S.

Hadley in Roosevelt's southern strategy gave these hearings special significance to the South. Taft, however, sought to stave off "a battle royal" over Missouri by intervening personally with the committee to work out a compromise with the Roosevelt forces. The resultant agreement gave Roosevelt twenty delegates and recognized Hadley's faction in the state. In a bid for party unity, the agreement denied Taft's own secretary of commerce and labor, Charles Nagel, a place on the delegation.[25]

The North Carolina quarrel involved but six of the state's twenty-four delegates in three congressional districts. Since they were all cut-and-dried affairs touching only rival Roosevelt factions, the contests came as a welcomed relief from the heated altercations involving other parts of the South. The Roosevelt bandwagon led by Richmond Pearson and Zeb V. Walser remained in control of the state Republican apparatus following the May 15 state convention and brought a solid delegation to Chicago. Pearson, who attended the Princeton University annual commencement in early June before traveling to Oyster Bay and the national convention, said in an interview in New York that Roosevelt could count on his state. Moreover, as TR heaped praise on Pearson and Walser for achieving a great victory in North Carolina, Taft continued to put his confidence in National Committeeman Duncan and former Congressman Morehead. But the initiative had passed so completely from their hands that not a single Taft challenge was offered to the committee. The Chicago *Tribune* reported that the all-Roosevelt disputes were settled in the third and ninth districts "without argument by the attorneys and without a roll call"; former Senator Marion Butler, now for Roosevelt, was one of those seated in the third. Two days later, on June 15, Roosevelt gained official control of his only southern state, when the North Carolina fourth district contest, which had been postponed to the last case on the docket, was finally resolved among its TR contestants.[26]

When the committee reassembled on Friday, June 14, contests were heard from Alaska, Oklahoma, South Carolina, and Tennessee. In every instance, the administration steamroller decided in favor of the Taft claimants. The Oklahoma fight, which involved a single district, was a replay of contests from the deep South where rival conventions had elected dual delegations. When the decision went to Taft, Heney again burst forth in strong ejaculations objecting to the presence of National Committeeman Grant Victor, a United States marshal in Oklahoma, on the grounds that he organized rival conventions and that he was a federal officeholder. The committee, however, rejected Heney's demand as the South Carolina contest from the first district around Charleston was called. John G. Capers, the state's national committeeman and sometime friend of both factions, announced that both slates from the district were for Taft and no Roosevelt challenge was present. Thomas L. Grant and a Negro, Aaron P. Prioleau, both solid for the president, were seated without fanfare, and the committee moved to the Tennessee disputes and the renewed antics of Heney.[27]

The single district fight in South Carolina grew from a tilt between Capers and Joseph W. Tolbert for control of the state GOP organization. "The selfish aspirations and candidacy on the part of Joseph W. Tolbert to be National Committeeman," wrote C. M. English, the Negro undertaker from Charleston, "and the ambition of a small politician [Capers?] who is mentally and politically weak, but who desires to be the biggest man in the state caused all the trouble." Capers and Tolbert both recognized the necessity of keeping the state for Taft, even though McHarg and Dixon hoped to lure a number of South Carolina delegates from the president before the convention opened. Dixon was overjoyed in April when he informed a confidant that six of the eighteen South Carolinians had expressed an intent to support the colonel, and "we have assurances that we will obtain all but three of them from this state." Yet the Roosevelt support was illusory for the most part. "Out of the claims and counter claims," reported the Charleston *News and Courier* on the eve of the Chicago conclave, "estimating the figures issued for both sides, the South Carolina delegation has figured a little in both columns, but the majority, if not all of them, are probably for President Taft." The upsurge in Taft sentiment resulted from a conference held in Spartanburg on June 11, in which Capers and Blalock used their influence to sway several undecided delegates for the administration. As Capers was proving his loyalty to the regular GOP by recommending the seating of Taft delegates, however, the Roosevelt Republican Progressive League at Charleston adopted a resolution denouncing the "unseating of Roosevelt delegates, etc., and of others generally favorable to him." The Roosevelt enthusiasts at home also disapproved the "steamroller methods" used by the National Committee and challenged the notion that Taft could rely on support from a majority of South Carolina Republicans.[28]

Next came four district contests from Tennessee. The at-large delegation selected at the May 15 state convention was solid for Taft and not challenged. Roosevelt, however, had made gains in several districts, although Sanders informed the White House in March that he was "making a strenuous effort to avoid contests because contested delegates are of doubtful value." Not only were the usual Roosevelt Progressive clubs active in the state, but Roosevelt followed an established pattern and sought to entice instructed delegates from the president. TR also remained convinced that "Governor Hooper was against us"; and he confessed to Judge John Allison of Knoxville an ignorance about what was happening in the state in his behalf. Yet as the Tennessee delegation left for Chicago, a Memphis newspaper reported that Taft had fifteen sure votes and Roosevelt one; the remaining votes were contested but would probably be claimed by the administration.[29]

The hearings over Tennessee were complicated by a continuing fight between Sanders, now a United States senator, and John W. Overall, United States marshal at Nashville, for the national committeemanship. Because the prize would be decided at the Chicago gathering, both men sought to influence as many delegates as possible independently of the Roosevelt-Taft conflict. Sanders, who continued a close liaison with the White House, eventually secured enough votes to win the coveted spot. When the first district contest, which contained no Roosevelt challenge, was called, the faction led by Congressman Sam R. Sells, a congressional ally of Sanders, was seated by the committee. An opposing group supported by former Congressman Z. D. Massey was denied recognition, although the Sells forces had been outnumbered in the county and district conventions. Franklin Murphy of New Jersey suggested a compromise, giving one vote to each faction, but the administration steamroller quickly proved it did not need a Roosevelt conflict to be effective. The second district conflict presented a three-way fight between two Roosevelt delegates, John C. Houk and Judge Hugh B. Lindsay, and two Taft slates representing opposing factions in state GOP politics. Although the Roosevelt men shouted "no" on the voice vote, the delegation headed by Congressman Richard W. Austin, another friend of Sanders and the administration, was seated.[30]

The Roosevelt clubs at home adopted strong anti-Taft statements after all the Rough Rider's claims from Tennessee were turned down, and several Progressive conventions were organized in protest. Rooseveltian ire reached red hot proportions when the Tennessee ninth district decision went against them. This district, which contained eight counties along the Mississippi River in far west Tennessee, was a straight-out Roosevelt-Taft contest, although the two Taft delegates, J. B. Tarrant and J. W. Brown, represented the Sanders wing of the party. W. F. Poston, who became the Bull Moose candidate for governor, and G. Tom Taylor, state treasurer and later Bull Moose national committeeman, were the Roosevelt aspirants rejected on a voice vote. Then, reported the news services:

"This is plain stealing," howled Heney.

"Sit down," answered Taft members of the committee.

"Order!"

"Plain stealing," shouted Heney again.

"We can't be scared by the hooting of an owl," cried another member.

"Plain stealing," Heney continued to yell, only to be answered with loud "cat calls." Following this outburst by the fiery Californian, a "two-fisted, hard drinking young lawyer, [who] true to the traditions of the old West had killed a man in gunplay on the streets of an Arizona town" before Roosevelt appointed him a special prosecutor in a California graft case, the committee decided the tenth Tennessee district fight. No Roosevelt chal-

lenge was offered for the four-county district around Memphis, and the
Sanders delegation predictably received recognition.[31]

The knock-down, drag-out Texas fight came before the panel on the
following morning along with contests from Washington and Virginia.
Senator Dick had obtained a delay from the previous day on the Texas
cases over the strong objections of National Committeeman Cecil A.
Lyon. The Texan declared that the Taft managers did not have their briefs
ready for presentation and were merely stalling for time. The forty-man
delegation, by far the largest from the South, had challenges for the eight
delegates-at-large and for eleven of the state's sixteen congressional districts. Since Lyon's organization controlled party functions in Texas,
however, the Taft group appeared as the dissidents. Although Lyon and
McHarg argued that there were no contests in Texas, the steamroller
contended otherwise. Frederick C. Bryan, a Taft lawyer, likened Lyon's
hold on the Texas GOP to the rotten borough system in England and said if
his delegates were recognized, he would be both the beginning and the end
of the party in the state. William M. "Gooseneck Bill" McDonald, a Taft
Negro from Fort Worth and former associate of E. H. R. Green, told the
committeemen: "Most of the counties in Texas are inhabited chiefly by
prairie dogs, and of the 245 counties only about 100 contained a republican
party." The old enemy of Lyon and lily-whiteism said further: "All of the
populated counties are strongly for Taft and the only Roosevelt sentiment
is that which has been aroused by Col. Lyon." McHarg and Lyon protested
loudly as the steamroller refused even a roll call in rejecting their at-large
slate.[32]

Hardly two weeks had passed between the state convention in Fort
Worth and the start of the national committee hearings. And though
Roosevelt continued to trust Lyon to deliver a favorable delegation, it was
plain when the district contests were called that the president and MacGregor had control of the group from Texas. Throughout the hearings Heney
kept up a barrage of abuse directed at the Taft onslaught; the Taft
managers were moving so rapidly that even the prestigious Borah was
ruled out of order when he sought to offer a protest statement. Heney
shouted, "They are Mexicanizing America," as the committee again
refused a roll call when deciding the district contests. "It's more than plain
stealing," he continued, "it's treason." He nearly came to fisticuffs with
Massachusetts Senator Murray Crane during the Texas district hearings. In
one district after another the Taft delegates were seated against Heney's
colorful protests. In the third, however, the committee recognized the
Roosevelt representatives after Lyon read a statement that indicated
complete regularity in the proceedings that led up to the Roosevelt
convention. The sprawling fifteenth district, embracing twenty-five counties in southwest Texas, was also awarded to Roosevelt even though one of

the Taft claimants, Judge C. K. McDowell of Del Rio and the 1942 GOP candidate for governor, referred to Lyon as "a gentleman, but politically as the rottenest man that ever presided over a State Committee."[33]

Earlier, Lyon, who sat on the National Committee throughout the hearings as the Texas member, had voted to seat Taft delegates from other parts of the South in an effort to court votes for his own delegation. His strategy did not pay off, however, because the committee gave only four of the thirty disputed Texas seats to Roosevelt and the remaining twenty-six to Taft. Roosevelt fared even worse in Virginia and Washington, where he did not receive a single vote. In Virginia, which had twenty-four seats in the convention, challenges were offered for the four delegates-at-large and for sixteen delegates from eight of the state's ten congressional districts. Furthermore, the twenty Roosevelt claimants were Negroes representing the black-and-tan faction that held the pro-Roosevelt rival convention in Richmond on May 14. McHarg, therefore, apparently wishing to divorce himself from the all-black group as Roosevelt increasingly drifted toward a lily-white stance in the South, agreed to bunch all of the Virginia cases into one presentation as a time-saving measure.[34]

The black-and-tans under the leadership of Jesse M. Newcomb initiated a move after the Richmond gathering to win recognition at Chicago, although without help from the national Roosevelt campaign. But Congressman Slemp, with administration cooperation, used the post office patronage to whip several recalcitrant delegates into line for Taft: "Don't worry about your friends in Virginia," he told Hilles as the convention approached, "they will see you straight through." And solid they were for the president even though the would-be Roosevelt delegates put up a halfhearted argument before the committee. W. H. Brown, a Negro attorney favoring Roosevelt argued for the challengers, declaring that a lily-white stewardship in the state had held most of the county and district conventions in locations where Negroes could not attend. When L. P. Summers attempted to refute that position for the Taft group, several Negroes, with the boisterous approval of Heney, began "to shout protests against Mr. Summers' statement while the Chairman rapped his gavel for order." Another Taft advocate, D. L. Groner of Norfolk, told the committee that "these afterthought conventions" by the black-and-tans were not organized until weeks "after Mr. Roosevelt had begun his campaign." Groner produced affidavits from two Negroes who had attended the Richmond convention for Roosevelt, swearing they "were paid off at the door as they went out $1 and expenses." At the conclusion of his argument, all twenty Taft delegates were seated without a roll call, although "two or three Roosevelt members shouted 'no!' "[35]

Theodore Roosevelt rolled into Chicago on Saturday, June 15, the same day the committee completed its work. The old campaigner, "in a fighting mood," denounced the lopsided outcome of the hearings as well as the Taft steamroller. Although the committee had been in nearly continuous session since June 7, often under difficult circumstances, Roosevelt obviously had a justifiable complaint, or, as he phrased it in his statement of June 22, his opponents placed on the temporary roll "a sufficient number of fraudulent delegates to defeat the legally expressed will of the people, and to substitute a dishonest for an honest majority." The New York *Times* reported that 254 contests had been heard by the National Committee for the 1,078 convention seats or 24 percent of the total. Taft got 235 of the disputed contests and Roosevelt 19; the handling of TR's claims in the South hardly needs restating. Whatever the merits of Taft's contention that most if not all of his contests had little genuine value, the fact remains that Roosevelt and his southern supporters received no favors from the committee. Failure to do so also meant that he had no chance for the nomination once the convention roll was finalized. The Washington *Bee,* a major Negro organ that urged its readers to reject Roosevelt in 1912, commented dryly: "The vote previous to the nomination had completely shattered the Roosevelt forces and demoralized their ranks."[36]

William Jennings Bryan, who had had much experience with conventions, observed that Roosevelt would have handled Taft's supporters in the same way Taft did his if he had had a majority in the National Committee. La Follette, hardly a disinterested participant, later noted that TR's loud outcry had the dual effect of diverting attention from his own questionable contests and of discrediting the committee's actions. And Roosevelt broke precedent for a presidential contender by arriving in Chicago to take personal command of his nomination, while Taft stayed in Washington to play golf and watch the Senators play baseball with his son Robert.

The flamboyant Roosevelt stole the show before a huge crowd in the Chicago Auditorium one night before the opening session. He had spurned all suggestion of deferring to a compromise candidate and, though drifting rapidly toward a break with traditional Republicanism, he delivered a fighting speech, pounding the party for favoring Taft. The example of "delegates stolen" by an entrenched organization fitted neatly with his talk of a war on privilege and his notion of a New Nationalism. The southern contests were obviously on Roosevelt's mind as his fiery denunciations served to whip his enthusiasts into an uncontrollable frenzy. "The fraudulent delegates whom the national committee seated, for instance from California, from Washington, . . . from Alabama, from Texas, represent nothing but a deliberate attempt by certain discredited bosses to upset the free and honest expression of the people's will. The greatest issue before us is theft." The tilt with Taft was reduced to a conflict between "human rights on the one side and on the other special privilege asserted as a property right." Finally, in an outburst of righteous indignation, the famous words rang out: "We fight in honorable fashion for the good of mankind, fearless of the future, unheeding of our individual fates, with unflinching hearts and undimmed eyes, we stand at Armageddon and we battle for the Lord."[37]

The questionable southern conventions manufactured by McHarg and the turning away of Negro Republicans from the South were swept under the rug by Roosevelt and his lieutenants as they entered the convention prepared to fight for delegates. No sooner had the Reverend James R. Callaghan of St. Malachy's Roman Catholic Church in Chicago concluded the opening prayer, followed by a reading of the official call, a drab and drawn-out affair, than the great tug-of-war for mastery of the convention opened with the southern delegates, and especially those from Texas, figuring prominently in the proceedings. With Victor Rosewater of Nebraska, editor of the Omaha *Bee* and chairman of the Republican National Committee, the presiding officer until a temporary chairman and keynote speaker could be chosen, the historic confrontation started when Governor Herbert S. Hadley and former Indiana Congressman James E. Watson, floor managers for Roosevelt and Taft respectively, began to cross swords. The immediate question before the house was which delegates would be permitted to vote for the temporary chairman. Rosewater, a slight man with a weak speaking voice, had considerable difficulty controlling the swirling mass of partisan delegates, gallery spectators, and newspapermen. The challenge came from Hadley, suffering from tuberculosis and running a 103° temperature during the convention, who offered a motion to substitute a Roosevelt-approved list of seventy-two delegates for seats already authorized by the National Committee. Rosewater was certain to incur the wrath of whichever camp he failed to recognize; even before the assemblage opened, threats were made in anticipation of his rulings. Roosevelt's valet, James Amos, for instance, reported a conversation overheard outside TR's hotel suite in Chicago involving a former Rough Rider who vowed to "fill him full of lead" if he ruled in favor of Taft.[38]

Although Rosewater insisted the convention organize before a consideration of disputed delegates could be entertained, he permitted Hadley to state his motion over Watson's objections. Hadley argued for substitution of his list of seventy-two delegates from several states for an equal number of seats on the temporary roll held by Taft people. The Missouri governor, who was joined on the floor by New Jersey's Franklin Fort, drew heavily upon party precedent to advance Roosevelt's case. Significantly, Hadley told Nicholas Murray Butler, Taft's 1912 vice-presidential candidate and president of Columbia University, in April 1913 that he, Senator Borah, and Frank Kellogg decided Roosevelt had been cheated in twenty-four cases by the National Committee. But Roosevelt exploded into a rage when told that twenty-four seats would be contested on the convention floor. "On hearing the statement," reported Hadley, "Colonel Roosevelt cried with great vehemence: 'Twenty-four seats! Twenty-four? You must contest seventy-four if you expect to get anywhere.' So we raised the number to seventy-four." The total dropped by two in the convention, and amid a great uproar by Roosevelt's followers, Watson was joined by Congressman Sereno Payne of New York in a successful bid to delay Hadley's motion until after the temporary chairman had been named.[39]

Finally, a harried Rosewater, faced with a no-win situation as friend and foe hurled insults at the chair, ruled Hadley's attempt to seat the Roosevelt delegates out of order, as he did Watson's motion to table. Then, said Rosewater, the only business before the house was selection of a temporary chairman. Although a scattering vote was cast for several candidates, only Root and McGovern were placed in formal nomination by the Taft and Roosevelt camps, respectively. During the numerous seconding speeches, however, J. E. Wood, a Negro delegate from Kentucky, rose to second the nomination of Root after Hadley had informed the convention that the Roosevelt men were firm for McGovern. Attempting to justify Negro participation in the Chicago deliberations, Wood began, "The Negro of this country has always looked to the Republican party for . . ." and was interrupted by another delegate yelling, "Postoffices." After the rowdy disruption subsided, he concluded his brief remarks: "But I stand here as a representative of my race to say to you that the negro is loyal and true, and he will obey the instructions of his constituency, and will cast his vote for Elihu Root." The Negro's loyalty to Taft in the proceedings did much to influence Roosevelt's rejection of black participation upon formation of the Bull Moose party a few weeks later.[40]

When the roll was called for voting on the nominees, pandemonium broke out as delegates on the floor clamored for a ruling from the chair on which personnel could properly vote. Although Rosewater kept slamming the gavel and ordering the vote to proceed, the confusion became so intense that he was obliged to make a further ruling. Since the 1888 National Convention was the only previous time the temporary roll prepared by the National Committee had been challenged, he ruled that party precedent would be followed, with each delegate rising in his seat to cast an individual ballot. Therefore, Rosewater's failure to permit Hadley's motion to purge the roll meant that Taft's control of the convention was a foregone conclusion. Root received 558 votes to 501 for McGovern with three others getting a very few votes. The southern delegations recognized by the National Committee voted overwhelmingly for Root and Taft; 199 of the 252 votes from the eleven ex-Confederate states were cast for Root, 52 for McGovern, and 1 man in the Texas delegation failed to vote.[41]

Florida and Louisiana went solidly for Root. The North Carolina delegation, however, led by Richmond Pearson, cast twenty-one votes for McGovern and only three for Root, the most support given Roosevelt from the South. Two delegates from Alabama's third district, Byron Trammell and John B. Daugherty, went for McGovern, as did the four pro-Roosevelt Negroes from Mississippi, Banks, Locker, Gary, and

Howard. Powell Clayton was unable to prevent one Arkansas delegate from voting for the Roosevelt candidate; likewise, Newell Sanders of Tennessee lost one of his delegation, who bolted to McGovern. The South Carolinians, still wavering under an uncertain leadership, split eleven to seven in favor of Root. With Cecil Lyon disqualified by the National Committee, H. F. MacGregor produced thirty-one votes for Root, although eight of the Texans went for McGovern. Nor could Congressman Slemp prevent two delegates from the Virginia fifth from deserting the president; and, finally, six members of the Georgia delegation led by Clark Grier and John H. Boone voted for McGovern against the wishes of National Committeeman Jackson. Since Root won by a margin of fifty-seven votes, had even a fraction of the 176 disputed southern delegates awarded Taft by the committee gone the other way, Roosevelt might well have gained control.[42]

Before the vote, however, the already heated proceedings became more embittered when Walter L. Houser, La Follette's campaign manager, announced from the podium that La Follette "had entered into no combination and therefore endorsed neither candidate for Temporary Chairman." Yet McGovern readily agreed to accept the post after a previous understanding with Roosevelt, although La Follette considered it a betrayal, "not merely of my candidacy, but of the Progressive principles which the Wisconsin voters instructed these men to represent with fidelity." More important, McGovern announced he would seat some of the discredited Roosevelt delegates, including those from the South, if named to the job. But that is what might have been. As Root ascended the barbed-wire encased platform to give his keynote address, he was greeted by a delegate shouting loudly: "Receiver of stolen goods." After delivering a reaffirmation of Republicanism, Root declared that the assembly would be governed by the rules of the 1908 convention until permanent rules could be adopted. The fireworks started anew when Watson offered a motion to name the all-important working committees, including the Credentials Committee that would rule on disputed contests arising on the convention floor. The Roosevelt forces were up in arms as Hadley reintroduced a substitute motion to recall his earlier resolution to eject the seventy-two Taft delegates. To stave off more wrangling, Root declared the convention adjourned with an understanding that Hadley's motion would be first on the following day's agenda. The assemblage had been in session seven continuous hours, the longest time ever to select a presiding officer for a GOP national convention.[43]

A nearly empty convention hall on June 19 heard Root, characterized by William Allen White as "a man then in his sixties, probably the most learned, even erudite, distinguished, and impeccably conservative Republican in the United States," ring down the gavel for order. Both sides had agreed to limit debate on Hadley's motion to one and a half hours each.

The seventy-two Roosevelt delegates at stake were from eleven states, although La Follette for one did not think their recognition would affect the eventual outcome. Thirty-four of them or 47 percent were from the South: Alabama, two; Tennessee, four; Arkansas, two; and Texas, twenty-six. The southern delegates had already been a cause célèbre during the hearings, but Hadley and his cohorts were prepared to argue again for the Alabama ninth district, the Arkansas fifth, the Tennessee second and ninth districts, the at-large delegation, and nine districts in Texas in addition to the others.[44]

Hadley, who, to the annoyance of Roosevelt, had received overtures from the Taft managers about being a compromise presidential nominee, opened the debate. The entire effort was termed "farcical" by the New York *Times,* which thought both camps rehashed old arguments without presenting new evidence. Nonetheless, Hadley got an "uninterrupted hearing as he described the burglaries and piracies." And the convention came alive with enthusiasm when he called the decision of the National Committee "nothing but naked theft." Amid the clamor, Hadley proceeded to read the minority report signed by fourteen Roosevelt members on the committee which detailed the hearings from their point of view. In response to a shouted request from the floor, the Missouri governor read the names of the fourteen dissenters, including W. C. Monday of Tennessee, Capers of South Carolina, who had broken with Taft, Wight of Louisiana, and Lyon of Texas. Then, Kansas Governor Henry J. Allen, a Roosevelt man who assisted Hadley with his presentation, declared he could support the party nominee only "upon the condition that his nomination is not accomplished by fraud and thievery." Moreover, Allen, termed "a spellbinder who riddled the Taft argument," restated the Roosevelt position on the southern contests while he blasted the notion that the seventy-two be referred to the Credentials Committee: "If you make a Credentials Committee, selecting members from all the southern states, who have not earned their right to a seat here—selecting a Credentials Committee from the contested delegations, do you think we will have any better chance than we have upon the temporary roll?"[45]

It was no doubt impossible to sway the votes of the highly charged partisans by verbal persuasion. Yet Watson and several Taft speakers rose to protest Hadley's list; although time was devoted to all of the contests, most of their attention was directed at the massive Texas group. James A. Hemenway of Indiana, a former congressman and senator, stated the Taft argument by stressing the need for party regularity and therefore the legality of the temporary roll. "Take the Alabama cases," he said, while referring to the South: "When the National Committee decided those contests—What did we hear? That Mr. Roosevelt himself said he expected to win only one of them. . . . What were they filed for? To furnish a basis for what; and what are the gentlemen doing here today—hollering fraud where there is no fraud." But of all the southerners, Cecil Lyon's Texans excited the Taft camp to its wildest fury. Thomas H. Devine of Colorado, a Taft advocate, started a violent ruckus by saying "that the action of the Roosevelt forces in stirring up contests in the south was a most damnedable thing," while he crowed about Lyon being replaced on the National Committee by MacGregor: "He talks about a steamroller. There is not one extant that begins to compare with the roller Lyon runs in Texas," he said, as Root wielded the gavel for order amid the rising din.

Finally, the seemingly endless debate over the seventy-two ceased, but not before a great demonstration lasting nearly an hour erupted "spontaneously" for Hadley. It was nothing short of a presidential boomlet for the border state governor which later turned into a wild outburst for Roosevelt. A certain madness ran through the hall with fights, yelling, an attractive wife of a Chicago lumber dealer "in a white dress" leading a charge for TR, and policemen being knocked to the floor before order returned. The New York *Times* called it "a remarkable demonstration," and even the South Carolinians got into the action along with most other delegations with Roosevelt supporters: "The Roosevelt men in South Carolina were trying frantically to drag their colleagues out of their chairs and stampede them into joining the demonstration." When calm was restored, the undaunted Watson renewed his motion to refer Hadley's list to the Credentials Committee. Then Governor Charles S. Dennen of Illinois, a Roosevelt man, moved a substitute motion that no challenged delegate on the list should have the right to vote on selection of the credentials personnel or on the report of the committee. Wild disorder reigned as Root ordered a roll call after Watson moved a nondebatable motion to table Dennen's proposal; it became instead the crucial vote on accepting or rejecting the seventy-two delegates. It carried by a vote of 567 to 507, thereby bringing another defeat to Roosevelt. And since the Taft forces could now proceed unimpeded to a formal organization of the convention, including formation of the Credentials Committee, Roosevelt was virtually eliminated from further consideration. Although he received nine votes less in the total count than during the Root-McGovern contest, Roosevelt's vote from the eleven ex-Confederate states remained unchanged.[46]

The vote of several delegations was challenged, resulting in long, drawn-out individual roll calls. Hadley rose to a point of order while Arkansas was being polled and asked "if individuals whose titles to seats here are challenged are to vote upon this question." Root, however, ordered the roll to continue, indicating that he would rule on the motion at the end of the vote. The often bitter challenges by both Roosevelt and Taft partisans caused several delegation chairmen to have difficulty keeping discipline. Richmond Pearson, for instance, announced when his state was called: "I have been instructed by resolution to cast the vote of North

Carolina 23 to 1 in favor of Roosevelt in all motions preliminary to the ballot for nomination for President. I therefore announce the vote of North Carolina in accordance with the resolution, 1 yea and 23 nay." But John C. Matthews of the fourth district was on his feet like a shot challenging the vote and demanding a poll of the delegation; the changed vote stood twenty-two against, two for. The Texans also had difficulty voting, as did

Table 5–1
Vote of Southern Delegates on Organization of
1912 GOP Convention

	Southern Vote for Temporary Chairman			Southern Vote on Watson's Motion to Table		
	Root	McGovern	N.V.	Yeas	Nays	N.V.
Alabama	22	2		22	2	
Arkansas	17	1		17	1	
Florida	12			12		
Georgia	22	6		24	4	
Louisiana	20			20		
Mississippi	16	4		16	4	
N. Carolina	3	21		2	22	
S. Carolina	11	7		11	6	1
Tennessee	23	1		23	1	
Texas	31	8	1	29	9	2
Virginia	22	2		21	3	
Total	199	52	1	197	52	3

SOURCE: *Proceedings of the 1912 Republican National Convention*, pp. 148–66.

the tempestuous Californians and Powell Clayton's Arkansas group. Finally, after the tally was announced, Root made his momentous but not unexpected ruling: "To hold that a member whose seat is contested may take no part in the proceedings of this body would lead to the conclusion that if every seat were contested as it surely would be if such a rule were adopted, there could be no Convention at all, as nobody would be entitled to participate." The committees—their personnel already designated at earlier delegation caucuses—were quickly appointed before adjournment at 5:47 P.M., after the convention had been in session for six hectic hours.[47]

Immediately, the newly formed Credentials Committee went into extended sessions adjudicating contests referred to the whole body. Although it was soon obvious that the "solid fourteen" on the committee for Roosevelt were powerless to check the Taft onslaught, rulings were handed down on numerous cases, including fifty-eight disputes from the South: Alabama, two; Arkansas, two; Louisiana, four; Mississippi, twelve; North Carolina, two; Tennessee, two; Texas, thirty-two; and Virginia, two. But when the convention opened on Thursday, June 20, it remained in session a scant few minutes because the committee was not ready with an official report. Former Congressman Charles H. Cowles of North Carolina, moreover, was the lone southern member voting with the minority. And Roosevelt, who was hopelessly outmaneuvered in the committee deliberations, finally informed his advisers that he was "through" and commenced preparing for his bolt from the GOP. According to Amos Pinchot, Roosevelt's decision to abandon the party was influenced in part by the southern Negroes deciding "they would stick to Taft since he seemed to be the more Republican of the two candidates" and taking advantage of the credentials battle to advance their own interests. But the real catalyst for action came during the late evening of June 20, when two millionaires, George W. Perkins and Frank Munsey, informed Roosevelt that they would finance a third-party candidacy.[48]

All of Friday, June 21, was taken up with delegate contests even though the convention had become an all-Taft show. Yet when the Credentials Committee offered a majority report to the whole house on the ninth Alabama contingent, the "solid fourteen" presented a Roosevelt substitute. The two fought-over delegates at stake were before the convention, which forced Root to make another unpopular ruling, when the unquenchable Heney rose to a point of order and inquired if the seventy-two could vote on their seating. "The gentlemen from the ninth district of Alabama whose seats are contested," Root declared, "and whose right to sit is involved in this report will not be permitted to vote." The remaining seventy, however, could cast a ballot under the edict. Then the test vote on credentials came over the objections of Hiram Johnson on a motion to table the committee's minority report, which carried by a vote of 569 to 499. The ninth Alabama vote was essentially the same cast throughout the convention by each side although there was a slight increase in Taft support. Roosevelt's southern count dropped from fifty-two to forty-four votes primarily because the Georgia Negroes went over to Taft, as well as defections in the North Carolina, Virginia, and South Carolina delegations. Although other credentials cases, including Arkansas and Georgia, were considered before adjournment, there were no additional roll calls. Roosevelt's strength had peaked as many of his southern supporters like others across the country not willing to bolt the GOP commenced to look for a safe haven.[49]

Additional contests were heard when the convention reassembled on June 22 for its final session. Although minority reports were offered in several disputes, no roll calls were allowed as the Taft steamroller gave every contest to the president from Mississippi, North Carolina, Oklahoma, Washington, Virginia, and the District of Columbia. "Every time a motion was offered by the Taft people," wrote William Allen White, "a thousand toots and imitation whistles of the steamroller engine pierced the air sharply, to be greeted with laughter that swept the galleries." While the Washington cases were being debated as Root hurried the body toward the nominating speeches, Perry W. Howard of the Mississippi delegation gained a bit of notoriety when he rose to a point of order. "The point of order is that the steamroller is exceeding the speed limit," he called out with a laugh when recognized, which brought down the house. "The Chair," Root replied, "with a broad grin, sustains the point of order. But unless you let the steamroller run for a while there isn't a chance of our getting home for Sunday." The same urgency to nominate Taft prevailed as Root announced that managers for both sides had agreed to abandon a number of contests filed with the Credentials Committee, including ninety-eight from the South: Arkansas, ten; Mississippi, eight; North Carolina, four; South Carolina, two; Tennessee, two; Virginia, sixteen; Florida, twelve; Georgia, twenty-four; and Louisiana, twenty. The row over credentials reached its inevitable conclusion when the massive Texas contests were decided for Taft on a voice vote following a jarring but futile debate that retraced the worn fight btween Lyon and MacGregor.[50]

No sooner had the permanent roll been completed to the total satisfaction of the Taft camp than the fateful moment arrived. The convention was in "wild disorder" as Root, who had been made permanent chairman, turned the podium over to Governor Henry J. Allen of Kansas, the man picked by the colonel to say farewell and lead Roosevelt's delegates out of the convention. Unbelievable confusion ruled the hall as Allen, a forceful speaker, rang out the ultimatum: "We do not bolt. We merely insist that you, not we, are making the record. We have pleaded with you for ten days. . . . We plead with you no longer. WE SHALL SIT IN PROTEST."

After he declared that Roosevelt's followers were through with the convention, Allen answered the cry of radicalism leveled at them: "Let me tell you, no radical in the ranks of radicalism ever did so radical a thing as to come to a National Convention of the great Republican party and secure through fraud the nomination of a man whom they knew could not be elected." Unmoved, Root ordered the chairman of the Resolutions Committee to present the platform as the convention raced toward adjournment. The document contained several progressive clauses, but in the main it was a conservative appeal to the nation; among other things it "invited the intelligent judgment of the American people upon the administration of William H. Taft" because the country had "prospered and been at peace under his Presidency." Peace within the Grand Old Party was shattered as the Roosevelt men sat in stony silence when the states were called for a vote on the platform. Only two votes—one each from Arkansas and Texas—were cast from the South against it while 212, the highest pro-Taft vote yet from the region, were registered in favor; thirty southern delegates were "present but not voting" as Roosevelt's Dixie supporters joined their northern colleagues in silent indignation.[51]

Nor did Roosevelt's southern loyalists take an active role when the Taft phalanx began to make the presidential nominations. Although TR did not join Taft and La Follette in allowing his name to be placed in formal nomination, he had intended like Taft to have southerners participate in the nominating speeches. He had maintained a correspondence with Dr. Redmond about having his kinsman, Perry W. Howard, deliver a seconding address, but the decision to stand moot in the convention aborted his scheme to give the southern Negro recognition in the campaign. Taft likewise had no speakers from the South following his nomination by Warren G. Harding of Ohio. He had contracted with Senator William O. Bradley of Kentucky to make a seconding speech, but poor health prevented Bradley from speaking. Arrangements had also been made for a Georgia Negro, W. F. Penn from Atlanta, to second the nomination as a concession to the South, but, reported the *Official Proceedings,* he "considerately refrained from doing so on account of the lateness of the hour."[52]

When Taft received 561 votes and the nomination on the first ballot, both Negroes and whites from the South gave him an overwhelming support, to the disgust of Roosevelt. Taft got 209 votes from the region, including the solid vote of Florida, Georgia, and Louisiana. Roosevelt, on the other hand, garnered but two votes—one each from North Carolina and Tennessee—from southern delegations. Thirty-eight of the South's 252 votes were registered "present but not voting"—twenty-two of those being cast by Pearson's North Carolinians—and three were absent. The Texans under the charge of MacGregor gave thirty-one votes to Taft, while eight did not vote and one was absent. The pro-Taft vote went even higher among the southern contingent on the roll call for vice-president that followed immediately. Although ballots were cast for six candidates for second place on the ticket, the southerners voted only for James S. Sherman of New York, the choice of Taft and the Old Guard, or refrained from voting altogether. Nineteen did not vote and another nineteen were absent as the convention neared completion. Sherman got 214 ballots from the eleven ex-Confederate states, including the undivided vote of Arkansas, Florida, Georgia, and Louisiana. Most Roosevelt men had left for the big gathering later in the evening in Orchestra Hall, but the two Alabamians, eight Texans, and nine others from Mississippi, North and South Carolina, Tennessee, and Virginia stayed to the bitter end. By consistently casting a "present but not voting" tally, they gave Roosevelt a presence from the South that would stand him in good stead long after his managers had abandoned the convention.[53]

The new National Committee designated at the convention also reflected Taft's hold on the party. From the South only Richmond Pearson of

North Carolina, who replaced Edward C. Duncan, a Taft loyalist, was named to the committee by the Roosevelt forces. Four others, Barker, Clayton, Moseley, and Martin, all of whom opposed Roosevelt during the preconvention campaign, were renamed with the approval of Taft and Hilles. Henry S. Chubb of Florida, who had been on the committee since 1911 when he took the place of James N. Coombs, was also granted a full four-year term in payment of his services to the Old Guard. The Georgia delegation gave their support to Henry S. Jackson, who enjoyed the confidence of the state's Negroes, as a replacement for the Savannah postmaster, Henry S. Blun. Pearl Wight was replaced by Victor Liosel of Louisiana, as was Cecil Lyon of Texas by H. F. MacGregor, because of their activity in behalf of Roosevelt. The South Carolinians for Taft likewise saw to it that Joseph W. Tolbert was substituted for John W. Capers as a result of his outbursts during the credentials fight. And the sweep was complete when the Tennessee delegation, to the great satisfaction of Governor Hooper, elected Sanders over his opponent, John W. Overall.[54]

Even a cursory glance at the convention proceedings reveals that the southern delegates played a vital role in the outcome. Taft's papers in the Library of Congress, for instance, abound with "thank you" notes and telegrams sent to GOP politicians all over the South after the Chicago gathering. They are more than mere expressions of gratitude; the messages are recognition that Taft could not have won without the nearly solid support of the southerners. "I want to thank you . . . for the support which I had from you," Taft wrote to Henry S. Jackson of Georgia two days after the convention; and to Henry L. Johnson of the same state, he telegraphed, "your services were of inestimable value." "Your excellent work at Chicago for the cause was deeply gratifying to me," he informed Harry Beck, a delegate from Hillsboro, Texas, "and I wish you to know that I deeply appreciate your energy and loyalty." Similar missives were sent to Joseph W. Tolbert, L. P. Summers of Virginia, former Governor Henry C. Warmouth of Louisiana, J. D. Adams of South Carolina, H. Clay Evans of Tennessee, and Congressman Slemp—to name a few. Taft had every reason to be grateful to his southern loyalists. They had cast 209 of the 561 required votes for his first ballot nomination. Roosevelt's followers, on the other hand, had an understandable complaint that eleven states in the Democratic South accounted for 37 percent of what they viewed as a stolen victory.[55]

The Negro delegates from the South and elsewhere overwhelmingly supported Taft, resulting in considerable hostility within the Roosevelt camp. They were held in line for the president through the efforts of such key Negro politicians as James C. Napier of Tennessee, who had been named register of the treasury in 1910 by Taft. Napier was a close political ally of Governor Hooper and a former Nashville city councilman, and he stayed on as register for several months into Wilson's administration.

Roosevelt had offered to appoint him to a diplomatic post in Brazil, and Taft wanted to make him minister to Liberia; Napier declined both posts to become register upon the resignation of William T. Vernon. But in 1912, Napier thought Taft had earned the support of Negro America because "the colored people of this country never had a firmer friend." Before the Chicago conclave Napier urged the Negro delegates to "stand like *a stone wall* by the instructions from the pledges to your constituencies." Otherwise, he had informed one of the black delegates: "A change or wavering from instructions will go far toward establishing a feeling of distrust of us both as representatives and as voters, not only among those who gain from what may be termed the wavering instability of the knavish capriciousness of our minds."[56]

Napier traveled to Chicago with another Negro in the administration, Whitefield McKinlay, Taft's collector of customs in the District of Columbia. Although neither man was an official delegate, both worked skillfully among the black delegates on Taft's behalf. Yet McKinlay had doubts about the loyalty of Negroes to traditional Republicanism following the convention. "The colored men I met from the different states," he wrote a week or so afterward, "seemed as bitter toward the President as they were toward Roosevelt on account of the Brownsville matter, and it is going to take a great deal of education to overcome it." Following the Progressive convention in August, he told former Governor P. B. S. Pinchback of Louisiana that he feared "a large number of Negroes will vote for Wilson." But McKinlay had no sympathy with those blacks threatening to desert the party: "I cannot understand how any unselfish, selfrespecting colored man can vote the Democratic ticket, regardless as to who [sic] is at its head." Still, McKinlay thought in 1913 that Taft "owed a great debt of gratitude to the colored delegates who stood by him in the convention."[57]

Other segments of the black community soon joined in a defense of the delegates, though there was no outpouring of support for Taft or Roosevelt among Negroes. When Roosevelt had made a speech at Baltimore imploring Negroes not to sell their votes "to the highest bidder," John Mitchell of the Richmond *Planet* thought "he would have done well to have saved his advice for his own people" at Chicago. "After all," his editorial continued, "the colored people of this country are about what the white people of this country have made them." And when Roosevelt's Bull Moose gathering turned away Negro delegates from the South in August, the Montgomery *Colored Alabamian* commented acidly: "We told you so." The widely circulated Washington *Bee,* which also opposed Roosevelt throughout 1912, agreed with Napier and McKinlay that the Negro delegates owed a firm loyalty to Taft at Chicago. Nor did the *Bee* think they were for sale: "The colored delegates . . . are business and professional men . . . [who] are of high standing in their respective communities . . . . Many of them are worth from $10,000 to $20,000 each, and a few are worth more than

$100,000." Such delegates, the paper argued, simply could not be bought and would remain committed to Taft and the GOP in the coming fight with Roosevelt and the Bull Moosers. Most of the delegates displayed an honest devotion to the president because "they are the chosen representatives of the Afro-American people, and they will be held to strict accountability by the rank and file of the race if they betray their trusts."[58]

Roosevelt, however, had his own view of the southern blacks: "If the Negro delegates last month had been willing to stand by the Progressive cause," he wrote later, "and follow the lead of the great northern states, the Republican party would now be the Progressive party of the country; but seven-eighths of the Negro delegates, and about the same proportion of white men representing Negro districts in the South went for Taft. I do not blame the colored men in question. I know that they have not had the chance that . . . the colored men of the North have had." W. O. Hart, a visitor at the Chicago gathering, noted: "The large number of colored delegates at the convention reminded me somewhat of the Louisiana legislature during reconstruction times, and it was a curious note how carefully the colored delegates were watched. It was very seldom that one moved from his seat without being accompanied by another person." That many of the southern delegations were held in line through promises of money and jobs as well as fear of the Taft steamroller hardly needs restating. Roosevelt and the Progressives, moreover, like the Bourbon South, saw them as fraudulent representatives of a "rotten borough system," a point stressed in the weeks ahead, albeit with questionable campaign results.[59]

Chapter 6

"The Best White Men in the South"

Taft had not been formally nominated when the Roosevelt enthusiasts were called to order in Orchestra Hall, one block from the GOP convention, to launch the Progressive party. Those southerners who followed the parade into the rump convention and who would be expected to form a branch of the new movement at home were faced with an impossible dilemma from the outset. They had been sent to Chicago by "after-thought conventions" not recognized by the official Republican organization; they had been rejected by the Republican National Committee and by the party's national convention; and now they were helping to create a new political party most of whose leaders, including Theodore Roosevelt himself, had been spurned by the Grand Old Party. All other considerations aside, it would be difficult indeed to sell white southerners with their long antipathy to Republicanism on a party led by discredited Republicans seeking a new political future.

As TR appeared on the stage following a nominating speech by William Pendergast of New York, the New York *Times* reported, "The crowd went wild with enthusiasm. Men flung their hats in the air and women tossed their fans and gloves about." And the southerners were in the middle of things from the start. A thunderous applause greeted Hiram Johnson as he entered the hall with the huge California delegation, saying Roosevelt would "break the solid south and be elected in spite of the bosses." The Mississippi delegates for Roosevelt attracted considerable comment when they entered the auditorium in a body, stating that Dr. Redmond had been elected their national committeeman for the new party and apparently oblivious to its soon to be announced policy on the Negro. Richmond Pearson, Oscar Hundley, and Pearl Wight were members of the Notification Committee that escorted Roosevelt to the podium. The old campaigner talked about theft in the other convention as he accepted the unanimous nomination for the presidency from the Orchestra Hall throng. "I recognize you," he told his hearers, "as the lawfully elected delegates to the Republican National Convention." He urged them to return home and "find the sentiment of the people" and invited them to return in August for a mass convention of the Progressive party. The southerners departed convinced of the righteousness of their cause; like their northern counterparts they were certain Taft had been nominated by a combination of fraud and ruthless machine politics.[1]

Hilles thought Roosevelt was bluffing and would not run in November on a third-party ticket. The Orchestra Hall episode had been a gesture "to cover his tracks." Taft issued a statement following the GOP convention proclaiming that a great victory had been achieved and the party saved from certain disaster. "All over this country patriotic people," the president said, "are breathing more freely, that a more serious menace to our republican institutions has been averted." Roosevelt and his followers, however, were not interested in helping salvage the Republican party. During a stopover in Toledo on his return to Oyster Bay, he gave out a statement of his own on June 24 announcing the names of eighteen managers who would serve as organizers of the new party. Although Pearson was the only southerner on the official list, Roosevelt's lieutenants—nearly all of them with lifelong Republican affiliations—in the eleven ex-Confederate states joined actively in forming the Bull Moose party in the weeks following Chicago. GOP politicians in all sections of the country were now forced to declare for or against the new movement. Simply put, the time for decision had arrived, and the southern wing of the party rejected by the Republican National Convention lost no time in jumping on the Progressive bandwagon.[2]

Some of the first organizing activity in the South took place in Georgia, where a struggle for control developed from the beginning between white and Negro groups. The Roosevelt Georgia White League under the direction of J. St. Julian Yates even tendered an invitation to hold the party's national convention in Atlanta instead of Chicago. Yates, twenty-five years of age and a native of Aiken, South Carolina, was a salesman and newspaperman until his death in 1929. His organization began to tout Seaborn Wright of Rome, Georgia, the 1896 Populist candidate for governor and former Democratic member of the state legislature, as a vice-presidential candidate with Roosevelt. Wright had a long association with reform movements across the South, and he reportedly believed in white supremacy but also demanded justice for the Negro. Independent-minded Democrats were urged to join the White League, and Clark Grier, who was not a delegate to the Progressive National Convention, joined the chorus by informing Dixon that "Georgia can be carried if Progressive Democrat is placed on the ticket." Grier, who found himself in hot water with the GOP organization after his actions at Chicago, expressed a desire to affiliate with the new movement as well as asking Dixon to use his influence in the Senate to block confirmation of all Georgia appointments until he received "fair treatment." But Roosevelt and Dixon passed over both Yates and Grier as their representatives in the state. They relied instead upon Charles W. McClure and Roger Dewar, who conferred with the colonel at Oyster Bay during early July. Julian Harris, a delegate to the Bull Moose convention and Georgia member of its Credentials Committee, which was forced to rule upon contesting delegates from the state, was also an early member of the official Roosevelt team.[3]

Both factions sent out a call for a state convention to meet July 24 in Atlanta; in addition, a Negro group organized for Roosevelt. At the same time GOP National Committeeman Jackson was assuring reporters of his confidence that Taft would be reelected and that the Republican party in Georgia would make a straight fight, both white factions for Roosevelt were vying with each other to denounce the Negro. The Yates group, reported the Atlanta *Journal,* took "an emphatic stand for unmixed white as the color of the new Roosevelt party," while the McClure-Dewar organization—which was recognized by the national campaign—announced that no Negroes would be allowed to enter the Atlanta convention. The regular Bull Moose group headed by Charles W. McClure, an Illinois native and founder-owner of a 5 and 10 cent store chain, adopted a pro-woman's-suffrage stance as well as putting out a statement encouraging Negroes "who believed in Progressive principles" to form their own party in Georgia: "The white organization will not affiliate with them though it will lend what advice and aid it can." In an effort further to discredit the Roosevelt Progressive White League, the "regulars" declared that "any Roosevelt organization in this state other than itself exists solely for the aggrandizement of its promoters." Several Negro conventions were held around the state for TR, even though Ben Davis's Atlanta *Independent* called on Georgia blacks to ignore the new party while denouncing both Roosevelt and "his army of villifiers, character assassins, and bribers." The Democratic press took a jocular attitude toward these meetings and reported that white Republicans showed no interest in them.[4]

A split developed among the white Progressives at the state convention in Atlanta's Aragon Hotel. Neither group, according to newspaper accounts, had an overabundance in attendance. About "thirty loyal Bull Moosers" held a meeting presided over by Dean E. Ryman behind closed doors and elected a delegation to the upcoming convention in Chicago. This group, which held authorization from Dixon and had delegates present from every congressional district in Georgia, put out a contingent headed by William J. Tilson, McClure, Dewar, and Julian Harris. Tilson, who was subsequently named state chairman, had been born and reared in east Tennessee but practiced law in Atlanta following graduation from the Yale Law School in 1896; he was active in state GOP politics until 1912, and his brother, Quillin Tilson, also a Republican, served eleven terms in Congress from a Connecticut district. The Yates meeting in an adjoining room with Dr. Horace Grant officiating had twenty-five or thirty present, including half a dozen women, and got up another delegation to Chicago led by Grant and Yates. As a sidelight, J. R. Race, who was named state secretary by this group, was fined $300 in a local police court later the same day for being a "blind tiger"; he was the manager and president of the Southern Club in Atlanta, and it was alleged that this organization had been selling whiskey illegally.[5]

Meanwhile, the Negro groups that met in several parts of the state, including Atlanta, Savannah, and Thomasville, also picked delegates to the Chicago gathering. They, too, were poorly attended, and a state convention that had been announced to meet on July 29 in Atlanta was apparently not given press coverage. Another meeting in Savannah formed a branch of the party in that part of the state and, reported the Atlanta *Journal,* had "eleven Negroes and one white man present." The Negroes were given short notice by national Roosevelt headquarters, as was the white faction led by Yates and Grant. Dewar made a trip to Oyster Bay following the Atlanta conclave and upon his return issued a statement that he would be campaign manager of the Bull Moose party in the state. Julian Harris put out a press release on August 1, saying the delegation chosen by the "meeting presided over by D. E. Ryman, is the delegation which will be seated by the national convention of the Progressive party."[6]

While the Progressives were organizing, the regular GOP leadership set about purging those connected with the new movement from the federal patronage. Grier's reappointment to the Dublin post office and the vacillations of State Chairman Johnson caused concern for Hilles and Taft as well as evoking vociferous protests from administration loyalists in the state. Although Georgia Negroes remained firm for Taft, and Henry L. Johnson campaigned for him throughout Ohio, Ben Davis, himself a delegate to the GOP National Convention, blasted Hilles in the *Independent* and boldly called on the president either to order him to get rid of the Roosevelt men or fire him. Matters came to a head on August 20, one week before a session of the GOP Executive Committee, when word went out that "at the committee meeting the administration will be endorsed and the committee will be purged of all Bull Moosers." Yet Walter H. Johnson, who resigned the chairmanship in September, called the meeting to order on August 27 that named electors and laid plans for the campaign. Resolutions were adopted "reading Clark Grier out of the party" and asking that National Committeeman Jackson be made the "arbiter of party affairs in Georgia." Taft, however, grew disenchanted with Jackson as the campaign progressed and even indicated that he would find another adviser in the state if reelected. "It might not be possible to carry Georgia for Taft," the wavering Colonel Johnson told the committee, "but it was the duty of all republicans to vote for the principles of the regular organization."[7]

The Bull Moose organizers in Alabama also held a state convention on July 24, the same day as the Georgians, after several weeks of campaigning for Roosevelt. Joseph O. Thompson, who attended the Orchestra Hall gathering after being turned aside by the Republican convention, returned home on June 25 to lead the Roosevelt crusade. The Birmingham *Age-Herald* reported that he was "more than ever, if possible, possessed of the opinion that Roosevelt will sweep the country." He was soon joined in the organizational work by Judge Hundley and William R. Farley, a local official with the Bureau of Commerce and Labor. Thompson proclaimed instantly that a "third party movement" would be organized in Alabama "just as soon as the Democrats in Baltimore completed their work"; moreover, he said the party would be born within the next "thirty or sixty days." A call went out three weeks later for the state convention or mass meeting to meet on July 24 in the Birmingham City Hall. Signed by Thompson, Hundley, Farley, "and other leading Republicans of the state," it appealed to all "who believe in this great state of ours and a new party unfettered, . . . which shall promote the well being of the honest farmer, wage earner, professional man, and business man alike."[8]

Meanwhile, like their colleagues in Georgia, the GOP regulars set about stripping federal office from all connected with the new party. Truman H. Aldrich informed the White House on July 1 that Thompson was campaigning for Roosevelt and asked his removal as revenue collector. National Committeeman Prelate D. Barker also wrote to Hilles urging that something be done about the patronage. But if the president was slow to act in Georgia, the opposite was true in Alabama. Judge Hundley wrote to Dixon on July 11 complaining: "Taft is removing every man who took any part for Roosevelt in the Chicago convention and is reappointing all of his henchmen." The Montana senator wrote in return asking for any information that might help him block Senate confirmation of the appointees. And Byron Trammell, the Dothan postmaster who supported TR at Chicago, sent an urgent although futile appeal to Dixon trying to save his own neck from Taft's retaliation. The Roosevelt men were particularly upset with the reappointment of Oscar D. Street as U.S. attorney; it was Street, Hundley reminded Dixon, "who misrepresented our position as to the ninth district." But the cries of anguish did them no good; their third-party activity cost not only Farley his position but brought the removal of Thompson himself after Secretary of the Treasury Franklin McVaugh "received the President's authority to ask you to send your resignation."[9]

Thompson acted as chairman and presiding officer when the mass convention of Bull Moosers met a few days later. The Democratic Birmingham *Age-Herald,* which accused Roosevelt of building a personal party rather than a Progressive one, referred to the 150 whites and 17 Negroes making up the convention "as the Alabama Republican faction of the Roosevelt persuasion." Nonetheless, an Alabama Executive Committee for the Progressive party was formed and a twelve-man delegation to Chicago designated. The conventioneers also adopted resolutions praising TR and calling for adoption of a woman's suffrage amendment and announced that the party in Alabama would await action at the national convention before taking an official name. A major rift developed, however, over putting Negroes on the all-white contingent to Chicago. Joseph T. Thomas, a Negro physician from Birmingham, was steamrolled when he asked to speak on the existence of political equality. A few hisses were heard as he spoke, and except for the intervention of Dr. J. W. Hughes, a former Birmingham postmaster, the Negroes might have been thrown physically from the auditorium. Incredibly, as W. H. Mixon, one of the Negro delegates at the GOP National Convention who refused money from Taft, was pleading for black representation in the new party, Thompson gave him a tongue-lashing because so few Negroes were present in the gathering.

After finalization of the delegation headed by Thompson, Hundley, Farley, and Hughes, and including the much exercised Trammell as a delegate from the third district, the Negroes announced they would hold a convention of their own. They met the next afternoon after resolving to make a fight. Their rump gathering put up a rival slate to Chicago and served notice that the white delegates to the national conclave would be challenged. "It should be noted," the *Age-Herald* commented, "that on the first day of its existence in Alabama the 'progressive party' suffered a split in its ranks." Surprisingly, Thompson had wanted to put Negroes on the regular delegation but had been overruled. The Bull Moose leader also refused to resign his federal post as expected and had to be bodily ejected from his office in the federal building at Birmingham by U.S. marshals a few days afterward. He fired a blast to waiting reporters while leaving, "calculated to get between the ribs of the President and Secretary McVaugh." When his replacement took over, Thompson refused comment on his future outside politics, but, reportedly, he was "the owner of valuable farm lands in Lowndes and other counties and will engage in the farm land business on a large scale."[10]

Charles J. Allinson, clerk of the U.S. District Court at Birmingham and Taft's campaign chairman in Alabama, indicated during mid-September that the president's reelection bid would be pushed vigorously. But the GOP effort was in more trouble than usual because of mass Negro defections from the party. The trouble arose in part because Barker and Long refused to appoint Dr. U. G. Mason, a Negro physician and delegate to the Republican National Convention, as revenue collector following Thompson's removal. The GOP hierarchy had been besieged with petitions for Thompson's job, and when the Negroes were passed over, several all-black Wilson-Marshall clubs were formed around the state. Taft's vote in November dropped to a miserable 9,000 after a high of 25,000 in 1908 at the same time Roosevelt polled better than 20,000 votes in the state. Nor were Alabama Negroes who deserted to the Democrats favorably disposed toward the Bull Moosers; after their rejection at the Progressive National Convention, one such group adopted a resolution declaring that "Roosevelt is too dictatorial and has not the brains and boots of Napoleon." Nonetheless, Thompson and the new movement ignored the Negro while organizing the state in anticipation of a Roosevelt visit in September. At the same time, however, a directive went out that every federal officeholder would be expected to pay as much as he was willing to give to Taft's campaign. And when the state Progressive Executive Committee met on August 24 to launch the campaign by naming presidential electors and approving a platform, each committeeman subscribed one thousand dollars as the nucleus for a campaign fund.[11]

In Florida three separate conventions of Bull Moosers met on July 27, three days after similar meetings in Georgia and Alabama. In many respects, events in Florida leading to formation of a third-party movement and the personnel involved were a replay of earlier GOP divisions. Charles H. Alston and Henry L. Anderson led rival Negro and white delegations to the Progressive National Convention, while Chubb remained loyal to Taft straight through the November election even though he could only drum up 4,279 votes for the Republicans. But it was Anderson who led the colonel's third-party fortunes in the state, although he had failed to secure a favorable delegation for Roosevelt in the GOP convention. Anderson announced in early July that after receiving letters from many prominent Floridians he was convinced that 80 percent of Florida's Republicans would join the new party. Therefore, on July 7, the future Bull Moose national committeeman sent out a call for a meeting in Ocala of a state convention, which would nominate candidates for Congress in all three districts and at-large, choose a gubernatorial nominee, and pick a delegation to Chicago.[12]

A native of Mayfield, Kentucky, and a graduate of Wabash College in Indiana, Anderson had been a prominent attorney in Jacksonville and Ocala since 1885; he remained active before the Florida bar "until ten days before his death" at age eighty-six in 1945. In 1912, however, he attempted to head off trouble over Negro participation in the Progressive party by arranging for an all-black convention to meet in St. Augustine concurrently with the gathering for Roosevelt at Ocala. Anderson acted as presiding officer and keynote speaker at the latter meeting in which a full delegation to Chicago and electors were chosen. William C. Hodges of Tallahasse was tapped to run for governor against Park Trammell, and nominations were made for secretary of state, commissioner of agriculture, state treasurer, superintendent of public education, attorney general, and judge of the supreme court. Hodges, who had been given the nomination by the earlier Roosevelt convention in May, addressed the Ocala meeting in which he challenged Trammell to a joint debate and declared that the Bull Moose in Florida would abolish all county and state taxes. In his keynote speech, Anderson hurled a scathing denunciation at Chubb and Taft for their handling of Republican affairs in the state. He "bitterly arraigned the Republican party for its 'betrayal of the interests of the people; for its refusal to revise the tariff downward; for its friendship with the trusts; for its theft of the nomination at Chicago; and for its general duplicity, having outlived its usefulness.' " In conclusion, Anderson charged that Taft had appointed John M. Cheney, state director of the census and loyal party worker, to the federal bench "to repay National Committeeman Chubb for his delivery of the Florida vote to the Taft column."[13]

Try as they might, Anderson and the Bull Moosers were unable to avoid a clash with the Negroes. Word had gone out that no Negroes would be admitted because they were holding their own convention in St. Augustine and were selecting a separate delegation to Chicago. Yet many Negroes, led by Alston, the black attorney from Tampa who had been cast out by the GOP National Committee, were in Ocala for the opening session. Alston reportedly meant to disrupt the proceedings as much as possible, and extra police were present to turn his followers aside; several Negroes, however, were allowed to enter the galleries as spectators. The Negro protest was the outgrowth of an agreement between Alston and Chubb to play havoc with the new party in Florida. That Chubb had no love for the Progressives was obvious when he told Hilles he could "not understand how any honorable man will retain membership on the national committee when he is not heart and soul in favor of the reelection" of the president. "You can count on me at all times," he assured Taft's campaign director. And at Ocala, Chubb schemed with Warren Shields, an official with the U.S. Land Office at Gainesville, to invade the hall with a number of Negroes. But when H. C. Groves, a white delegate, sought to have Alston and the Negroes seated on the convention floor, his motion was loudly ruled out of order. Anderson and the Ocala assemblage remained all white and loyal to Roosevelt's new brand of southern politics.[14]

About one hundred persons, most of them Negroes, left the Anderson meeting to form another convention under the tutelage of Alston. A racially mixed delegation headed by Groves and Alston was selected to the national convention and nominations made for the state's congressional seats. This gathering, also in Ocala, resolved to await advice from their executive committee before making further nominations for state office. Ben Davis and the *Independent* scored Alston for holding "the Bull Moose convention" and speculated that he would "soon settle down to his law practice in Tampa." Roosevelt, the paper said, was attempting to ride two horses in the campaign, and it prophesied that Florida Negroes would "see through his shallow artifice" of appealing to the black man in the North while disowning him in the South.[15]

Meanwhile, with only thirty delegates present, the Negro wing of the Roosevelt Progressive party met in a state convention at St. Augustine. Perfect harmony prevailed at the gathering, which met on the same day as the Ocala convention and had been preplanned and orchestrated by Anderson. A number of "enthusiastic speeches" were made praising Roosevelt and predicting a bright future for the party in Florida. A resolution was drafted indicating that the Negroes would support the state ticket and congressional nominees of the Anderson convention, and an agreement was adopted whereby the two conventions would correlate their activities by wire. Then, surprisingly, although it no doubt resulted from poor communications, Alston and several delegates named at the rump meeting in Ocala were chosen as representatives to Chicago. In the end, however, none of them, not even Anderson and his all-white contingent, were recognized by the Progressive National Committee.[16]

Three days later, on July 30, the Bull Moose was established in Virginia when two conventions were held in Roanoke and Richmond. Jesse M. Newcomb, the white leader of the state's black-and-tans who had not been recognized at the GOP convention, stated on June 28 that a Roosevelt party would be formed in the state. Then "the Executive Committee of the Roosevelt wing of the Republican party" opened a campaign headquarters in a Richmond hotel, and on July 23 this faction sent out a call for a state convention to meet in Richmond to select a delegation to Chicago. In the meantime, however, Dixon informed Newcomb that U.S. Attorney Thomas L. Moore had been tapped as Progressive national committeeman and would direct the colonel's fortunes in the Old Dominion; furthermore, Dixon said Hiram Johnson was running things for Virginia and that he (Dixon) "had nothing to do with it." Newcomb was also told "it would be better not to recognize any former republican organizations while working for the new party." Virginia newspapers began to carry press releases in mid-July issued by Moore saying a Progressive organization independent of the black-and-tans would be formalized. After conferring with prominent Progressives Moore issued a call on July 10—one week after Newcomb and the Negroes had resolved to make a fight of it—for the Roanoke meeting. It was directed at "the people of Virginia without reference to past party differences," and a special plea was made "for all independents to join the movement."[17]

Moore also lashed out at Slemp, who still retained Taft's confidence and continued to act as administration adviser on appointments and said he would not be reelected in November. Slemp had sinned in Bull Moose eyes because he had gotten up delegates to the GOP National Convention "contrary to the will of the people." Although Slemp later refused to stand for reelection and Dr. J. M. Daugherty announced as a Progressive for his seat, a coalition of GOP regulars and Bull Moosers in the ninth district who recognized his value as a southern Republican in Congress afforded him the nomination. Nor did Slemp's continued leadership of the lily-whites prevent the regulars from making overtures for Negro support as the Bull Moose momentum swelled in the state and several newspapers came out for the new party. J. R. Pollard, the Negro lawyer from Newport News who had been turned aside by the GOP at Chicago, termed it the "double squeeze" when Roosevelt and the Progressives commenced their drive to exclude the southern Negro. He took over the black-and-tan movement for Roosevelt after Newcomb issued a statement canceling the already announced meeting in Richmond. Pollard indicated that it would be held as scheduled. Virginia Negroes, he said further, "know our power and how to exercise it"; they had already proved their loyalty to Roosevelt and if the delegation to be chosen at Richmond was not seated in the Progressive National Convention, Pollard and the black-and-tans "intended to raise a big rumpus." The decision to abort the Negro convention, according to Pollard, had come about following a conference between Newcomb and Moore in which they resolved "to patch up their differences and leave us out in the cold."[18]

When the Negro or Pollard convention assembled on July 30, "the attendance was small but those present were enthusiastic," reported the Richmond *Virginian*. Although Moore had been placed in charge of the new party, John M. Parson, one of the original Roosevelt men in Virginia, traveled to New York for a personal conference with Dixon and was told that the Negro faction would not be recognized at Chicago. Yet it was decided to name six delegates at the Richmond conclave to contest the all-white Moore contingent for the twelve seats allotted to Virginia; the Negroes were prepared to concede one-half of the delegation in a futile fight for recognition. The decision to proceed in the face of certain rejection had been reached at a mass meeting of Negroes for Roosevelt, which met on the previous evening and was poorly attended. Pollard presided over the convention that named but four of the announced six delegates; it adjourned without further deliberation after naming a solid Negro delegation composed of Pollard, Henry Mallory of Richmond, W. H. Brown of Norfolk, and P. W. Harris of Petersburg. A second convention was called for August 12 following the national convention to create a permanent organization should recognition be extended at Chicago.[19]

The Moore faction convened in Roanoke on the same day as the black-and-tan meeting. It "will go down in history as the most harmonious political gathering ever assembled," reported the *Virginian* further, as the white Progressives named a full delegation to Chicago, adopted a party platform, chose electors, and fashioned a state organization, electing Moore state chairman in addition to his duties as national chairman. The unanimously drafted platform was "entirely in accord with the sentiments and principles outlined by Theodore Roosevelt, the father of the Bull Moose party." The forty-seven-year-old Moore, who had been appointed U.S. attorney by Roosevelt in 1902, was named to head the delegation. The representatives chosen at this convention were seated without fanfare at Chicago, and the four Negroes named at Richmond did not attempt to challenge the "regulars." Moore, as a member of the Provisional National Committee, joined in the effort to recognize other all-white delegations from the South, although he did object to proposals for limiting party membership to whites only.[20]

With less than a week before start of the national convention, state gatherings met in rapid succession throughout the country. Arkansas held an organizational convention on July 30 in Little Rock. A call signed by

J. A. Comer, A. S. Flower, Harry Trieber, W. S. Holt, and several other prominent Arkansas Democrats and Republicans had been issued two weeks earlier. But when the important Pulaski County Convention assembled on July 26, the state's Progressives split into warring factions over the ever-present issue of Negro representation. A lily-white faction headed by E. B. Downie bolted the county gathering when Winfield S. Holt, a Connecticut native and former Little Rock postmaster, recommended a delegation to the state convention that included several Negroes. Although Holt and Downie fought each other until November, Arkansas, unlike other southern states, permitted Negroes to have a role in the official party apparatus. Dr. H. M. Suggs, a Negro physician from Little Rock, was seated as an at-large delegate at Chicago. Enthusiastic claims by sponsors of the state convention—most of whom had been rejected as Roosevelt delegates by the GOP in Chicago—failed to impress the state's Democrats in any numbers. Congressman Joe Robinson ridiculed reports that the new party had a strong chance of carrying Arkansas; Robinson, who had conferred with Wilson at Sea Girt, New Jersey, thought the state would remain solidly Democratic.[21]

The fight engendered by the Pulaski County group was carried over into the state convention, although the Holt faction was ultimately recognized by Roosevelt and the Progressive National Committee. The staunchly Democratic *Arkansas Gazette,* which enjoyed jabbing at the movement, editorialized about the state confab: "It was thoroughly demonstrated that the new progressive party is a one-man party, and it would seem that if Roosevelt sent word for the members to jump into the Arkansas River they would do so with great loyalty and enthusiasm." Several mass meetings around the state returned partial Negro delegations, and when they were not expelled, E. B. Downie and the lily-whites bolted the convention. Harry King Cochran was named national committeeman after a racially mixed contingent headed by Comer was selected and a platform adopted. The latter document, said the *Gazette,* "in effect approves the Declaration of Independence, the Constitution and the Ten Commandments." It also demanded federal aid for drainage and levee construction, a popular issue among Arkansans, and came out against a proposed grandfather clause to the state constitution. The Democrats, however, continued to poke fun at the Bull Moosers following adjournment of the organizing convention, calling them "Moosevelts," and "Senator Jeff Davis likened them to a 'lot of old women at a quilting' who 'take snuff and fuss.' "[22]

Although Downie and the lily-whites did not hold a separate convention, the struggle continued among Roosevelt's Arkansas supporters. Downie, a Kansas native, who practiced law in Little Rock following graduation from the University of Arkansas Law School and served the Southwestern Bell Telephone Company as legal counsel, 1914–1945, blasted the "regulars" following the Little Rock meeting: "The new party in this state will be a miniature republican party since it came out squarely for giving prominence to the Negro." His faction did, however, proceed with plans to organize a Progressive Club that would "work for the election of Theodore Roosevelt and Hiram Johnson without coming under the contaminating influence of the Bull Moose leaders and their black-and-tan followers." But so few recruits flocked to the lily-white banner at the club's first meeting on August 29 that the press predicted an early death for the movement. In the meantime, Comer announced for the "regulars" following their return from the national convention that the "official Bull Moose party in Arkansas" would adhere to the policy regarding the Negro as outlined in Roosevelt's letter to Julian Harris on the eve of the Chicago convention. Yet Comer worked to conciliate the Negro and made a statement praising Bishop J. M. Conner, one of the Arkansas Negro delegates at Chicago, for his actions on behalf of TR. And when formally launching the campaign, Comer emphasized that several distinguished speakers would come into the state and that Roosevelt himself would appear.[23]

As his managers were making the planned Roosevelt visit a high point of the Bull Moose campaign, Powell Clayton, Harmon L. Remmel, and the GOP organization commenced to organize for Taft. Remmel got the ball rolling on August 8 with a rally in Little Rock's Forest Park; Clayton was out of the state and could not attend. Judge Andrew Roland, Republican candidate for governor in the September 20 general election, was the major speaker. Like Remmel, he denounced Roosevelt and the Bull Moose crusade in strong language. But, reported the *Gazette,* "a band was placed on the stage to keep the crowd awake." Although Roland, a native of Arkansas and a son of a Confederate veteran, was soundly trounced by the Democrat, Joe Robinson, Remmel and Clayton sent a number of speakers around the state predicting victory for the much maligned Republicans. The unprepared Bull Moosers did not field a candidate in the early gubernatorial contest but concentrated their efforts instead on the presidential canvass. Taft expressed great satisfaction with Remmel's conduct of the Arkansas campaign, but when "the whip was cracked" over postmasters and other federal officeholders suspected of supporting the new party, the National Civil Service Reform League issued a scathing indictment of the administration's conduct in the state. Yet in November, Remmel and his organization were able to get four Republicans returned to the legislature, a judge elected in Independence County, and a second-place finish secured for Taft behind Wilson.[24]

The recognized Bull Moose faction in Mississippi under the tutelage of Benjamin F. Fridge met on August 1, two days after the Arkansas group, to organize for Roosevelt. Considerable confusion reigned prior to the state convention, however, as a black-and-tan faction at odds with the regular GOP organization also sought acceptance by national headquarters. This group, composed of Negroes and whites and spearheaded by F. S. Swain, a white druggist in Brookhaven, and A. J. Wade, a Negro graduate of Alcorn College, issued a call on July 20 for a state convention. The call was rescinded a few days later "on account of many appeals to us from our many faithful Republican friends that are coming in from all parts of the state urging us to stay with the old party." Seven days later, Swain and his followers reissued their summons for a Roosevelt meeting after "refusing to be kicked out" by an organization that "based its creed upon the sinking sands of race and color." This on-again-off-again activity prompted Roosevelt to telegraph his press secretary, O. K. Davis, asking about the Mississippi situation. By mid-July it was clear that Roosevelt and Dixon had decided to divorce themselves from the state's black-and-tan element. Accordingly, Fridge's lily-white faction, which held authorization from Dixon, sent out a call for another convention to meet in Jackson to select a delegation to Chicago. Fridge, a lifelong Democrat, minced no words concerning the Negro and the new party: "All white citizens of Mississippi, irrespective of previous political affiliations, who believe in progressive government, by the people and for the people are hereby urged to meet at the Edwards House."[25]

The Negro–lily-white tug-of-war in the name of Progressivism was manifest at the two Jackson conventions. The former group met first on July 31, quickly naming a twenty-man delegation that was half white and half Negro, choosing electors, and drafting a platform. Few whites were present, but Swain, who was made state chairman, read several letters from Mississippi whites who condemned the lily-white movement. The platform, reported the New Orleans *Picayune,* contained twelve planks "in line with the progressive ideas expressed by Colonel Roosevelt"; however, the Negro group added a proviso against "any effort to launch a party upon a creed of color or racial distinctions." Fridge and the lily-whites were obviously unmoved by the pleas for racial justice when their convention opened the next day, also to organize for Roosevelt. That body not only reaffirmed its credentials from Dixon but pledged "to eliminate the African from the party"; by doing so, Fridge stated from the podium, "a large number of the best citizens of the state" would be attracted to the cause. The platform carried a condemnation of the Negro as well as the usual Progressive planks, including an endorsement of woman's suffrage. After naming an all-white delegation, the assembly adjourned with Fridge offering a prophecy: "I consider the mixed convention held here yesterday as a joke and have no hesitation in saying that I do not believe it will be recognized at Chicago."[26]

When Fridge returned from the national assembly to start the fall campaign, the Birmingham (Ala.) *News* reported: "The Bull Moose is not going to set the woods on fire in Mississippi." Even worse for the future of the Republican and Progressive parties, not only in Mississippi but throughout the South, Dr. Redmond and other black leaders joined in the movement to persuade Negroes to vote for Wilson following their rejection at Chicago. Yet the Progressives under Fridge's urging proceeded with plans for a fall campaign. At least one Bull Moose newspaper was established at Purvis "in the Pine Belt," and a stable of speakers financed by national headquarters was sent around the state whipping up enthusiasm for Roosevelt. Even with his openly racist appeal for white votes only, Fridge and the Mississippi Bull Moosers were able to give Roosevelt but 3,627 votes in November. Not to be outdone, however, a Republican campaign under the direction of L. B. Moseley got under way in September, although Taft did even worse, getting only 1,511 votes in the state. Moseley was unable to attend national party functions, but both he and Taft made repeated bids to retain the loyalty of the Negroes. At a meeting of the GOP State Executive Committee on September 24, when the Republican hierarchy was restructured, Moseley saw to it that A. L. Granbury, a Negro, was named secretary of the committee. The same gathering appointed W. O. Ligon of Gloster, a United States marshal, as state chairman as well as naming electors. But in November, the meagerness of the combined Roosevelt-Taft vote left little doubt that Mississippi Negroes still enjoying the franchise had gone to Wilson.[27]

In Louisiana the Bull Moose drive from the beginning was dominated by John M. Parker's defection from the Democrats and subsequent affiliation with Roosevelt. Shortly after the GOP National Convention, Parker joined Pearl Wight in sending out a call for a Progressive State Convention at the urging of Theodore Roosevelt, Jr., who presumably spoke for his father. Although Parker did not officially terminate his leadership of the Good Government League, a reform group in Democratic politics, until August 3, he indicated a preference for TR from the outset: "I am for Roosevelt, because I believe he is one of the most progressive men in the United States and does things." Roosevelt and the national campaign were of course overjoyed at the future governor's decision to join the movement. Instructions were issued by TR for Pearl Wight and Edward J. Thilborger, his captains in Louisiana, to make Parker as comfortable as possible in his associations with former Republicans. Parker received broad press exposure in the weeks leading up to the national convention, and he was widely touted to be the body's permanent chairman. But as he departed for Chicago, Parker said "no" to the speculation, "so that he might make a fight from the floor as 'a plain delegate' for a strictly white man's party and for the federal control of levees and waterways."[28]

The New Orleans *Picayune* accurately forecast that the new party in Louisiana would be a white organization before the August 2 state convention: "The convention will be a Lily White meeting. It will not send a mixed delegation to the national convention." Not a single Negro was present when Thilborger called the completely harmonious meeting into session. General William J. Behan, former Democrat and a leader among the sugar planters in southern Louisiana, delivered a ringing address praising Roosevelt and roasting Wilson. But it was Hugh S. Suthon, the former GOP gubernatorial nominee, who spoke out on the tariff for benefit of the Democratic planters: "He said there was no excuse for Louisiana to consider further what he called the imposture of clinging to the Democratic party and its platform of tariff for revenue only. He declared that party intends to abandon the protective feature all together." A platform was thereupon adopted calling "for a reasonable protective tariff as against a system of tariffs for revenue only." Two years later, Louisiana Democrats and Bull Moosers joined forces in the third district to elect Whitmell P. Martin to Congress because of his stance on the tariff and sugar. In addition to the usual Progressive features in the platform, another resolution demanded "the building and maintenance of the Mississippi levees by the Federal Government." The body elected an all-white thirty-man delegation to Chicago with the admonition to support Roosevelt as "the only man who could break the solid south."[29]

The stands on the Negro and tariff issues enabled the Bull Moose to gain great momentum in the state under the able direction of Parker and Wight following the national convention. No position had been taken in the state assemblage on the Negro because none were present. The party's strength seemed certain, however, when "L. D. Jarvis, of Tensas, a parish in which but one white Republican has lived for many years, it was stated, was elected to the state convention by thirty-seven in bull moose convention assembled." Moreover, "wholesale desertions from the Taft organization" took place, including Henry N. Pharr, the 1908 GOP gubernatorial candidate and president of the influential American Cane Growers Association. Frightened by the rapid acceleration in Progressive sentiment after Roosevelt's tour of the state in September, the GOP regulars under the generalship of Victor Liosel and Armand Romain filed "injunction proceedings against the State Contest Board and the Secretary of State, jointly to restrain them from putting the electors of the Bull Moose Progressives on the state ticket." The state supreme court, however, on October 26, refused the writ of mandamus and permitted the electors on the official ballot, thus paving the way for creation of the South's only viable Bull Moose organization—one that twice elected a U.S. congressman, nearly elected a governor in 1916, and later supplied Roosevelt with a vice-presidential running mate.[30]

Liosel and Romain mounted a reelection effort for Taft in addition to fighting the Progressives in court. Both men had conferred with Hilles following the GOP National Convention regarding the manipulation of patronage in the state for Taft's benefit; and Romain, who was scheduled to take over as state chairman, was later placed in charge of the president's Louisiana campaign. A lawyer and New Orleans native, Romain was a graduate of Tulane University and had served in the state legislature during the 1890s; he was also a son-in-law of H. Dudley Coleman, a one-term Republican congressman, 1891–1893, and a prominent leader of the party until his death in 1926. Romain, who had served as military governor of a Cuban province during the Spanish-American War, died in 1918. The campaign committee he appointed was reportedly all white, although Taft had personally written to several black leaders in the state soliciting support. Romain kicked off Taft's second bid for the White House with a GOP rally on September 10 in New Orleans' St. Charles Hotel. That meeting had "about 25 to 30 Taft followers," reported the New Orleans *Picayune* "among whom were a sprinkling of officeholders, most prominent of whom were U.S. Marshal Victor Romain, National Committeeman from Louisiana, Collector of the Port Clarence S. Herbert, and Surveyor of the Port E. J. Rodriguez." Although later GOP caucuses for Taft were better attended and Romain was able to funnel $5,000 from the state into the national campaign, the Parker-Wight bandwagon was strong enough to win second place for TR behind Wilson. Even the Negroes deserted Taft, giving him a fourth-place finish, with Eugene V. Debs and the Socialists coming in third.[31]

In North Carolina, where Roosevelt received his highest southern vote, the Bull Moosers had completely eclipsed the regular GOP by August 1, when a Progressive State Convention met in Greensboro. Sentiment for the new movement was so strong among the state's Republicans that many sought to usurp the established party machinery for Roosevelt's campaign. But Richmond Pearson and James N. Williamson, who retained the support of Roosevelt and Dixon, prevailed upon a meeting of TR backers on July 8 to issue a call for a separate state conclave. A resolution was adopted, however, to placate the dissidents: "The decision would be left to the individual voter of the various precincts to decide whether Taft or Roosevelt is the rightful nominee of the party. The precinct primaries will elect delegates to the state convention . . . in Charlotte and this convention will select electors who will cast their ballots for either Taft or Roosevelt in accordance with the vote of the precinct primaries." Both men realized the importance of establishing the new party independently of the GOP as a means of sidestepping old animosities held by the southern voter. J. N. Williamson of Burlington, who worked with Pearson through the November election, was the wealthy owner and operator of several textile mills. He consistently advised a break with the GOP as the only avenue for attracting Independents and Democrats.[32]

At the same time TR was declaring he "would make a strong fight in North Carolina," Dixon admonished Pearson to keep the third party distinct. "I know how some of the old line Republicans of North Carolina," Roosevelt's campaign manager wrote as the campaign progressed, "may feel about going into the new party but my own mind is perfectly clear that is the only thing to do. It is daily becoming more apparent to everyone that to attempt longer to work within the old republican organization puts us in a false attitude." Marion Butler was among those joining the exodus into the North Carolina Bull Moose. Though TR was personally delighted to have his support, several Democrats, reported the Charlotte *Daily Observer,* said "that they were glad to see Mr. Butler taking such an active part in the Roosevelt campaign, for they believe it will help the democratic cause." Congressman Robert N. Page even issued a statement proclaiming, "Mr. Butler's activity would enthuse the Democrats and dispel any apathy in the ranks." Nonetheless, the Roosevelt men counseling an independent party held a convention that in reality was a mass meeting of Roosevelt enthusiasts as scheduled in Greensboro under the direction of Pearson and Williamson. With about fifty delegates present, Williamson was made state chairman and Pearson officially designated national committeeman, although he had been acting in that capacity for some time. A delegation to Chicago was named and instructed for Roosevelt after the new party had been formally organized, complete with its own Executive Committee. Before adjourning, the meeting drafted a resolution creating a committee "for the purpose of naming a time and place for a State Progressive Convention and employing whatever means they think best to aid in the election of Theodore Roosevelt to the Presidency."[33]

The Republican regulars were faced with dilemma as the Roosevelt movement mushroomed. At a meeting of the State Executive Committee on August 7 to set the date for a state convention, resolutions were adopted supporting Taft and Sherman as well as binding all delegates in the September convention to support the national ticket. State Chairman Morehead informed Taft of the action and speculated that a majority of the state's Republicans opposed the stance, "but it appeared proper to the committee to maintain the autonomy of the party in the State regardless of election results. While favorable results in this State are not at all within the range of probability, we are anxious that the party be maintained in its integrity, strong in the hope that if this is done, something may be accomplished after the passing of this dementia of the moment." But when the state convention met in Charlotte to name electors and to nominate Thomas Settle, a prominent party man since Reconstruction, as its gubernatorial candidate, about 400 Roosevelt delegates led by six of the principal Republican leaders of the state, called another convention to meet at the same time as the regulars. The action of the bolters, which further compounded the problems facing Morehead, came after the GOP Executive Committee made good its ultimatum to bar everyone from the convention who had not endorsed Taft. Butler, furthermore, was on hand to give the dissenters a spellbinding speech, although he had failed earlier to gain a compromise between the regulars and Bull Moosers. The rump convention not only protested the action of the committee and declined to have any further relations with the Taft convention, but also agreed to endorse the gubernatorial candidate and electors named by the official Progressive apparatus in the state.[34]

The state convention summoned by Pearson and Williamson met one day earlier in Greensboro and nominated Dr. Cyrus Thompson of Onslow County for governor. Pearson had never been in doubt about the rightness of Roosevelt's candidacy, although he lamented Morehead's stand which precluded cooperation between the two parties. Following his return from the Progressive National Convention, he thought the Republicans had no chance in North Carolina: "I do not believe that President Taft will receive 5,000 votes in the entire state. There are whole districts where he will hardly black the board." Thus buoyed, the less than two hundred persons attending the Greensboro convention completed the state organization and named a slate of electors after listening to a rousing address by Everett Colby, a New Jersey state senator, who had been imported for the occasion.[35]

The regulars commenced to fight back by having Pearson, who was still Republican national committeeman, thrown off the National Committee by Hilles. Although his official removal two weeks after the state Bull Moose convention was anticlimactic, a move against him had been under way since early July, when Edward C. Duncan, who subsequently replaced him, had called at the White House. After Morehead and Duncan had agreed to bury old differences, Taft and Hilles entrusted the ill-fated North Carolina campaign to them. The Bull Moosers, on the other hand, had a vigorous campaign going several weeks earlier with a generous flow of money from national headquarters. Two days after the Progressive National Convention, W. S. Pearson, who became state secretary of the party, informed Dixon: "I immediately returned to Greensboro without stopping to go to my home in Charlotte and secured a headquarters, and hung out a big Bull Moose over the entrance of the old Benbow Hotel in the heart of the city and proceeded to get the counties into line." By early October, reported the Charlotte *Daily Observer,* "the Bull Moose state headquarters are in full swing here [at Lexington]. A force of stenographers is busy sending out Progressive dope about Zeb Vance Walser, State Chairman, who is a busy man." Although the GOP leadership established campaign headquarters in the major cities, Roosevelt's sweep through North Carolina in October enabled the Bull Moosers to overshadow their efforts.[36]

The Tennessee Bull Moose was christened at a convention in Nashville on August 2 under the auspices of the state's Republican treasurer, G. Tom Taylor. Roosevelt had picked him as provisional national committeeman following a conference on July 1 at Oyster Bay. Taylor was soon joined by John C. Houk, another GOP delegate rejected at Chicago, in sponsoring a Progressive conference that issued a call for the gathering. To the chagrin of Hooper and the Republican regulars, Taylor announced that a full ticket including the most obscure offices in the state would be put out by the Bull Moose assembly in Nashville. The former Republicans flocking to the new party, however, were sharply divided on the issue of nominating a candidate to oppose Hooper's reelection. While Sanders strove to block all Tennessee confirmations in the Senate, Hooper and his friends initiated a drive to keep a Bull Moose opponent from the field after he "had learned the horrible details of the Nashville convention." In addition, W. J. Oliver, who refused to join the movement, started a drive to have Roosevelt scotch any plan for a state ticket. Although failure to resolve the impasse eventually split the Tennessee Progressives, Roosevelt remained adamant: "I do not see how it is possible for me to take any position that will directly or indirectly endorse Governor Hooper, or fail to support any Progressive candidate against him. . . . He must either be for us or against us, so far as I am concerned."[37]

Finally, Hooper hit upon the idea of "being on the ground when the Bull Moosers meet" to persuade old allies to his view. The Progressive convention, however, chose not only to ignore him and his plea that an opposition ticket "would destroy any chances of Republican victory in Tennessee," but singled him out for ridicule: "He saw twenty-three dummy delegates from Tennessee sitting at Chicago," said Henry B. Anderson, the meeting's temporary chairman and later a federal judge, "casting their votes for a man who had hardly any real friends in the state, and he never lifted a hand. The neutrality of the Governor of Tennessee was about on a par with the neutrality of the Republican National Convention." When the gathering nominated W. F. Poston of Alamo for governor to oppose Hooper and Benton McMillin, the Democratic nominee, about thirty delegates bolted to hold a separate convention at the Hermitage Hotel. Meanwhile, the original assembly in the House Chamber at the State Capitol nominated a delegation to Chicago and drafted a platform. Among other planks, reported the Memphis *Commercial Appeal,* "it eulogizes Roosevelt, denounces Taft's nomination as a steal, declares against any man who stands for Taft [a hit at Hooper], favors woman's suffrage, and numerous fads and fancies." As the body led by Taylor and Houk adjourned, Poston, heretofore an anti-Hooper Republican, threw down the gauntlet for the GOP regulars: "Both my feet are firmly on the platform," he told reporters, "and I am going to canvass the state from Bristol to Memphis."[38]

John W. Farley, a Memphis lawyer and an organizer of the Piggly-Wiggly food chain across the South, presided over the bolting faction that named a rival Bull Moose organization empowering it to send its own delegation to Chicago. After displaying the usual outburst for Roosevelt, the dissident Moosers who wanted to give Hooper solid Republican-Independent Democratic support invited him to address the convention. Although barred from the Taylor convention, the beleaguered governor seized the opportunity to state his position without equivocation: "He would vote for Taft," said the New Orleans *Picayune,* "without imposing his views on others." Moreover, "he entered upon his duties as governor with a determination that he would take no part in a Republican factional fight, and that he intends to live strictly up to that determination." Judge Hugh B. Lindsay and Oliver, both supporters of Hooper, were given charge of the new State Committee, even though Roosevelt had already made his views clear on a state ticket. Yet the convention went further, adopting a resolution that denounced Taylor and Houk by name as well as their handling of Progressive affairs in Tennessee. But they held the confidence of Roosevelt and Dixon, which explains why none of the Farley-Lindsay-Oliver group was seated in the national convention when it met three days later.[39]

Although Poston campaigned as promised and TR entered the state flaying Hooper and Sanders, one correspondent told Taft not to despair because in Tennessee "Roosevelt didn't have any more chance than a bowlegged girl in the town in which she was raised." Hooper, who enjoyed the support of the state's Negroes as well as Independent Democrats, won reelection by a majority of 8,000 votes; Poston polled 4,483 votes and did not carry a single Tennessee county. The Progressives ran candidates for Congress in four of the state's ten districts, although none of them were very strong in championing the national Progressive campaign or in identifying themselves with Roosevelt. Taft also received a larger vote in Tennessee than TR because of Hooper's support and because the president exerted great pressure on GOP congressional candidates to do nothing to alienate sympathetic Democrats in the gubernatorial contest. The Republicans spent considerable sums of money in both the presidential and state races; Sanders informed Hilles that he was throwing his personal fortune into the fray after the campaign war chest had been exhausted. Roosevelt's steadfast refusal to support Hooper or at least to refrain from naming a Bull Mooser to oppose him cost the Progressives dearly in the Volunteer State. Yet for all their exertions, Wilson polled a higher vote in the state than Roosevelt and Taft combined.[40]

South Carolina and Texas, although both were represented in the Progressive National Convention, did not formally organize for the new party until afterward. A group of South Carolina Negroes "announced themselves for the third term hunter," reported a Democratic newspaper, in late July and even issued a call for a state convention. John G. Capers, who had supported Roosevelt during the preconvention campaign, refused to leave the GOP for the Bull Moose party, even though most of the Negroes endorsing the movement were his former associates: "The national Progressive party in Charleston for the most part is composed of members of the so-called Capers wing of the party in this state, and other republicans who supported Roosevelt up to the time of the republican

convention in Chicago." John Gill, a Negro leader at Manning, organized
a branch of the party in Clarendon County and optimistically told reporters: "One third of the Democrats and two thirds of the Republicans are
going to vote for the new Progressive party." But when Dixon appointed
L. W. C. Blalock, an associate of Capers and former revenue collector, as
Progressive national committeeman and organizer for the state, the
Negroes canceled their state convention.[41]

Edmund Deas, another Negro leader, Chairman of the Republican
Executive Committee and known as the "Duke of Darlington," maintained that the state conclave had been aborted because it took $1500 to
hold such a convention and that his committee did not have the money.
Dixon not only withheld organizing funds but informed the Negroes that
they would not be recognized in Chicago. Yet a number of them appeared
at the convention. "In the South Carolina case before the Progressive
National Committee," noted the New York *Times,* "the enthusiastic
Negroes who were anxious to hitch their destinies to Roosevelt's star made
the initial mistake of calling themselves 'Progressive Republicans,' a fatal
error because the Colonel wanted to go fishing for Democrats in the
South." Although several newspapers indicated that South Carolina would
have no representation in the national gathering, the official roll lists
Lawrence E. Gray of Westminister as a lone delegate. Progressive rejection of the South Carolina Negroes along with similar southern delegations
failed to lure whites in any numbers as anticipated, which prompted the
Charleston *News and Courier* to comment: "There are so many southern
Democrats supporting the Bull Moose that it would cost as much as a
dollar to give each of them a dime." And the blacks, too, became miffed
following their humiliation at the hands of Roosevelt and the Progressive
leadership. Dr. Alonzo C. McClennan, a Negro physician and onetime
student at the U.S. Naval Academy who operated an all-black hospital in
Charleston, stated during an interview: "The anti-Roosevelt feeling is
general and gaining in intensity every day. He did not think TR would get
many Negro votes in the state."[42]

Meanwhile, J. W. Tolbert, who retained control of the GOP machinery
as well as command of the Taft campaign, called the Republican State
Executive Committee into session in late September to combat the Bull
Moose menace. Although Taft received less than six hundred votes in
South Carolina in the general election, the committee selected electors but
declined to put out a state ticket. Following the example of other states,
the committee was purged of those going over to the Progressives. The
Republicans as usual failed to generate much steam in overwhelmingly
Democratic South Carolina, but the mere curiosity of the Bull Moosers
enabled them to attract considerable attention following the Chicago
convention. B. Sherwood Dunn, an Aiken lawyer, who assumed control of
the new party following a conference with Dixon, officially launched the

Bull Moose at a convention in Charleston on October 4 as a white man's party.[43]

About fifty delegates, including Blalock, who had stepped aside in favor of Dunn, attended the gathering which nominated electors but refused to name a state ticket because "it is too late to hold a primary, and the Progressive party wished to be strictly regular in its proceedings"; the national party platform was adopted as the state document. Several "genuine Bull Moose rallies" were organized around the state, such as one in Charleston on October 24 that attracted "an estimated one hundred persons." But Dunn apparently had difficulty receiving both money and cooperation from a national headquarters preoccupied with matters in states more important to the campaign. He was obliged to telegraph Dixon on October 10 to stop sending such "dope" as "thirty-five thousand 'Contract with the People' of [sic] sixteen page pamphlet of the Chicago platform, which will not be read because of general illiteracy of our people." Furthermore, Roosevelt's labor record "will do more good," Dunn thought, "as our support will come chiefly from cotton mill operatives, railroad men and laboring classes to whom we are addressing our campaign. We have four typewriters working and are going into a whirlwind campaign with enthusiasm working fifteen hours daily and we want what we want when we want it." For all the brave talk, however, the South Carolina Bull Moosers delivered but 1,293 votes to Roosevelt in November—by far his poorest showing in the eleven ex-Confederate states.[44]

The Texans, too, failed to organize until after the national convention because of restrictions imposed upon political activity by the state's election laws. Cecil Lyon, however, who had been in the Roosevelt vanguard from the start and a member of the Progressive National Committee since the Orchestra Hall affair, and several members of the GOP Executive Committee represented the state with a contingent in the Chicago assembly. Therein lay both the outlines of a renewed Roosevelt-Taft tug-of-war and the shape of the Texas campaign until November. Lyon and his lily-white allies looked upon rejection of his delegation by the GOP in Chicago as naked theft and fraud; he was still chief of the state's Republican apparatus, and he saw no difficulty in using the party machinery for the Bull Moose crusade. Although he had been discarded along with Richmond Pearson and Pearl Wight by Hilles and the National Committee, Lyon sought to retain his hold over Lone Star Republicans by changing the party's official name from "Republican" to "Progressive." But Hilles and Taft continued to recognize MacGregor, who campaigned for Taft in other parts of the country and in Texas, as their man. At the same time Lyon and the Bull Moosers were organizing a campaign by opening headquarters in various parts of the state, W. M. McDonald, the Negro leader, was telegraphing the White House that "the third party cannot make headway in Texas." The Texas Negroes remained loyal to Taft following their snubbing by the Progressives, enabling the president to run ahead of Roosevelt in the state, even though the combined Republican-Progressive vote was roughly 10,000 less than Taft had received in 1908.[45]

The Republican State Executive Committee—with Lyon as chairman although no longer national committeeman—held a stormy session in Dallas on August 13, one day before the state convention, which resulted in the long-anticipated split. The fracas started when Taft members demanded Lyon's removal as chairman because of his pro-Roosevelt activities. Lyon not only ignored the challenge but rammed through a resolution changing the name of the party because Bull Moose "adherents control this state organization, and this power should be brought to bear exclusively for the good of the Progressive movement, and also as an endorsement of the Texas Republican organization of Johnson and Roosevelt, and the Chicago Bull Moose platform." That was too much for MacGregor, who immediately made plans for a separate convention. Meeting the same day as the Lyon faction and the Democrats, who nominated O. B. Colquitt as their gubernatorial candidate, the Taft loyalists, numbering approximately three hundred, about one-third of whom were Negroes, named Judge C. K. McDowell as state chairman. They also adopted a platform that declared for Taft, "who for the last four years, despite bickerings from within and opposition from without, has guided honorably and non-partisanly the destinies of our matchless republic." Taft electors were selected, and C. W. Johnson, a longtime U.S. commissioner and federal officeholder, was named to oppose Colquitt. The meeting became bitterly divided when Harry Beck, who had the support of the blacks, waged an unsuccessful fight for the gubernatorial nomination. But the real struggle was with the Progressives, and the San Antonio *Daily Express* reported that the gathering adjourned with Johnson offering "caustic criticism of the 'war and political activities' of Roosevelt."[46]

The larger and more clamorous Lyon convention adopted a resolution changing the party name: "That the political organization in Texas heretofore and now known as the Republican party of Texas is now and hereafter known as the Progressive party of Texas." Before serious business could be taken up, several delegates carried a large "Progressive State Convention" banner to the front of the auditorium and hastily tacked it over the "Republican State Convention" streamer already in the building. Although five Negroes were in attendance among the 250 delegates, resolutions were adopted approving Roosevelt's stand at the national convention reading the Negro out of the party. One of the Negroes, B. F. Wallace of Palestine, delivered an impassioned address attempting to stave off the antiblack stance: "White men," he said, "need not fear Negro domination, or anything that would retard the progress of Roosevelt or Johnson, whose interests the honest Negroes of Texas have at heart." But Lyon had been too long in the lily-white fight to permit Negroes a voice in the new party.

After all, J. A. Winters of Fort Worth told the gathering, "no party can be built in Texas to accomplish anything that will permit Negro affiliations." The legal cloud raised by the name change was lifted later when Texas Secretary of State C. C. McDonald, declared that he "was pretty sure the Roosevelt and Johnson electors . . . can get on the ballot by petition, this to be filed with the Secretary of State within the required time. This is the procedure followed by the Socialists and organizations of that sort."[47]

Even though Lyon and the lily-white Republicans had never attracted a following among Texas Democrats in the past, plans were laid for a statewide Progressive organization. Bull Moose committees were planned in every congressional district, county, and precinct as well as the selection of only "good men" on county tickets; yet only two of the state's sixteen congressional districts had a Progressive candidate in November. Lyon was named both national committeeman and state chairman, the only Bull Moose leader in the South to hold both posts. In addition to adopting a lengthy platform, the assembly at Lyon's urging posted a slate of electors and named a complete ticket for state office. Edward C. Lasater of Fulfurrias was chosen to oppose Colquitt and Johnson in the race for governor. A prominent rancher in extreme south Texas, Lasater was president of the powerful Texas Cattle Raisers Association; along with J. M. Parker, he was appointed to a post in the Food Administration during World War I. A longtime associate of Lyon in the state's lily-white movement, Lasater predicted a bright future for the party as he thanked the convention: "The opposition party to the Democrats was born here today and the dominating party of Texas is in need of a strong opposition." Furthermore, he gave his assurance that "the Progressive movement would endure and that its leaders were working for ultimate victory."[48]

When the Negro delegations from Alabama, Florida, and Mississippi arrived in Chicago to press their claims for seats, Roosevelt and the Bull Moose leadership faced a perplexing situation: how to dissuade them without alienating the northern Negro and his sympathizers. The Negro contingent gotten up by J. R. Pollard in Virginia as well as the Georgia group apparently bowed to the inevitable and did not challenge the lily-white groups from their states, although several northern delegations had Negroes as did those from Arkansas and West Virginia. Roosevelt, however, settled the controversy on August 1, when his oft-quoted letter to Julian Harris of Georgia stating the official party policy was released to the press. It was a long letter—one in which TR reviewed repeated GOP attempts to build a party based upon Negro representation over the past forty-five years: "The sentiment of the southern Negro collectively has been prostituted by dishonest politicians, both white and black, and the machinery does not exist (and can never be created as long as present political conditions are continued) which can secure what a future of real justice will undoubtedly develop, namely, the right of political expression by the Negro who shows that he possesses the intelligence, integrity and self-respect which justify such right of political expression in his white neighbor. . . . It would be worse than useless to try to build up the Progressive Party in these Southern States where there is no real Republican Party, by appealing to the negroes or the men who in the past have derived their sole standing from leading and manipulating the negroes."

Rhetoric was included about helping the Negro by appealing "to the best white men in the South" before the concluding exercise in practical politics: "Our only wise course from the standpoint of the colored man himself is to follow the course that we are now following toward him in the North and to follow the course we are following toward him in the South."[49]

"Northern colored men will not support the Bull Moose party," commented the Washington *Bee,* because "they have decided to defend their brethren in the south against attacks of the [new] party." Yet Roosevelt's message to the southern Negro was final: he was not needed in the Bull Moose crusade for a Progressive America. And at Chicago, the Provisional Progressive National Committee went through the façade of hearing contests from three southern states, even though the Negro had been systematically excluded from the party's organizing drive in the eleven ex-Confederate states. The Alabama case involving a challenge from twelve Negroes led by Dr. Joseph Thomas came first on August 3, two days after start of the convention. Hundley, the state's national committeeman, charged that twenty-four delegates had been chosen by a large majority in the state convention and "the negroes [sic] had no basis for their claim." But Thomas maintained that the state's blacks had been promised representation on the delegation by J. O. Thompson, and "when we saw the convention was not going to give the colored man anything we selected our own delegates right in the corner of the convention hall in Birmingham, where it was held." That did it; the committee voted for the all-white Hundley-Thompson contingent after Dixon pointed out that by their own admission, the Negroes "were chosen by only a small minority of the state convention."[50]

In the Florida case, C. H. Alston, the Negro attorney from Tampa denied a seat in the GOP convention, argued that blacks had been refused a role in the Bull Moose State Convention but that Harry L. Anderson had "urged the negroes to hold a separate meeting in St. Augustine." Anderson thereupon "admitted he endeavored to keep the negroes out of the white convention [because] my experience in Southern politics had showed me that white men will not follow negro political leaders." Finally, the committee decided that the movement was on such thin ice in the state that both delegations were disallowed, causing Florida to be the only state not represented in the national gathering; Anderson, however, was permitted to continue as national committeeman. A challenge had been anticipated by the breakaway white group from Georgia led by J. St. Julian Yates, but the dissidents did not respond when called. Yet Cecil Lyon, anxious to avoid any hint of "steamroller tactics," sponsored a successful resolution for "the contest to be considered without prejudice before the credentials committee if the contestants appear." The Mississippi contest came last, with Perry W. Howard speaking for the Negro delegates and pleading with the committee "not to discourage the 90,000 negro voters of that state by refusing them recognition." He asked with great force: "Would you have Roosevelt the cause of taking from us the liberty that Abraham Lincoln has given us?" Meanwhile, strong sentiment developed among certain northern members either to give the Negro a measure of recognition or to throw out both delegations as had been done with Florida. Fridge asked his fellow committeemen "not to embarrass" or "disgrace" him at home by turning away his all-white delegation. His faction was finally seated, but not before the committee adopted a resolution rapping his call for a state convention that would have made the Bull Moose in Mississippi a party for whites only. The committee had again rejected the Negro's leadership but left the door ajar for his support at the polls.[51]

Unlike the cataclysmic events involving the South in the Republican National Convention, the region played no important role in the three-day Progressive gathering. "It was not a convention at all," reported the New York *Times:* "It was an assemblage of religious enthusiasts." Roosevelt totally dominated the August 5–7 meeting, and, because "he refused to budge" on the Negro question as outlined in his letter to Harris, there was nothing for "the one thousand serious, earnest, almost fanatical men and women" to do but rubber stamp his decisions. The National Committee had already fixed the issue of southern representation; yet several speakers, including Roosevelt himself, made repeated references to the South's importance in the campaign. Former Senator Albert J. Beveridge of Indiana, who gave the keynote oration, played on the theme that southerners since the Civil War had not been for Democrats but against Republicans. Amid an atmosphere bordering on fanaticism, the recently named Progressive candidate for governor continued the call for southern support: "They want to be free of that political bondage; and the Progressive party is here to deliver them. They want to be free because they want to take part in solving the nation's real problems of today, and today our real problems are economic and national." Echoes of the New Nationalism! In conclusion, he proclaimed that "Our God is Marching On," as the great concourse rose in a body singing "The Battle Hymn of the Republic."[52]

The second day, August 6, opened with delegates and onlookers roaring out stanzas of "America" and was monopolized with Roosevelt's "A Confession of Faith"—a fighting speech interrupted by applause and cheers at least 145 times. Escorted to the platform by a committee of fifteen, including J. M. Parker, Julian Harris, J. N. Williamson, Jr., and former Governor W. M. O. Dawson of West Virginia, Roosevelt rang out an impassioned appeal to the South: "And, friends, it was of real significance that this convention should have opened by the drums and the fifes of men who in their youth dared all. . . . And beside the men of blue stood the men of gray. . . . And we are facing the future, both Americans, and we are all Progressives as all good Americans should be." Although the address was a catalog of Progressive hopes and the party's "Contract with the People," Roosevelt also offered concrete proposals for southern consumption: improvement and flood control along the Mississippi—"just as the nation has gone into the work of irrigation in the west, so it should go into the work of helping reclaim the swamp lands of the South"—and for the Louisiana sugar interests, he declared for a "Scientific Revision" of the tariff. When a black delegate shouted an inquiry, he deviated from his prepared text to speak out on the "Negro Question." The answer, which ran to eight pages of typescript in the *Convention Proceedings,* was by and large a restatement of the Harris letter and his previous utterances: "I have taken the action which so far as I am able to judge in my own soul, I believe with all my heart is the only action that offered any chance of hope to the black man in the South, and which has already given the black man in the North a better chance than he ever had before."[53]

It was a "motley crowd," writes Arthur S. Link, composed of "social and economic reformers, disgruntled politicians and bosses, representatives of big business, idealists, suffragettes, and sundry others," that handed Roosevelt and Johnson the nomination one day later. The handful of Negroes among them, however, split into rival factions over a proper response to Roosevelt's unbending stance. One group led by Dr. W. A. D. Venerable of St. Louis wanted to denounce the new party entirely, while the other with Bishop J. M. Connor of Little Rock as its spokesman sought to endorse the Bull Moosers. Consequently, the Negroes went off in different directions, and if they were divided, the remaining partisans were united upon a common goal as the assembly neared completion. Roosevelt and Hiram Johnson were nominated by acclamation "under a suspension of the convention rules amid scenes which fluctuated between the solemn and impressive and the merely spectacular and melodramatic." The 174 southern delegates listed on the *Official Roll* were thus deprived of casting an individual ballot for the ticket, although such leaders as Parker, Wight, and Lyon gave the South a conspicuous role in the gathering. Roosevelt further acknowledged the South's influence by asking A. T. Hamilton, a delegate from Rome, Georgia, to offer one of several seconding speeches: "I thank God that there is a Dixie Land, because Theodore Roosevelt's mother lived in Georgia. If she had not been born in Georgia we might never had had the reform in America that the people will have," he said, following the Chicago social worker, Jane Addams, to the rostrum.

Ironically, another contender with strong ties to Georgia and the South, Woodrow Wilson, Roosevelt's most formidable opponent, delivered his formal speech accepting the Democratic nomination on the same day the Bull Moosers put their stamp of approval on TR. And the New Jersey governor tellingly portrayed himself "as a progressive southerner, with a gentlemanly concern for the public weal." Clearly, not only Progressives but Republicans as well faced a difficult southern campaign in the weeks ahead.[54]

The cardinal event in the South for both Bull Moosers and Republicans during the campaign was Roosevelt's visit to Arkansas, Tennessee, Georgia, Louisiana, and North Carolina in late September and early October as part of his celebrated transcontinental tour. While the attention he gained on the swing handed the southern Bull Moose an advantage, local Republicans all over the nation were hampered by Taft's inactivity before the election. The president, writes Paolo E. Coletta, "retired to Beverly at the end of the congressional session late in August and abandoned his party. Neither he nor the members of his cabinet actively participated in the campaign." After a brief address at his formal notification ceremony at the White House on August 1, he virtually withdrew from the fight for votes. Yet he remained highly critical of the Rough Rider: "As the campaign goes on and the unscrupulousness of Roosevelt develops," he informed Mrs. Taft, "it is hard to realize we are talking about the same man whom we knew in the presidency. . . . I look upon him as I look upon a freak, almost, in the zoological garden, a kind of animal not often found." As the electioneering progressed, it became clear that Taft was out of the running, which caused Roosevelt to increase his vitriolic attacks on Wilson and to heap continual scorn upon the Old Guard. At no time was this more apparent than as he prepared to spread his Progressive gospel throughout the southland.[55]

Numerous Arkansas Republicans were dispirited enough to "join hands with Bull Moosers" in welcoming Roosevelt to Little Rock on September 25 to open his southern tour. After speaking on the west coast, he arrived in the Arkansas capital by way of Kansas and Oklahoma to address the progressive-minded Lakes-to-Gulf Waterways Association. Eugene V. Debs had spoken one day earlier, saying TR "loved only himself" and stating a desire to debate the former president "on the same stage." But Roosevelt took no notice of the Socialist challenge as he called for a deepening of the Mississippi River with equipment and engineers working on completion of the Panama Canal. After lauding Senator James P. Clarke and Governor-elect Joe T. Robinson, the chief Bull Mooser traveled to New Orleans, making speeches at Memphis and several Tennessee whistlestops.[56]

The Memphis address before a nonpartisan group, the Interstate Levee Association, was billed as nonpolitical although Roosevelt took time to announce: "Mr. Wilson is about as much a Progressive as Mr. Taft." But at Jackson, Tennessee, he expounded the Progressive doctrine before a large crowd from several counties. In New Orleans there was a parade through the city's celebrated French Quarter as well as a plug for the only real Bull Moose organization in the South. Accompanied by "many old time Republicans and some newer ones, and a few converts from the Democrats," Roosevelt took care to emphasize that the "Progressive party had come to stay, and had no more connection with the democratic and republican parties." After an appeal to the sugar planters and agricultural interests in general, he moved north to Atlanta, where he visited his mother's home—even viewing a crib used by her as an infant—again proclaiming his loyalty to the "men who fought in the grey." Yet when interviewed at the end of the southern trip, Roosevelt was far from optimistic: "I am no prophet. I have been told that we have an excellent chance in Tennessee and that there is a strong Progressive party sentiment in Louisiana. I can't make any prediction as to what we may do. I found Georgia extremely friendly, but I can't say anything about our chances there."[57]

Roosevelt next traveled through east Tennessee on his way to North Carolina, where he hoped to give Pearson's organization a shot in the arm. At Chattanooga, Senator Sanders's hometown, he "flayed both Sanders and Hooper" for their support of the Old Guard. At Knoxville, however, on the same day, September 30, he ran into trouble with his assaults on Hooper and, reported the Knoxville *Banner,* "a middling lively time" took place: "Colonel Roosevelt had hardly begun to speak when a score of men began to shout Governor Hooper's name. The Colonel stopped short. The cries grew louder, and in a moment there was an uproar." Then, regaining his composure, he stated his position before the "tumultuous crowd": "I am pinning by faith," he shouted when the noise had partially subsided, "to the Commandment, Thou Shall not Steal." Again the crowd became unruly at the suggestion that Hooper had assisted in stealing the GOP nomination from him at Chicago, and the fracas started anew. Although Roosevelt spent most of his time in Tennessee attacking Hooper rather than pleading the Progressive platform, he took a different tack in North Carolina. Before an estimated seven thousand in the City Auditorium at Raleigh, he spoke about the fight at Armageddon and the need for eliminating the "middle man" from both business and politics. He also lashed out at the American Tobacco Company, contending that only the Progressives had a plan to check runaway trusts. He was reportedly "hoarse and weary" during the North Carolina junket: "When Colonel Roosevelt reached Raleigh tonight (October 1) he had travelled 10,373 miles on his present trip. The former President left New York on September 2, and has spoken in 27 states in 30 days."[58]

Roosevelt's swing through the South was not enough for him to carry one of the eleven ex-Confederate states as he had hoped or to affect Democratic dominance in the region. Although scientific analyses of election returns lay decades in the future, even the most cursory examination of the 1912 statistics reveals a nearly nonexistent appeal by Roosevelt and Taft to the southern voter. Wilson got 1,035,044 or 16.4 percent of his 6,293,019 popular votes in the South. Significantly, he did not capture a majority in any state outside the old Confederacy: 126 of his 435 electoral votes, more than one-fourth the total, came from the area. Roosevelt received the second highest vote in Alabama, Georgia, Louisiana, Mississippi, North and South Carolina, and Virginia, but he got only 6.4 percent or 258,048 votes of his total 4,119,507 in the eleven states. Taft, on the other hand, came in second behind Wilson in Arkansas, Tennessee, and Texas, getting but 5.4 percent of his national vote in the South while carrying only two states, Utah and Vermont. The Socialist candidate, Debs, came in ahead of both TR and Taft in Florida, and in Louisiana and Mississippi he ran third. Taft and Roosevelt carried but forty-four counties of the 1,059 comprising the eleven states, the remainder going to Wilson; but in the Bull Moose–GOP contest, Roosevelt won 655 counties over Taft, while Taft took second place in 389 and they actually received a tie vote for second place in fifteen. In three states, Florida, Louisiana, and South Carolina, neither Taft nor Roosevelt won a single county. Even though their combined vote was highest in Tennessee, neither came close to breaking the solid South, and in several southern states their vote bordered on the insignificant.

If Progressives came out second best in their southern fight with Republicans in the presidential canvass, the new party fared worse in local contests. Neither party made an appreciable showing in six states—Florida, Mississippi, North and South Carolina, Tennessee, and Texas—holding gubernatorial elections concurrently with the Taft-Roosevelt fight. Only the Socialists ran a candidate against the Democrats in Mississippi and South Carolina; Bull Moosers and Republicans did not offer a state ticket in November 1912 in either state. In Florida the Progressive candidate for governor, W. C. Hodges, did not win a single county though he took second place in nineteen of the state's forty-eight counties; W. R. O'Neal, the GOP nominee, likewise carried no counties. The Bull Moose candidate in North Carolina, Iredell Mears, who had replaced Dr. Thompson on the state ticket, actually won five counties in his race against Thomas Settle, the Republican standard-bearer, and Governor Locke Craig; Settle also carried five counties although in the remainder of the state he ran second in thirty-six counties to fifty-four for Mears. And in Tennessee, where Roosevelt had plotted Hooper's defeat, the Republican incumbent triumphed handily over Benton McMillin, the Democratic challenger; Poston, the Progressive supported by TR, did not carry a single county. Even in Texas, where Cecil Lyon supposedly controlled the GOP vote, the new party did poorly in the gubernatorial race. Edward C. Lasater, the Progressive candidate, did not carry any counties, although Roosevelt managed to win two; and C. W. Johnson won but three for the

Republicans, one more than Taft. The Texas Bull Moosers did even worse in their search for second place behind Governor Colquitt when Johnson ran ahead of Lasater in 136 of the state's 243 counties.

Table 6–1

1912 Presidential Voting in the South

	Wilson	Roosevelt	Taft	Counties won by TR	Counties won by Taft	COUNTIES TR over Taft	Taft over TR
Alabama	82,438	22,689	9,731	3	0	56	11
Arkansas	68,869	21,673	24,297	0	1	28	47
Florida	36,417	4,535	4,279	0	0	20	28
Georgia	94,019	22,010	5,190	4	2	123	23
Louisiana	60,435	9,323	3,834	0	0	49	11
Mississippi	57,164	3,627	1,511	0	0	74	5
N. Carolina	144,407	69,130	29,139	8	3	74	25
S. Carolina	48,357	1,293	536	0	0	30	9
Tennessee	133,025	53,725	59,444	14	3	35	61
Texas	219,559	26,755	28,853	2	2	128	107
Virginia	90,354	23,288	21,777	1	1	38	62
Total	1,035,044	258,048	188,591	32	12	655	389

SOURCE: Robinson, *Presidential Vote*, pp. 46–53; *World Almanac, 1913*, pp. 721–66.

While standing at Armageddon in the South, the Progressives carried but thirty-two counties in the presidential race and only five counties, all of them in North Carolina, in state elections; the Republicans, on the other hand, won twelve and fifty-seven, respectively. Nor did either party do better in the congressional contests. Although pressed for time following creation of the party, the Progressives put up candidates in twenty-one districts in addition to several at-large races in Alabama, Florida, North and South Carolina, Tennessee, Texas, and Virginia; none, however, were successful. The Republicans offered congressional nominees in twenty-one districts located in seven southern states; only three, Sam R. Sells, Richard W. Austin, and C. Bascomb Slemp, were elected. In terms of elected officials, Republican strength in the South remained about the same: Tennessee retained its GOP governor and two congressmen; Sanders was still in the Senate although his appointed term would end in January 1913; and Slemp was reelected to a fourth term by the Virginia ninth district. The usual fistful of Republicans was elected to legislatures in all southern states but Florida, Louisiana, Mississippi, and South Carolina; and the Progressives even returned a scattering to the Arkansas, North Carolina, and

Tennessee legislatures. The Bull Moosers—most of whom were former Republicans hoping lightning would strike under the Roosevelt banner—not only failed to win at the polls in the South, but had also failed to affect the GOP in a material way as the region's chief opposition party.[59]

Chapter 7

1914: Victory, Defeat, and Amalgamation

"Notwithstanding the magnificent tribute of 4,119,582 votes," noted Amos Pinchot, "Roosevelt was discouraged by his 1912 defeat, and quickly lost interest in the new party." He was clearly not a man to lead lost causes, although other Progressive leaders, including George W. Perkins, Jane Addams, Albert J. Beveridge, and Hiram Johnson, proceeded with plans to mold the Progressive party into a permanent organization. While professional politicians—North and South—who had supported TR were reassessing their allegiance to the movement, a general sorting out within the party took place in the weeks following the November debacle. Gradually the unlikely combination of the wealthy Perkins working with a number of northern dilettantes and would-be social reformers gained influence in the party hierarchy. With an eye to rebuilding for the 1914 off-year elections and the 1916 presidential race, a call was sent out for a massive Progressive convention on December 6, 1912, in Chicago. But with a Democrat soon to enter the White House, one who possessed impressive progressive credentials, the prospect seemed bleak indeed that the new party could be refashioned into a winning machine.[1]

Fifteen hundred delegates assembled in Chicago for the organizational meeting and cheered wildly as Roosevelt denounced the Republican party, stating grandly that "no honest man could be a member of it." Nor was the old fire gone as he reaffirmed the Progressive credo: "We stand for every principle set forth in our platform. We stand for the purging of the roll of American public life by driving out of politics the big bosses who thwart the popular will, who rely on corruption as a political instrument and who serve the cause of privilege." The colonel scotched a move initiated by Gifford Pinchot and a group of western radicals to drive Perkins from a position of influence in the party councils because of his close ties with Wall Street. He not only singled out Perkins for praise but also several others identified with the eastern branch of the party, including William Flinn, Charles Sumner Bird, and magazine publisher Frank Munsey. The South was not mentioned by Roosevelt, who also informed the assemblage that Progressives were the heirs of Lincoln, a statement hardly calculated to win southern support. Later, however, Beveridge of Indiana renewed an old theme when he followed TR to the podium: "The Progressive party," he said, "was the only one in which the voters of both North and South could meet on common ground." With Senator Dixon presiding, the body also approved a plan advocated by Jane Addams to build a permanent organization and to create an educational network for getting the party's message to the public.[2]

No southerner shared the limelight with Roosevelt at Chicago, even though several southern states reported Bull Moose activity following the November election. In Texas, Cecil Lyon set about organizing a committee in every county and seeking to increase membership in Progressive clubs across the state as a prelude to the 1914 state and congressional campaigns. The Progressive party in North Carolina, reported Zeb V. Walser, "received about eighty-five percent of the old Republican vote," and "a thorough state-wide organization" was being built in anticipation of the next campaign. And in Arkansas, J. A. Comer issued a call for the State Committee to meet on December 21 in Little Rock "for the purpose of discussing ways and means of fully organizing this state." The party in Florida set out to create an organization in every voting precinct under the direction of H. L. Anderson, still acting as its shogun. "We aspire," he optimistically stated in the *Progressive Bulletin,* a party organ designed to place all Bull Moose endeavors in a favorable light, "to achieve the first break in the south [by] hard, systematic work." But in Alabama and Georgia, party leaders resolved to wait until after the Chicago confab before proceeding with organizational plans. J. O. Thompson, however, was confident of the party's prospects because there "is hardly a family in Alabama but has one Bull Moose voter and many more our well wishers." The Virginians, still led by Thomas L. Moore, promised to retain the state organization as well as those at city and county levels and to organize "any counties not already organized and to extend same to voting precincts."[3]

The South was fully represented at a meeting of the Progressive National Committee that convened upon adjournment of the conference, although several southern committeemen had turned their seats over to proxies. Only C. W. McClure of Georgia, B. F. Fridge of Mississippi, and G. Tom Taylor of Tennessee were present. The remainder sent substitute representatives. Although most of the meeting dealt with establishing a permanent headquarters in New York with a publicity branch in Washington, the committee took time to resolve a factional struggle in South Carolina. An affidavit was presented from the State Executive Committee certifying that T. H. Wannamaker had been elected national committeeman following the Chicago convention. Yet B. Sherwood Dunn, who had directed the Bull Moose campaign in the state, was present and contended that Wannamaker had been improperly chosen. But Senator Dixon told the committee he had appointed Dunn provisional committeeman "in order to start a Progressive organization in South Carolina." Following debate on the issue, including appointment of a committee of three to hear the conflicting arguments, Wannamaker was recognized, thereby completing the party's organization in the South.[4]

Republicans and Progressives alike in the eleven ex-Confederate states were still licking their wounds following the election. Nor did 1914 hold out much promise for either party; off-year elections in the South were bad enough for Republicans, but with the dissident vote split and the Democrats riding high in the patronage saddle, their voter appeal plunged to new lows. A major problem continued to be failure to field candidates, which further reduced minority party visibility in the region. Five states, Alabama, Arkansas, South Carolina, Tennessee, and Texas, elected governors in 1914, and only in Alabama and Texas did both parties put up a candidate. Neither made a nomination in South Carolina, and in Tennessee the Bull Moosers did not offer anyone against Hooper although he lost his bid for a third term. A. J. Kinney, Republican mayor of Green Forest, Arkansas, ran for governor in his state's September election, even though the Progressives did not nominate a candidate. Thus in five possible gubernatorial contests during 1914, the Progressives ran two candidates and the GOP four.

Because of restrictive clauses in state election laws designed to inhibit Negro voting, the Republicans had ceased to exist legally in Georgia and Louisiana. And in Florida both parties were outlawed for failure to garner a requisite number of votes under the recently enacted Bryan Election Law. Nor did either party put up an appreciable number of candidates in the South's nearly one hundred congressional districts. The GOP had aspirants in thirty-eight districts while the Bull Moosers fielded but twelve in Alabama, Arkansas, Georgia, Louisiana, Tennessee, Texas, and Virginia. In Florida and Mississippi neither put up candidates. Again, Republican and Progressive failure to press the congressional races and to make nominations whenever possible weakened the appeal of both throughout the South. Yet the Republicans reelected Sells, Austin, and Slemp from their Appalachian enclaves in Tennessee and Virginia; the party also returned James J. Britt from a district in the mountains of western North Carolina; and in Louisiana, Whitmell P. Martin won as a Progressive because of disenchantment by the sugar planters with the Democratic tariff of 1913.[5]

The poor southern showing by both parties in 1914 notwithstanding, the Bull Moosers underwent considerable reorganization prior to the off-year elections. John M. Parker, still acting as the party's chief southern strategist, directed much of the retooling activity, especially in Louisiana, where he exploited dissatisfaction with the Underwood Tariff. After traveling through twenty of the state's parishes during the summer of 1913, he informed A. J. Beveridge that Bull Moose sentiment was strong in Louisiana and would continue to intensify "if our Progressive Congressmen and Senators vote according to our platform." Furthermore, "we are not idle in this section of the woods," he told the Indiana statesman, "but those of us who have the welfare of the party at heart, believe deliberate action in securing the best men, of far more importance to our cause throughout the south, than simple organization with a lot of political barnacles and disgruntled politicians." Parker was overjoyed when Charles Buck, a German native but a resident of New Orleans since 1852, affiliated with the Louisiana party; Buck had served a single term in Congress during the 1890s; in addition to being a lifelong Democrat, he was the only thirty-third degree Mason in Louisiana. But men of Buck's standing were apparently not arriving in great numbers because Parker complained to Beveridge about the slowness of his work in late August and insisted that the party structure could be "perfected only if we got the best men in the country with us." Although blacks were not included in his reorganization schemes, the "best man" appeal of Roosevelt and the southern reformers was awakening a degree of noblesse oblige in the region's Bull Moosers. B. F. Fridge, for instance, addressed a Progressive gathering at Newport, Rhode Island, in July 1913, asking for party support to have Congress allot pensions for indigent Negroes. Ironically, he again called for a white man's party in the South, and by late twentieth-century standards his language was blatantly racist, indicating anew that the southern Negro would be required to seek his political solace elsewhere.[6]

In the midst of Parker's drive to upgrade the southern Bull Moose, two important tests of Republican and Progressive strength came when Arkansas and Virginia held gubernatorial elections. In Arkansas a special election was held on July 23, 1913, to elect a successor for Governor Joseph T. Robinson. Although he had been elected to the Governor's Mansion the year before, Robinson was forced to resign following his election by the state legislature to the United States Senate in January, where he remained until his death in 1937. In the summer of 1913 both Republicans and Progressives were faced with choosing a candidate to run against Judge George W. Hays, winner of the special Democratic primary and the next governor. The Bull Moosers, anxious to make a good showing and to test the party's strength, acted first, holding a convention on June 24 in Little Rock. In addition to nominating Colonel George W. Murphy for governor, the more than one hundred delegates representing fifteen counties named Harry M. Trieber to replace Harry K. Cochran as national committeeman. J. A. Comer, who had been in the forefront of the Roosevelt movement in Arkansas from its inception, acted as presiding officer and told the gathering: "The campaign to be waged by the Progressive party in this brief contest . . . is to educate the people of the state in the principles advocated by the national organization." Murphy, a former officer in the Confederate army, vowed to fight an active and vigorous campaign upon accepting the nomination. As a lifelong Democrat "he renounced no principle he ever advocated, would fight against nothing he ever fought for, and would fight for nothing he ever fought against."[7]

Well known as a criminal lawyer throughout Arkansas and the Southwest, Murphy had been elected attorney general of the state in 1900 and 1902 following a distinguished career before the bar. The *Progressive*

Bulletin called him "a first class citizen," commenting that he enjoyed a wide personal following in the state. The Republicans found themselves in a quandary over choosing the right man to oppose Hays and the Bull Moose nominee. The aged Powell Clayton, then living in Washington, had informed H. L. Remmel in May that he was unable to propose a GOP candidate: "I think though that it is very essential at this juncture that you should put out a good ticket, and give it all the assistance you can. Of course your candidate for Governor should be a friend of yourself and myself." But one day before the Republican State Convention on July 1, Remmel told reporters that many Republicans wanted to make no nominations but instead to draft resolutions supporting Murphy. That would not be an endorsement of the Bull Moosers, Remmel continued, but "an endorsement of Colonel Murphy, who we believe is entirely honest in his purpose and a man of unimpeachable integrity, and because in 1904 . . . he supported the Republican candidate for governor, while holding the office of attorney general as a Democrat, saying he had rather vote for a honest Republican than a dishonest Democrat."[8]

Murphy was quickly forgotten by the GOP convention, which tapped Harry H. Myres for the governorship. The forty-six-year-old Myres, an Iowa native and lawyer who had been the party's nominee previously, was superintendent of the government reservation at Hot Springs. He was in Washington at the time of his nomination conferring with Wilson's secretary of interior, Franklin K. Lane, about his Democratic successor and had to telegraph his acceptance to the convention: "There is no personal sacrifice that I would not make for the betterment of the state and her people. Let my friends command me." After that noble rhetoric, the convention heard a speech by Judge John I. Worthington of Boone County, "who said he could not vote for a Bull Moose, Democratic donkey or anything else but an elephant." The gathering adopted a platform lambasting the Democrats for "handing around state offices" and forcing the cost of a special election on the taxpayers. The GOP document ignored the state's Progressive party candidate, choosing to concentrate its fire upon Democratic handling of the state's finances. Yet in a gesture toward Progressivism, the Republicans came out in favor of "the commission form of government for the cities of Arkansas and abolition of the fee system in county offices."[9]

Both Murphy and Myres, as well as the Socialist candidate, Emile Webber, campaigned widely for the election. Although Hays and the Democrats were confident of victory from the outset, Comer, who acted as Murphy's campaign manager, made repeated statements claiming that private polls guaranteed victory for the Bull Moosers. And Murphy, who ended his wide-ranging campaign at Argenta, told a crowd estimated at four hundred in the city park that he was "fighting for the interests of the common people," that Powell Clayton and the Republicans were crooks, and that the Democratic organization was guilty of "hookworm politics." Myres, on the other hand, closed "his whirlwind tour" in Hot Springs, cheerfully predicting that his Republican vote would be the the the highest in the state's history. In the end, however, Murphy came in third behind Hays and Myres, and the GOP remained the second party in Arkansas. The Progressives under Murphy and Comer had exerted Herculean efforts in the special election, even admitting Negroes and women to the June nominating convention in a drive to expand the party's electoral base. But, alas, it was not enough to overcome the Democratic hold on the state; Hays carried every county, receiving a clear plurality over his opponents. The final tally stood: Hays, 41,150; Myres, 11,887; Murphy, 6,747; Webber, 2,910.[10]

In Virginia, the outburst of enthusiasm that had driven the Arkansas Bull Moosers was lacking when the Old Dominion elected a governor the following November. The party under the leadership of Thomas L. Moore did not enter a candidate in the contest, although many representatives from all the districts in the state attended a meeting of the State Committee in Richmond. The Richmond *Virginian* reported that a host of resolutions was adopted authorizing the state chairman to summon "an advisory committee to consider the question of calling a state convention for the purpose of making nominations for state offices and for the legislature in the coming campaign." But no such convention met. Nor did Slemp and the Republicans exert themselves to oppose Henry Carter Stuart, one of the great landowners of southwestern Virginia and winner of the Democratic primary. Stuart, a native of Russell County in Slemp's ninth district, had crossed swords with the Republican chieftain earlier, and Slemp had little inclination to reopen the fray. Three years before, in 1910, Stuart had challenged Slemp in an all-out effort to break GOP domination of the district, when a number of leading politicians had been imported, including Roosevelt, who spoke for Slemp. "It was estimated that each side spent from $100,000 to $250,000—an enormous sum for a single congressional district. . . . When it was all over, Slemp was found to be the winner by 227 votes." In the 1913 gubernatorial canvass only the Socialist and Socialist-Labor parties put up candidates against Stuart, who won by a 60,000-vote margin.[11]

Parker sponsored a giant Progressive rally at New Orleans on November 15—one of several held in various parts of the country—before the 1914 campaigns got under way in earnest. It was part of his plan for strengthening the Bull Moose in the South, and party leaders from throughout the region attended the confab, which was highlighted by an address from Albert J. Beveridge in the city's Athenaeum. Speaking in the "finest meeting place in New Orleans," Beveridge recognized "the abiding hostility to the Republican party in the south before giving a powerful defense" of the Bull Moose stance on the tariff and the Progressive program. His remarks fitted well with Parker's drive to build up the party in the Gulf states and to discredit the region's Republicans.

The GOP National Committee one month later drafted resolutions reducing the number of southern delegates in the next national convention. The long-standing issue had been responsible for vociferous denunciations of the GOP by Roosevelt and his followers during the 1912 campaign. But by 1916 when the ruling took effect sharply curtailing representation from the southern "rotten boroughs," the Bull Moose bolt was already spent, not only in the South but nationally. Yet the Progressive cry for reform had wrought a long-needed reform in national politics.[12]

In 1914, however, Tennessee opened the campaign in the South when its GOP State Convention met on April 15 to nominate Hooper for a third term. Republican conventions were also held in Alabama, Arkansas, North Carolina, and Texas before the year was out, and the Progressives held parleys in several other southern states. The Nashville meeting nominated a recalcitrant Hooper, who did not want to run again because of ill health and the knowledge that no Tennessee governor had been elected to a third term since the Civil War; yet, when it became certain that Independent Democrats would again support him, the governor bowed to party demands and prepared to wage his usual tough campaign. He was handed a party platform that endorsed a prohibition amendment to the U.S. Constitution and put Tennessee Republicans on record as favoring the National Committee's scheme for reapportioning southern delegates in the forthcoming national convention. Hooper's Democratic opponent, Thomas C. Rye, a lawyer and district attorney, was nominated on May 28 by the party's state convention on a platform "against the repeal of the prohibition laws now in force and pledging the party to enact any additional legislation necessary to secure their rigid enforcement." Although Rye and the Democrats looked to Wilson for aid in ousting Hooper, the governor personally felt "it would help the campaign if Washington would send in outsiders to attempt to control Tennessee politics." But prohibition continued to be the major issue in the state, and though the anti-Prohibition or Independent Democrats nominated Hooper at their convention on April 22, the moderate liquor stance of the regulars and the pull of party regularity cut deeply into any support Hooper might expect from dissatisfied Democrats. The Independents also nominated Judge S. C. Williams for the state supreme court, but, reported the Memphis *Commercial Appeal*, "the crowd was not large enough to make the necessary show in the Ryman Auditorium and the House of Representatives was used for the state convention."[13]

Hooper's defeat in November notwithstanding, he supported Williams, who won his election to the state's high court on August 10 with combined Independent Democrat-Republican backing. Some east Tennessee stalwarts, however, objected to the party's support of Williams, and all of

Hooper's diplomatic efforts were needed to bring about Republican harmony. Thus, when J. S. Beasley, GOP state chairman, convened the State Executive Committee in Nashville on June 23 to chart the campaign, Hooper, who continued to ignore the Bull Moosers, pleaded "that all resources must be centered upon the judicial fight in August and predicted that east Tennessee would roll up a tremendous majority for Williams." Beasley also opted for the judge, telling a Nashville audience two weeks before the election that "a vote for Sam C. Williams is a vote to sustain the administration of Governor Hooper." The state chairman, a Nashville lawyer and former GOP congressional candidate, had managed the 1910 and 1912 campaigns for Hooper as well as remaining chief of the party until 1916. Williams, on the other hand, who had been appointed to the Tennessee Supreme Court by Hooper in January 1913, was a Vanderbilt graduate and lifelong Democrat. He went on to a distinguished career before his death in 1947, serving as dean of the Emory University Law School and writing several books, including the widely heralded, *The History of the Lost State of Franklin,* "a comprehensive study of a phase of frontier history that had received scant attention from historians."[14]

In contrast to the GOP momentum in Tennessee, Progressive and Republican activity was practically nonexistent in Mississippi. There was no gubernatorial contest in 1914, and the iron grip of the Democrats enticed no minority party other than the Socialists to offer congressional candidates. Although several constitutional amendments were on the ballot, the absence of appreciable politicking was due in large part to GOP and Bull Moose failure to run candidates for the limited number of offices available. Yet Fridge, who appeared to be the state's only Progressive spokesman, managed to keep the new party organization intact after 1912. In May 1913, he had summoned a specially appointed committee into session long enough to draft a statement upon the death of Dr. J. C. French of Natchez, who had been Bull Moose state chairman. But when invited to address a Progressive conference at New Orleans in June 1914, he was less than optimistic about the party's chances: "He said there was nothing but Bilbo in Mississippi, and admitted that the Progressive party had little hope of winning any important office this fall." Nor did L. B. Moseley and the Republicans make any ripples during the year, which prompted the New Orleans *Picayune* to report after the November election: "The only opposition met with by the democrats in Mississippi came from the socialists, but the total vote polled by the opposition was negligible. Interest in many districts was at a low ebb, and it was thought not more than one-third the full vote was polled."[15]

Conditions were similar in Florida, where there was also no gubernatorial contest, even though Senator Duncan U. Fletcher was running for reelection without opposition. And, as in Mississippi, only the Socialists put up congressional candidates. "The election," editorialized the Jacksonville *Times-Union,* "has attracted less attention than any we have ever known. In the first place there is no opposition except from the Socialists. The Republican party in Florida seems to have gone out of business. Then the prolonged session of Congress made it impossible for them to come home and campaign." Besides the usual Democratic majorities, a prime concern for Republicans and Bull Moosers alike was the recently enacted Bryan Election Law. Passed by the legislature in 1913, the law, drafted by United States Senator Nathan P. Bryan, took supervision of all primaries from control of party executive committees and placed them directly under state control. Furthermore, the statute closely regulated the registration process that allowed state and county officials the power to levy fees for primary candidates.[16]

This first step toward legalization of the Democratic white primary and its restrictive features caused all minority parties in the state to demand its repeal or modification. The Negro Republican leader, Joseph E. Lee, spoke out in March 1914, demanding changes in the law because it gave the Democrats a monopoly over the state's election process. And H. L. Anderson, Progressive national committeeman, filed legal proceedings to block Secretary of State H. Clay Crawford from implementing its provisions. He was joined in the fight by the Florida Socialists, although all efforts proved unsuccessful. Upon his return from Chicago in October, Anderson told reporters in Jacksonville that the Progressives in Florida did not "expect to begin aggressive plans for the future." And, he continued, the struggle over the Bryan Law "and other arrangements his party had not made, would mean no active work soon."[17]

Anderson's decision not to pursue an active campaign in 1914 was undoubtedly influenced by Bull Moose failure to attract members. After asking an editorial question, "What happened to the vanishing Bull Moose herd," a Democratic paper summarized voter registration totals in Duval, Orange, and Osceola counties. The Progressives had attracted only sixty-two registrants—fewer than either Independents or Socialists—in all three counties, while Democrats numbered 11,873 and Republicans 3,955. "Democratic registration," the Jacksonville paper continued, "amounts to nearly one third of the vote cast for Wilson in the entire state. The republican registration is rather more than two-thirds of Taft's vote in all Florida, while the Bull Moose registration is only about one seventieth of Roosevelt's vote."[18]

The Tennessee Bull Moosers, also having difficulty attracting converts, held a state "conference" on June 9 to decide upon a candidate to oppose Hooper and Rye. Meeting in Nashville, the group failed to pick a nominee, but adopted a resolution: "That the nomination of a full state ticket depends upon whether Theodore Roosevelt enters the race for governor of New York." Roosevelt, however, recently returned from his bone-wracking trip through the Brazilian jungle, announced on June 8 that he

would not run for office in 1914. Yet, Harry B. Anderson, state chairman
and reportedly desirous of the Progressive gubernatorial nomination in
1916, went ahead with plans for a state nominating convention to be held in
September. Hooper, worried over "the sulking attitude of the Bull Moose
contingent," developed a series of meetings around the state seeking
accommodation. His efforts were obviously successful when Frank L.
Snedeker, secretary of the Shelby County Hooper Club, wrote on August
27: "We are definately [sic] informed by Hon. H. B. Anderson that the
Bull Moose party will not have a candidate in the field. It is generally
understood that this action means an endorsement of your candidacy."
The change in plans forced Anderson to cancel the already planned
Progressive convention as Hooper made ready to concentrate upon his
ill-faced campaign against Rye.[19]

The Bull Moose leadership in Arkansas followed suit on June 17 when a
meeting of the State Executive Committee decided not to offer a candidate
against Governor Hays. Colonel George W. Murphy, who had gone down
to defeat in the 1913 race for governor, made a powerful address during the
deliberations at Little Rock "extolling the virtues of the party and asserting
that the party strength in Arkansas had increased since the last election."
He also demanded a change in the state's election statutes that would
afford the Progressives a degree of representation at the polls. Although
the Arkansas GOP was waging a vigorous campaign for the September
election and had already scheduled a state convention, the Bull Moose
gathering contented itself with a resolution by Sid B. Redding directing the
committee "to issue a call for a state convention should they later deem it
necessary." Redding, who had been in the forefront of the Roosevelt
movement since early 1912, was clerk of the U.S. District Court at Little
Rock; born in Kentucky and educated in Missouri and New Mexico, where
his grandfather had been appointed attorney general by Hayes, he had
been a member of the GOP State Committee from 1898 until the schism of
1912. Long identified with the party in Arkansas, he was appointed clerk in
1901 by Judge Trieber.[20]

Roosevelt's refusal to run for governor of New York in 1914 notwithstanding, the Arkansas Bull Moosers followed the lead of their brothers in
Tennessee and resolved not to call a state convention until TR's intentions
became fully known. Yet they rejected "amalgamation," as the term
became known, an issue that developed into a controversy among Republicans and Progressives after 1912 both nationally and in the South. Sooner
or later, the argument ran, the warring factions of the GOP would be
forced to "amalgamate" or join forces if Wilson and the Democrats were
to be defeated. And a form of coalition did come in 1916, when Roosevelt
decided to throw his support behind Charles Evans Hughes and the
Republican platform. But in 1914, many party leaders at the state level
went along with the national policy that Progressives "avoid entangling

alliances" with other groups and Republicans in particular, who sought to lure them back into the fold. Accordingly, the Progressive meeting at Little Rock, reported the *Arkansas Gazette,* "was strong in its denunciations of the republican party and declared there can never be any alliance with that party." Although not strong enough to offer a candidate for governor, the committee held the door ajar that a prominent man "not now openly affiliated with the party" would be nominated later for the United States Senate. That nomination, however, did not materialize as the party continued its downward slide; and in November the Progressives ran but one candidate for Congress in the third district composed of ten counties in extreme northwestern Arkansas.[21]

The Louisiana Bull Moosers, however, were a beehive of activity as the State Committee, now chaired by Parker, met in New Orleans on June 18 to chart the fall campaign. They, too, were concerned lest Roosevelt's projected fusion with Republicans in New York might interfere with organizing efforts in the state. Understandably, a sigh of relief went up when Roosevelt announced he would campaign for Frederick M. Davenport, the Progressive nominee for governor in the Empire State, thereby giving up his vendetta with Boss William Barnes and his alleged connections with Tammany Hall. The fear of being forced into agreements with the GOP that would thwart efforts to build a white man's party in the South thus eliminated, Parker told the gathering: "The fight in Louisiana would be waged on the principle that the present administration's foreign policy was not decisive and that the tariff has worked a hardship on Louisiana." But Wilson's vacillating stance on the convulsions in Mexico was nothing compared to his signing the Underwood Tariff into law during Christmas of the preceding year. Tariff reform had been a bulwark of the 1912 Democratic campaign, and the "competitive tariff" enacted meant the removal of protection from trusts, which hit the Louisiana sugar interests squarely in the pocketbook. Although several southern groups, including sugar producers, Texas sheep raisers, and some southeastern textile manufacturers, fought the measure in Congress, its provision placing sugar on the free list spelled disaster for several southern Louisiana counties. The Parker-Wight drive to attract large numbers of Democrats was helped further when the Louisiana GOP was officially outlawed because of its failure to poll 10 percent of the vote in 1912.[22]

"Every mention of Col. Roosevelt's name was greeted with deafening applause," the *Picayune* reported, as a procession of speakers addressed the June 18 meeting in the New Orleans Hippodrome. Nor did the Negro issue go untouched as Harry N. Pharr, a former GOP candidate for governor, told the assembly: "If New York and Maine and other states wish to have Negroes in their councils it is within their rights as defined by the platform of the progressive party, but in Louisiana and the south the progressive party is strictly a white man's party." Discussion of the new tariff, however, motivated the sizable numbers of Democrats present to wild applause. "A man named Wilson," Pharr continued, "was responsible for the enactment by Congress of a tariff bill that practically wrecked Louisiana and came near disrupting the democratic party." The assembly roared approval.

Democrats, not only in Louisiana but throughout the country, became alarmed at the burgeoning strength of the party. "The trouble with the Progressive party in Louisiana," editorialized the Charleston (S.C.) *News and Courier,* "is that it was born under suspicious and not very inspiring circumstances. It was not born of the yearning for more righteous living, for general uplift and for social justice which is supposed to be true blue Progressive." In addition, "the spirit which has caused them to get out of the Democratic party will soon cause them to get back into it again. The shift will come as soon as they perceive that the local interests which they have placed above party principles have nothing to gain from progressivism." The Louisiana Democratic State Executive Committee met on July 7 to help that process along by drafting a set of resolutions reading all Democrats out of the party "who were making sweet eyes at the progressives."[23]

"The fight has gotten so bitter here in Louisiana," Parker wrote as the campaign progressed, "that the combined opposition of State, National, and local politicians" made it impossible for him to accept speaking engagements outside the state. But, he thought, the party had an excellent chance to win the third district congressional fight and possibly to elect one other congressman. Much of the hassling stemmed from efforts by northern Louisiana Democrats in the legislature to secure passage of Bull Moose exclusion bills designed to keep Progressives from voting in subsequent Democratic primaries. "Their scheme would have been fine if it had worked," said the *Picayune,* but they failed on a close vote, "and as a result the Bull Moosers can do just as much Progressive voting as they like this fall and still vote in the Democratic primary in 1916." Parker remained in close touch with Roosevelt from the moment of his return from South America, and in early July he visited Sagamore Hill bringing encouraging reports on the outlook in Louisiana. Although TR thought the gains in Louisiana would be useless without success in other sections of the country, he announced on July 5, to the joy of Parker and his associates, that he would tour southern Louisiana on behalf of Progressive candidates during the fall.[24]

In Virginia, where there was no gubernatorial contest in 1914, neither Republicans nor Progressives put up much of a fight in the congressional races except in Slemp's ninth district. Since the inauguration of Wilson, both U.S. Senators, Claude A. Swanson and Thomas S. Martin, as well as Governor Stuart, had bombarded Postmaster General Burleson to appoint Democratic postmasters in the district when vacancies occurred. The undermining of Slemp's congressional courtesy was part of a renewed assault by Democrats to capture his seat and return the state to solid party control. But he was nominated for another term on July 9, when an enthusiastic convention met at Bristol. The veteran congressman met opposition from Bull Moosers in the district who nominated J. L. Rose in a rump convention to run for Congress. Yet most Progressives in the ninth joined with Republican stalwarts to endorse Slemp's selection. Statewide the Republicans ran candidates in five of ten congressional districts; only Rose, whose vote was insignificant, carried the Progressive standard. The GOP managed to return several members to the state legislature in addition to reelecting Slemp.[25]

No doubt other Progressives would have run except for Roosevelt's adamant stand against amalgamation: "There is no use to attempt a coalition with Republicans in Virginia, or anywhere else," he informed Percy S. Stephenson, a Norfolk lawyer and leading Bull Mooser, "as long as the party is under its present leadership. . . . Let me suggest that you advise them to endorse Progressives instead of Progressives to endorse them." A Southampton County native and graduate of William and Mary, Stephenson had been prominent in the Virginia GOP since 1906 when appointed U.S. commissioner at Norfolk. He was reappointed to 13 consecutive terms, and when he died in 1953 he was the oldest commissioner in the country. At the same time Stephenson was undecided about mounting a Progressive campaign, most Virginia politicians, including Slemp, were watching a September 22 special referendum on prohibition. Always an adroit politician, Slemp declared his support for the measure at an early date, and it carried by an overwhelming plurality. The Democratic leadership, which ignored the lone Progressive candidate, was greatly disappointed at Slemp's reelection in November. A vigorous effort had been made to restore the district and some of the "strongest campaigners in the State," reported a Richmond newspaper, "including Gov. H. C. Stuart, Attorney General Garland Pollard and Congressman Carter Glass . . . did yeoman service on the stump to stem the tide of republican votes." Yet he managed to hold his seat by a 699-vote margin over Rose and R. Tate Irvine, his Democratic challenger.[26]

In South Carolina, both Republicans and Bull Moosers were less visible than in Florida and Virginia. The state elected a governor, the archdemagogue Coleman L. Blease, but only the Socialists offered a state ticket, and the scholar must probe in vain for the scantiest newspaper mention of other parties. Aaron Prioleau, a Negro and former officeholder from Charleston, who fought black endorsement of Roosevelt in 1912, ran for Congress in the first district; and two additional Republicans contested the state's seven congressional seats. The Bull Moosers under their new national committeeman, T. H. Wannamaker, were totally inactive during 1914. Yet several party leaders gathered at the railroad station in Spartanburg on September 9 to greet Roosevelt, who stopped for a few minutes to shake hands on his return from campaigning in southern Louisiana. He was seemingly uninterested in the South Carolina Progressives and could offer them no encouragement: "To one of those who remarked that he hoped to vote for Roosevelt in 1916," commented the Charleston *News and Courier,* "the Colonel said that he preferred not to be a candidate and did not know that he would be." The same newspaper reported that "a very light vote was polled in the general election" as the Democrats swept every office in the state with mammoth majorities.[27]

Republicans in Alabama and Arkansas held conventions during mid-July to map out the fall campaign. A long-smoldering fight between lily-whites and Negroes for control of the Arkansas GOP was temporarily patched up at a state convention on July 14 in Little Rock. The troubles stemmed in part from H. L. Remmel's announcement in June that he might step down as state chairman. Long associated with the aging Powell Clayton and the Negroes, Remmel was immediately opposed by Harry H. Myres, the GOP standard-bearer in the 1913 special election, who was now firmly identified with the lily-whites. Matters came to a head at a meeting of the State Committee one day before the convention when a group of Pulaski County Negroes challenged the credentials of several white delegates. J. E. Bush, a Negro, former receiver of public monies at Little Rock, and prominent businessman, pressed the black-and-tan claims and informed the convention that the Negroes would organize a rump convention if denied justice. Yet the committee refused to act, referring the contest to the convention proper, even though Remmel sided with the Negroes because the county convention had been held in Little Rock's Marion Hotel which denied them admission; Myres, however, defended the lily-white position in a strongly worded statement. Party harmony was further threatened by a three-way fight for the gubernatorial nomination: A. C. Curtis of Lonoke, supported by Remmel; Andrew Kinney, Republican mayor of Green Forest, who had the backing of Myres; and R. I. Floyd, a young attorney newly arrived in Little Rock, who had been active in Republican politics.[28]

The convention "made the Negroes of Pulaski County understand that a 'lily white' party . . . is perfectly acceptable to the Republicans of Arkansas" before nominating Kinney. The nomination came after Myres made a speech in support of the nominee "in which he scolded blind servility to leadership"; he "was roundly cheered during his talk and was later nominated for the U. S. Senate by acclamation." But the Myres-lily-white sweep was not complete as "Remmel exhibited his old time strength" by being renamed state chairman. Following an outward show of harmony, the contesting groups adopted a platform supporting a woman's suffrage amendment to the federal Constitution.

As both candidates prepared to launch a vigorous speaking campaign, the *Arkansas Gazette* noted: "The biennial educational canvass conducted by Arkansas Republicans just preceding each state general election in hopes of attracting a vote or two has started." The absence of Bull Moose opposition notwithstanding, neither Kinney nor Myres did well, though both spoke widely. The Republicans did not carry a single county as Hays won by a 55,000-vote margin over Kinney and Daniel Hogan, the Socialist candidate, in the September 14 gubernatorial contest. Later, Myres, the perennial Republican candidate, was beaten handily by Senator James P. Clarke for a second term in the November election. The drive to make the Arkansas GOP a white man's organization had not attracted new voters because the Democrats were in such control, commented the *Gazette,* "that in many precincts no election was held and in practically all precincts where held a very light vote was polled."[29]

The Alabama Republicans named a full state ticket headed by O. D. Street for governor on July 22 in Birmingham. Like the party in Arkansas, the GOP leadership pursued a strict lily-white policy, and this was its first state convention without a Negro delegate. Although J. O. Diffay and other Negro leaders threatened to form a rival party, a bolt did not occur at the convention when the State Committee eliminated the Negro by not allowing counties that cast less than 100 votes for Taft or Roosevelt to send delegates. Diffay, a wealthy real estate broker, and Dr. Ulysses G. Mason, a Negro physician and a graduate of Edinburgh University in Scotland, led an abortive move to have Alabama Negroes "take some action to retain their political activity." But the Republican conclave, which also nominated Alex C. Birch of Birmingham to oppose Oscar W. Underwood for the Senate, rejected all Negro participation in 1914. The *Colored Alabamian* blamed Alabama Negroes themselves for their exclusion from the convention because they had bowed to pressure and chose white delegates instead of blacks in the district gatherings. Several GOP chieftains—including P. D. Barker, O. D. Street, T. H. Aldrich, and Pope M. Long—refused to discuss the matter with reporters as the party adopted a platform that "urged rigid enforcement of all laws on the liquor question, but did not mention woman's suffrage which had been interjected into state politics."[30]

If the GOP was back in business as usual, the Alabama Bull Moosers were anything but tranquil when their convention met two weeks later in Birmingham. "After drifting under a clear sky and with all aboard in a joyful frame of mind, the Progressive bark," said the Birmingham *Age-Herald,* "ran on a rock, Prohibition and divided in halves." The row started when Judge Hundley doubted the wisdom of making "it a Progressive football" when a move was instituted to strike a prohibition plank from the platform. Thompson, however, delivered a "hot response" in favor of a party position on the issue, and though Hundley reminded the convention "that Mr. Roosevelt, himself, had declared against Prohibition," the plank remained by a narrow two-vote margin. A provision was also inserted favoring woman's suffrage at the insistence of Judge Hundley, whose wife was state leader of the suffragettes. Amid the denunciations of both Democrats and Republicans, the convention presided over by Milford W. Howard, a former Populist congressman, nominated a full state ticket headed by Dr. E. H. Cross for governor and A. P. Longshore for the Senate seat held by Oscar W. Underwood.[31]

As the party was laying plans for a rejuvenated Bull Moose in Alabama, Street resigned as Republican nominee for governor; the former U.S. attorney notified the GOP State Committee that business reasons prevented him from staying on the ticket and asked to be withdrawn. He was replaced by James B. Shields, probate judge of Walker County and onetime postmaster at Jasper, at a meeting of the committee on August 27. Shields completely overshadowed Cross and the Progressives by a vote of 13,695 to 3,795 in the contest with Charles Henderson, the Democrat chosen to succeed Governor Emmet O'Neal, by a whopping 64,275 votes in the November election. The fifty-three-year-old Cross, who had not been active in Progressive or GOP politics, was a native of Marysville, Ohio, and first settled at Gadsden in 1886 after traveling all over the Southeast by horse and buggy as a drug salesman. Apart from his brief political career, he operated a drugstore at Gadsden until his death in 1952. His running mate for the Senate, Longshore, did some better, receiving 4,263 votes; Longshore was a lifelong Republican and a lawyer at Columbiana except for the Bull Moose interlude. He had also served in the Alabama legislature and as probate judge of Shelby County.[32]

Failure to reach an agreement on amalgamation or at least a joint appeal to the voters in 1914 cost both Republican and Progressive candidates in Alabama. Yet individual candidates in both parties received roughly the same vote, which indicated a certain voter loyalty. Cross and Longshore had a mere 468-vote spread in the statewide tally, while Birch, the GOP senatorial candidate, got but 1,375 fewer votes than Judge Shields. Like Longshore, Birch was a Republican stalwart who remained active in party councils until the 1930s; he was a graduate of the University of Alabama and the Washington and Lee Law School and served as U.S. commissioner and federal attorney. Furthermore, the Republicans ran six candidates and the Progressives two in the state's nine congressional contests. In the seventh district, where "as is generally known, there is little difference in strength between the democratic and anti-democratic vote" a tight race developed. The district, composed of eight counties stretching across north central Alabama, had been represented by John L. Burnett since 1899 when he took over from the Populist, Milford W. Howard. A tremendous effort was made to amalgamate, contrary to the stated position of both state organizations, although the plan fell apart when the Progressive candidate refused to withdraw in favor of the Republican. In a close race, Burnett won reelection by a 1,500-vote margin, but, reported the *Age-Herald* further: "It is generally agreed that had the anti-democratic forces fused . . . Mr. Burnett would have been in danger."[33]

Efforts at amalgamation also collapsed in Texas when both parties held nominating conventions on August 11. Meeting on the same day because of the state's election statutes, each convention asked the other to support its nominees in an exchange of public telegrams: "While the light holds out to burn," Cecil Lyon taunted the GOP "the vilest sinner may return, Come, Sinner, Come." The Republicans retaliated similarly: "Come humble sinner, in whose breast a thousand thoughts resolve, Come, with your sins and guilt oppressed and make this resolve, the door is open." The refusal to merge notwithstanding, the GOP gathering at Fort Worth drafted a platform that advocated a popular referendum on prohibition as well as adoption of the initiative, referendum, and recall. The party also wanted to limit public officials in Texas to one term of four years and passed a resolution lamenting the death of Mrs. Woodrow Wilson before naming a state ticket headed by John W. Philp. Prior to 1914, Philp had been active in the party and a prominent Dallas businessman; a graduate of Southwestern University and the University of Tennessee, he was appointed postmaster at Dallas by Harding, and after 1929 he joined the Hoover administration as an assistant postmaster general. In addition, the Republicans named local tickets in several counties and made nominations for twelve of the state's seventeen congressional seats.

In the meantime, Lyon whipped the Bull Moosers into line at their convention in Waco, although a dissident faction offered a challenge to his hold on the party. The bosom friend of Roosevelt had retained the dual posts of national committeeman and state chairman since 1912, which caused the Bexar County organization to start a move to bar Lyon from keeping both jobs. His grip on the party was unassailable, however, and the move not only failed but the convention passed a resolution praising his handling of its affairs. The Bull Moosers likewise adopted a lengthy platform that sidestepped the divisive liquor issue. The Democrats were blasted for "placing raw materials, which are the source of wealth in this State on the free list, while retaining a tariff without corresponding reductions on the manufactured product." Sheep ranchers in central Texas, like the Louisiana sugar planters, were up in arms over the tariff, and this denunciation of the tariff no doubt contributed to the election of William Bierschwale of Fredericksburg to the legislature in November as its only non-Democratic member. That the party would remain a white organization was restated: "The Progressive party in Texas shall be officered, controlled, and governed by white voters exclusively and [we] denounce the insincerity of the Democrats in inviting negroes into their recent primaries." After declaring Roosevelt "America's greatest and grandest representative," the convention named F. M. Etheridge of Dallas to oppose Philp and James E. Ferguson, winner of the Democratic primary. Etheridge, another Dallas businessman, had been an unsuccessful candidate for congressman-at-large in 1912.[34]

Nowhere in the South was the Progressive party's poverty more evident than in Texas. Etheridge had been out of the country at the time of the convention and was unaware of his nomination: "Imperative and monopolizing professional engagements as well as extraordinary conditions with which we are confronted have prevented me from presenting my candidacy to you as otherwise I would have done," he announced on election eve. And in the general election his miserable 1,794 votes raised the question if Texas in fact had a Bull Moose party. Nor did Philp, who received 11,411 votes, and the Republicans do much better, although he conducted a wide-ranging speaking tour. Moreover, E. O. Meitzen, the Socialist nominee, got 25,000 votes—more than Philp and Etheridge combined—to come in second behind the Democrats. More important, Ferguson, the Temple banker and businessman who with his wife Miriam would dominate Texas politics for more than a decade, received a whopping 230,000 votes. The Republican-Progressive vote together amounted to only 5 percent of the total cast. Not even the Dallas *Morning News* could explain the poor showing except to remark: "As usual all Democratic candidates for state office, congress, and legislature were elected, the sole exception being William Bierschwale. . . . The democratic ticket has received a somewhat larger proportion of the votes than in 1912. The socialists about the same proportion and the republican and progressive parties have scored losses."[35]

Two weeks after the Texas conventions, the North Carolina Bull Moosers met to make a nomination for the U.S. Senate seat held by Lee S. Overman. Because the next gubernatorial election was in 1916, the August 18 "Conference of the Progressive or Roosevelt Republicans," reported the Raleigh *News and Observer*, met amid a "frosty" atmosphere. Zeb V. Walser, Progressive state chairman, had previously rejected an overture from Duncan and Morehead for a fusion agreement with the GOP. The State Committee, he proclaimed, "all with one accord oppose anything like organic union or amalgamation. They believe the State should be more united for Col. Roosevelt than it was in 1912. They think the vote for the Republican ticket in 1912 represented mainly a desire for regularity and the liquor influence, and that the vote is now practically solid for Progressive principles." With only forty-eight delegates present, the Bull Moose meeting in Greensboro selected Charles H. Cowles, the former GOP congressman, as its nominee for the Senate.

His selection was attacked by Martin Douglas, a candidate for Congress in the fifth district. Douglas, a twenty-six-year-old lawyer from Greensboro, objected to Cowles because he could not get the onetime congressman "to say straight out that he was a Progressive"; moreover, Douglas, who withdrew from the Bull Moose contest, "was a son of the late Justice R. M. Douglas, a brother of postmaster R. D. Douglas, and a grandson of Stephen A. Douglas, the 'Little Giant' of Illinois and famous opponent of Lincoln." His objections notwithstanding, Cowles was endorsed enthusiastically after "the oratory of Chairman Walser pulsated the air." Instead of drafting a formal platform, the Progressives adopted three resolutions: "one hurrahing for protection of the old time republican stripe," another calling for all state primaries to be held on the same day, and "a general boost for Roosevelt." The Republican convention that met two days later on August 20 in Raleigh refused to nominate anyone for the Senate and did everything possible to lure Bull Moosers back to the Republican standard. About two hundred delegates attended the conclave which reportedly transacted its proceedings "in an orderly business-like manner." Morehead and Duncan had not only sought a rapprochement with the Bull Moosers but they also played down the North Carolina organization's closeness to Taft in 1912. Although the stormy Charlotte convention two years earlier was composed of "revenue officers, postmasters, and other federal officeholders by grace of Taft," matters were much different in 1914; now, remarked the *News and Observer,* "a tameness prevails over the GOP that is pitiful to behold. There are no offices to squabble over and no pie to distribute."[36]

That assessment proved correct as the Republicans did everything possible to get the Progressives back into the party. No speaker mentioned Roosevelt or Taft by name, and Elihu Root was the only nationally prominent Republican praised in the assembly. Frank Linney, elected state chairman to replace Morehead, engineered the peace moves, and at his insistence no senatorial nomination was made. Instead, a committee was formed to make a nomination later in the campaign if it thought feasible to do so as a means of reducing friction with the Bull Moosers over the Cowles candidacy. Linney, who became the GOP candidate for governor two years later, was a well-known lawyer and solicitor of the seventeenth judicial district since 1908; later he was appointed U.S. attorney for North Carolina by Harding, a post he continued under Coolidge. He was an organizer of the white Republican party in the state and state chairman until 1920. Also assisting him in the 1914 drive to divorce the party from its Taft moorings was Gilliam Grissom, who was named secretary of the State Executive Committee. Grissom, subsequently appointed internal revenue collector by Harding, ran for governor in 1936 against Clyde R. Hoey, when, though defeated, he made the best showing of any previous Republican gubernatorial candidate in the state, receiving over 140,000 votes to Hoey's 332,000.[37]

The Progressive decision to go it alone in North Carolina resulted not only in a humiliating defeat for Cowles but also in failure to elect candidates to the state legislature. That was a bitter pill to swallow in a state that regularly returned a sizable minority delegation to both houses. The Republicans, moreover, showed increased strength in 1914, actually raising their legislative delegation by three members although they were still grossly outnumbered by the Democrats. In addition, the GOP was heartened by James J. Britt's defeat of veteran Congressman James M. Gudger in the tenth district. Even though Governor Craig expressed regret at Gudger's defeat, he said it was no great surprise. Britt won, commented the *News and Observer,* because hundreds of Democrats stayed away from the polls "and have only themselves to blame for the loss of the district." The tenth lay in the mountains of western North Carolina, where formidable GOP strength was traditional, and as late as 1909–1911 it had been represented by a Republican, John G. Grant, in the Sixty-first Congress. Britt was able to recapture it in 1914 by making the most of a local depression in the lumber industry and by blaming Wilson and the Democrats for the war in Europe.[38]

After much delay, the Bull Moosers in Georgia held a convention on October 3 to make last-minute nominations for the U.S. Senate. Because of the death of Augustus O. Bacon in February 1914 and the expiration of Hoke Smith's first term, both Senate seats were up for grabs in November, although no state offices were at stake. As early as March 27, the Progressive Executive Committee had met to consider nominations but could not reach agreement on who the candidates should be. The state's Republican leadership remained silent throughout 1914 and offered no candidate for either seat; most of the GOP officeholders appointed by Taft had been turned from office by Wilson, which further reduced the party's clout among Georgia Negroes. Even Henry L. Johnson, the black leader and recorder of deeds in Washington, was removed in June 1914, after heavy pressure had been exerted by Hoke Smith. Johnson quietly resumed his law practice in Atlanta, became active in the national Negro Odd Fellows movement, and like other Republicans did not take part in the off-year elections.[39]

If the Republicans were quiescent in 1914, the state's Progressives were stirred to action following the August 19 Democratic primary. The nomination of Hoke Smith for the regular term and Congressman Thomas W. Hardwick for the remainder of Bacon's term caused the Bull Moosers to summon the October convention. The gathering at Rome, with about thirty members present, nominated C. W. McClure to oppose Smith for the long term and Rufus G. Hutchens to oppose Hardwick for the short term. Hutchens, a Rome lawyer, had been defeated in the Democratic primary when he ran against Hardwick, and his affiliation with the Bull Moosers came after consultation with McClure and other party leaders. Harry G. Hastings, an Ohio native and president of H. G. Hastings Company, a leading seed and nursery business, was confirmed to replace McClure as national committeeman. The platform adopted declared for the preservation of white supremacy, which made it easier for Hutchens and other Democrats to vote with the Progressives. Furthermore, the document favored free textbooks for schoolchildren, prohibition, and a measure giving farmers "reasonable advances at moderate rates of interest"; and it took the Democrats to task for failure "to provide an efficient system of rural credits distinct from the national and regional bank system."[40]

McClure and Hutchens took the Bull Moose platform with its appeal to the state's farmers in reminiscently Populist rhetoric on a wide-ranging speaking tour before November. In fact, Hardwick accused Hutchens of being in league with Tom Watson and said that he was spending large sums to buy votes. After 1910, all Georgia politics had been enlivened by Watson's virulent attacks on many of the state's Democrats, including Hardwick; the old Populist did not hesitate to use the pages of his *Watson's Jeffersonian Magazine* to heap abuse upon him along with Hoke Smith and especially "Professor Woodpile Wilson." The late but energetic entrance of the two Progressives into the 1914 contest caused the Atlanta *Constitution* to remark that the off-year campaign "has been a trifle more vigorous than usual." Yet they ran without the support of Roosevelt, who declined to be quoted on any current topic when he stopped briefly in Atlanta while on his way to speak in Louisiana. Later, however, after the Progressives had compiled a respectable vote, the colonel was moved to write McClure: "That's really an extraordinary showing! . . . I only wish the other states of the country had done relatively as well as Georgia and Louisiana." His change of heart came when twenty-six Georgia counties reported Progressive victories; McClure got 28,420 votes to 61,107 for Hoke Smith and Hutchens 28,163 to Hardwick's 61,876. Clearly, Hutchens's switch to the Bull Moose standard following the Democratic primary and a strong campaign by both candidates had enabled the party to consolidate much of the state's dissident vote.[41]

But it was Roosevelt's decision to campaign personally for Progressive candidates in the Louisiana sugar belt and Hooper's struggle for reelection in Tennessee that highlighted the Republican-Progressive campaign in the South. Although John M. Parker had received a commitment from Roosevelt shortly after his return from South America, his arrival in Louisiana coincided with the third district convention at New Iberia that selected W. P. Martin as its Bull Moose candidate for Congress. The district, composed of eight parishes along the Mississippi River and Gulf Coast, had received the individual attention of Parker as well as national Progressive leaders for more than a year. Here, where Democratic disenchantment with the Underwood Tariff was strongest, the Progressives had scented victory since 1912 which brought forth several would-be candidates. A three-cornered fight for the nomination developed between Edwin S. Broussard, a Democratic prosecuting attorney at New Iberia and after 1920 a United States senator, Wilson T. Peterman, the Democratic sheriff of St. Mary's Parish, and Martin, scion of a wealthy plantation family and judge of the fourteenth judicial district. Moreover, it took

Martin, a lawyer and graduate of the University of Virginia who remained in Congress until his death in 1929, 116 ballots and twelve grueling hours to win in the deadlocked convention. The September 6 gathering also made nominations for local offices before adjourning to await the arrival of Roosevelt one day later.

Amid the glare of newspaper publicity, Roosevelt spoke first in the French Opera House at New Orleans. Every seat was filled, said the *Times-Picayune,* "and the police had some difficulty with the crowds" as he smote the Democrats for selling out the sugar planters. Their position on the tariff was pronounced "backward and reactionary" as "he declared for a tariff for revenue only; another part pledged that no American industry would be injured." Then, after castigating Wilson for his proposed $25,000,000 settlement to Colombia for U.S. acquisition of the Panama Canal, Roosevelt left for the third district in the company of Martin and Parker. Louisiana Republicans remained sullenly unresponsive as the colonel rode a horse over part of his tour while speaking in Franklin, Jeanerette, and New Iberia before returning to New Orleans. His message was unfailingly the same: that the Democrats had deserted the state and that Louisiana deserved much from the Progressive party because of its continued loyalty. Blacks, however, who remembered Brownsville and Roosevelt's record on the South, were not impressed with his trumpeting through the state. Ben Davis's Atlanta *Independent* not only thought Roosevelt was still anti-Negro but accused him of remaining as dictatorial as ever because he indicated that Parker would be his 1916 running mate. And the Negro paper unhesitatingly prophesied that "the electoral vote of this section will not be cast for him."[42]

Yet Roosevelt's trip through Louisiana gave the Progressives a boost in the third district as well as opening the way for Parker's election as governor six years later. Significantly, many Bull Moosers in the state, including Parker, Martin, and Broussard, who fought Wilson on the sugar issue, were not hurt by their association with Roosevelt but enjoyed distinguished careers after 1920 as Democrats. But in 1914, with only the state's eight congressional seats and a few judicial and municipal offices at stake, the Democrats had Progressive opposition besides Martin in only the first and second districts. The Republicans, moreover, were forced to sit out the election. Although GOP State Chairman C. S. Herbert blasted the Democrats for "manipulating the election laws as to make it impossible for us to get . . . on the official ballot," he urged Louisiana Republicans "to support Progressive candidates where they see fit." Both the Republican and Progressive National Committees, reported the New Orleans *Times-Picayune,* were watching the Louisiana fight: "The republicans were assured that Martin would win easily. They are not especially anxious to see a Progressive elected but are more interested in seeing the democratic majority in the house reduced." Predictably, the Democrats had no

difficulty in Louisiana except from Martin, who swept the third from
Henry I. Gueydan by a vote of 6,030 to 4,604. The other Progressives,
Louis H. Burns and Louis Le Bougeois in the first and second districts,
received inconsequential votes, as did two Socialists in the seventh and
eighth districts. Though Martin's victory caused rejoicing among Progressives all over the country, Democrats and Republicans had little to fear in
the future. In the sweep of history, his election was a fluke resulting from
political expediency because the Progressive drive in Louisiana had been a
one-issue fight. Martin won reelection as a Progressive in 1916 because of
Parker's prominence on the national stage, but by 1918 he, too, had
rejoined the Democrats, thereafter returning the state to the solid South.[43]

Meanwhile, the Republican campaign to reelect Hooper in Tennessee
had encountered difficulties, although he had no Bull Moose opponent.
When numbers of Independent Democrats began returning to the regular
party, the Memphis *Commercial Appeal* noted: "Probably the most interesting feature that the Tennessee political campaign has furnished thus
far . . . is that the Republican party is getting back to its moorings. It's the
same old party of ten years ago in spite of what wholesome influence
fusionism may have lent it." Nor did he have total support from his own
party, particularly on the Prohibition issue; Jesse M. Littleton, who was
elected mayor of Chattanooga in 1914, cautioned "sane, sensible people
not to lose their balance in this age of Puritanism," while blasting "those
fanatics who recently at the behest of Gov. Hooper poured pure whisky
into the Cumberland River in the very shadow of Old Hickory's statue."
What was worse, several prominent Progressives came out openly for the
Democrat Rye, including Thomas W. Poston, the party's 1912 candidate
for governor. And J. C. Benson, chairman of the Henderson County
Progressive Committee, urged all Bull Moosers to oppose Hooper because
"he is a standpat Republican and appointed Sanders to the U. S. Senate
and upheld him even when Sanders joined in the combination to defraud
Roosevelt at Chicago." Hooper's wide-ranging campaign in the state
notwithstanding, he was defeated by a 21,000-vote margin, thereby ending
a notable career in southern politics and putting the Tennessee statehouse
once again under solid Democratic control.[44]

All over the South Democrats were returned to office with their usual
lopsided majorities. The epic battles raging in Europe with the outbreak of
World War I produced an understandable indifference to the off-year
elections; although most Americans stood by the president in November,
voter disenchantment with some administration policies culminated in
startling gains for the Republicans nationally. The Democrats actually
gained seats in the Senate, but in the House of Representatives the GOP
picked up sixty-nine members, reducing their majority to an uncomfortable thirty-four. The Progressives elected only nine members to the House,
including Martin, in spite of Roosevelt's campaigning. The party virtually

disappeared after the election, receiving only half its 1912 vote and losing eight congressional seats.

The Progressive party for all practical purposes was not only moribund nationally and the disastrous schism among Republicans healed after 1914, but the dream of building a viable white opposition party in the South had also evaporated. Southern Negroes had both shunned Bull Moose candidates and deserted the GOP in numbers when numerous state organizations embraced lily-whiteism as a counter to the Progressive challenge. The lone Progressive victory in Louisiana was not the work of renegade Republicans nor even of reformers wanting to build a new party but of dissident Democrats motivated by local economic interests. Furthermore, Bull Moose rejection of proffered amalgamation agreements on the state level resulted in a diminished vote in several states. Their failure to field candidates in others was hardly a strategy calculated to perpetuate the party in the South or elsewhere. And in every southern state where Bull Moose and Republican candidates opposed each other, the Republican came in ahead of the Progressive, except in Louisiana. The message of 1914 for the South was unmistakenly clear: the Democrats remained in unchallenged command in all eleven ex-Confederate states except for a few isolated pockets, while the Republicans had reestablished themselves as the region's chief opposition party.

Chapter 8

"We Denounce the Colonel in Unmeasured Terms"

With the possible exception of John M. Parker, who was keen as ever for the Bull Moose crusade, few Republican or Progressive leaders in the South had much heart after 1914 to renew the fight. Early 1915 was a period of intense soul-searching by members of both parties in all sections of the country as the approaching national conventions necessitated the reassessment of long-held views. The disastrous results of 1914 were particularly harsh for the Progressives, who realized that their party was not only disintegrating but that their haughty attitude toward amalgamation needed reexamination. Although Progressive hard-liners argued to the last against reconciliation, many party leaders acknowledged the need for rejoining the Grand Old Party. Yet there was never a consensus on how to handle the problem. Some wanted a return with no strings attached, while others viewed amalgamation as a means for securing the GOP nomination for Roosevelt. All were agreed, however, that if Roosevelt could not win over the Old Guard, Progressive support should go to Charles Evans Hughes and not Elihu Root, whom they considered unacceptable for the 1916 GOP nomination. Compounding any meeting of the minds was Roosevelt's refusal to commit himself or to permit his name to be used in primaries or factional disputes within the party. Although most Republican leaders were opposed to offering him the GOP nomination, Roosevelt devoted most of his time and energy to attacking Wilson and the Democrats throughout 1915 for failure to protect America's national honor as the war intensified in Europe.[1]

Even though William Allen White and other Bull Moosers objected to his criticism of administration foreign policy, Roosevelt was successful in converting the party to preparedness. He continued a policy of conciliation toward the GOP and counseled the Progressives against active politicking before 1916: "My own view is that we have got to get on with the fight on the one hand, and that on the other hand there should be very little activity on our part for a year to come," he wrote to Parker, while agreeing that "it was impossible for us to support the Democrats under the Wilson regime." Roosevelt felt a continued loyalty toward Parker and the Louisiana Progressives, although he had written off the remainder of the South after 1912: "If the South had done as well as the North; if we had carried three southern states," he informed Richard Washburn Child of Boston during the summer of 1915, "the triumph of the party would have been assured."

His disappointment with the region notwithstanding, Roosevelt did not abandon Parker, who intended to build upon Progressive gains in Louisiana to launch a campaign for governor in 1916, and he accepted an invitation to visit Parker's summer retreat at Pass Christian, Mississippi, during June 1915. Accompanied by several naturalists as well as officials of the Audubon Society, the two Progressive warriors spent a week aboard Parker's yacht *Daisey* touring bird sanctuaries along the Louisiana and Mississippi coasts. Although the sojourn supposedly had no political overtones, it did serve to bolster Parker's standing in national party circles. Later, however, the friendship dissolved into caustic criticism by Parker after Roosevelt and George W. Perkins led the Bull Moosers back into the Republican fold at the 1916 Republican National Convention [2]

Since the Louisiana gubernatorial election was scheduled for April 18, 1916, it was necessary for Parker to start his campaign shortly after Roosevelt's departure for New York. After the turn of the new year, Progressive and Republican leaders in every southern state as well as in the nation at large were required to make plans for the 1916 campaign. Seven states—Arkansas, Florida, Georgia, North and South Carolina, Tennessee, and Texas—besides Louisiana elected governors and thus required party nominations. Before the year was out, the Republicans put up candidates in all seven except Georgia and South Carolina. The Progressives, however, offered no gubernatorial candidates other than Parker when the party dissolved following the Chicago conventions. In addition, U.S. senators were up for election in six states, and Republican candidates ran in all but Mississippi and Virginia. Minority party activity also increased when the GOP made its usual congressional nominations across the South. Nonetheless, after the Progressives decided to hold a national convention in 1916, every southern state held a state convention or Executive Committee meeting to send delegates, Roosevelt's advocacy of a low party profile notwithstanding. The Republicans, too, anxious to heal what they viewed as a lingering party schism, called conventions in all but Mississippi to elect national convention delegations and to hold out the olive branch.

Following the pattern of 1912, the Florida GOP acted first, on February 9, when its state convention assembled in Palatka. Henry S. Chubb, who was renominated national committeeman pending his confirmation at Chicago, called the meeting to order with "a powerful address which brought forth applause." The completely harmonious gathering, reported the *Florida Times-Union*, "was one of the largest and most enthusiastic and representative republican conventions held in years." The eight-man delegation—greatly reduced in size as were all southern contingents under the ruling of the Republican National Committee affecting the "rotten boroughs"—was sent to Chicago uninstructed. Chubb felt that "it was folly for the party to have divided in 1912" and that a "conciliatory candidate" should be named as the best scheme for defeating the Democrats. The refusal to endorse any presidential contender was part of the politics of amalgamation authorized by the national leadership. Yet the Florida platform adopted at the assembly contained a strongly worded denunciation of the Democrats in both state and nation.[3]

The convention at Palatka also nominated a full state ticket headed by George W. Allen, a well-known Key West banker, for governor; the 1912 gubernatorial nominee, William R. O'Neal of Orlando, was tapped to oppose Governor Park Trammell, who had defeated Nathan P. Bryan for the U.S. Senate in the Democratic primary. Nominations were also made for all three of the state's congressional seats at district conventions later in the year. Although the Florida GOP remained silent about the Bull Moosers throughout the campaign, a resolution adopted by a local gathering at Dade City called on "all Florida voters to vote against candidates who had supported passage of the Bryan Election Law." Allen, a native of Jacksonville but educated in New York, held a string of federal jobs in Florida dating from 1879 when Hayes appointed him collector of internal revenue. He also served several terms in the state legislature in the 1880s; twice previously, in 1896, when he declined the honor, and in 1900, when he was beaten by William S. Jennings, Allen received the gubernatorial nomination. In 1916 he was again overwhelmingly defeated by Sidney J. Catts, a Baptist minister from Alabama, who capitalized on anti-Catholic sentiment in the state to win the Democratic nomination.[4]

Republican conventions met the following month in North Carolina and Virginia. The North Carolina gathering on March 2 named an uninstructed delegation to Chicago, but the otherwise smooth-running convention was disrupted by a bitter factional dispute between E. C. Duncan and former Senator Marion Butler over selecting a new national committeeman. Butler, a Bull Moose adherent in 1912, "returned to North Carolina," said the Raleigh *News and Observer,* "making the proposition that Duncan, twelve years the national committeeman, and his own personal enemy step down and out. In consideration of this he would do likewise, thus healing the Taft-Roosevelt split in the party." Although the convention was treated to a lively outburst when Duncan "declined this obstinately, treating Butler's offer as an impertinence," the assembly went along with Butler and elected John M. Morehead to the coveted spot. Morehead had not only supported Taft but he had been GOP state chairman until 1914 when replaced by Frank A. Linney as a conciliatory gesture toward the Progressives. But he had broken with Duncan in his support of the Old Guard, which prompted party approval and its rejection of Duncan. Since North Carolina would hold a primary on June 6, which included for the first time every elective office in the state, the convention made no nominations for state office. A month later, therefore, on April 8, the State Executive Committee met to endorse a full ticket headed by Linney for governor and Zeb V. Walser for attorney general. The selection of Walser, who was Progressive state chairman, was designed as a peace offering to the Bull Moosers. The committee refrained from making any presidential recommendations; the party leadership had intended to endorse Judge J. C. Pritchard, a personal friend of Roosevelt and a favorite son, until a ruling by the state's attorney general blocked the plan.[5]

The continued lily-white orientation of the North Carolina GOP prompted the Negroes to convene a self-styled Negro Republican State Convention on April 24 in Raleigh. "A long Preamble and Resolutions," according to a Raleigh paper, was drafted condemning the regulars for "shutting them out of the councils of the state since the democrats put into effect the constitutional amendment which prevents the illiterate negro [sic] from voting." To dramatize their position, a rival delegation to the national convention was authorized and instructed to insist "on the Negro having proper representation in the councils of the Republican organization of the southern states." Blacks were also ignored in the district conventions that named district delegates; these gatherings, like the state convention, refused to instruct, but, reported the New Orleans *Times-Picayune,* most of the delegation was leaning to Massachusetts Senator John W. Weeks, who ultimately received 105 votes on the first ballot at Chicago. The sentiment for Weeks notwithstanding, the state's Republicans gave Roosevelt a landslide majority, to the chagrin of the Negro, in the June 6 primary. Roosevelt carried all but two of the state's ten districts, both of which went to Charles Evans Hughes. Under North Carolina law, however, the national convention delegates were bound by the primary results and Roosevelt even received the at-large delegation because of his statewide plurality. The new apportioning scheme for the convention allotted twenty-one votes to the state; after the primary Roosevelt had seventeen and Hughes four, though neither had campaigned or permitted use of his name in the state.[6]

The North Carolina Bull Moosers did not hold a formal convention in 1916 although the state was fully represented in the Chicago conclave. And if Tar Heel Republicans were solicitous about amalgamation, Roosevelt's followers were determined to fight on alone. A meeting of the State Executive Committee on April 5 at Greensboro named a complete contingent and instructed the delegates to support and vote for Theodore Roosevelt. Headed by Walser, the group was ordered to oppose harmony with the GOP. A committee of fifteen was authorized to call a convention later in the campaign if thought necessary. That assembly, however, did not materialize after Roosevelt pulled the rug from under them by informing Dr. A. T. Pritchard, the son of Judge Jeter C. Pritchard: "But it is not possible for me to allow the use of my name in the primaries of any state." After passing his regards to the father whom he had once appointed to the federal bench, Roosevelt concluded: "Mr. Perkins tells me that he has talked with you on the telephone . . . and that you understand the situation thoroughly."

The North Carolina Progressives understood perfectly, though they were obviously overjoyed at Roosevelt's showing in the Republican preferential primary. Walser, on the other hand, while allowing himself to be courted by the Republicans, carried the fight to Chicago, apparently unaware of Roosevelt's decision to spurn another Progressive nomination. Walser and National Committeeman James N. Williamson, Jr.—who later told John M. Parker he would fight to the end to prevent "the Progressives from being swallowed up by the Republicans"—were hesitant to give up the hope of power even as the party came apart at Chicago. They not only rejected conciliation in North Carolina, but when a Bull Moose "conference" met one day before the national convention they opposed amalgamation by the national party. The state's delegation was "ready to break up the meeting," said the *News and Observer,* "because of the compromise talk. The North Carolinians wanted to lay down the law to fellow partymen from the outset. They would go so far and no further." Butler, who had assumed a go-between role among the warring factions, asserted on the eve of the national convention that "the Bull Moose people favor a fight rather than any compromise." And like other diehard Progressives, the North Carolina Bull Moosers were hopelessly saddened by Roosevelt's final turning away. While still in Chicago, the delegation adopted a parting resolution: "We . . . strayed from the pastures of our fathers and traveled on a Bull Moose special to Chicago to be deserted and left to shift for ourselves as best we could. WE DENOUNCE THE COLONEL IN UNMEASURED TERMS." The state organization that had given the most in all the South—Louisiana included—had gotten in the last salvo.[7]

Virginia Republicans held a convention in Roanoke on March 29, four days after the North Carolina Progressive meeting at Greensboro, and like other southern organizations got up an uninstructed delegation. By convention time, however, its delegates were reportedly for Hughes. Slemp, who not only won reelection in the ninth district but remained undisputed chief of the Virginia party, acted as southern spokesman in the drive to have the New Yorker seek the nomination. A former reform governor in the Empire State and a Supreme Court justice since 1910 when appointed by Taft, Hughes became an increasingly attractive candidate as the GOP searched for a popular alternative to Roosevelt. Yet his secluded position on the court precluded any active solicitation for the nomination, although numerous Republican politicians urged him to do so. Always the gentleman and proper statesman, Hughes was named without his formal sanction, and he did not resign from the court until June 10, after the nomination had been tendered by the convention. Therefore, in response to an earlier plea from Slemp and the Virginians that he be a presidential contender, he informed the veteran congressman in an oft-quoted letter: "I am entirely out of politics, and I know nothing whatever of the matters to which you refer. I am totally opposed to the use of my name in connection with the nomination and selection or instruction of any delegates in my interest, either directly or indirectly."[8]

The Roanoke convention also declined to offer a candidate for the U.S. Senate seat held by Claude A. Swanson, who was running for reelection. Inasmuch as the governorship was not at stake until 1917, there was little to do but hand out the olive branch to the Bull Moosers and draft the usual resolutions denouncing the Democrats. The Wilson administration was censured for its foreign policy, while the Virginia Republicans went on record for "a strict and real neutrality toward all warring nations, but a firm and resolute maintenance of our American rights at all times." The GOP State Committee was given the task of acting on a senatorial nomination later in the year, after the convention ratified the idea of supporting a strong independent Democratic candidate. The intended nominee, Henry St. George Tucker, a former Democratic congressman, onetime gubernatorial candidate, and author, refused to accept the GOP offer, leaving Swanson unopposed. Percy S. Stephenson, Progressive state chairman, followed Tucker's lead and turned aside any suggestion of cooperation with the Republicans. Like the North Carolinians, Stephenson and the Virginia Bull Moosers were prepared to go it alone prior to the national convention. Stephenson, reported the Richmond *Times-Dispatch,* "was bitterly opposed to the Martin-Slemp combination in Virginia. He is [also] bitterly opposed to what he alleges to be the combination between Republican National Committeeman A. H. Martin and some Democratic leaders." Nonetheless, the GOP managed to elect sixteen members to the next legislature, and though nine candidates entered the congressional races, only Slemp was successful.[9]

The Georgia Republicans were as quarrelsome and tempestuous as ever when dual conventions met two weeks later on April 12 and named rival delegations to Chicago. The fight started at a State Committee session in Macon a month before that had been called to fix the time for a state convention. Two factions, headed by State Chairman Walter H. Johnson and National Committeeman Henry S. Jackson, renewed their struggle for control of the state party at the meeting, and the argument got so heated that police and firemen were called to quell the fisticuffs. According to the Atlanta *Journal:* "There were several fights in the hall and Negroes attending the committee meeting carried one fight to the streets outside. The Negroes were arrested, charged with being intoxicated and having violated the state's prohibition laws. It was said the firemen were prepared to use streams of water from their hose, but that it did not become necessary." Unable to agree, the Johnson faction scheduled a convention in Macon, while Jackson and his group announced a meeting for Atlanta.[10]

Both Georgia conclaves were much too concerned with internal matters

to heed presidential politics. Yet on the eve of national convention
hearings to decide which delegation would be recognized, the Johnson
faction was supporting Elihu Root and the Jackson delegates Hughes.
Jackson's people were finally accepted by the GOP National Committee
and Jackson was reelected national committeeman, which gave him control
of the party over the next four years. In addition to naming a delegation,
the Johnson assembly completely reorganized the State Committee with
Johnson as state chairman and adopted a platform with a strongly worded
antilynching plank. Although Georgia elected a governor in 1916, this
convention did not name a candidate to oppose the Democrat Hugh M.
Dorsey. The Jackson convention in Atlanta not only selected an uninstructed contingent to the national meeting, but, unlike their counterparts,
named a state ticket, headed by Roscoe Pickett of Jasper. Pickett, a
Republican member of the state senate, was a graduate of the University of
Georgia and a highly respected member of the bar; prior to his death in
1954, he maintained a law practice at Jasper for forty-five years and,
besides his Republican activities, he edited for many years the official
journal of the National Association of Claimant's Attorneys. The Republican nominee, however, bowed out of the race before November, leaving
Dorsey without opposition; 1916 was not a good year for the GOP in
Georgia as Hughes polled a mere 11,294 votes in the state to Wilson's
127,763.[11]

Bull Moose conventions also met in other parts of the South during
April. The Florida party, still under the direction of H. L. Anderson, held
a convention on April 15 at Atlanta Beach, insisting that fusion with
Chubb's Republicans was out of the question. A unanimous resolution of
the Progressive State Committee two weeks earlier had declared against
amalgamation because Anderson thought "the Progressive party repre-
sents the need of another strong white party which can figure in the politics
of the south." Through this means he thought "the administration of state
government will be greatly bettered." Therefore, the April 15 convention
enthusiastically endorsed Roosevelt for the nomination and instructed its
delegation to support him at Chicago. Knowing full well that he was
anathema to many Republicans following the fiasco of 1912, Anderson and
the Florida party were in effect burning their bridges behind them. Yet,
after Roosevelt abandoned the party in June, throwing his support to
Hughes, the Rough Rider was moved to inform Anderson, who had fought
against great odds in one of the most Democratic of southern states: "I
thoroughly sympathize with the position of the Progressive party in the
south. It is as you say pathetic; but my dear sir, it is the fault of southerners
only that such should be the case. The Progressive party in the south in
point of numbers was imponderable . . . [it] made less headway in the
south than in any other part of the country." Be that as it may, the Bull
Moose convention in April proceeded in good faith for the 1916 campaign.

Not only were delegates instructed for Roosevelt but a platform was adopted annihilating the Democratic administration and presidential electors were chosen.[12]

Three days later, on April 18, the hotly contested gubernatorial election in Louisiana took place between John M. Parker and the state's attorney general, Rufus G. Pleasant. As the state conventions were meeting throughout the first weeks of spring, political observers in Louisiana and the lower South watched intently as Parker waged the first viable statewide campaign for the Progressives in the region. He had opened the race on November 1, four months after Roosevelt's sojourn at Pass Christian, with a fighting speech at Crowley in the sugar belt. At Ruston on March 29, Parker announced that he would be returned by the thinking people of the state because of his Progressive principles. In an effort to counteract his appeal to the sugar interests, Pleasant consistently spoke against protective tariffs and in favor of tariffs for revenue only. According to the *Times-Picayune,* he also proclaimed an abiding interest in "the farmer and laboring man, when Parker had nothing to offer but honeyed words"; Parker was also accused of catering to blacks after the Republicans came out in his support. As the Bull Moose campaign began to pick up steam, Pleasant called Parker's candidacy "only part of a well laid scheme of Theodore Roosevelt's to break the solid Democratic south and become the dictator of the Republican and Progressive parties." But Wilson T. Peterman, Parker's manager, quickly refuted the Democratic mischievousness: "If there are ten thousand qualified Negro voters in Louisiana, who registered them," he asked. Nor did Parker play to the Republican gallery by rejecting the whites' only posture of southern Progressivism. "Mr. Pleasant should know," Peterman continued, "that Mr. Parker will not receive the Negro vote whether it be one thousand or one hundred. Mr. Parker said at Bogalusa, and he has said it all over the state, 'the only use I have for the Negro in politics is to put him in his place.' "[13]

In the face of unrelenting Democratic pressure, Parker himself declared before the election: "I beg to say I am a Progressive. The policy of my administration will be non-partisan and non-political. . . . Even though it were in my power I would not turn over this state to the Republican party." Most Democrats, however, including Congressman Ladisias Lazaro, running for reelection in the seventh district which was adjacent to Martin's and partially in the sugar-growing region, were skeptical. "It is plain," Lazaro wrote during the campaign, "that the Progressive party, which was an offshoot of the Republican party, is going back to that party, and that the fight from now on is between the Democratic and Republican parties." The *Times-Picayune* took a swing at Pleasant for injecting the Negro issue into the race, and, three days before the election, editorialized that throughout the campaign Parker's "high character, public spirit, public service . . . have been testified to by leading men of the state." His wide-based support notwithstanding, Parker lost by a vote of 48,068 to 80,807, although the campaign hurled him to the forefront of national Progressive politics. Furthermore, his strength was concentrated in the sugar-producing region; all sixteen parishes carried by him were either in Martin's third district or immediately surrounding it; and his vote in Democratic north Louisiana was inconsequential while he failed to carry metropolitan New Orleans. "Dear John," Roosevelt wrote afterward, "It was not in the cards to win. You and I have got to make up our minds that we are a little too far ahead on some things."[14]

As the campaign was in progress, the lily-white wing of the GOP called a state convention into session on March 23 at New Orleans. This group named an all-white but uninstructed delegation to Chicago; later, however, the delegates were reportedly in favor of Hughes as the national campaign intensified. Although no Republican candidates were entered in the April 18 election because of the party's legal status, all factions were anxious to achieve recognition at the national convention and to gain the patronage that would follow a national GOP victory. Therefore, the lily-whites, who claimed to represent the Republican party of Louisiana, selected a twelve-man contingent headed by Armand Romain, lawyer and national committeeman; Samuel A. Trutant, banker and broker at New Orleans; E. F. Dickinson, sugar planter of Matthews; and Dr. Charles F. Bogani, physician and real estate broker of Opelousas. But when another GOP group dominated by Negroes named a rival delegation, the *Times-Picayune* commented with customary Democratic contempt for all southern Republicans: "A fight between the opposing delegates from Louisiana is a regular event, sure to come as an exciting prelude to every regular convention and this year, as in the past, the credentials committee [at Chicago] will hold a special session to decide who's who in republican circles in Louisiana."

The opposing convention, called by Walter L. Cohen, Negro leader and confidant of the deceased Booker T. Washington, met nine days after the election on April 27, also in New Orleans. This group officially designated itself "The Old Republican Party of Louisiana" and charged that the earlier GOP meeting was invalid because it had been convened in a hotel that denied admittance to Negroes. Whereas the lily-white assembly met under hurried circumstances, the Cohen convention had 405 delegates present from thirty-five parishes and the seventeen wards of New Orleans. A full delegation was named for the state's twelve seats at the national convention under the plan of reduced southern representation; it was not only divided equally between white and black delegates but it was also admonished to reject any accommodation with the lily-whites and "to insist upon full recognition or carry the fight to the floor of the convention." Nor was the delegation instructed for the presidential balloting, although some of the Negroes reportedly favored Roosevelt, of all people, for the GOP nomination. They were simply told to "favor any man the states who elect the president want."[15]

The Louisiana Bull Moosers, however, did not hold a convention until May 15 because they were preoccupied with the Parker-Pleasant race, although public notice of the gathering appeared in state newspapers several weeks earlier. A full delegation was named to Chicago led by Parker and Pearl Wight and charged to support "the Hon. Theodore Roosevelt for President of the United States as a man and a citizen best fitted to uphold the manhood and citizenship of all American citizens." The platform also reconfirmed the principles of 1912 and pledged cooperation with the new Democratic administration in Louisiana. The later section was the outgrowth of a well-received speech before the assembly by Parker, who already had his eye on the 1920 gubernatorial contest when he would again be a reform candidate. In glowing language, the convention took time to praise "those stalwart, fearless, and honest men of the Independent Democracy, who voiced their sentiments and assisted our state candidates." And at Parker's insistence the party obligated itself "to assist Governor Pleasant and the state administration in those reforms to which we jointly agreed and to support all measures for which those necessary and just laws are needed for the general prosperity of the state." Several speakers singled out the seventh district for "holding the Democrats to such a narrow victory" and predicted that it would elect a second Bull Moose congressman from the state in November. Before adjourning, the three hundred delegates not only reelected Wight to the Progressive National Committee but also vowed "to remain organized and to organize the party further."[16]

Meanwhile, the Arkansas Bull Moosers met on April 21 in Little Rock amid a struggle between J. A. Comer and Winfield S. Holt for control of the party. Comer, state chairman and intrepid Roosevelt man, had the backing of the strong Little Rock–Pulaski County delegation for national committeeman to succeed Harry M. Trieber, who had bowed out. In the convention, however, he lost out to Holt, who was also secretary of the State Committee, on a close vote; Comer was allowed to continue as state chairman and as a delegate to the national convention. The future Ku Klux Klan leader in the state stayed with Roosevelt to the end, and even after the colonel's rejection of the party at the national convention, Comer returned from Chicago claiming that he would be the Progressive candidate for president in spite of the Hughes nomination. Although the Little Rock gathering did not instruct its delegation other than to vote as a unit, Roosevelt was endorsed for the Progressive nomination.

Though Negro papers in other states, such as the Washington *Bee,* the Richmond *Planet,* and the *Colored Alabamian* were loudly proclaiming that no self-respecting Negro would support the Progressives in 1916, the Arkansas Bull Moosers admitted Negroes to their state convention and again seated Bishop J. M. Connor, the Negro clergyman, on the official delegation to Chicago. And the party held out the hope of amalgamation with the state's Republicans. Although the hand of friendship was not openly extended, a resolution expressing "the hope that all elements opposed to the democratic administration may unite under one leader and upon the same platform" certainly pointed in that direction. The platform also scored Wilson's "European and Mexican policies" in addition to catering to the state's depressed rice growers by advocating "restoration of a protective tariff." Though never on the scale of the Louisiana protest over sugar, the Bull Moose leadership in Arkansas had attempted to stir up support among the rice producers since 1913 and enactment of the Underwood Tariff. Nominations for the governorship and state offices were deferred until after the national convention, causing the *Arkansas Gazette* to speculate: "Evidently it was desired to determine whether consolidation with the Republican party is reached."[17]

For the first time in Arkansas history, the election for state office was held concurrently with the presidential canvass in November, and the Republicans lost no time in putting up a candidate to oppose Charles H. Brough, winner of the March 29 Democratic primary. Wallace Townsend, a future GOP national committeeman and leader of the state's lily-white faction, was given the bid for the governorship at the state convention on April 26, six days after the Progressives had refrained from making a nomination. That convention was wracked with the ongoing fight between lily-whites and Negroes for mastery of the party. The long-festering sore had surfaced again at the Pulaski County convention when A. C. Remmel, the county chairman, blocked Negro efforts to gain recognition. Although Little Rock city police were called to eject blacks from the Marion Hotel, a segregated facility, where the county convention assembled, several Negroes were nonetheless put on the county's delegation. The state convention, however, voted 235 to 18 following a protracted debate not to seat black-and-tan delegations from Pulaski and Hempstead counties. The controversy spilled over to the gubernatorial nomination with Townsend, the lily-white candidate, defeating the former party standard-bearer, Andrew Kinney of Green Forest, who had the support of the Negroes, by a vote of 171 to 129.

Harmon L. Remmel, who had been acting head of the party since the death of Powell Clayton, not only engineered the lily-white capture of the convention but was also reelected national committeeman. At no time was the lily-white victory more complete than in the selection of delegates to Chicago: "The convention refused to nominate a negro [sic] to one of the four delegates at-large to the national convention thereby breaking a precedent of 32 years standing." The blatant rejection of the Negro, particularly the refusal to recognize him on the official delegation, precipitated a crisis for the party later in the campaign. Although Arkansas Negroes remained disfranchised in large numbers, "a well-organized plan," reported the *Arkansas Gazette,* was implemented to have blacks "boycott the Republican party." Harry H. Myres, who led the black-and-tan forces at the convention, fought lily-white ascendancy every step of the way, and he even sponsored a move to instruct the delegation for Roosevelt. That, too, was turned down along with his other motions, and the delegation was sent to Chicago uninstructed, although Remmel later referred to the colonel "as one of the great galaxy of Republican leaders" in the convention debates. The platform, unlike most of those adopted by southern organizations in 1916, "made no reference to the proposed consolidation with the Republican party." The convention made only one other nomination for state office besides Townsend; Durand Whipple was selected to run for the state supreme court. Remmel, however, mounted a last-minute campaign for the unexpired term of Senator James P. Clarke, who died unexpectedly on October 1. But 1916 was a bad year for all Republicans in Arkansas: Townsend, Whipple, and Harmon ran considerably behind Hughes and the national ticket, which received but 47,000 votes to 112,000 for the Democrats.[18]

In a strictly chronological sense, the on-again, off-again Bull Moosers in South Carolina held a state convention on May 2 at the city council chamber in Columbia. T. H. Wannamaker, the approved national committeeman, stated on April 29 that he was going through the formality of calling a convention but that a state ticket would not be named; he also criticized the state's Democrats for not allowing the Progressives to "vote in the democratic primaries under the oath requiring all voters to support the national and state nominees of the party." In the May 2 gathering, his remarks were broadened to censure them for "barring white men of other parties from participation in the democratic primary by which municipal, county and state affairs are controlled." In other respects, reported the Atlanta *Constitution,* the platform "was patterned closely after that of the national organization." Wannamaker and John Canty of Camden were elected delegates-at-large and empowered to appoint the remaining delegates, which meant that South Carolina held no district conventions as did other southern states. The convention did not instruct its delegation, although Roosevelt sentiment was reportedly strong in the assembly which met behind closed doors. The failure to endorse a candidate notwithstanding, Wannamaker told reporters after the meeting: "It is as certain as anything can be which has not already happened that Mr. Roosevelt will be the nominee of the republican convention on a progressive platform. This, of course, means the uniting of the progressive and republican vote, and nothing but a miracle can prevent us from sweeping the country." Seven additional white men accompanied the two at-large delegates to Chicago where they reelected Wannamaker national committeeman and announced "it was Roosevelt or nothing" on the eve of the national convention.[19]

Both parties held delegate-naming conventions across the South in rapid succession throughout May. With the short time remaining before the national conventions opened on June 7, all of them were concerned with gauging the ever-shifting sands of presidential politics. Roosevelt had coerced the Progressive National Committee during January into adopting a resolution asking loyal Bull Moosers to rejoin the GOP as the only means of defeating Wilson. At another time he thought the party should nominate Henry Cabot Lodge, a man clearly unacceptable to Progressives everywhere. The colonel no doubt wanted the GOP nomination for himself as he traveled about the nation preaching preparedness and denouncing Wilson's timidity toward the axis powers. But the Republican pros would have no part of Roosevelt and set about securing the party banner for the recalcitrant Hughes. Another presidential boomlet in early March was started for the aging Elihu Root, who was a more than willing candidate. Taft thought him the man of the hour and therefore refused to join the Hughes bandwagon during the preconvention maneuvering. As convention time neared, however, Roosevelt became convinced that a candidate must be chosen who could unite Republicans and Progressives for the fall campaign. Root was not that man—nor Lodge—which caused Roosevelt to join other politicians of both parties in bowing to the inevitable and agreeing to support Hughes once the Supreme Court justice resolved to accept the nomination.

Nevertheless, Benjamin F. Fridge called his miniaturized Progressive party of Mississippi into session on May 2 at Jackson, certain that Roosevelt should have his support. A delegation composed of "dyed-in-the-wool Roosevelt men" and headed by Fridge was named. The convention, which met "in the parlors of Edwards House, some thirty or forty delegates being present and holding proxies for perhaps 200 others who found it inconvenient to come to Jackson," came out for "a lily white party of progressive ideals and invited the young men of the state to join hands with them." At the same time the Mississippians were whooping it up for Roosevelt and restating their allegiance to an all-white party, the colonel was again flirting with Dr. S. D. Redmond, the Negro physician whom he had spurned in 1912. Among other things he was asked to stay in touch with Roosevelt's secretary while in Chicago, although he was not a member of the Fridge delegation. Yet unaware that their position was being undermined, the convention adopted a platform emulating Roosevelt's stand on several issues, including support for military training schools, national flood control, and uniform liquor laws.[20]

The Tennessee Republicans who gave Hughes 116,000 votes in November, second only to North Carolina in the South, assembled the next day in Nashville. Through the strenuous efforts of Governor Hooper, who had waged a program of reconciliation for several months, the convention was completely harmonious. Hooper, however, was not concerned with the Bull Moosers but with the ever-present struggle between the state's congressional delegation and the Tennessee GOP organization for control of the party. He not only conferred with Congressman Sam R. Sells in Washington and Nashville but also with former Postmaster General Frank H. Hitchcock, who gave his blessing to Hooper's plan. The difficulty stemmed in part from a contest between Sells and former Senator Newell Sanders for the national committeemanship that was "threatening to tear the party apart." After Sells expressed a willingness to go to any reasonable length in preventing a party rupture, it was agreed that John W. Overall, a Hooper confidant, would be the committeeman. "[You have] made a splendid fight," E. W. Essary, a party functionary, informed Hooper, "to divorce the state organization, and the national committeeman, from domination and control of congressional members."[21]

Sanders attempted to control the convention but, commented a Chattanooga paper, "he was unable to do so." Hooper's plan for a united front in November dominated the assembly. A pro-woman's suffrage plank was added to the platform at his insistence, and though the document said nothing about the Progressives, it declared for maintenance of all prohibition laws. Although Hooper, who had the continued support of James C. Napier and the Tennessee Negroes, did not want to be on the Chicago delegation or to receive a party nomination, he was given the nomination for the U.S. Senate. He conducted a vigorous but losing campaign against Kenneth D. McKellar, who had beaten the veteran Luke Lea in the Democratic convention. Hooper's candidate for governor, Overall, a popular Republican leader and former U.S. marshal in middle Tennessee, won the nomination over Chattanooga Mayor Jesse M. Littleton. The delegation to Chicago was uninstructed, although Hooper and his followers made no secret of their admiration for Hughes. Joseph O. Thompson, the Alabama Bull Moose captain, wrote Hooper a long letter asking him to use his influence for Roosevelt at the convention. The Tennessee Republicans not only rejected the colonel but added insult to injury by naming Colonel A. M. Hughes one of its delegates-at-large. "It is established in Washington and Tennessee," the Chattanooga *Daily Times* said, "that if one man ever had an abhorrence for another it is Col. Hughes' antipathy for Roosevelt. It had to do with then President Roosevelt's gross injustice to Hughes when the latter was postmaster at Columbia."[22]

In the week following Hooper's pouring oil on the troubled waters of Tennessee Republicanism, Bull Moose conventions met in Virginia, Georgia, and Alabama. Everywhere in the South there was a certain sameness about these assemblies during 1916. With the constant decline in party strength casting doubt on its future, there was little to be done but rubber stamp Roosevelt for the presidency, select a predetermined slate of delegates to the national convention, and hope for the best. Florida's H. L. Anderson summed up the urgency of keeping the party intact when he informed John M. Parker: "The men who have formed the Progressive party in the south have a task to perform. We must cooperate for mutual protection—Amalgamation means extinction." Therefore, the Virginia convention at Roanoke on May 12 particularly was a cut-and-dried affair because the State Committee had already declared for Roosevelt at an April 8 meeting in Richmond. Nevertheless, the meeting went through the formality of naming a twenty-four-man delegation with one-half vote each and instructing them to vote for Roosevelt. Then, after several speakers lambasted "the alleged maladministration" of the Democrats in general, a platform "severely arraigning the Democratic party in Virginia was passed unanimously." Although the Progressive convention, which was dominated by National Committeeman Percy S. Stephenson, said nothing about the Virginia GOP, the delegation announced before entraining for Chicago that Hughes was completely unacceptable.[23]

In Georgia a rift developed between two Bull Moose factions at the May 13 state convention in Atlanta that was not resolved until the national convention. The expected resolution for Roosevelt also pledged the party to support any candidate he might endorse if he failed to receive the nomination. C. W. McClure, the former national committeeman and 1914 senatorial candidate, explained to the press later: "That if Colonel Roosevelt should receive the nomination of the republican party at the Chicago convention that the Georgia wing of the progressive party would at once unite with the republicans in his support, and that the same result would also come about if Colonel Roosevelt does not run, but endorses the republican nominee." McClure's willingness to patch up differences with the GOP notwithstanding, he soon found himself in hot water with his fellow conventioneers. When a two-pronged challenge led by Roger A. Dewar of Atlanta was made to McClure's hold on the Georgia party, the convention agreed to let the National Committee settle the issue and to refrain from entering a candidate in the governor's race. First, Dewar, who had conducted the state's only Bull Moose campaign for Congress in 1914 over the strong objections of McClure, wanted to chair the Chicago delegation instead of McClure; second, McClure wanted to resume his post as national committeeman—relinquished for the 1914 campaign—though Harry G. Hastings, who had taken over upon his resignation, wanted to stay on the committee.

Once in Chicago, the insurgents were able to eclipse McClure completely. Yet, one of his cohorts, Harry S. Edwards of Rome, who had the backing of Roosevelt and George W. Perkins, was retained as state chairman. Nevertheless, Dewar was acknowledged as delegation chairman and Hastings as national committeeman by the Progressive National Committee. Dewar's delegation had two women, Mrs. W. H. Felton of Cartersville and Mrs. Helen D. Longstreet of Gainesville, in addition to McClure, who remained an at-large member despite his other difficulties. "Regardless of the suffrage problem or any of the various phases of agitation connected with it," reported the Atlanta *Constitution,* "certain it is that Georgia could not be more worthily represented in any convention than by these two women who love and have served the state." McClure's loss of prestige resulted because many of the state's Bull Moosers did not share his eagerness to rejoin the GOP. "We favor an honorable alliance, but not a surrender," another at-large delegate, James L. Sibley, proclaimed on the eve of the national gathering: "The progressive party must be preserved if any headway is to be made in the south for thousands have joined the party so as to secure two parties in this section, no progress can be made here unless the progressive party is out in front and leading the way." McClure later joined Sibley, Dewar, and Hastings in urging John M. Parker to continue the Bull Moose fight in the South after Roosevelt had thrown over the party for Hughes and amalgamation.[24]

The Alabama Progressives held a convention on May 17 and "ratified without any dilatory tactics the programme arranged in advance by the executive committee of the party." The gathering that met in Birmingham's Manufacturer's Hall did not bother with a platform but adopted a slogan: "Roosevelt and Americanism." Surprisingly, reported the Birmingham *Age-Herald,* "at no time during the proceedings was the name of President Wilson mentioned or his policies assailed." The governorship was not at stake in 1916 which freed the Bull Moosers from having to make nominations for state office. They did, however, endorse Roosevelt and instructed the Alabama contingent to Chicago, headed by J. O. Thompson, George S. O'Bear, J. F. Lovingood, and Oscar R. Hundley to vote for him. Although the Birmingham assembly was wild for Roosevelt, Judge Hundley—still acting as Bull Moose leader in the state—announced before the national convention that his group would "possibly support Hughes if the republicans rejected TR." Like most other southern Progressives, the Alabamians thought Elihu Root was taboo: "We want Roosevelt first because he is Roosevelt, second, because in our opinion he is more certain of success than any other individual. It is our opinion that only two men have a chance to defeat Wilson—Roosevelt and Hughes." "Roosevelt and Americanism," Hundley said at the convention, "is a phrase which, emanating from Alabama, will sweep the country. It is the shortest platform on record. . . . We cannot fail to win with such a patriotic call."[25]

In contrast, the state's Republicans assembled three days later, also in Birmingham, heaping fire and brimstone on Wilson for "his policies in regard to the European war, Mexico and the tariff." The platform also "takes the hide off" the Democratic state administration, although the Republicans refused to join in denouncing "hyphenated Americans." "Owing to the fact that many of the republicans of Alabama are of Teutonic extraction," reported the *Age-Herald* further, some of the leaders thought "there was no necessity of embarrassing the German republicans with such discussions." But their racial understanding did not include the Negro and his sharing in the Alabama GOP. In fact, the lily-white element was in such command that not one Negro was among the 257 delegates present from every district in the state. That such actions were driving blacks out of the GOP became increasingly obvious when the Montgomery *Colored Alabamian* editorialized: "The Negroes of Alabama have got to fight the white Republicans as well as the Democrats if they ever hope to enjoy their full political rights." Even so, the convention remained all white on the pretext "that no negroes [sic] had attempted to conform with the regulations of the republican party and stand for election as delegates." And when Ulysses G. Mason and J. O. Diffay, Negro leaders who had been spurned in 1914, announced they would hold a black-and-tan convention later to name a rival delegation, the lily-white leadership reported that "it would not receive any consideration from the credentials committee in Chicago."

The Alabama convention was not only ruled by the lily-whites but the old officeholding faction dominated by Pope M. Long and Oscar D. Street was in complete charge, Democratic control of the national administration notwithstanding. When former Congressman M. W. Howard challenged the delegate selection process, he quickly learned, said the Birmingham *Age-Herald,* "the steamroller of the federal officeholders, which has controlled the republican party in the south since the war, still is in excellent condition." Howard, who had supported black participation, was denied a place on the state's uninstructed delegation. Charles B. Kennamer of Guntersville, the convention's presiding officer and a member of the officeholding faction, asserted that the delegation would have "an open mind" toward all candidates: "However," he continued, "we will be influenced by whatever action such states as New York, Massachusetts and Illinois will take, and we will vote for the strongest man likely to win the nomination." He had been U.S. attorney under Roosevelt and Taft, and he later reassumed the post under Harding, Coolidge, and Hoover; Kennamer was a graduate of the Georgetown University Law School and an Alabama native. The assembly also remained cool toward amalgamation with the Bull Moosers. A resolution inviting "the active cooperation and support of all the patriotic citizens of our beloved state" was the nearest they could come to conciliation. Yet some party leaders indicated privately that they would rather support Roosevelt for the GOP nomination than have the Progressives enter a separate candidate. Oscar D. Street was tapped for national committeeman after "Maj. P. D. Barker of Mobile refused reelection," although Pope M. Long stayed on as state chairman.[26]

The staggering Democratic majorities in Texas as elsewhere in the South made the feeble efforts of Republicans and Progressives appear useless in comparison to the campaign to reelect Wilson and Governor James E. Ferguson. Democratic hold on the state's electorate was heightened in 1916 by the roles of two native sons: Colonel Edward M. House, as the president's confidant and personal envoy for world peace, and Postmaster

General Albert S. Burleson, who played a conspicuous part in the administration. With that advantage, Lone Star Democrats expected little competition from either party; yet both held conventions on the same day, May 23, to choose personnel for the Chicago gatherings. Meeting at Waco, the Progressives were required to reorganize their high command following the death of Cecil A. Lyon in April 1916. Lyon had been both national committeeman and state chairman and because of his close friendship with Roosevelt had exercised a free hand in the state. Therefore, a major yet difficult job for the convention was finding replacements for Lyon and creating a new state organization at the same time the party was decaying nationally. Henry L. Borden, a Houston lawyer who had been the party candidate for attorney general in 1912 and one of the state's leading Bull Moosers, was made national committeeman; and Judge J. M. McCormick of Dallas, who drifted back into the regular party after 1916, took over as state chairman. Under their leadership the Texans entered the 1916 fray supporting "the principles of true Americanism and preparedness as typified by Col. Roosevelt" and opposing the "vacillation policies of the Wilson administration."[27]

The platform adopted at Waco said nothing about amalgamation. And though the delegation headed by Borden and McCormick went to Chicago uninstructed, the assembly declared for Roosevelt: "The exigencies of this nation are such as to imperatively require the election of Theodore Roosevelt to the presidency as an essential to the restoration of the confidence of the American people." Borden, however, arrived in Chicago for the national convention claiming he was for "a reunited party." But at the time of the state convention, the new committeeman was in New York conferring with Roosevelt and telegraphing to his comrades in Waco: "The Colonel's hat went into the ring yesterday and the Spring drive has started." Obviously, the shift in Borden's position during the short interval had been influenced by TR's own change of heart regarding the nomination. Once the national Bull Moose crusade crumbled at Chicago, the Texas party, like others across the South, simply vanished from the political scene. Many Progressives were Republicans at heart as well as Roosevelt's followers, and when his star faded they followed the lead of such men as McCormick and returned to the GOP.[28]

The Republican convention at Fort Worth also named an uninstructed contingent to Chicago. The gathering, "one of the largest and whitest . . . held in many years," ran into difficulty over naming the national convention delegation. Because of the Terrell Election Law, the body named forty delegates, although the state was entitled to only twenty-six votes in the convention under the reduced representation scheme implemented by the GOP National Committee. "The conflict between Texas state law and the official call was considered by the national committee," said James B. Reynolds, its secretary, "when it fixed the representation of the southern states." At Chicago the committee seated all forty men, although the state cast only the allotted twenty-six votes in the presidential balloting. Yet another controversy arose when Charles J. Hostrasser, a delegate at Fort Worth from Hearne, attempted to get through a resolution condemning National Committeeman H. F. MacGregor, who was also presiding officer, for "his lily-white methods." Hostrasser also sought to have several Roosevelt men put on the official delegation, and when he failed in both ventures, he withdrew, "shouting in protest as long as his voice could be heard."

Approximately sixty people followed him into a rump convention at the Fort Worth City Hall. There a rival at-large delegation equally divided between whites and Negroes was chosen and instructed for Roosevelt and the insurgents were admonished to support Ed McCarthy of Galveston for national committeeman at Chicago in place of MacGregor. Although Secretary Reynolds acknowledged that Hostrasser had filed a notice to contest the regular delegation before the National Committee, the group did not appear in Chicago. The *Arkansas Gazette* indicated that "most of the secessionists were Negroes." Even so, several Negroes were among the estimated seven hundred delegates attending the main convention which endorsed MacGregor for another four-year stint. He had worked hand-in-glove with Hilles on Taft's behalf in 1912, and though the Texas delegates were not officially instructed, it is significant that a majority voted for the former president on the first ballot at Chicago before switching to Hughes. The gathering was silent about amalgamation, although the Bull Moosers were welcomed back at a second GOP convention in August that named Rene B. Creager to run against Governor James E. Ferguson. In May, however, the Republican platform was content with abusing Wilson and the Democrats for "blowing hot and cold" with American honor "at home and abroad." The protective tariff was also approved in the platform and a plank inserted declaring for preparedness. "The reunited Republicans" became the GOP battle cry for the November campaign, yet the lily-white–black-and-tan confrontation among Texas Republicans continued throughout the 1920s. The issue raised by Hostrasser at Fort Worth did not end in the state until 1932 and the final break of the Negroes with the Grand Old Party.[29]

Republican activity in South Carolina, on the other hand, was nearly nonexistent during 1916, and though the state held a gubernatorial election, the party did not offer a candidate. The Charleston *News and Courier* reported on May 26, three days after the Texas conventions, that a full delegation had been named: "The Palmetto delegation is composed of 11 delegates under the new plan of representation adopted by the Republican national executive committee, which cut this state down from 18 to 11." Yet the scholar searches the state's newspapers in vain for any prior indication of a Republican convention. Joseph W. Tolbert, the planter from Ninety-six, was not only national committeeman and state chairman, but he also led the contingent to Chicago. There was apparently some opposition to his hold on the party, but he won reelection to the National Committee with only one dissenting vote in Chicago. Although several Negroes on the delegation favored Roosevelt, the same newspaper later reported: "The Colonel will hardly poll ten percent of the total southern vote in the GOP convention if he is nominated at all. The Roosevelt vote in all the rest of the south will probably not exceed the vote he will get from North Carolina and he will not poll a majority of that state's ballot." Accordingly, Tolbert and the Old Guard favored former Vice-President Charles W. Fairbanks to oppose Wilson. Their preconvention maneuvering notwithstanding, the South Carolina GOP, which remained primarily a Negro organization, maintained its minority party status by giving Hughes a mere 1,558 votes in November.[30]

The Tennessee Bull Moosers waited until June 3, just four days before the national convention, to declare for Roosevelt. That organization had been confronted with difficult choices throughout because of Governor Hooper and the state's sizable Republican vote. Great pressures were again exerted for them to return to their traditional party moorings and to keep a united front. But Roosevelt's reticence toward another Progressive nomination compounded their problems and hastened a growing amalgamation sentiment. Although several Georgia and Tennessee leaders planned a joint Bull Moose conference in April and even took steps to establish a Roosevelt newspaper in the area, the Tennesseans went their own way in 1916. The first move toward reconciliation occurred when State Chairman Harry B. Anderson attended the GOP State Convention on May 3 and made a plea for harmony. He was joined on the Republican podium by William Barker, secretary of the Progressive State Committee, who likewise called for a united front to face the Democrats. Moreover, Roosevelt's attitude placed his Tennessee followers in an intolerable position. When Anderson asked him to intervene with several recalcitrant party members, he replied tartly that he could not "put myself in the position where I was asking them to nominate me."

Yet Roosevelt informed Foster V. Brown, a former GOP congressman from Tennesseee and onetime attorney general of Puerto Rico: "If I am nominated and accept the nomination, it will be with the determination to treat the past as completely past and to give absolutely fair play to all my supporters." Caught in the crossfire, Anderson halfheartedly called the Nashville convention into session and quickly secured a delegation to the national convention. The gathering not only instructed for Roosevelt but adopted a platform that endorsed the reelection of G. Tom Taylor as national committeeman. But, reported the Chattanooga *Daily Times,* the forty delegates present set about increasing membership on the State Executive Committee, which "brought out the fact that an amalgamation between the progressive and republican parties is expected." And the Republicans were more than willing to join in a healing effort. Immediately after the national convention, on June 11, the Tennessee GOP committee adopted a resolution opening "its membership to at least ten or more members of the Progressive state committee for the sake of harmony." G. Tom Taylor, perhaps the state's leading Bull Mooser, thereupon resigned as Progressive national committeeman and announced his intention to vote for Hughes. Yet many Tennessee Progressives were slow to abandon the new party. C. A. Dagley, who had taken over as secretary of the state committee, took issue with Taylor's position, declaring "that unless Charles Evans Hughes comes out soon with a statement that sounds good to the Progressives, he can expect little support from members of that party next November." Their differences notwithstanding, the bulk of Bull Moosers closed ranks with the Republicans, although their united front was not enough to carry the Volunteer State for Hughes and Overall.[31]

The national conventions opened with great fanfare and amid an electrically charged atmosphere on June 7, four days after the last southern convention at Nashville. All of the eleven ex-Confederate states had Progressive and Republican representatives on hand for the unfolding spectacle, although with the exception of John M. Parker most of them took a back seat in the deliberations. "Each side," wrote the noted scholar John A. Garraty, "had one mighty asset the other lacked. The Republicans had a powerful organization, but no candidate of national stature or appeal. The Progressives were woefully lacking in experienced workers at the precinct level, but they had in Roosevelt a proved and colorful national leader." Before the conventions could proceed with the business at hand, the respective national committees assembled to hear an assortment of disputed contests, including several from the South. First, the Progressives found themselves with a procedural problem when Charles D. Hilles, still GOP national chairman, and other Republican leaders asked the Bull Moosers to refrain from nominating Roosevelt until after the Republicans had acted. That request brought on a serious division at a June 5 committee meeting as George W. Perkins, representing Roosevelt's interests at Chicago, advocated a wait-and-see policy. Another faction, typified by Victor Murdock of Kansas, Hiram Johnson, and Parker, was opposed to accommodation and urged the Progressives to press on with Roosevelt's selection. "There should be no understanding," Johnson told the committee, "that the Progressive convention should wait indefinitely upon the Republicans. The time will come for action and when that time comes we must be ready to act, and it must be understood that we will not mark time indefinitely for the other to act at their own pace." Throughout the days that followed, the Bull Moosers were bitterly divided on how to resolve the issue, although in the end they nominated Roosevelt on their own initiative. Before breaking up, the Progressive committee settled any dispute that might arise from contesting delegations by approving the temporary roll which had been presented by the State delegation chairmen.[32]

The Republicans not only sought a quick amalgamation agreement, but their National Committee was plagued with several tiresome contests. Sixty-two of the convention's 987 seats were at stake and, reported the New York *Times,* "a majority are from southern states, involving rows between 'lily white' regular and 'black and tan' contesting factions." The southern cases did not attract the attention they had generated in 1912, although contests from every state in the region except Arkansas and North Carolina constituted fifty-five of the total heard. Nor does that figure include the entire fifteen seats for Virginia; here twice the number of authorized delegates appeared, and on a motion by Hilles the Virginians were allowed to settle among themselves who would be seated. One delegate each was contested from Florida, Mississippi, and Texas; in the Florida dispute George W. Bean of Tampa was seated over former Negro officeholder, C. H. Alston. The inflated figure for the South, however, was produced when the entire Alabama, Louisiana, and Georgia delegations were contested—a total of forty-five seats.

The Alabama regulars successfully beat off a challenge from the state's black-and-tan faction after Oscar D. Street informed the committee that a majority of Alabama Negroes voted for the Democrats. But in the Louisiana cases, which caused the committee more concern than any others, the impasse was bridged by an amicable agreement that allowed both delegations to be seated with one-half vote each. That arrangement "also contemplates," commented the *Times,* "the resignation of National Committeeman Victor Liosel. Each faction has a candidate for the place, but it was said today the choice would probably go to Armand Romain of New Orleans who is a member of the regular delegation." Although Louisiana Negroes under Walter L. Cohen won a partial reprieve, Romain's connections with the lily-whites placed that faction in the driver's seat for the next four years. The Georgia disputes were as nasty as ever with the decision going to the contingent headed by National Committeeman Henry S. Jackson. Although Walter H. Johnson employed "three New York, one Richmond, one Washington, and three Georgia lawyers" to argue his case, the committee ruled against his delegates on the basis of "irregularity." The rejected Georgians thereupon loudly requested the National Committee to adopt a resolution condemning lily-whiteism in the South, but it was brushed aside. The black-and-tan at-large delegation and two districts from Texas withdrew their contests without a hearing for the sake of harmony. Even though the committee ruled consistently for lily-white delegations, southern Negroes were not without representation in the convention. The Mississippi contingent had three Negroes, and W. I. Saunders of the troublesome ninth Alabama district had the distinction of being the only delegate recognized by the convention over the objections of the National Committee.[33]

Although the Georgia Negroes and others appealed to the GOP convention for relief, the credentials committee, which was formed on the first day, June 7, refused all appeals except the single Alabama case. And the southerners were all but forgotten as the Republicans, intent upon patching over the troubles of 1912, rushed toward the nomination of Charles Evans Hughes. "We did not do very well," Warren G. Harding said at the opening of his keynote address, "in making harmony the last time we met." The future president pleaded with the delegates to "forget the old differences, and find new inspiration and new compensation in a united endeavor to restore the country." When the convention reconvened on June 8, the credentials committee report, which, unlike four years earlier, contained no minority report, was adopted without opposition. The southern lily-white delegations with the exception of Saunders and a handful of Negroes from Louisiana and Mississippi were seated without fanfare. The platform, presented by Senator Henry Cabot Lodge of Massachusetts, said nothing about the South, although it also reflected the compromise spirit flowing through the hall. "It was progressive enough not to alienate the advanced elements of the party and conservative enough for the Old Guard; it was adopted without significant debate." After listening to hell-raising speeches from "Uncle Joe" Cannon and Senator William E. Borah of Idaho, the assembly responded to a request from the Progressive convention and appointed a special committee to work on mutual problems. Composed of Utah Senator Reed Smoot, Senator W. Murray Crane of Massachusetts, Borah, Columbia University President Nicholas Murray Butler, and A. R. Johnson, a former Ohio congressman, this famous committee, according to Butler and Hilles, "might be found to hold the fate of the party in their hands."[34]

The Progressive convention opened a few blocks away in the Auditorium with a keynote address by Raymond Robins that emphasized a "Let's Be Patient" theme. The gathering, reported the New York *Times,* "was an indescribable hubbub" as clamor for Roosevelt's immediate nomination rent the air. A radical faction headed by Victor Murdock of Kansas, who would later head the party, led "the Teddy Racket," urging his selection without waiting for the Republicans. Yet the Robins-Perkins-Johnson wing counseled restraint, and a motion by James R. Garfield, second son of the president and Roosevelt's secretary of the interior, drove through a resolution for a conference committee to meet with the GOP. Garfield's proposal excited the radicals to the wildest fury until a Missouri delegate announced that he had a communication from Sagamore Hill. Then, after party secretary Oscar K. Davis read a letter dated June 8 from TR to W. P. Jackson of Maryland, a former senator and the state's GOP national committeeman since 1908, convention chairman Robins was empowered to appoint the committee. The Jackson letter was a straight appeal for harmony between the two conventions, as Roosevelt, still seeking the Republican endorsement, quoted Lincoln's Civil War rhetoric in appealing for "a common effort to save our common country." Thus armed, Robins overcame the objections of Murdock and designated a distinguished panel of Roosevelt followers to the five-man embassy: Perkins, Johnson, Parker—representing the South and the radical faction—Horace S. Wilkinson of New York, and genial, well-liked Charles J. Bonaparte of Maryland, a son of Napoleon's brother Jerome and attorney general in Roosevelt's cabinet.[35]

The committee held extended sessions during the evening of June 8 9, and, though the talks were always civil and courteous, GOP preoccupation with Hughes rendered them useless. Both sides readily agreed to the outline of a joint platform but stalled miserably when the negotiations turned to a presidential candidate. The Progressives were dead set on Roosevelt as the best man for the presidency and could think of no other nominee. John M. Parker, according to Butler, who later penned a first-rate account of the deliberations, likewise spoke for Roosevelt: He "harped on the old and tireless string of carrying the solid south for Republican principles. His argument was that this could be done if Republican principles were nicknamed Progressive, and if the candidate were Roosevelt. He was certain that Roosevelt could carry Louisiana, North Carolina, and probably other southern states, and if the Republican party were given a Progressive veneer so as to overcome the long-time antipathy of the southerner to the very name 'Republican,' all that could be hoped for would be speedily accomplished." Butler, obviously unimpressed with Parker and southern Republicanism, next recounts that Senator Borah informed all present that the GOP convention would never nominate Roosevelt "and they might as well accept the fact." Unable to reach common agreement, the talks broke up at 3:30 A.M. after six and one-half hours of continuous deliberation.[36]

Smoot, a powerful leader in the Mormon church, immediately took the podium when the Republicans reconvened on June 9 to report on the plenary sessions. Speaking with a sharp, clear voice, he read a prepared statement indicating that both sides agreed the two parties should unite but that the Progressives wanted Roosevelt to receive the nomination. Smoot's remarks were greeted with applause, but Harding, the GOP permanent chairman, simply stated that since the committee "had not asked for its discharge it is authorized to continue its work." Without further comment, he ordered the clerk to call the roll for presidential nominations as the next order of business. New York Governor Charles S. Whitman put Hughes's name before the assembly first after Alabama passed and Arizona yielded to the Empire State; the wild demonstration that followed, with the

Mississippi delegates leading the bandwagon across the floor, made it clear that Hughes was the convention favorite. Ten additional names were presented and seconded, including New Mexico Senator Albert B. Fall's formal nomination of Roosevelt. But the Republicans were in no mood to consider him. "Hisses and cries of, 'Throw him out' " greeted the speech: "In the prayer of every American praying for success here today, although in the heart of that American may be the favored name of some favored son, there is yet whispered the name of one great American." On the first ballot, however, Hughes led the field with 253½ votes—far short of the necessary 494—as the southerners scattered their 174 ballots among fourteen candidates. Ominously, Roosevelt received only 65 votes—fewer than Elihu Root, Theodore Burton of Ohio, Albert B. Cummins of Iowa, John W. Weeks of Massachusetts, former Vice-President Charles W. Fairbanks, and Lawrence Y. Sherman of Illinois.[37]

As the Republicans prepared for a second ballot before adjournment, the Progressive convention continued its hassling over waiting for the GOP or pushing for Roosevelt's nomination. Although more practical politicians such as Walter Brown of Ohio and William Flinn of Pennsylvania had stood at Armageddon long enough and wanted to rejoin the Republicans at any cost, the assembly continued to await events down the street. In the meantime, the Progressives adopted a platform, which, according to the New York *Times,* stressed "Americanism, preparedness, protection, woman [sic] suffrage"; it said nothing about the South, although the protective tariff was again approved as "essential to our national prosperity." But getting Roosevelt on one of the national tickets was the order of the day, and his poor showing on the first Republican ballot caused the Bull Moose radicals to press anew for action. As the wrangling dragged on, Edward R. Gunby, a Florida delegate, reported the *Times,* "aroused the crowd to some excitement when he declared that all the army engineers in the country were not enough to rebuild the bridges the Progressives had burned behind them when they left the Republican party. He likened the Colonel to Saul of Tarsus, and became so mixed up when the crowd began to laugh that he began to refer to the Colonel as 'Tall of Sarsus.' That was enough and he had to sit down." Speaker after speaker joined in the chorus for Roosevelt although their rhetoric was soon overshadowed by the Republicans as Harding ordered the roll called for another ballot.[38]

Hughes's vote increased to 328 on the second ballot, far outdistancing that of any other candidate. Roosevelt's strength peaked at 81 votes, while the remaining field stayed about even except for Weeks of Massachusetts whose tally dropped from 105 to 79; Sherman was also a big loser on the ballot. The southern vote was again so scattered and confused that it is difficult to determine what if any trends were present in the region; Hughes, Root, Burton, Fairbanks, and du Pont gained while Roosevelt and Weeks lost southern delegates. Faced with the inevitability of a

Hughes nomination, the Republicans adjourned without another ballot in the hope that agreement could be reached with the Bull Moosers. The night of June 9–10 was filled with endless political discussions as the conference committees met twice. Another standoff resulted when the Progressives would not abandon Roosevelt and the Republicans were unwilling to suggest an alternative to Hughes. Moreover, Johnson and Parker withdrew from the committee deliberations when it became apparent that Roosevelt was giving up the fight. The colonel talked over a private wire to Chicago during much of the night with conferees from both parties. When Nicholas Murray Butler asked if he could suggest a compromise candidate acceptable to each convention, Roosevelt suggested Massachusetts Senator Henry Cabot Lodge.[39]

Though Roosevelt insisted Lodge was "straight as string," it was obvious from the start that he would never receive endorsement from either party. Again, Smoot took the podium as the GOP gathering was called together for its final session to report on the conference meetings. But he had no sooner read a letter from the colonel vouching for Lodge than Harding curtly announced: "The business in order before the convention is that of balloting for the nomination of a candidate for President." The southerners thereupon joined heartily in putting Hughes over the top. The Alabama, Florida, and Georgia delegations cast a solid vote for Hughes before Illinois clinched the nomination on the alphabetical roll call; Louisiana, Texas, and Virginia also registered an undivided Hughes vote, and though a majority of the remaining southern vote went to him there were some defections. Six and one-half votes from Mississippi and Tennessee went to Roosevelt, who got but a total eighteen votes; the South Carolinians cast five votes for Senator du Pont of Delaware; and the North Carolina delegation gave Lodge seven ballots, his only vote in the convention. Charles W. Fairbanks, who had been vice-president under Roosevelt, was again given second place on the ticket with 836 votes; all but six southern votes from Alabama, Arkansas, and North Carolina went to the vice-presidential nominee. All of the southern dissidents voted for onetime Senator Elmer J. Burkett of Nebraska. Their work finished, the Republicans adjourned to prepare for a heated campaign against "this man Wilson" and to see whether the Bull Moosers would again go it alone or close ranks behind Hughes.[40]

When the Progressives assembled the same morning at ten o'clock, however, the Lodge proposal was loudly shouted down. The Republican conference report was likewise rejected by a vociferous outcry. Parker, who had been leading the radicals throughout, thereupon pleaded with the delegates to reject all overtures for compromise: "Nominate your man and go before the people on a platform of Americanism," he said as the convention rules were suspended for the Roosevelt nomination. Bainbridge Colby of New Jersey made the formal presentation, and Raymond

Robins put the question: "All in favor of Colonel Roosevelt's nomination by acclamation please rise." Immediately, "the immense throng rose in a roar," reported the wire services, "as leaders on the stage and delegates on the floor shrieked hysterically, hugged each other and threw hats in the air." The deed accomplished, an adjournment was called to await news from Oyster Bay, where, according to H. L. Stoddard, Roosevelt "sincerely believed it was his patriotic duty to refuse another Progressive party nomination and to endorse the Republican nominee."[41]

The southerners, who had been taking a back seat, were elated as the South was recognized through Parker's nomination for the vice-presidency when the convention reconvened at three o'clock. "It is proper that a man from the southern states should be made the running mate of our leader," Hiram Johnson proclaimed while seconding the nomination and Judge W. E. Howell of Louisiana told the assembly that "in the interests of the party and its work in the south, Mr. Parker would accept." But the nomination, which "carried with a tremendous ovation and not a dissenting voice," brought little comfort to either Parker or the South. For he had no sooner thanked his fellow delegates for the honor, telling them that their convention was "a protest against the ability of a few men to control the destiny of 100,000,000 people," than the Roosevelt bombshell arrived: "I cannot accept at this time. I do not know the attitude of the candidate of the Republican Party toward the vital issues of the day. Therefore, if you desire an immediate decision, I must decline the honor." The Bull Moose faithful sat in dumb disbelief as they listened to the colonel's telegram. Roosevelt was clearly on the road to amalgamation with Hughes and the GOP—the very circumstance H. L. Anderson of Florida had forecast to mean extinction for Progressives in the South. It is little wonder that the southerners joined the sullen, disquieted exodus as the delegates "tore up photographs of the Rough Rider, threw Roosevelt badges on the floor and stamped on them, and drifted out of the convention hall in angry disorder." The Bull Moose crusade as well as the schism among Republicans in the South ended when the disappointed conventioneers spilled out into the hot Chicago afternoon.[42]

Chapter 9

Epilogue: Amalgamation at Last

"The delegates filed out," reported the New Orleans *Times-Picayune*, "with the last words of Colonel Roosevelt and patriotic airs ringing in their ears." And most of them marched out of the Progressive party forever. Immediately, the dejected Bull Moosers split into two major groupings: those who agreed with Roosevelt that their first job was the defeat of Wilson and who were therefore willing to close ranks behind Hughes; and the radical faction led by such men as Parker, Victor Murdock, Gifford Pinchot, and Mathew Hale who felt "sold out" by Roosevelt but who wanted to maintain the party organization intact. The southerners on the National Committee—Joseph O. Thompson of Alabama, Winfield S. Holt of Arkansas, Harry L. Anderson of Florida, Harry G. Hastings of Georgia, Pearl Wight of Louisiana, Benjamin F. Fridge of Mississippi, James N. Williamson of North Carolina, T. H. Wannamaker of South Carolina, G. Tom Taylor of Tennessee, Henny L. Borden of Texas, and Percy S. Stephenson of Virginia—were widely separated following the Chicago conventions. Parker continued his protest and ultimately led his followers into the Democratic camp in November, but most southern leaders either remained neutral or came out for Hughes. Yet, as H. L. Stoddard wrote, all of them were obliged to look on helplessly as "the Colonel bowed his head and unprotestingly accepted the condemnation of those who did not see the real issue before the country as he plainly saw it." The Progressive National Convention dissolved on Saturday, Stoddard continues, and the "following Tuesday Roosevelt dined with Hughes, the Republican nominee, in New York and pledged his full support."[1]

Unwilling or unable to accept the inevitable, Parker joined in a move to reconstruct the party at a meeting of the National Committee on June 26—two weeks after his nomination for the vice-presidency. "I am going to Chicago on the 26th," he wrote to John C. Houk of Tennessee, "to do all that lies in my power to see that the Progressive party is kept in existence, to place my nomination unreservedly in the hands of the Executive Committee, urging they select as strong a ticket as possible." He also telegraphed several southern committeemen, including those from Kentucky, New Mexico, and Oklahoma, asking for their proxies at the meeting. But not all of the southerners supported Parker and the radical position; Bainbridge Colby, for instance, held the proxy for Anderson of

Florida though Parker had specifically requested it. When the committee voted thirty-two to six for a pro-Hughes resolution after a hot six-hour debate, Parker was not even able to control his own state. Pearl Wight, the onetime Taft referee in Louisiana, joined with committeemen from Alabama, Arkansas, Texas, Georgia, and Virginia to support the measure, while the vote of Florida, Mississippi, and South Carolina was not cast; G. Tom Taylor of Tennessee, who had already left the Bull Moosers to rejoin the GOP did not attend the session. North Carolina therefore, in all the South, was the only state that refused to stand behind Hughes. Although the southern Progressives overwhelmingly favored amalgamation, Parker announced at the meeting that he would seek the vice-presidency with or without Roosevelt. A plan to substitute Victor Murdock, Progressive national committeeman and leader of the party's tiny delegation in Congress, for Roosevelt was turned down.[2]

Roosevelt sent a lengthy letter to T. H. Wannamaker on June 24, expressing his utmost admiration for Parker and the southern Bull Moosers, but he wanted the party to disband because "to perpetuate the Progressive Party organization at present would mean . . . the risk of seeing the Progressive organization seized by unworthy persons." In Roosevelt's mind the party was dead. Yet Parker and his cronies addressed a call to "the Patriotic Men and Women of America" for another Progressive convention to meet on August 2 in Indianapolis to select a revised national ticket. Several southern delegates joined in the meeting which opted to continue the party machinery in spite of Rooseveltian displeasure by naming an Executive Committee "to cooperate with the fifteen members of the National Committee who refused to vote for the endorsement of Charles E. Hughes at Chicago, June 26." After the diehards found themselves unable to agree on a presidential nominee, authorization was granted for Parker to be on the ballot alone "in every state where there is a nucleus of an organization left." Parker, who received a scattered vote in several states and even came in third in Louisiana, opened his campaign at Cleveland, Ohio, criticizing both the Railroad Eight Hour Law and "the men who betrayed the Progressive Party." And the Prohibition party approached him during the campaign to form a joint national ticket with their presidential candidate. Although the offer was spurned at first, a merger between the two organizations was later worked out as Parker continued his speaking tour in several midwestern and eastern cities. Finally, on October 14, at the formal notification ceremony of his nomination in New York, Parker launched a biting attack on Roosevelt, announcing that he supported Wilson for reelection and would "stump the country at his own expense" for the president.[3]

As Parker went around the country looking for votes and castigating Roosevelt and Perkins for destroying the party, conventions met in at least two southern states. The Progressives simply ceased existence throughout the South after the national conventions, but the Louisiana party held one last assembly on August 2. Even here Parker was required to struggle to prevent an endorsement of Hughes, though the body finally approved a slate of electors and accepted Parker's plan for continuation of the party. A similar convention that had been scheduled to meet in Texas before the Bull Moose disintegration did not assemble. The Texas GOP, however, hoping that the "re-united Republicans" would win in November, met on August 8 in San Antonio. Unlike their counterparts in many southern states, the Texas Negroes were strong enough to block a pro-literacy plank in the platform gotten up by a group of Bull Moosers who had rejoined the party. Rene B. Creager, a Brownsville attorney who controlled the Texas GOP until his death in 1950, was nominated to oppose Governor James E. Ferguson with Negro support. Amalgamation was also the order of the day in Tennessee, where one of Hooper's correspondents told him that since "TR was for Hughes, it was time for the Tennessee GOP to quit fighting."[4]

It was business as usual after 1916 for the Republicans throughout the South. All eleven members of the GOP National Committee—Oscar D. Street of Alabama, Harmon L. Remmel of Arkansas, Henry S. Chubb of Florida, Henry S. Jackson of Georgia, Armand Romain of Louisiana, Lonzo B. Moseley of Mississippi, John M. Morehead of North Carolina, Joseph W. Tolbert of South Carolina, Jesse M. Littleton of Tennessee, Henry F. MacGregor of Texas, and Alvah H. Martin of Virginia—were identified with the Old Guard to the man. Six—Chubb, Jackson, Moseley, Tolbert, MacGregor, and Martin—had been on the committee previously and had fought for Taft in 1912. "The Republican National Committee," Albert J. Beveridge wrote later, "was found to be overwhelmingly dominated by the same 'bosses' and reactionaries who had helped to commit the 'crime of 1912.' " Nowhere was this truer than in the South, where the committeemen, who presumably spoke for the party rank and file, had been battling the Bull Moose insurgents for the past four years. Charles D. Hilles, who had been national committeeman since 1912, was replaced by William R. Willcox following the Hughes nomination. The southern chiefs were therefore compelled to work with the onetime head of New York's Public Service Commission who was picked to manage the 1916 campaign. "Willcox had proved to be an able public servant," writes Hughes's biographer, "but in politics he was a novice who did not speak the language of professionals," and this contributed to the difficulties of the southerners.[5]

The disenchantment of the committeemen notwithstanding, 1916 represented another failure for the southern GOP. Although Hughes managed to get slightly more than the combined Roosevelt-Taft vote in 1912, the *Arkansas Gazette* commented on election eve: "The Republicans do not appear to be making much effort to poll a large vote [in the South] except in Texas and North Carolina." The New Yorker campaigned extensively across the nation but never in the South. In only five states—Arkansas, Florida, North Carolina, Tennessee, and Virginia—did his vote exceed the Roosevelt-Taft total four years before; moreover, Taft had gotten a greater vote in every southern state except Alabama, Florida, and North Carolina in 1908. The Republican tally in Louisiana, where Parker admonished his followers to support Wilson, fell to a miserable 6,466 votes, though Whitmell P. Martin, running as a nominal Progressive, retained his seat in Congress. Hughes got 8,301 votes over the combined strength of Roosevelt and Taft in the South but interestingly he won ninety-four counties whereas they had carried but forty-four. And the GOP did no better in the congressional races: Britt retained his North Carolina seat after a long and bitter challenge against his Democratic opponent before the Congress while Slemp and the two Tennesseans were handily returned by their Appalachian constituencies. The state and senatorial contests were equally disappointing, indicating that the Bull Moose–Republican schism extending over four years had failed to affect Democratic domination in any manner whatsoever. "President Wilson," said the *Gazette,* one day after the election, "was given the usual substantial majority in the southern states . . . and Democratic state tickets were elected by customary majorities."[6]

The southern Progressives for all their hopes had failed to build a white opposition party in the South, and the Hughes vote in the region suggests that Republican strength actually increased slightly after the Bull Moose crusade had ended. The Progressive party ceased to function as a viable political machine when its National Committee voted to endorse Hughes, although Parker and the radicals carried on the charade of a campaign until November. Finally, after protracted negotiations, those remnants of the national party that had not been reabsorbed into the GOP affiliated with the Prohibition party in April 1917 as a final act of defiance. The small success of the party in Louisiana had been the work of disgruntled Democrats whose leaders soon rejoined that party. Elsewhere in the South the Progressives had made no significant impact upon either Republicans or Democrats; they simply disappeared from the political scene through amalgamation into other parties and without notice from the southern mainstream.

Undoubtedly, the most significant long-term influence of the 1912–1916 schism among southern Republicans was its contribution to the ongoing Negro revolt against the GOP. In 1916, formal Negro protest movements were organized in North Carolina, where the Republican gubernatorial candidate was an avowed segregationist, and in Louisiana, Arkansas, and Alabama as a result of developments in the preconvention campaign. Much of the difficulty stemmed from a growing lily-whiteism across the South and the resultant loss of Negro participation in party councils. The reduction in size of Republican delegations by the National Committee

Table 9-1
Southern Presidential
Voting Statistics, 1908–1916

	Taft in 1908	TR and Taft in 1912	Hughes in 1916	TR and Taft Counties in 1912	Hughes Counties in 1916	Wilson in 1912	Wilson in 1916
Alabama	25,561	32,420	28,660	3	3	82,438	99,409
Arkansas	56,684	45,970	47,135	1	0	68,869	112,189
Florida	10,654	8,814	14,611	0	0	36,417	55,984
Georgia	41,355	27,200	11,980	6	1	94,019	127,724
Louisiana	8,958	13,157	6,466	0	0	60,435	79,875
Mississippi	4,315	5,138	4,253	0	0	57,164	80,422
N. Carolina	114,887	98,269	120,890	11	24	144,407	168,383
S. Carolina	3,963	1,829	1,558	0	0	48,357	61,846
Tennessee	117,977	113,169	116,257	17	43	133,025	153,408
Texas	68,506	55,608	64,673	4	9	219,559	287,430
Virginia	52,568	45,065	49,358	2	14	90,354	102,825
Totals	505,428	446,639	465,841	44	94	1,035,044	1,329,495

SOURCE: Robinson, *Presidential Vote*, pp. 46–53; *World Almanac, 1913*, pp. 721–66.

sharply cut the number of places open to Negroes for recognition; federal appointments, already limited under Roosevelt and Taft, became virtually nonexistent under the Wilson administration. This, coupled with the anti-Negro stance of the Bull Moosers unquestionably caused Negro leaders in the South and throughout the country to question their traditional alliance with the GOP. Yet massive Negro defections to the Democrats lay in the future because, noted Elbert W. Tatum, "in 1916 it was thought by most political observers that the Negro vote went solidly for Hughes." Although several Negro leaders in the South encouraged their followers to support Wilson in 1916, Alexander Heard has observed that the president's "segregation policy and southern background barred a wholesale change of party." The groundwork had been laid, however, for the black exodus to the Democrats over the next decade and a half that would deprive southern Republicanism of its longest and most consistent element of support.[7]

Notes

Chapter 1

1. Theodore Roosevelt to J. M. Parker, July 13, 1912, Theodore Roosevelt Papers, Manuscripts Division, Library of Congress, Washington, D.C., hereafter cited as TR Papers; Arthur S. Link, "Theodore Roosevelt and the South in 1912," *North Carolina Historical Review* 23:3 (July 1946): 314; C. Vann Woodward, *Origins of the New South, 1877–1913* (Baton Rouge: Louisiana State University Press, 1951), p. 478.

2. Wilbur J. Cash, *The Mind of the South* (New York: Knopf, 1941), pp. 128–31; Alwyn Barr, *Reconstruction to Reform: Texas Politics, 1876–1906* (Austin: The University of Texas Press, 1971), p. 176; Everett R. Boyce, ed., *The Unwanted Boy: The Autobiography of Governor Ben W. Hooper* (Knoxville: University of Tennessee Press, 1963), p. 130; Paul E. Isaac, *Prohibition and Politics: Turbulent Decades in Tennessee, 1885–1920* (Knoxville: University of Tennessee Press, 1965), pp. 191–94; William Ivy Hair, *Bourbonism and Agrarian Protest: Louisiana Politics, 1877–1900* (Baton Rouge: Louisiana State University Press, 1969), pp. 275–79; Thomas D. Clark and Albert D. Kirwan, *The South since Appomattox* (New York: Oxford University Press, 1967), pp. 108ff.; Guy R. Hathorn, "The Political Career of C. Bascom Slemp" (Ph.D. dissertation, Duke University, 1950), pp. 89–93.

3. Delegate strength for each southern state in 1912 was: Alabama 24, Arkansas 18, Florida 12, Georgia 28, Louisiana 20, Mississippi 20, North Carolina 24, South Carolina 18, Tennessee 24, Texas 40, Virginia 24 *(Official Report of the Proceedings of the Fifteenth Republican National Convention Held in Chicago, Illinois, June 18, 19, 20, 21, and 22, 1912* [New York: Republican National Committee, 1912], pp. 305ff.).

4. Wilson carried every county in the South except Alabama 4, Arkansas 1, Georgia 3, North Carolina 10, Tennessee 24, Texas 2, Virginia 2 (Edgar E. Robinson, *The Presidential Vote, 1896–1932* [Stanford: Stanford University Press, 1934], pp. 133ff.).

5. Seth M. Scheiner, "President Theodore Roosevelt and the Negro, 1901–1908," *Journal of Negro History* 67:3 (July 1962): 169–73; Willard B. Gatewood, *Theodore Roosevelt and the Art of Controversy: Episodes of the White House Years* (Baton Rouge: Louisiana State University Press, 1970), passim; J. Leonard Bates, *The United States, 1898–1928: Progressivism and a Society in Transition* (New York: McGraw-Hill, 1976), p. 75; Dewey Grantham, Jr., "Dinner at the White House: Theodore Roosevelt, Booker T. Washington, and the South," *Tennessee Historical Quarterly,* 17:2 (July 1958): 112–18; Uniontown (Ala.) *Negro Leader,* May 3, 1912.

6. Grantham, "Dinner at the White House," pp. 115–16; Raleigh *News and Observer,* February 1, 1912; TR to Charles G. Washburn, November 20, 1915, TR Papers, quoted in Etling Morison, ed., *The Letters of Theodore Roosevelt* (Cambridge: Harvard University Press, 1954), VIII, 981; Edmund Morris, *The Rise of Theodore Roosevelt* (New York: Coward, McCann, and Geoghegan, 1979), p. 727.

7. Richard B. Sherman, *The Republican Party and Black America from McKinley to Hoover, 1896–1933* (Charlottesville: University of Virginia Press, 1973),

pp. 38–45; Scheiner, "Roosevelt and the Negro," pp. 174–76; Gatewood, *Roosevelt and the Art of Controversy,* pp. 62–89.

8. George E. Mowry, *The Era of Theodore Roosevelt and the Birth of Modern America, 1900–1912* (New York: Harper and Row, 1958), pp. 166–67; Sherman, *The Republican Party and Black America,* pp. 38ff.; Whitefield McKinlay to TR, February 14, 1903, TR to Whitefield McKinlay, March 4, 1903, W. C. Crum to Whitefield McKinlay, September 22, 1903, Whitefield McKinlay Papers in Carter G. Woodson Collection, Manuscripts Division, Library of Congress, Washington, D.C., hereafter cited as McKinlay Papers.

9. Emma Lou Thornbrough, "The Brownsville Episode and the Negro Vote," *Mississippi Valley Historical Review* 44:3 (December 1957): 469–93; James A. Tinsley, "Roosevelt, Foraker, and the Brownsville Affray," *Journal of Negro History* 41:1 (January 1956): 43–65; Sherman, *The Republican Party and Black America,* pp. 55–63; Chicago *Daily Tribune,* May 13, 14, 1912; Richmond *Planet,* May 28, 1912.

10. John M. Blum, *The Republican Roosevelt* (Cambridge: Harvard University Press, 1962), pp. 43–46; Scheiner, "Roosevelt and the Negro," pp. 182–84; *Proceedings of the Thirteenth Republican National Convention Held in Chicago, Illinois, June 21, 22, 23, 1904* (Minneapolis: Republican National Committee, 1904), p. 165.

11. Henry F. Pringle, *The Life and Times of William Howard Taft* (New York: Farrar and Rinehart, 1939), I, 347; Paul D. Casdorph, "The Bogus Delegation to the 1860 Republican National Convention," *Southwestern Historical Quarterly* 65:4 (April 1962): 480–84; Malcolm Moos, *The Republicans: A History of Their Party* (New York: Random House, 1956), pp. 67–68.

12. *Official Report of the Proceedings of the Fourteenth Republican National Convention Held in Chicago, Illinois, June 16, 17, 18, and 19, 1908* (Columbus, Ohio: Republican National Committee, 1908), pp. 95–110; Chicago *Daily Tribune,* June 18, 1908.

13. *Proceedings of the 1908 Republican National Convention,* p. 182; Pringle, *Taft,* I, 370–77; Everett Walters, *Joseph Benson Foraker: Uncompromising Republican* (Columbus: Ohio History Press, 1948), pp. 323–47; Robinson, *Presidential Vote,* pp. 69–77.

14. Paolo Coletta, *The Presidency of William Howard Taft* (Lawrence: The University Press of Kansas, 1973), p. 30; Pringle, *Taft,* I, 389–91.

15. New York *Times,* October 16, 17, 20, 25, 1909; San Antonio *Daily Express,* October 17, 18, 1909; A. Ray Stephens, *The Taft Ranch: A Principality* (Austin: The University of Texas Press, 1964), pp. 162–64.

16. New York *Times,* October 28, 29, 1909, November 1, 1909; New Orleans *Daily Picayune,* November 1, 1909.

17. New York *Times,* November 1, 2, 1909.

18. Ibid., November 11, 1909; Richmond *Virginian,* November 11, 1909; Atlanta *Journal,* November 6, 1909.

19. Leslie H. Fishel, Jr., "The Negro in Northern Politics, 1870–1900," *Mississippi Valley Historical Review* 42:3 (December 1955): 466; Gordon B. McKinney, "Southern Mountain Republicans and the Negro, 1865–1900," *Journal of Southern History* 61:4 (November 1975): 513–16; Rayford W. Logan, *The Betrayal of the Negro from Rutherford B. Hayes to Woodrow Wilson* (New York: reprint, Collier Books, 1965), p. 347.

20. Sherman, *Republican Party and Black America,* pp. 2–4; *Colliers Magazine,* June 1, 1912; Paul D. Casdorph, "Norris Wright Cuney and Texas Republican Politics, 1883–1896," *Southwestern Historical Quarterly* 68:4 (April 1965): 455–64; Augusta A. Wheaton, *The Negro from 1863 to 1963* (New York: Vantage Press, 1963), pp. 67–68; Samuel D. Smith, *The Negro in Congress* (Chapel Hill: University of North Carolina Press, 1940), passim; Joseph J. Boris, ed., *Who's Who in Colored America: A Biographical Dictionary of Notable Living Persons of Negro Descent in America* (New York: Who's Who in Colored America Publishing Co., 1927), I, 128–33.

21. George H. Mayer, *The Republican Party, 1854–1966* (New York: Oxford University Press, 1967), p. 213; Robert D. Marcus, *The Grand Old Party: Political Structure in the Gilded Age, 1880–1896* (New York: Oxford University Press, 1971), p. 28; *Proceedings of the Republican National Convention Held at Chicago, Illinois, Thursday, Friday, Saturday, Monday, and Tuesday, June 2d, 3d, 4th, 6th, and 7th, 1880* (Chicago: Republican National Committee, 1880), pp. 165–69; *The Nation,* June 10, 1880.

22. Horace S. Merrill and Marion G. Merrill, *The Republican Command, 1897–1913* (Lexington: University of Kentucky Press, 1971), pp. 303–04; Paul D. Casdorph, "Texas Delegations to Republican National Conventions, 1860–1896" (M.A. thesis, The University of Texas, 1961), pp. 127–28; Henry F. Pringle, "Theodore Roosevelt and the South," *Virginia Quarterly Review* 9:1 (January 1933): 22–23; *Colliers Magazine,* May 4, June 1, 1912.

23. Vincent P. De Santis, *Republicans Face the Southern Question: The New Departure Years, 1877–1897* (Baltimore: Johns Hopkins University Press, 1959), p. 13; Thomas R. Cripps, "The Lily White Republicans, the Negro, the Party, and the South in the Progressive Era" (Ph.D. dissertation, University of Maryland, 1967), pp. 13–15; Tom Dillard, "To the Back of the Elephant: Racial Conflict in the Arkansas Republican Party," *Arkansas Historical Quarterly* 33:1 (Spring 1974): 9–10.

24. Sherman, *Republican Party and Black America,* pp. 32–35; Dallas *Morning News,* March 9, 1892; San Antonio *Daily Express,* September 11, 1902; Galveston *Daily News,* April 14, 1892; TR to Pearl Wight, January 26, 1912, TR Papers; Alexander J. Simpson, Jr., "George L. Sheldon and the Beginnings of the Lily White Movement in Mississippi, 1909–1932" (M.A. thesis, Mississippi State University, 1962), p. 38.

25. Robert L. Schuyler, ed., *Dictionary of American Biography, Supplement* (New York: Scribners, 1958), II, 514–15; Benjamin S. Phillips, "Administration of Governor Parker" (M.A. thesis, Louisiana State University, 1933), pp. 1–10; William D. Lewis, *The Life of Theodore Roosevelt* (New York: John C. Winston Co., 1919), p. 428.

26. Bruce L. Clayton, "An Intellectual in Politics: William Garrott Brown and the Idea of a Two Party South," *North Carolina Historical Review* 62:3 (July 1965): 320–25; Joseph F. Steelman, "Republicanism in North Carolina: John Motley Morehead's Campaign to Revive a Moribund Party, 1908–1910," *North Carolina Historical Review* 62:2 (April 1965): 155–58.

27. *Biographical Directory of the American Congress, 1774–1961* (Washington, D.C.: U.S. Congress, 1961), pp. 465, 1839; *Official Congressional Directory, 55th Congress* (Washington, D.C.: U.S. Congress, 1897), p. 126; Ethel M. Armes, *The Story of Iron and Coal in Alabama* (Birmingham: Birmingham Chamber of

Commerce, 1910), pp. 267–68.

28. Steelman, "Republicanism in North Carolina," p. 155; Moos, *The Republicans*, pp. 266–67; Mayer, *The Republican Party*, p. 318; *Official Congressional Directory, 62nd Congress* (Washington, D.C.: U.S. Congress, 1913), p. 99; *Biographical Directory of the American Congress, 1774–1961*, pp. 267–301.

29. Monroe Billington, *The Political South in the Twentieth Century* (New York: Scribners, 1975), pp. 11–15; George B. Tindall, *The Persistent Tradition in New South Politics* (Baton Rouge: Louisiana State University Press, 1975), pp. 46–47; Stanley P. Hirshson, *Farewell to the Bloody Shirt: Northern Republicans and the Southern Negro* (Bloomington: Indiana University Press, 1962), pp. 200–35; De Santis, *Republicans Face the Southern Question*, pp. 198–214.

30. Billington, *The Political South*, pp. 2–6; Carl Resek, ed., *The Progressives* (New York: Bobbs-Merrill, 1967), p. xi; Otis L. Graham, Jr., *An Encore for Reform: The Old Progressives and the New Deal* (New York: Oxford University Press, 1967), pp. 33–36.

31. Jack Temple Kirby, *Darkness at the Dawning: Race and Reform in the Progressive South* (Philadelphia: J. B. Lippincott, 1972), pp. 1–3; Tindall, *The Persistent Tradition*, pp. 65–66; Arthur S. Link, "The Progressive Movement in the South, 1870–1914," *North Carolina Historical Review* 23:2 (April 1946): 179–81.

32. Kenneth W. Hechler, *Insurgency: Personalities and Politics of the Taft Era* (New York: reprint, Russell and Russell, 1964), passim; Anne F. Scott, "The Southern Progressives in National Politics, 1906–1916" (Ph.D. dissertation, Radcliffe College, 1957), pp. 110–14; R. W. Austin to B. W. Hooper, February 15, 1912, Ben W. Hooper Papers, University of Tennessee Library, Knoxville, hereafter cited as Hooper Papers; Richmond *Virginian*, January 16, 1912.

33. Alan B. Gould, "Secretary of the Interior Walter L. Fisher and the Return to Constructive Conservation: Problems and Policies of the Conservation Movement, 1909–1913" (Ph.D. dissertation, West Virginia University, 1969), p. 443; James Penick, Jr., *Progressive Politics and Conservation* (Chicago: University of Chicago Press, 1968), pp. 1–10; Alpheus T. Mason, *Bureaucracy Convicts Itself: The Ballinger-Pinchot Controversy of 1910* (New York: Viking Press, 1941), pp. 27–28; Arthur S. Link and William B. Catton, *American Epoch: A History of the United States since the 1890s* (New York: Knopf, 1967), pp. 94–96, 103.

34. Willard B. Gatewood, "Theodore Roosevelt and Arkansas, 1901–1912," *Arkansas Historical Quarterly* 22:1 (Spring 1973): 14–16; William H. Harbaugh, *Power and Responsibility: The Life and Times of Theodore Roosevelt* (New York: Farrar, Straus, and Cudahy, 1961), pp. 334–37; *Yearbook of Agriculture, 1911* (Washington, D.C.: U.S. Department of Agriculture, 1912), pp. 1–5; *Areas Administered by the National Park Service and Related Properties as of January 1, 1972* (Washington, D.C.: U.S. Department of the Interior, 1972), pp. 1–8.

35. Hechler, *Insurgency*, pp. 158–59; Martin L. Fausold, *Gifford Pinchot: Bull Moose Progressive* (Syracuse: Syracuse University Press, 1961), pp. 32–33; Elmo R. Richardson, *The Politics of Conservation: Crusades and Controversies, 1897–1913* (Berkeley: University of California Press, 1962), pp. 70–82; *Congressional Record, 61st Congress* (Washington, D.C.: U.S. Congress, 1909), Vol. 45, pt. 1, pp. 837–41.

36. Hechler, *Insurgency*, pp. 65–67; Richard Lowitt, *George W. Norris: The Making of a Progressive* (Syracuse: Syracuse University Press, 1963), pp. 168–79; Norman L. Zucker, *George W. Norris: Gentle Knight of American Democracy*

(Urbana: University of Illinois Press, 1966), pp. 6–8.

37. Russell B. Nye, *Midwestern Progressive Politics: A Historical Study of Its Origins and Development, 1870–1958* (New York: Harper and Row, 1959), pp. 252–54; *Congressional Record, 61st Congress,* Vol. 45, pt. 4, pp. 3436–39.

38. F. W. Taussig, *The Tariff History of the United States* (New York: reprint, Capricorn Books, 1964), pp. 407–08; Lewis L. Gould, "New Perspectives on the Republican Party, 1877–1913," *American Historical Review* 74:4 (October 1972): 1079; Kirk H. Porter and Donald B. Johnson, *National Party Platforms, 1840–1968* (Urbana: University of Illinois Press, 1972), p. 158; Claude G. Bowers, *Beveridge and the Progressive Era* (New York: The Literary Guild, 1932), pp. 333–35.

39. David W. Detzer, "The Politics of the Payne-Aldrich Tariff of 1909" (Ph.D. dissertation, University of Connecticut, 1970), p. iv; Richard C. Baker, *The Tariff under Roosevelt and Taft* (Hastings, Nebr.: Democrat Printing Co., 1941), pp. 77ff.; *Congressional Record, 61st Congress,* Vol. 44, pt. 5, p. 806; Vol. 44, pt. 2, p. 1301; Vol. 44, pt. 5, pp. 4754–55.

40. Joseph L. Gardner, *Departing Glory: Theodore Roosevelt as Ex-President* (New York: Scribners, 1973), pp. 185–89; Helene M. Hooker, ed., *History of the Progressive Party, 1912–1916* by Amos R. E. Pinchot (New York: New York University Press, 1958), pp. 112–14; Hermann Hagedorn, ed., *The Works of Theodore Roosevelt,* 20 vols. (New York: The National Edition, Scribners, 1926), VII, 5 ff.

41. *Arkansas Gazette,* October 8, 9, 10, 11, 1911; Nashville *Banner,* October 8, 10, 1911.

42. Oscar T. Barck, Jr., and Nelson M. Blake, *Since 1900: A History of the United States in Our Times* (New York: Macmillan, 1968), p. 76; George E. Mowry, *Theodore Roosevelt and the Progressive Movement* (New York: reprint, Hill and Wang, 1960), pp. 188–93; Harbaugh, *Power and Responsibility,* pp. 404–07.

43. Austin *Daily Statesman,* March 13, 14, 1911; Dallas *Morning News,* March 14, 1911; New Orleans *Daily Picayune,* March 11, 1911.

44. Dallas *Morning News,* March 13, 14, 15, 1911; New Orleans *Daily Picayune,* March 10, 11, 12, 13, 1911.

Chapter 2

1. Pringle, *Taft,* II, 756–58; Coletta, *Presidency of Taft,* p. 223 (quote).

2. George W. Norris, *Fighting Liberal* (New York: Collier Books, 1945), p. 148; Pringle, *Taft,* II, 757.

3. Memphis *Commercial Appeal,* March 29, 1912; Chicago *Daily Tribune,* March 27, 1912; Paul D. Casdorph, "The 1912 Republican Presidential Campaign in Mississippi," *Journal of Mississippi History* 33:1 (February 1971): 3; Howard W. Smith, "The Progressive Party and the Election of 1912 in Alabama," *Alabama Review* 9:1 (January 1956): 6.

4. TR to William E. Glasscock, January 5, 1912, TR to Julian Harris, January 19, 1912, TR to John M. Parker, February 9, 1912, TR to J. W. Pritchard, January 19, 1912, TR to Richmond Pearson, January 30, 1912, TR Papers; Harlan Hahn, "The Republican Party Convention of 1912 and the Role of Herbert S. Hadley in

National Politics," *Missouri Historical Review* 59:4 (July 1965): 410; Paul D. Casdorph, "Governor William E. Glasscock and Theodore Roosevelt's 1912 Bull Moose Candidacy," *West Virginia History* 28:1 (October 1966): 8–15.

5. Richmond *Virginian,* January 25, 30, 1912; San Antonio *Daily Express,* August 12, 1908; *Biographical Directory of the American Congress, 1774–1961,* p. 715; John A. Garraty, *Right Hand Man: The Life of George W. Perkins* (New York: Harper and Row, 1960), pp. 254–58.

6. Memphis *Commercial Appeal,* March 19, 1912; Atlanta *Independent,* May 4, 1912; Victor Rosewater, *Backstage in 1912* (Philadelphia: Dorrance, 1932), p. 123.

7. New York *Times,* January 26, 1912; Richmond *Virginian,* January 3, 1912; W. H. Taft to G. W. Wickersham, February 5, 1912, Charles D. Hilles Papers, Sterling Library, Yale University, New Haven, Connecticut, hereafter cited as Hilles Papers.

8. Emmett J. Scott to C. D. Hilles, February 26, 1912, Hilles Papers; Cripps, "Lily White Republicans," pp. 337–39; Benjamin Brawley, *A Social History of the Negro Problem in the United States and a Study of the Republic of Liberia* (New York: reprint, Collier Books, 1970), p. 351.

9. *Biographical Directory of the American Congress, 1774–1961,* p. 1307; Coletta, *Presidency of Taft,* pp. 230–31; Cripps, "Lily White Republicans," p. 338; David Needham, "William Howard Taft, the Negro, and the White South" (Ph.D. dissertation, University of Georgia, 1970), pp. 230–31.

10. *Who Was Who in America, 1949–1950* (Chicago: A. N. Marquis Co., 1950), II, 342; Norman M. Wilensky, *Conservatives in the Progressive Era: The Taft Republicans of 1912* (Gainesville: University of Florida Press, 1965), pp. 28–30.

11. Bella C. La Follette and Folla La Follette, *Robert M. La Follette, 1855–1925* (New York: Macmillan, 1953), I, 313–22; Moos, *The Republicans,* pp. 320–21; Paul D. Casdorph, *A History of the Republican Party in Texas, 1865–1965* (Austin: Pemberton Press, 1966), p. 98.

12. Eugene Roseboom, *A History of Presidential Elections* (New York: Macmillan, 1959), pp. 360–63; Tom Daley to C. D. Hilles, February 1, 1912, Hilles Papers; John M. Morehead to C. D. Hilles, December 20, 1911, February 3, 1912, John M. Morehead Papers, Perkins Library, Duke University, Durham, North Carolina, hereafter cited as Morehead Papers.

13. Robert S. Maxwell, ed., *Great Lives Observed: La Follette* (Englewood Cliffs, New Jersey: Prentice-Hall, 1969), pp. 112–15 (quotes); Robert M. La Follette, *Autobiography: A Narrative of Political Experiences* (Madison: reprint, University of Wisconsin Press, 1963), p. 259; Arthur S. Link, *Wilson: The Road to the White House* (Princeton: Princeton University Press, 1947), p. 349.

14. Bella and Folla La Follette, *La Follette,* I, 415–43; Richmond *Virginian,* February 6, 1912; New York *Times,* February 6, 1912; Fausold, *Pinchot,* pp. 55–79; Hooker, ed., *History of the Progressive Party* by Pinchot, pp. 136–40.

15. George N. Green, "Republicans, Bull Moose, and Negroes in Florida, 1912," *Florida Historical Quarterly* 43:2 (October 1964): 155–57; *Arkansas Gazette,* February 15, 1912; Atlanta *Independent,* February 17, 1912; Tampa *Morning Tribune,* February 7, 1912.

16. Hathorn, "Slemp," pp. 87–89; *Biographical Directory of the American Congress, 1774–1961,* p. 1765; James I. Robertson, Jr., *The Stonewall Brigade* (Baton Rouge: Louisiana State University Press, 1963), pp. 244-45.

17. Virginius Dabney, *Virginia: The New Dominion* (Garden City, N.Y.: Doubleday, 1971), pp. 433–34; William A. White, *A Puritan in Babylon: The Story of Calvin Coolidge* (New York: Macmillan, 1938), p. 25; *Biographical Directory of the American Congress, 1774–1961*, p. 1609; W. C. Pendleton, *Political History of Appalachian Virginia* (Dayton, Va.: Shenandoah Press, 1927), passim.

18. Philip A. Bruce, ed., *History of Virginia* (New York: Macmillan, 1926), I, 181–82; Richmond *Virginian*, January 16, 1912.

19. Richmond *Virginian*, February 8, 1912; *Who Was Who in America, 1897–1942* (Chicago: A. N. Marquis Co., 1942), p. 731; *Proceedings of the 1912 Republican National Convention*, p. 328.

20. Richmond *Virginian*, February 8, 1912; C. B. Slemp to C. D. Hilles, February 7, 1912, A. H. Martin to C. D. Hilles, February 8, 1912, Hilles Papers.

21. Dabney, *Virginia*, pp. 428–29; Michael S. Patterson, "The Fall of a Bishop: James Cannon, Jr. versus Carter Glass, 1909–1934," *Journal of Southern History* 39:4 (November 1973): 493–95.

22. Dabney, *Virginia*, pp. 432–33; John S. Ezell, *The South since 1865* (New York: Macmillan, 1963), p. 253; William Larsen, *Montague of Virginia: The Making of a Southern Progressive* (Baton Rouge: Louisiana State University Press, 1965), pp. 135–37.

23. Larsen, *Montague of Virginia*, pp. 138–49; Andrew Buni, *The Negro in Virginia Politics, 1902–1965* (Charlottesville: University of Virginia Press, 1967), pp. 17–55.

24. Robinson, *Presidential Vote*, p. 354; Buni, *Negro in Virginia Politics*, pp. 51–54.

25. Dabney, *Virginia*, pp. 455–58; Bruce, ed., *History of Virginia*, VI, 3–4; Buni, *Negro in Virginia Politics*, pp. 59–60.

26. G. L. Hart to C. D. Hilles, February 3, 1912, L. P. Summers to W. H. Taft, February 26, 1912, Hilles Papers; Richmond *Virginian*, February 13, 17, 26, 1912.

27. Richmond *Virginian*, February 29, 1912; Richmond *Planet*, March 23, 1912; Lyon G. Tyler, *Men of Mark in Virginia* (Washington, D.C.: Men of Mark Publishing Co., 1906), V, 313–14.

28. TR to J. C. Pritchard, January 19, 1912, TR Papers; John M. Morehead to C. D. Hilles, February 8, 1912, Hilles Papers; *Biographical Directory of the American Congress, 1774–1961*, p. 1484.

29. New Orleans *Daily Picayune*, September 19, 1912; Charlotte *Daily Observer*, August 12, 1912; Raleigh *News and Observer*, February 12, 1912; Joseph F. Steelman, "Richmond Pearson, Roosevelt Republicans, and the Campaign of 1912 in North Carolina," *North Carolina Historical Review* 63:2 (Spring 1966): 122–23; *Biographical Directory of the American Congress, 1774–1961*, p. 1440.

30. Raleigh *News and Observer*, January 18, 1912; J. M. Morehead to C. D. Hilles, December 20, 1912, Morehead Papers; *Who's Who in America, 1912–1913* (Chicago: A. N. Marquis Co., 1912), p. 1484.

31. Cripps, "The Lily White Republicans," p. 342; Robert S. Rankin, *The Government and Administration of North Carolina* (New York: Crowell, 1955), p. 25; Hugh T. Lefler and Albert R. Newsome, *North Carolina: The History of a Southern State* (Chapel Hill: University of North Carolina Press, 1963), p. 40.

32. Raleigh *News and Observer*, January 18, 1912.

33. Ibid., March 9, 1912; New Orleans *Daily Picayune,* September 19, 1912; *History of North Carolina* (New York and Chicago: Lewis Publishing Co., 1919), V, 74.

34. W. H. Taft to George W. Wickersham, February 5, 1912, J. M. Morehead to C. D. Hilles, February 3, 8, 1912, Hilles Papers.

35. Raleigh *News and Observer,* February 1, 1912.

36. Ibid., January 29 (Page quote), February 20, 1912; Steelman, "Pearson and the Campaign of 1912," pp. 124–27.

37. Raleigh *News and Observer,* February 23, 1912; Charlotte *Daily Observer,* May 16, 1912; Helen G. Edmonds, *The Negro and Fusion Politics in North Carolina, 1894–1901* (Chapel Hill: University of North Carolina Press, 1951), pp. 61–62; Robert F. Durden, *The Climax of Populism: The Election of 1896* (Lexington: University of Kentucky Press, 1966), p. 169; *Biographical Directory of the American Congress, 1774–1961,* p. 639.

38. Raleigh *News and Observer,* February 29, 1912; Charlotte *Daily Observer,* February 29, 1912; *National Cyclopaedia of American Biography* (New York: White, 1922), XVIII, 400; Steelman, "Pearson and the Campaign of 1912," p. 126.

39. Raleigh *News and Observer,* February 6, 1912 (Pearson quote); Medill McCormick to P. D. Conner, February 21, 1912, Hilles Papers; TR to Richmond Pearson, January 20, 1912, TR Papers; Robert M. Warner, "Chase S. Osborn and the Progressive Movement" (Ph.D. dissertation, University of Michigan, 1957), p. 286.

40. Verton M. Queener, "The East Tennessee Republican Party, 1900–1914," East Tennessee Historical Society *Publications* 22 (1950): 94–97; Verton M. Queener, "The East Tennessee Republicans as a Minority Party, 1870–1896," East Tennessee Historical Society *Publications* 15 (1943): passim; E. Merton Coulter, *William G. Brownlow: Fighting Parson of the Southern Highlands* (Chapel Hill: University of North Carolina Press, 1937), passim; Daniel M. Robison, *Bob Taylor and the Agrarian Revolt in Tennessee* (Chapel Hill: University of North Carolina Press, 1935), passim.

41. Queener, "East Tennessee Republican Party, 1900–1914," pp. 120–25; Boyce, ed., *Unwanted Boy,* pp. 54–67.

42. Stanley J. Folmsbee, Robert E. Corlew, and Enoch L. Mitchell, *History of Tennessee* (New York: Lewis Historical Publishing Co., 1960), II, 219–23; Eric R. Lacy, "Tennessee Teetotalism: Social Forces and the Politics of Progressivism," *Tennessee Historical Quarterly,* 24:3 (Fall 1965): 224–27.

43. Boyce, ed., *Unwanted Boy,* pp. 67–96; Isaac, *Prohibition and Politics,* pp. 189–94; John T. Moore and Austin P. Foster, *Tennessee: The Volunteer State* (Chicago and Nashville: S. J. Clarke Publishing Co., 1923), pp. 616–17.

44. Ben W. Hooper to Sam R. Sells, January 8, 1912, Hooper Papers; Knoxville *Journal and Tribune,* January 11, 12, 1912.

45. Knoxville *Journal and Tribune,* January 23, 1912; Newell Sanders to W. H. Taft, February 7, 1912, Hilles Papers; *Biographical Directory of the American Congress, 1774–1961,* p. 1560; Rufus Terral, *Newell Sanders: A Biography* (Kingsport, Tenn.: Kingsport Press, 1935), passim.

46. Knoxville *Journal and Tribune,* January 29, 1912; Memphis *Commercial Appeal,* August 3, 1912; Boyce, ed., *Unwanted Boy,* p. 129; *Who's Who in the South, 1926–1927* (Chicago: A. N. Marquis Co., 1927), p. 38.

47. Knoxville *Journal and Tribune*, January 23, 1912; Ben W. Hooper to Newton C. Myres, January 6, 1912, Hooper Papers; John W. Overall to James A. Fowler, January 30, 1912, Lee Brock to W. H. Taft, February 7, 1912, Hilles Papers.

48. Knoxville *Journal and Tribune*, January 28, 1912 (quotes); Memphis *Commercial Appeal*, August 4, 1912; Will T. Hale and Dixon L. Merritt, *A History of Tennessee and Tennesseans: The Leaders and Representative Men in Commerce, Industry, and Modern Activities* (Chicago: Lewis Publishing Co., 1913), pp. 1023–24.

49. John F. Fort to William E. Glasscock, January 19, 1912, William E. Glasscock Papers, West Virginia and Regional History Collection, West Virginia University Library, Morgantown, hereafter cited as Glasscock Papers; John F. Fort to B. W. Hooper, January 19, 1912, New York *Times* to B. W. Hooper, January 24, 1912, C. F. Millican to B. W. Hooper, January 29, 1912, J. Tom Daniel to B. W. Hooper, January 31, 1912, Hooper Papers.

50. B. W. Hooper to John F. Fort, January 25, 1912, John F. Fort to B. W. Hooper, February 1, 1912, Hooper Papers; New York *Times*, February 11, 1912; Pringle, *Roosevelt*, pp. 553–54; Casdorph, "Glasscock and Roosevelt's 1912 Candidacy," pp. 8–15.

51. Thomas H. Russell, *The Political Battle of 1912* (New York: n.p., 1912), pp. 25–31; New York *Times*, February 13, 1912 (Taft quote); Hoyt L. Warner, *Progressivism in Ohio, 1897–1917* (Columbus: Ohio State University Press, 1964), p. 318.

52. R. W. Austin to B. W. Hooper, February 15, 1912, B. W. Hooper to R. W. Austin, February 16, 1912, B. W. Hooper to W. B. McKinley, February 20, 1912, Hooper Papers; James A. Fowler to C. D. Hilles, February 3, 1912, Hilles Papers.

53. James A. Fowler to Newell Sanders, February 23, 1912, Hooper Papers; New York *Times*, February 28, 1912.

54. W. J. Oliver to B. W. Hooper, February 29, 1912, B. W. Hooper to W. J. Oliver, February 29, 1912, Hooper Papers.

55. Knoxville *Journal and Tribune*, March 3, 1913; Memphis *Commercial Appeal*, April 25, 1912; Knoxville *News-Sentinal*, July 22, 1912; Knoxville *Journal*, November 3, 1936; P. M. Hamer, *Tennessee: A History* (Washington, 1933), IV, 665–66.

Chapter 3

1. Robinson, *Presidential Vote*, p. 314; Charleston (S.C.) *Evening Post*, March 25, 1912; Charleston (S.C.) *Evening News and Courier*, August 31, 1912.

2. David D. Wallace, *South Carolina: A Short History, 1520–1948* (Chapel Hill: University of North Carolina Press, 1951), pp. 630–34; William F. Guess, *South Carolina: Annals of Pride and Protest* (New York: Harper and Row, 1960), pp. 288, 302–03; Clark and Kirwan, *The South since Appomattox*, pp.124–26.

3. Charleston (S.C.) *Evening Post*, January 26, 1912; Blum, *The Republican Roosevelt*, pp. 44–45; undated newspaper clippings, William Howard Taft Papers, Manuscripts Division, Library of Congress, Washington, D.C., hereafter cited as Taft Papers; J. C. Hemphill, *Men of Mark in South Carolina* (Washington, D.C.: Men of Mark Publishing Co., 1907), pp. 62–64; J. C. Garlington, *Men of the Times:*

Sketches of Living Notables (Spartanburg, S.C.: Garlington Publishing Co., 1902), pp. 72–73.

4. Charleston (S.C.) *Evening Post,* January 26, 1912; *Who's Who in America, 1938–1939* (Chicago: A. N. Marquis Co., 1938), p. 2483; Margaret Watson, *Greenwood County Sketches* (Greenwood, S.C.: Attic Press, 1970), p. 391.

5. Charleston (S.C.) *Evening Post,* February 20, 1912; Columbia *State,* May 4, 1912; John G. Capers to C. D. Hilles, February 19, 1912, Hilles Papers.

6. Wilmot L. Harris to C. D. Hilles, February 26, 1912, J. D. Adams to C. D. Hilles, February 27, 1912, Hilles Papers.

7. Charleston (S.C.) *Evening Post,* March 1, 1912; Charleston (S.C.) *News and Courier,* May 9, 1912.

8. TR to Julian Harris, January 19, 1912, August 1, 1912, TR Papers; *Who's Who in America, 1936–1937* (Chicago: A. N. Marquis Co., 1936), p. 1110; Arthur S. Link, "Correspondence Relating to the Progressive Party's 'Lily White' Policy in 1912," *Journal of Southern History* 12:4 (November 1944): 481–88.

9. Atlanta *Independent,* February 17, 1912; Paul Lewinson, *Race, Class, and Party: A History of Negro Suffrage and White Politics in the South* (New York: Oxford, 1932), p. 172; Olive H. Shadgett, *The Republican Party in Georgia from Reconstruction through 1900* (Athens: University of Georgia Press, 1964), pp. 152–54.

10. E. Merton Coulter, *Georgia: A Short History* (Chapel Hill: University of North Carolina Press, 1947), pp. 369–99; Dewey W. Grantham, *Hoke Smith and the Politics of the New South* (Baton Rouge: Louisiana State University Press, 1958), pp. 170–201; Clark and Kirwan, *The South since Appomattox,* pp. 111–12.

11. Coulter, *Georgia,* p. 382; C. Vann Woodward, *Tom Watson, Agrarian Rebel* (New York: reprint, Oxford University Press, 1963), pp. 370–71, 430; Robinson, *Presidential Vote,* p. 161.

12. Knoxville *Journal and Tribune,* February 13, 1912; Franklin M. Garrett, Atlanta Scrapbook of Obituaries, 1923–1932 (copy in Georgia Department of Archives and History), p. 30.

13. Savannah *Press,* April 18, 1923, November 3, 1939; *Colliers Magazine,* April 27, 1912.

14. *Colliers Magazine,* May 4, 1912; Cornelius V. Troup, *Distinguished Negro Georgians* (Dallas, Tex.: Royal Publishing Co., 1962), pp. 178–79; Shadgett, *History of the Republican Party in Georgia,* pp. 113–14; John Dittmer, *Black Georgia in the Progressive Era, 1900–1920* (Urbana: University of Illinois Press, 1977), pp. 93–94.

15. H. L. Johnson to C. D. Hilles, February 2, 1912, H. S. Jackson to C. D. Hilles, February 3, 1912, Hilles Papers; W. H. Taft to Alexander Ackerman, September 17, 1912, Taft Papers.

16. Atlanta *Independent,* February 17, 1912; *Arkansas Gazette,* February 15, 1912; Allen D. Candler and Clement A. Evans, eds., *Georgia: Comprising Sketches of Counties, Towns, Events, Institutions, and Persons, Arranged in Cyclopaedic Form* (Atlanta: State Historical Association, 1906), II, 505–06; *City of Atlanta, 1892–1893* (Atlanta: Inter-City Publishing Co., 1893), p. 85.

17. Tampa *Morning Tribune,* February 7, 1912; Cripps, "Lily White Republicans," pp. 339–40.

18. Green, "Republicans, Bull Moose, and Negroes in Florida," pp. 153–54;

Birmingham *Age-Herald,* January 17, 1912; *History and Facts of the Regular Reorganized Republican Party of Florida* (n.p.: The Regular Reorganized Republican Party of Florida, 1927), p. 11 (quote); Tampa *Morning Tribune,* January 27, 1912.

19. Robinson, *Presidential Vote,* p. 156; H. D. Price, *The Negro and Southern Politics: A Chapter in Florida History* (New York: New York University Press, 1957), pp. 12–13; Kathryn A. Hanna, *Florida: Land of Change* (Chapel Hill: University of North Carolina Press, 1948), pp. 330–31; C. Vann Woodward, *The Strange Career of Jim Crow* (New York: reprint, Oxford University Press, 1974), pp. 84–85.

20. Price, *The Negro and Southern Politics,* pp. 13–18; Carleton W. Tebeau, *A History of Florida* (Coral Gables: University of Miami Press, 1971), pp. 293–340; William T. Cash, *History of the Democratic Party in Florida, Including Biographical Sketches of Prominent Florida Democrats* (Tallahassee: Florida Democratic Historical Association, 1938), pp. 98–125.

21. Green, "Republicans, Bull Moose, and Negroes in Florida," p. 153; Tampa *Morning Tribune,* February 7, 1912; Jacksonville *Florida Times-Union and Citizen,* July 29, October 19, 1898, January 8, 1904; Henry S. Chubb to C. D. Hilles, February 8, 1912, Hilles Papers.

22. H. S. Chubb to C. D. Hilles, February 7, 1912, Hilles Papers; Jacksonville *Florida Times-Union and Citizen,* October 19, 1898; Harry G. Cutler, *History of Florida: Past and Present, Historical and Biographical* (Chicago: Lewis Publishing Co., 1923), II, 185; Francis P. Fleming, *Memoirs of Florida* (Atlanta: Southern Historical Association, 1902), II, 470–71.

23. Tampa *Morning Tribune,* February 8, 9, 1912; H. S. Chubb to C. D. Hilles, February 8, 1912, Hilles Papers; Needham, "Taft, the Negro, and the White South," p. 232.

24. Orlando *Evening Star,* January 23, 1946; Orlando *Sentinel,* March 14, 1937; Eldon H. Gore, *From Florida Sand to the City Beautiful: A Historical Record of Orlando, Florida* (Orlando: J. M. Cox, 1957), pp. 218–19; William F. Blackman, *History of Orange County, Florida* (Deland, Fla.: E. O. Painter Printing Co., 1927), pp. 22–28.

25. Tampa *Morning Tribune,* February 7, 1912; H. S. Chubb to C. D. Hilles, February 7, 1912, Hilles Papers.

26. Jacksonville *Florida Times-Union,* June 19, 1945; Frank Knox to John H. Dickinson, February 16, 1912, TR Papers.

27. *Colliers Magazine,* April 6, 1912, described the referee as "technically an 'advisor of the Post Office Department,' to decide matters of dispute, record, etc. Familiarly, the President's Referee is his official dispenser of patronage for the state. Some states have one Referee, some two. Often in Northern States they are members of Congress, but in the unrepresented south, they dispense offices, untroubled by elected representatives of the people."

28. Birmingham *Age-Herald,* January 9, 1912; *Colliers Magazine,* April 6, 1912; Blum, *The Republican Roosevelt,* pp. 45–47; Thomas M. Owen, *History of Alabama and Dictionary of Alabama Biography* (Chicago: S. J. Clarke Publishing Co., 1921), IV, 1667.

29. Birmingham *Age-Herald,* January 10, 12, 1912; Owen, *History of Alabama,* III, 869–70.

30. Birmingham *Age-Herald,* January 12, 1912; Albert B. Moore, *History of Alabama* (Tuscaloosa: Alabama Bookstore, 1951), pp. 650–54; James B. Sellers, *The Prohibition Movement in Alabama, 1702–1943* (Chapel Hill: University of North Carolina Press, 1943), pp. 101–04.

31. Moore, *History of Alabama,* p. 654; David Allen Harris, "Racists and Reformers: A Study of Progressivism in Alabama, 1898–1911" (Ph.D. dissertation, University of North Carolina, 1967), pp. 157–60; Robinson, *Presidential Vote,* p. 133; Sheldon Hackney, *Populism to Progressivism in Alabama* (Princeton: Princeton University Press, 1969), pp. 288–323.

32. Birmingham *Age-Herald,* January 12, 1912.

33. P. D. Barker to C. D. Hilles, February 2 (two letters), 3, 26, 1912, Hilles Papers; unsigned White House Memorandum, January 29, 1912, Taft Papers; Owen, *History of Alabama,* III, 99.

34. Birmingham *Age-Herald,* January 13, 1912 (Hundley quote); Pope M. Long to C. D. Hilles, February 2, 1912, Hilles Papers (Long quote).

35. Birmingham *Age-Herald,* January 17, 1912.

36. Ibid., February 7, 1912; *Biographical Directory of the American Congress, 1774–1961,* p. 465; Owen, *History of Alabama,* III, 16; Armes, *Coal and Iron in Alabama,* p. 267.

37. Birmingham *Age-Herald,* February 21, 22, 23, 25, 26, 1912; P. M. Long to C. D. Hilles, February 26, 1912, Hilles Papers; Charleston (S.C.) *Evening Post,* February 26, 1912.

38. Birmingham *Age-Herald,* February 27, 1912; TR to O. R. Hundley, February 21, 1912, TR Papers.

39. Robinson, *Presidential Vote,* p. 214; John K. Bettersworth, *Mississippi: A History* (Austin, Tex.: Steck Co., 1959), pp. 376–77; Woodward, *Origins of the New South,* pp. 321–22.

40. Bettersworth, *Mississippi,* pp. 376–77; Vernon L. Wharton, *The Negro in Mississippi, 1865–1890* (New York: reprint, Harper and Row, 1965), pp. 210–12; Albert D. Kirwan, *Revolt of the Rednecks; Mississippi Politics, 1875–1925* (New York: reprint, Harper and Row, 1965), p. 72.

41. Chicago *Daily Tribune,* March 29, 1912; *Colliers Magazine,* June 1, 1912; *Who Was Who in America, 1961–1968* (Chicago: A. N. Marquis Co., 1968), p. 684.

42. Memphis *Commercial Appeal,* March 29, 1912; Jackson *Clarion Ledger,* August 18, 1912; Charles H. Wilson, *God! Make Me a Man: A Biographical Sketch of Dr. Sidney Dillon Redmond* (Boston: Meador Publishing Co., 1925), passim.

43. Casdorph, "The 1912 Campaign in Mississippi," pp. 5–6; TR to Joseph M. Dixon, June 11, 1912, TR Papers; J. M. Dixon to P. W. Howard, July 14, 1912, Joseph M. Dixon Papers, University of Montana Library, Missoula, hereafter cited as Dixon Papers; Norfolk *Journal and Guide,* February 11, 1912; G. J. Fleming and C. E. Burckell, eds., *Who's Who in Colored America* (Yonkers, N.Y.: Who's Who in Colored America Corp., 1950), p. 273.

44. William F. Holmes, *The White Chief: James Kimble Vardaman* (Baton Rouge: Louisiana State University Press, 1970), pp. 262–65; Harbaugh, *Power and Responsibility,* pp. 443–45; Kirwan, *Revolt of the Rednecks,* p. 235.

45. Dunbar Rowland, *Encyclopaedia of Mississippi History* (Madison, Wis.: S. A. Bryant, 1907), III, 256–57; *Hinds County Gazette,* February 16, 1912; B. F. Fridge to J. M. Parker, January 29, 1912, J. M. Parker Papers, Southern Historical

Collection, University of North Carolina Library, hereafter cited as Parker Papers; see also, *Official and Statistical Register of the State of Mississippi* (Jackson: State of Mississippi, 1912).

46. TR to J. M. Parker, February 9, 1912, TR to Pearl Wight, January 20, 26, 1912, TR Papers; Matthew J. Schott, "John M. Parker and the Bull Moose Progressive Party in State and Nation" (M.A. thesis, Tulane University, 1960), pp. 77–86.

47. *Who Was Who in America, 1897–1942* (Chicago: A. N. Marquis Co., 1942), p. 1343; Alcée Fortier, *Louisiana: Comprising Sketches of Counties, Towns, Events, Institutions, and Persons Arranged in Cyclopaedic Form* (Atlanta: Southern Historical Association, 1903), III, unpaged.

48. Schott, "Parker and the Bull Moose Party," pp. 83–85; Frank Knox to TR, February 15, 1912, Frank Knox Papers, Manuscripts Division, Library of Congress, Washington, D.C., hereafter cited as Knox Papers.

49. Charles L. Dufour, *Ten Flags in the Wind: The Story of Louisiana* (New York: Harper and Row, 1967), pp. 239–40; Robinson, *Presidential Vote*, p. 218; Woodward, *Strange Career of Jim Crow*, pp. 84–85.

50. Hair, *Bourbonism and Agrarian Protest*, pp. 263–68; Edwin A. Davis, *Louisiana: The Pelican State* (Baton Rouge: Louisiana State University Press, 1969), pp. 233–34; Henry E. Chambers, *A History of Louisiana* (New York: American Historical Society, Inc., 1925), I, 708–10.

51. *Colliers Magazine*, May 25, 1912; New Orleans *Daily Picayune*, March 9, 1912; Fortier, *Louisiana*, III, 35.

52. New Orleans *Daily Picayune*, October 23, 1939; John S. Kendall, *History of New Orleans* (Chicago: Lewis Publishing Co., 1922), III, 946–47; William M. Deacon, *Reference Biography of Louisiana Bench and Bar* (New Orleans: Cox Printing and Publishing Co., 1922), p. 69.

53. New Orleans *Daily Picayune*, January 11, 12, 25, 26, 1912.

54. New Orleans *Daily Picayune*, January 26, 1912; *Colliers Magazine*, May 25, 1912; unsigned White House Memorandum, January 30, 1912, Taft Papers; A. E. Perkins, *Who's Who in Colored Louisiana* (Baton Rouge: A. E. Perkins Co., 1930), p. 113; Fortier, *Louisiana*, III, 262–63.

55. *Colliers Magazine*, May 25, 1912; New Orleans *Daily Picayune*, March 9, 1912; unsigned White House Memorandum, January 29, 30, 1912; W. H. Taft to Pearl Wight, February 29, 1912, Taft Papers.

56. *Proceedings of the 1912 Republican National Convention*, p. 153; Fortier, *Louisiana*, III, 197.

57. New Orleans *Daily Picayune*, March 9, 1912; Chicago *Tribune*, June 6, 1912.

58. San Antonio *Daily Express*, February 10, 15, 1912; Ernest W. Winkler, *Platforms of Political Parties in Texas* (Austin: The University of Texas, 1916), pp. 458–59; *Proceedings of the 1904 Republican National Convention*, p. 139.

59. Richmond *Virginian*, February 19, 1912; New York *Times*, February 18, 1912; San Antonio *Daily Express*, February 17, 1912; Casdorph, *Republican Party in Texas*, p. 99; Weldon Hart and James A. Clark, *The Tactful Texan: A Biography of Governor Will Hobby* (New York: Random House, 1958), pp. 13–18, 154.

60. San Antonio *Daily Express*, February 15, May 22, 1912; Austin *Statesman*, May 26, 1924; H. F. MacGregor to C. D. Hilles, February 8, 1912, Hilles Papers; William H. Atwell, *Autobiography* (Dallas: Warlick-Law Printing Co., 1935), pp. 7–10.

61. Seth S. McKay, *Texas Politics, 1906–1944: With Special Reference to the German Counties* (Lubbock: Texas Tech Press, 1952), pp. 9–24; Robinson, *Presidential Vote,* p. 330; Casdorph, *Republican Party in Texas,* passim.

62. Rupert N. Richardson, *Texas: The Lone Star State* (Englewood Cliffs, N.J.: Prentice-Hall, 1958), pp. 281–83; Lawrence D. Rice, *The Negro in Texas, 1874–1900* (Baton Rouge: Louisiana State University Press, 1971), pp. 137–39; Lewis L. Gould, *Progressives and Prohibitionists: Texas Democrats in the Wilson Era* (Austin: The University of Texas Press, 1973), pp. 5–8.

63. *Who Was Who in America, 1951–1953* (Chicago: A. N. Marquis Co., 1953), p. 757; Albert B. Paine, *Captain Bill McDonald: Texas Ranger* (New York: J. J. Little and Ives Co., 1909), pp. 273ff.; Oscar K. Davis, *Released for Publication: Some Inside Political History of Theodore Roosevelt and His Times, 1898–1919* (New York: Houghton Mifflin, 1925), p. 377.

64. Frank Knox to TR, February 15, 1912, Knox Papers; San Antonio *Daily Express,* February 20, 21, 1912; Cripps, "Lily White Republicans," pp. 342–44.

65. H. F. MacGregor to C. D. Hilles, February 8, 1912, Emmett Scott to C. D. Hilles, February 26, 1912, Hilles Papers; San Antonio *Daily Express,* August 12, 1908.

66. San Antonio *Daily Express,* February 26, 28, 1912; Knoxville *Journal and Tribune,* February 23, 1912.

67. San Antonio *Daily Express,* February 26, 29, 1912.

68. Webster Flanagan to C. D. Hilles, February 8, 1912, Hilles Papers; Walter P. Webb, ed., *The Handbook of Texas* (Austin: Texas State Historical Association, 1952), II, 288–89; San Antonio *Daily Express,* March 6, 1912; Memphis *Commercial Appeal,* March 6, 1912.

69. Dumas Malone and Allen Johnson, eds., *The Dictionary of American Biography* (New York: Scribners, 1958), II, 187–88; *Biographical Directory of the American Congress, 1774–1961,* p. 705; Robinson, *Presidential Vote,* pp. 134–35; Hiram Stutterfield to W. H. Taft, March 2, 1912, Hilles Papers; TR to Durand Whipple, March 5, 1912, TR Papers; see also Powell Clayton, *The Aftermath of the Civil War in Arkansas* (New York: Neale Publishing Co., 1915).

70. Dillard, "To the Back of the Elephant," pp. 5–13; David Y. Thomas, *Arkansas and Its People* (New York: American Historical Society, 1930), III, 35–37; Marvin F. Russell, "The Rise of a Republican Leader: Harmon L. Remmel," *Arkansas Historical Quarterly* 36:3 (Autumn 1977): 234–36.

71. John W. Graves, "The Arkansas Negro and Segregation, 1890–1903" (M.A. thesis, University of Arkansas, 1967), p. 113; James H. Fain, "Political Disfranchisement of the Negro in Arkansas" (M.A. thesis, University of Arkansas, 1961), pp. 53–75.

72. J. Morgan Kousser, *The Shaping of Southern Politics: Suffrage Restrictions and the Establishment of the One-Party South* (New Haven: Yale University Press, 1975), pp. 123–25; John G. Fletcher, *Arkansas* (Chapel Hill: University of North Carolina Press, 1947), p. 288; Graves, "Arkansas Negro," pp. 92–97; Woodward, *Strange Career of Jim Crow,* pp. 84–85; Thomas, *Arkansas and Its People,* III, 36; Sidney R. Crawford, "The Poll Tax" (M.A. thesis, University of Arkansas, 1944), pp. 29–43.

73. Graves, "Arkansas Negro," pp. 116–20; Kousser, *Shaping of Southern Politics,* p. 129; Cal Ledbetter, Jr., "Jeff Davis and the Politics of Combat," *Arkansas Historical Quarterly* 33:1 (Spring 1974): 29–30; see also Charles Jacob-

son, *The Life Story of Jeff Davis: The Stormy Petrel of Arkansas Politics* (Little Rock: Parke-Harper Publishing Co., 1925).

74. *Arkansas Gazette,* February 18, 20, 23, March 11, 20, 1912.

75. Ibid., February 28, March 1, 11, 14 (Cochran quote), 1912; *Arkansas Democrat,* March 3, 1912; *Tribute to Henry King Cochran* (n.p., n.d.), copy in Arkansas History Commission, Little Rock.

76. Memphis *Commercial Appeal,* March 27, 1912; *Arkansas Gazette,* March 27, 1912; *Proceedings of the Thirty-ninth Annual Session of the Bar Association of Arkansas Held at Hot Springs, May 1 and 2, 1936* (Little Rock: Bar Association of Arkansas, 1936), pp. 192–93; *Who's Who in Little Rock, 1921* (Who's Who Publishing Co., 1921), p. 43; Charles C. Alexander, *The Ku Klux Klan in the Southwest* (Lexington: University of Kentucky Press, 1965), pp. 113–15.

Chapter 4

1. *World Almanac and Encyclopaedia, 1913* (New York: Press Publishing Co., 1913), p. 719; Link, *Wilson,* pp. 405–08, 417; Gould, *Progressives and Prohibitionists,* pp. 70–73; Ezell, *The South since 1865,* p. 387.

2. William H. Harbaugh, ed., *The Writings of Theodore Roosevelt* (New York: Bobbs-Merrill, 1967), p. 331; Chicago *Daily Tribune,* March 8, 9, 1912; Paul G. Goodwin, "Theodore Roosevelt: The Politics of His Candidacy, 1904, 1912" (D.S.S. dissertation, Syracuse University, 1961), p. 419; Harbaugh, *Power and Responsibility,* pp. 419–24.

3. Garraty, *Right Hand Man,* p. 256; Gardner, *Departing Glory,* pp. 223–27; George W. Perkins to William B. McKinley, April 29, 1912, George W. Perkins Papers, Butler Library, Columbia University, New York, hereafter cited as Perkins Papers; Victor Rosewater, *Backstage in 1912: The Inside Story of the Republican Convention* (Philadelphia: Dorrance, 1932), pp. 118–20; Chicago *Daily Tribune,* March 1 (Pinchot quote), 8, 9, 1912.

4. Birmingham *Age-Herald,* February 28, 29, 1912; Birmingham *News,* March 5, 6, 1912; P. D. Barker to C. D. Hilles, March 4, 1912, Hilles Papers; J. M. Dixon to O. R. Hundley, March 2, 1912, Dixon Papers.

5. Birmingham *Age-Herald,* March 8, 1912; Memphis *Commercial Appeal,* March 8, 1912.

6. Charleston (S.C.) *Evening Post,* March 24, 25, 1912; Charleston (S.C.) *News and Courier,* March 29, 1912; Memphis *Commercial Appeal,* March 29, 1912; Washington *Bee,* April 22, 1912; J. W. Tolbert to C. D. Hilles, March 13, 1912, Hilles Papers; W. H. Taft to Sam R. Sells, June 2, 1912, Taft Papers.

7. Charleston (S.C.) *News and Courier,* April 21, May 2, 3, 1912; *Charleston, South Carolina, City Directory, 1913* (Charleston: Walker, Evans, and Cogswell, 1913), p. 20; J. D. Adams to C. D. Hilles, June 7, 1912, J. R. Levy to J. W. Tolbert, June 2, 1912, Hilles Papers.

8. Richmond *Virginian,* March 9, 1912; Raleigh *News and Observer,* March 17, 19, 1912; TR to Richmond Pearson, March 2, 3, 1912, TR to Z. V. Walser, June 7, 1912, TR Papers; *History of North Carolina: Brief Biographies of Leading People for Ready Reference Purposes* (Asheville: Evening News Publishing Co., 1906), unpaged; *History of North Carolina* (New York and Chicago: Lewis Publishing Co., 1919), V, 295.

9. Raleigh *News and Observer,* March 16, 17, April 28, May 1, 4, 1912; W. H. Taft to J. M. Morehead, March 16, 1912, C. D. Hilles to J. M. Morehead, April 13, 1912, Taft Papers.

10. Knoxville *Journal and Tribune,* March 3, 1912 (Sanders quote); Memphis *Commercial Appeal,* March 4, 1912; O. K. Davis to J. M. Dixon, March ?, 1912, Dixon Papers; Boyce, ed., *Unwanted Boy,* pp. 129–32.

11. Knoxville *Journal and Tribune,* March 3, 1912; TR to W. J. Oliver, March 1, 1912, TR Papers; W. J. Oliver to B. W. Hooper, March 4, 1912, B. W. Hooper to W. J. Oliver, March 14, 1912, Hooper Papers.

12. Boyce, ed., *Unwanted Boy,* p. 130; R. W. Austin to C. D. Hilles, March 3, 1912, Hilles Papers.

13. Memphis *Commercial Appeal,* March 13, 1912 (Saloon quote); Nashville *Banner and Tribune,* March 13, 1912.

14. Richmond *Virginian,* March 12, 24, 1912; Richmond *Planet,* May 28, 1912; *Colliers Magazine,* April 13, 1912; G. L. Hart to C. D. Hilles, March 2, 1912 (quote); C. B. Slemp to C. D. Hilles, March 3, 1912, R. A. Fulwiler to C. D. Hilles, March 2, 1912, Hilles Papers.

15. Richmond *Virginian,* March 13, 1912; Memphis *Commercial Appeal,* March 11, 1912 (Slemp quote); J. L. Graves II, Wytheville, Virginia, to the author, January 5, 1972.

16. Link, *Wilson,* pp. 395–400; Gardner, *Departing Glory,* pp. 229–30; Chicago *Daily Tribune,* March 15, 1912; New York *Times,* March 8, 1912.

17. Birmingham *News,* March 14, 15, 16, 1912; TR to O. R. Hundley, March 5, 1912, TR Papers; Pope M. Long to O. D. Street, April 30, 1912, Oscar D. Street Papers, William Stanley Hoole Special Collections Library, Amelia Gayle Gorgas Library, University of Alabama, University, Alabama, hereafter cited as Street Papers.

18. Birmingham *News,* March 19, 1912; Birmingham *Age-Herald,* April 22, 1912 (McHarg quote); P. M. Long to O. D. Street, April 24, 1912, J. O. Thompson to R. R. McClusky, April 18, 1912, Street Papers; J. M. Dixon to O. R. Hundley, March 2, 1912, Dixon Papers.

19. Chicago *Daily Tribune,* March 20, 1912; New York *Times,* March 20, 1912; TR to Frank Knox, March 12, 1912, TR Papers; Morison, ed., *Letters of Theodore Roosevelt,* VII, 523.

20. J. W. Hair to J. M. Dixon, March 9, 1912, Dixon Papers; B. T. Washington to Charles Banks, June 7, 1912, Booker T. Washington Papers, Manuscripts Division, Library of Congress, Washington, D.C., hereafter cited as Washington Papers.

21. Charles Banks to B. T. Washington, March 1, 1912, E. J. Scott to Charles Banks, March 23, 1912, Washington Papers; TR to O. K. Davis, July 10, 1912, TR Papers; James W. Loewen and Charles Sallis, *Mississippi: Conflict and Change* (New York: Pantheon, 1974), p. 195.

22. Memphis *Commercial Appeal,* March 29, 1912.

23. Ibid.; Casdorph, "The 1912 Campaign in Mississippi," p. 5; Chicago *Daily Tribune,* March 29, 1912; White House Diary, April 8, 1912, Taft Papers.

24. La Follette, *Autobiography,* pp. 270–75; Rosewater, *Backstage in 1912,* passim; Goodwin, "Theodore Roosevelt," pp. 429–31; New Orleans *Daily Picayune,* March 28, 1912; New York *Times,* March 28, 29, 30, 1912; Chicago *Daily Tribune,* March 28, 29, 30, April 3, 10, 1912.

25. New Orleans *Daily Picayune,* March 9, 22, April 1, 1912.

26. Ibid., March 22, April 9, 1912; Albert Godchaux to W. H. Taft, April 13, 1912, White House Diary, April 19, 1912, Taft Papers.

27. C. D. Hilles to B. T. Washington, April 2, 1912, Washington Papers; Victor Liosel et al. to C. D. Hilles, March 20, 1912, Taft Papers; Charlotte *Daily Observer,* May 17, 1912; New Orleans *Daily Picayune,* April 12, 17, 23, 1912.

28. Cincinnati *Enquirer,* April 15, 16, 21, 1912; Chicago *Daily Tribune,* April 30, May 1, 1912; New York *Times,* April 30, 1912.

29. *Arkansas Gazette,* April 21, 1912; Chicago *Daily Tribune,* May 2, 1912; Raleigh *News and Observer,* April 23, 1912; Charleston *News and Courier,* May 3, 1912; Atlanta *Journal,* May 3, 1912; Gatewood, "Theodore Roosevelt and Arkansas," p. 22.

30. New Orleans *Daily Picayune,* May 3, 1912; *Colliers Magazine,* May 25, 1912.

31. Ibid.

32. New Orleans *Daily Picayune,* May 3, 1912.

33. *Arkansas Gazette,* April 4, 13, 15, 21, 25, 1912; Memphis *Commercial Appeal,* April 26, 1912; W. H. Taft to H. L. Remmel, April 28, 1912, Harmon L. Remmel Papers, Series 1, University of Arkansas Library, Fayetteville, hereafter cited as Remmel Papers.

34. Memphis *Commercial Appeal,* May 8, 1912; *Arkansas Gazette,* May 8, 1912.

35. Ibid.; Charlotte *Daily Observer,* May 17, 1912; *Arkansas Gazette,* March 28, May 17, 1912; Fay Hempstead, *Historical Review of Arkansas* (Chicago: Lewis Publishing Co., 1911), III, 1427.

36. Birmingham *Age-Herald,* April 28, 1912.

37. Ibid., May 12, 1912; Charlotte *Daily Observer,* May 12, 1912.

38. Montgomery *Colored Alabamian,* March 23, June 1, 29, 1912; Richmond *Planet,* April 20, 1912.

39. Chicago *Daily Tribune,* May 15, 1912; Baltimore *Sun,* May 7, 1912; Rosewater, *Backstage in 1912,* p. 119; George E. Mowry, *The California Progressives* (Chicago: reprint, Quadrangle Books, 1963), pp. 176–77.

40. Raleigh *News and Observer,* May 4, 10, 12, 1912; J. M. Dixon to L. L. Wren, March 5, 1912, L. L. Wren to J. M. Dixon, March 6, 1912, Dixon Papers; J. M. Morehead to W. G. Brown, March 6, 1912, Morehead Papers; Charlotte *Daily Observer,* May 15, 16, 1912.

41. Charlotte *Daily Observer,* May 16, 1912.

42. Memphis *Commercial Appeal,* April 25, 26, 28, 1912; Atlanta *Journal,* May 14, 1912.

43. R. W. Austin to C. D. Hilles, April 24, 1912, Taft Papers; Charlotte *Daily Observer,* May 14, 1912; Memphis *Commercial Appeal,* May 15, 1912.

44. Atlanta *Journal,* May 15, 1912; Memphis *Commercial Appeal,* May 15, 1912; Charlotte *Daily Observer,* May 15, 1912.

45. Henry S. Jackson to C. D. Hilles, March 14, 1912 (quote), Hilles Papers; Atlanta *Independent,* April 20, 1912; Atlanta *Journal,* May 3, 8, 1912.

46. Charlotte *Daily Observer,* May 8, 1912; Atlanta *Journal,* May 8 (Tilson quote), 9, 1912; TR to St. J. Yates, May 8, 1912, TR Papers.

47. Atlanta *Journal,* May 17, 18 (Yates quote), 1912; Memphis *Commercial Appeal,* May 19, 1912.

48. Goodwin, "Theodore Roosevelt," pp. 448–49; Gardner, *Departing Glory,*

p. 234 (TR quote); Chicago *Daily Tribune*, May 13, 14, 1912; Richmond *Virginian*, May 18, 1912 (Delegate quote).

49. Richmond *Virginian*, May 9, 1912.

50. C. B. Slemp to C. D. Hilles, May 13, 1912, Hilles Papers; Richmond *Virginian*, April 24, May 14, 16, 17, 1912; Richmond *Planet*, April 20, 1912.

51. G. W. Allen to W. H. Taft, March 4, 1912, Hilles Papers; Green, "Republicans, Bull Moose, and Negroes in Florida," pp. 154–55; *History and Facts of the Republican Party of Florida*, p. 11; Atlanta *Independent*, April 20, 1912.

52. Miami *Daily Metropolis*, May 18, 1912; Chicago *Daily Tribune*, June 9, 1912; New York *Times*, June 9, 1912; Green, "Republicans, Bull Moose, and Negroes in Florida," p. 153; Frank L. Mather, *Who's Who of the Colored Race, 1915* (New York: Who's Who in Colored America Corp., 1915), I, Addenda, xxvi.

53. Chicago *Daily Tribune*, May 29, 1912; Richmond *Virginian*, May 29, 1912; New York *Times*, May 22, 29, June 2, 3, 4 (TR quote), 5, 1912.

54. Chicago *Daily Tribune*, June 3–5, 1912; Rosewater, *Backstage in 1912*, pp. 119–20.

55. Casdorph, *Republican Party in Texas*, pp. 99–103; B. T. Washington to C. D. Hilles, March 29, 1912, Washington Papers; J. M. Dixon to C. A. Lyon, March 6, 1912, Dixon Papers; San Antonio *Daily Express*, March 17, 18, 22, 1912; Raleigh *News and Observer*, March 23, 1912.

56. New York *Times*, June 15, 1912; San Antonio *Daily Express*, May 29, 1912; Galveston *Daily News*, May 29, 1912; Winkler, *Platforms of Political Parties in Texas*, pp. 554–56 (Platform quotes); Casdorph, *Republican Party in Texas*, pp. 100–01; Barr, *Reconstruction to Reform*, pp. 189–91.

Chapter 5

1. Chicago *Daily Tribune*, June 2, 1912; Richmond *Virginian*, May 29, 1912; Casdorph, *Republican Party in Texas*, p. 101.

2. Chicago *Daily Tribune*, June 2, 1912; New York *Times*, May 27, 30, 1912; Rosewater, *Backstage in 1912*, pp. 134–35.

3. *Proceedings of the 1912 Republican National Convention*, pp. 165–66; New York *Times*, June 7–16, 1912; Chicago *Daily Tribune*, June 2, 3, 1912.

4. New York *Times*, June 8, 1912; Chicago *Daily Tribune*, June 8, 1912; Birmingham *Age-Herald*, May 30, 1912; TR to O. K. Davis, May 29, 1912, TR to O. R. Hundley, June 4, 7, 1912, TR Papers.

5. Frederick C. Bryan to O. D. Street, May 31, 1912, O. D. Street to Charles Dick, n.d., Street Papers; F. H. Hardy to C. D. Hilles, June 12, 1912, Hilles Papers; Birmingham *Age-Herald*, May 30, June 4 (Taft meeting quotes), 10, 1912; Miami *Daily Metropolis*, June 15, 1912 (Trammell quote).

6. Chicago *Daily Tribune*, June 8, 1912.

7. New York *Times*, June 8, 1912; Birmingham *Age-Herald*, June 10, 1912; Chicago *Sunday Tribune*, June 9, 1912 (TR quotes).

8. New York *Times*, June 8, 1912; Chicago *Daily Tribune*, June 8, 1912.

9. Chicago *Sunday Tribune*, June 9, 1912.

10. Memphis *Commercial Appeal*, June 10, 16, 1912; TR to C. T. Bloodworth,

June 7, 1912, TR Papers; H. L. Remmel to Powell Clayton, February 17, 1912, Remmel Papers; C. D. Hilles to Powell Clayton, June 18, 1912, Hilles Papers; Hempstead, *Historical Review of Arkansas,* pp. 729–31.

11. Chicago *Sunday Tribune,* June 9, 1912; New York *Times,* June 9, 1912.

12. Jacksonville *Florida Times-Union and Citizen,* September 29, 1897; Miami *Daily Metropolis,* June 1, 1912; "Confidential—The Florida Situation," undated typescript, Hilles Papers; *History and Facts of the Republican Party of Florida,* p. 11; *Notice and Statement in Support of Henry S. Chubb* (Jacksonville: Republican State Committee, n.d.), passim, copy in Hilles Papers; White House Diary, June 1, 1912, Taft Papers.

13. Chicago *Sunday Tribune,* June 9, 1912; New York *Times,* June 9, 1912.

14. Ibid.

15. TR (Secretary) to J. M. Dixon, May 13, 1912, TR Papers; Atlanta *Journal,* June 17, 1912; Atlanta *Independent,* June 8, 1912; Chicago *Daily Tribune,* June 17, 1912; Lewinson, *Race, Class, and Party,* p. 172.

16. H. L. Johnson to C. D. Hilles, June 13, 1912, Hilles Papers; Atlanta *Journal,* June 12, 17, 1912; Washington *Bee,* June 8, 1912; Atlanta *Independent,* June 22, 1912; Charlotte *Daily Observer,* June 18, 1912; Chicago *Daily Tribune,* June 18, 1912.

17. Chicago *Sunday Tribune,* June 9, 1912 (Lyons quote); Atlanta *Journal,* June 17, 1912 (Rucker quote); H. S. Jackson to W. H. Taft, June 10, 1912, Hilles Papers.

18. New York *Times,* June 13, 1912; New Orleans *Daily Picayune,* June 13, 1912; "Confidential—The Louisiana Situation," undated typescript, Hilles Papers.

19. New York *Times,* June 13, 1912 (Herbert quote); Chicago *Daily Tribune,* June 13, 1912; *Colliers Magazine,* May 25, 1912.

20. Chicago *Daily Tribune,* June 13, 1912; New York *Times,* June 13, 1912; Casdorph, "The 1912 Republican Campaign in Mississippi," pp. 7–8 (quote).

21. Memphis *Commercial Appeal,* May 28, 1912; New York *Times,* June 13, 1912.

22. W. A. Attawing to O. McHarg, April 20, 1912, B. T. Washington to Charles Banks, June 7, 1912, Washington Papers; TR to S. D. Redmond, June 11, 1912, TR Papers.

23. Chicago *Daily Tribune,* June 15, 17, 1912; W. H. Taft to L. B. Moseley, May 22, 1912, Taft Papers; Casdorph, "The 1912 Republican Campaign in Mississippi," pp. 8–10 (Delegates quote).

24. Chicago *Daily Tribune,* June 14, 1912 (Borah quote); New York *Times,* June 14, 1912; Hanes Walton, Jr., *The Negro in Third Party Politics* (Philadelphia: Dorrance, 1969), pp. 48–49.

25. New York *Times,* June 14, 1912.

26. Chicago *Daily Tribune,* June 14, 16, 1912; Charlotte *Daily Observer,* June 10, 1912; W. H. Taft to E. C. Duncan, May 13, 1912, Taft Papers; TR to Richmond Pearson, May 6, 1912, TR to Z. V. Walser, June 7, 1912, TR Papers; Steelman, "Pearson and the Campaign of 1912," pp. 129–31.

27. New York *Times,* June 15, 1912; Chicago *Daily Tribune,* June 15, 1912.

28. C. M. English to J. D. Adams, May 9, 1912, Hilles Papers; Charleston (S.C.) *News and Courier,* May 9, June 16, 1912; Chicago *Daily Tribune,* June 15, 1912; undated newspaper clipping, Taft Papers; W. H. Taft to W. L. Harris, June 2,

1912, Taft Papers; J. M. Dixon to R. E. Brown, April 20, 1912, Dixon Papers.

29. Newell Sanders to W. H. Taft, March 13, 1912, Hilles Papers; TR to Judge John Allison, May 15, 1912, TR to W. J. Oliver, May 14, 1912, TR Papers; Memphis *Commercial Appeal*, May 26, June 1, 6, 1912.

30. Knoxville *Banner*, June 4, 1912; New York *Times*, June 15, 1912; Chicago *Daily Tribune*, June 15, 1912; Memphis *Commercial Appeal*, June 3, 24, 1912; W. H. Taft to R. W. Austin, June 24, 1912, Taft Papers.

31. Chicago *Daily Tribune*, June 15, 1912; New York *Times*, June 15, 1912; Memphis *Commercial Appeal*, June 14, 1912; Mowry, *The California Progressives*, pp. 32–33; J. W. Farley to B. W. Hooper, June 16, 1912, Hooper Papers.

32. New York *Times*, June 16, 1912 (McDonald quote); Chicago *Daily Tribune*, June 16, 1912; Lewis L. Gould, "Theodore Roosevelt, William Howard Taft, and the Disputed Delegates of 1912: Texas as a Test Case," *Southwestern Historical Quarterly* 80:1 (July 1976): 44–47; Casdorph, *Republican Party in Texas*, pp. 100–01.

33. San Antonio *Daily Express*, June 17, 1912; Dallas *Morning News*, October 4, 1942; TR to C. A. Lyon, June 3, 1912, TR Papers; *The Texas Almanac, 1964–1965* (Dallas: Dallas Morning News, 1964), p. 511; New York *Times*, June 16 (Heney and McDowell quotes).

34. New York *Times*, June 16, 1912; Chicago *Daily Tribune*, June 16, 1912.

35. Richmond *Virginian*, May 27, 1912; New York *Times*, June 16, 1912 (quotes); C. B. Slemp to C. D. Hilles, May 13, 1912, W. H. Taft to C. D. Hilles, June 6, 1912, C. D. Hilles to W. H. Taft, June 7, 1912, Hilles Papers.

36. New York *Times*, June 16, 1912; Harbaugh, *Power and Responsibility*, p. 433 (TR quote); Goodwin, "Theodore Roosevelt," pp. 466ff.; Washington *Bee*, June 29, 1912.

37. New York *Times*, June 18, 1912 (TR quote); Coletta, *Presidency of Taft*, p. 236; La Follette, *Autobiography*, pp. 274–76; Harbaugh, *Power and Responsibility*, pp. 433–34; Ralph G. Martin, *Ballots and Bandwagons* (New York: Rand McNally, 1964), p. 158.

38. Gardner, *Departing Glory*, p. 281; New York *Times*, June 19, 1912; *Proceedings of the 1912 Republican National Convention*, pp. 1–32; Rosewater, *Backstage in 1912*, pp. 160ff.

39. Philip C. Jessup, *Elihu Root* (New York: Dodd, Meade, and Co., 1938), II, 191–92; *Proceedings of the 1912 Republican National Convention*, pp. 32–34; Nicholas Murray Butler, *Across the Busy Years* (New York: Scribners, 1939), I, 244; Richard C. Bain and Judith H. Parris, *Convention Decisions and Voting Records* (Washington, D.C.: Brookings Institution, 1973), p. 180.

40. *Proceedings of the 1912 Republican National Convention*, pp. 42–54; Martin, *Ballots and Bandwagons*, p. 139; New York *Times*, June 19, 1912.

41. *Proceedings of the 1912 Republican National Convention*, pp. 54–85; Rosewater, *Backstage in 1912*, pp. 168–69.

42. *Proceedings of the 1912 Republican National Convention*, p. 85; New York *Times*, June 19, 1912; Chicago *Daily Tribune*, June 19, 1912.

43. Jessup, *Root*, II, 187–89; New York *Times*, June 19, 1912; *Proceedings of the 1912 Republican National Convention*, pp. 88–102; La Follette, *Autobiography*, p. 276.

44. William Allen White, *Autobiography* (New York: Macmillan, 1946),

pp. 469–70; *Proceedings of the 1912 Republican National Convention,* pp. 104–06.

45. New York *Times,* June 20, 1912; *Proceedings of the 1912 Republican National Convention,* pp. 106–30.

46. New York *Times,* June 20, 1912; *Proceedings of the 1912 Republican National Convention,* pp. 130–47; Martin, *Ballots and Bandwagons,* pp. 152–53; *A Stolen Nomination for the Presidency: The Facts of the Chicago Convention of 1912* (New York: Progressive National Committee, 1912), pp. 4–6.

47. *Proceedings of the 1912 Republican National Convention,* pp. 148–66.

48. Hooker, ed., *History of the Progressive Party* by Pinchot, p. 162; *Proceedings of the 1912 Republican National Convention,* pp. 167–68; Garraty, *Right Hand Man,* pp. 262–63; New York *Times,* June 21, 22, 1912.

49. *Proceedings of the 1912 Republican National Convention,* pp. 169–238.

50. Ibid., pp. 329–34; New York *Times,* June 23, 1912; White, *Autobiography,* pp. 472–73.

51. *Proceedings of the 1912 Republican National Convention,* pp. 305–47; New York *Times,* June 23, 1912; White, *Autobiography,* p. 473; Arthur M. Schlesinger, Jr., ed., *History of American Presidential Elections* (New York: Chelsea House, 1971), II, 2185.

52. *Proceedings of the 1912 Republican National Convention,* pp. 377–401; *Colliers Magazine,* May 4, 1912; New York *Times,* June 23, 1912; TR to J. M. Dixon, June 11, 1912, TR to S. D. Redmond, June 11, 1912, TR Papers; Casdorph, "The 1912 Republican Campaign in Mississippi," pp. 7–9.

53. *Proceedings of the 1912 Republican National Convention,* pp. 402–07.

54. Ibid., pp. 374–75; *Proceedings of the 1908 Republican National Convention,* pp. 89–90; Cutler, *History of Florida,* II, 185; Birmingham *Age-Herald,* June 18, 1912; Atlanta *Journal,* June 18, 1912; Memphis *Commercial Appeal,* June 15, 1912.

55. W. H. Taft to Harry Beck, July 6, 1912, H. S. Jackson, June 24, 1912, Henry L. Johnson, June 22, 1912, J. W. Tolbert, July 8, 1912, L. P. Summers, July 8, 1912, H. C. Warmouth, July 8, 1912, J. D. Adams, July 8, 1912, J. H. Hawley, July 8, 1912, H. Clay Evans, July 8, 1912, C. B. Slemp, July 8, 1912, Taft Papers.

56. Washington *Bee,* December 2, 1911, May 18, 1912; Baltimore *Afro-American Ledger,* December 2, 1911; "James Carroll Napier," typescript, unsigned biographical sketch, Booker T. Washington to J. C. Napier, January 2, 1912, Walter S. Bachman to J. C. Napier, January 24, 1912, J. C. Napier to Dear Sir, May 31, 1912, James Carroll Napier Papers, Fisk University Library, Nashville, Tennessee, hereafter cited as Napier Papers.

57. Whitefield McKinlay to Dr. C. B. Purvis, May 1, 1913, W. McKinlay to P. B. S. Pinchback, August 16, 1912, W. McKinlay to J. C. Napier, May 31, 1912, McKinlay Papers.

58. Richmond *Planet,* April 20, June 22, 1912; Montgomery *Colored Alabamian,* August 10, 1912; Washington *Bee,* June 18, June 29, 1912.

59. TR to William H. Maxwell, July 30, 1912, TR Papers; Goodwin, "Theodore Roosevelt," pp. 490–92; Davis, *Released for Publication,* pp. 274–75; Martin, *Ballots and Bandwagons,* p. 139 (Hart quote); New York *Times,* June 23, 1912.

Chapter 6

1. New York *Times,* June 24, 1912 (TR quote); Davis, *Released for Publication,* pp. 315–17; Gardner, *Departing Glory,* p. 252; Jules Karlin, *Joseph M. Dixon of*

Montana: Senator and Bull Moose Manager (Missoula: University of Montana Press, 1974), pp. 159–60.

2. Karlin, *Dixon,* p. 160; New York *Times,* June 23, 1912; Chicago *Daily Tribune,* June 25, 1912 (Taft quote).

3. Atlanta *Journal,* June 22, 25, July 7, 1912; TR to Henry S. Edwards, July 24, 1912, TR to Henry W. Brady, July 24, 1912, TR Papers; Julian Harris to J. M. Dixon, July 9, 1912, Clark Grier to J. M. Dixon, July 2, 1912, Dixon Papers; Franklin M. Garrett, Obituary Scrapbook—Atlanta, 1929–1932 (copy in Georgia Department of Archives and History, Atlanta), p. 52; Rebecca L. Felton, *My Memoirs of Georgia Politics* (Atlanta: Index Publishing Co., 1911), p. 663.

4. Atlanta *Journal,* July 11, 17, 18, 20, 24 (Bull Moose quote), 1912; Atlanta *Independent,* July 13, 29, 1912; *Who's Who in America, 1930–1931* (Chicago: A. N. Marquis Co., 1930), p. 1497.

5. Atlanta *Journal,* July 26, 27, 1912; Atlanta *Independent,* July 26, 1912; *Roll of Delegates and Alternates to the First National Convention: The Coliseum, Chicago, Illinois, August 5, 6, and 7, 1912* (New York: Progressive National Committee, 1912), p. 4; *A Standard History of Georgia and Georgians* (Chicago: Lewis Publishing Co., 1917), V, 2556–57.

6. Atlanta *Journal,* July 8, 20, 22, August 1, 1912.

7. Ibid., August 21, 28, 1912; Atlanta *Independent,* August 17, 24, 1912; H. S. Jackson to W. H. Johnson, September 25, 1912, Hilles Papers; W. H. Taft to Alexander Ackerman, September 17, 1912, H. L. Johnson to W. H. Taft, July 2, 1912, White House Memorandum, July 2, 1912, Taft Papers.

8. Birmingham *Age-Herald,* June 27, July 10, 1912.

9. O. R. Hundley to J. M. Dixon, July 11, 1912, Byron Trammell to J. M. Dixon, July 8, 1912, Dixon Papers; T. H. Aldrich to W. H. Taft, July 1, 1912, Taft Papers; P. D. Barker to C. D. Hilles, July 15, 1912, Hilles Papers; Hackney, *Populism to Progressivism,* p. 118; Birmingham *Age-Herald,* June 24, 28, July 2, 24 (McVaugh quote), 1912; Birmingham *News,* July 27, 1912.

10. Birmingham *Age-Herald,* July 25, 1912; Birmingham *News,* July 27, 1912 (Thompson quote); Smith, "The Progressive Party in Alabama," pp. 9–11.

11. Isabell Leander to O. D. Street, September 3, 1912, Pope M. Long to U. G. Mason, July 18, 1912, W. S. Morgan to O. D. Street, July 22, 1912, Street Papers; Birmingham *News,* August 5, 1912 (TR quote); Birmingham *Age-Herald,* August 25, September 7, 29, 1912; *Alabama Official and Statistical Register* (Montgomery: Alabama State Department of Archives and History, 1903), p. 115; Robinson, *Presidential Vote,* p. 113.

12. W. H. Taft to H. S. Chubb, November 11, 1912, Taft Papers; Charlotte *Daily Observer,* July 8, 1912; New Orleans *Daily Picayune,* August 5, 1912; *Report of the Secretary of State, 1912* (Tallahasse: State of Florida, 1913), n.p.; Green, "Republicans, Bull Moose, and Negroes in Florida," pp. 162–63.

13. Jacksonville *Florida Times-Union,* October 9, 1900, June 19, 1945; Miami *Daily Metropolis,* June 29, 1912.

14. H. S. Chubb to C. D. Hilles, September 11, 1912, Hilles Papers; Miami *Daily Metropolis,* July 29, 1912; Jacksonville *Florida Times-Union,* July 27, 1912.

15. Miami *Daily Metropolis,* July 29, 1912; Atlanta *Independent,* August 17, 1912.

16. Miami *Daily Metropolis,* July 29, 1912; Green, "Republicans, Bull Moose, and Negroes in Florida," p. 114; John A. Gable, "The Bull Moose Years:

Theodore Roosevelt and the Progressive Party, 1912–1916" (Ph.D. dissertation, Brown University, 1972), pp. 184–85.

17. J. M. Dixon to J. M. Newcomb, July 15, 1912, Dixon Papers; Richmond *Virginian*, June 28, July 5, 10, 15, 23, 1912.

18. Richmond *Virginian*, July 11, 15, 30 (Pollard quote), August 21, 29, 1912; Frank H. Hitchcock to C. D. Hilles, September 23, 1912, Hilles Papers; TR to Thomas S. Forsyth, July 27, 1912, TR Papers.

19. Richmond *Virginian*, July 30, 31, 1912.

20. Ibid.; Tyler, *Men of Mark in Virginia*, pp. 313–14; New Orleans *Daily Picayune*, August 4, 1912; "Official Report of the Proceedings of the National Progressive Committee Held in Room 1102 of the Congress Hotel, August 3, 1912, Senator Joseph M. Dixon in the Chair" (typescript), TR Papers, passim.

21. *Arkansas Gazette*, July 14, 26, 27, 1912; Dallas T. Herndon, *Centennial History of Arkansas* (Little Rock: S. J. Clarke Publishing Co., 1922), pp. 275–76; Hempstead, *Historical Review of Arkansas*, pp. 729–31; *Roll of Delegates and Alternates to the National Convention*, p. 1.

22. *Arkansas Gazette*, July 31, 1912 (Davis quote); Memphis *Commercial Appeal*, July 28, 1912; Gatewood, "Roosevelt and Arkansas," pp. 22–23.

23. *Arkansas Gazette*, August 1, 6, 10, 11, 30, 1912; *In Memory of Edward B. Downie* (pamphlet, copy in Little Rock Public Library); *Who's Who in Little Rock, 1921* (Little Rock: Who's Who Publishing Co., 1921), pp. 52–53.

24. *Arkansas Gazette*, August 26, 31, 1912; White House Memorandum, September 12, 1912, Taft Papers; H. L. Remmel to W. H. Taft, July 10, 1912, J. Rich to W. H. Taft, September 11, 1912, Hilles Papers; W. H. Taft to H. L. Remmel, July 25, 1912, Remmel Papers.

25. Memphis *Commercial Appeal*, July 21, 24 (Fridge quote), 28 (Swain quote), 1912; Atlanta *Journal*, July 23, 1912; New Orleans *Daily Picayune*, August 1, 1912; TR to O. K. Davis, July 10, 1912, TR Papers; J. M. Dixon to B. F. Fridge, November 11, 1912, Benjamin F. Fridge Papers, Mitchell Memorial Library, Mississippi State University, Mississippi State, Mississippi, hereafter cited as Fridge Papers.

26. Memphis *Commercial Appeal*, August 2, 1912; New Orleans *Daily Picayune*, August 1, 1912; Birmingham *News*, August 4, 1912.

27. Birmingham *News*, August 4, October 10, 1912; New Orleans *Daily Picayune*, August 27, September 25, 1912; A. Tonnar to J. M. Parker, September 30, 1912, Parker Papers; L. B. Moseley to C. D. Hilles, September 13, 1912, Hilles Papers; W. H. Taft to Wesley Crayton, June 25, 1912, Taft Papers; J. M. Dixon to B. F. Fridge, November 11, 1912, Fridge Papers.

28. Birmingham *Age-Herald*, August 2, 1912 (Parker quote); New Orleans *Daily Picayune*, July 9, 12, 31, 1912; TR, Jr., to J. M. Parker, July 2, 1912, TR to J. M. Parker, July 31, 1912, TR Papers; Pearl Wight to J. M. Parker, July 11, 1912, Parker Papers.

29. New Orleans *Daily Picayune*, August 3, 1912.

30. Ibid., August 3 (Convention quotes), 15, October 17, 27 (Injunction quote), 1912; Henry E. Chambers, *A History of Louisiana* (New York: American Historical Society, 1925), II, 15–16.

31. New Orleans *Daily Picayune*, September 11, 15, 1912; C. D. Hilles to W. H. Taft, July 25, 1912, Armand Romain to C. D. Hilles, September 7, 1912, Hilles

Papers; W. H. Taft to J. Madison Vance, June 25, 1912, Taft Papers; *Report of the Louisiana Bar Association, 1918* (New Orleans: Louisiana Bar Association, 1919), p. 180; Fortier, *Louisiana,* III, 282–83.

32. J. N. Williamson, Jr., to Richmond Pearson, August 16, 24, 1912, Richmond Pearson Papers, Southern Historical Collection, University of North Carolina Library, Chapel Hill, hereafter cited as Pearson Papers; Charlotte *Daily Observer,* July 10, 1912; Hugh T. Lefler, *History of North Carolina* (New York: Lewis Historical Publishing Co., 1956), III, 365–66.

33. TR to A. H. Price, July 6, 1912, TR Papers; J. M. Dixon to Richmond Pearson, August 12, 1912, Marion Butler to Richmond Pearson, August 24, 1912, Pearson Papers; Charlotte *Daily Observer,* July 13, August 2, 1912.

34. Charlotte *Daily Observer,* August 8, 1912; Raleigh *News and Observer,* September 5, 1912; Jacksonville *Florida Times Union,* September 5, 1912; J. M. Morehead to W. H. Taft, August 12, 1912, Hilles Papers; Carl N. Degler, *The Other South* (New York: Harper and Row, 1973), p. 173.

35. Raleigh *News and Observer,* September 4, 1912; Charlotte *Daily Observer,* August 12, 1912 (Pearson quote); Jacksonville *Florida Times-Union,* September 4, 1912.

36. New Orleans *Daily Picayune,* September 16, 1912; Charlotte *Daily Observer,* July 9, October 10, 1912; W. S. Pearson to J. M. Dixon, October 2, 1912, Dixon Papers; J. M. Morehead to W. H. Taft, July 7, 1912, Thomas Settle to W. H. Taft, July 8, 1912, W. H. Taft to E. C. Duncan and J. M. Morehead, September 21, 1912, Taft Papers.

37. Memphis *Commercial Appeal,* June 23, 29, July 20, 24, 1912; Nashville *Banner,* July 21, 25 (Hooper quote), 1912; B. W. Hooper to N. Sanders, July 6, 15, 1912, J. W. Farley to B. W. Hooper, July 17, 1912, L. N. Dutro to B. W. Hooper, July 19, 1912, W. J. Oliver to B. W. Hooper, August 2, 1912, Hooper Papers; TR to W. J. Oliver, August 9, 1912, TR to G. Tom Taylor, August 2, 1912, TR Papers.

38. Memphis *Commercial Appeal,* August 3, 1912 (Convention quotes); New Orleans *Daily Picayune,* August 3, 1912; Boyce, ed., *Unwanted Boy,* pp. 128–30; *Who's Who in the South, 1927* (Chicago: A. N. Marquis Co., 1927), p. 38.

39. Memphis *Press-Scimitar,* November 6, 1942; Memphis *Commercial Appeal,* August 3, 1912, November 6, 1942; New Orleans *Daily Picayune,* August 3, 1912.

40. Foster W. Brown to W. H. Taft, October 2, 1912, N. Sanders to C. D. Hilles, October 15, 1912, W. H. Taft to A. M. Hughes, September 26, 1912, Hilles Papers; Boyce, ed., *Unwanted Boy,* p. 132; Edith S. Evans, "The Progressive Party in Tennessee, 1912" (M.A. thesis, University of Tennessee, 1933), pp. 98–111.

41. Charleston (S.C.) *News and Courier,* July 21, 30, 1912.

42. Ibid., August 4, 31 (McClennan quote), 1912; New York *Times,* August 3, 1912; *Dedication: McClennan-Banks Hospital, Inc., of Charleston County, 1959* (pamphlet, copy in South Carolina Historical Society, Charleston).

43. Charleston (S.C.) *Evening Post,* September 30, October 4, 1912; W. H. Taft to J. W. Tolbert, July 8, 1912, Taft Papers.

44. Charleston (S.C.) *Evening Post,* October 24 (Convention quote), 29, 1912; B. S. Dunn to J. M. Dixon, October 24, 1912, B. S. Dunn to W. M. Webster, October 10, 1912, Dixon Papers.

45. San Antonio *Daily Express,* August 14, 1912; Winkler, *Platforms of Political Parties in Texas,* p. 570; G. W. Perkins to A. G. Hawes, June 29, 1912, Perkins

Papers; H. F. MacGregor to C. D. Hilles, October 13, 1912, C. D. Hilles to H. F. MacGregor, July 6, 1912, Hilles Papers (McDonald quote).

46. New York *Times,* August 14, 1912; San Antonio *Daily Express,* August 15, 1912 (Lyon quote); Dallas *Morning News,* August 14, 1912; C. D. Hilles to H. F. MacGregor, July 6, 1912, Hilles Papers; Casdorph, *Republican Party in Texas,* pp. 106–08.

47. San Antonio *Daily Express,* August 14, 1912; Dallas *Morning News,* August 14, 15, 1912.

48. Ibid., *Who Was Who in America, 1897–1942,* p. 607; Casdorph, *Republican Party in Texas,* pp. 103–05 (Lasater quote).

49. TR to Julian Harris, August 1, 1912, TR Papers; Gable, "The Bull Moose Years," pp. 171–77; Morison, ed., *Letters of Theodore Roosevelt,* VII, 584; Charleston (W. Va.) *Daily Mail,* July 31, 1912; New York *Times,* August 7, 1912.

50. Washington *Bee,* August 10, 1912; "Official Report of the Proceedings of the Progressive National Committee," passim; Chicago *Daily Tribune,* August 4, 1912; New Orleans *Daily Picayune,* August 4, 1912.

51. Chicago *Daily Tribune,* August 6, 1912.

52. New York *Times,* August 6, 1912; "The First Convention of the Progressive Party Held at Chicago, August 5, 6, and 7, 1912" (typescript), TR Papers, pp. 112–14; George H. Payne, *The Birth of the New Party: Or Progressive Democracy* (New York: n.p., 1912), pp. 63–66.

53. "The First Convention of the Progressive Party," pp. 52–138; Harbaugh, ed., *The Writings of Theodore Roosevelt,* pp. 123ff.; Gardner, *Departing Glory,* pp. 260–63.

54. New York *Times,* August 8, 1912; Link, *Wilson,* p. 474; Schlesinger, ed., *American Presidential Elections,* III, 2227 (quote); *Roll of Delegates and Alternates to the Progressive Convention,* passim.

55. *Arkansas Gazette,* September 25, 1912; Nashville *Banner,* October 2, 1912; Coletta, *Presidency of Taft,* pp. 241–42 (Taft quote); Pringle, *Taft,* I, 834.

56. *Arkansas Gazette,* September 25, 26, 1912; New Orleans *Daily Picayune,* September 26, 1912.

57. New Orleans *Daily Picayune,* September 27, 28, 1912; *Arkansas Gazette,* September 21, 1912; Atlanta *Journal,* September 30, 1912.

58. Charlotte *Daily Observer,* October 1, 2, 1912; Nashville *Banner,* October 1, 1912; Raleigh *News and Observer,* October 2, 1912; Evans, "Progressive Party in Tennessee," p. 98.

59. *World Almanac and Encyclopaedia, 1914* (New York: Press Publishing Co., 1914), passim; Nashville *American,* November 14, 1912; Schlesinger, ed., *American Presidential Elections,* III, 2242; *Biennial Report of the Secretary of State, 1911–1913* (Little Rock: State of Arkansas, 1913), pp. 400–03, 420; *Report of the Secretary of State, 1912* (Tallahassee: State of Florida, 1913), passim; *Annual Report of the Secretary of State, 1912* (Baton Rouge: State of Louisiana, 1913), pp. 162–63; *Biennial Report of the Secretary of State, 1913–1915* (Memphis: State of Mississippi, 1915), pp. 8–9; *The Warrock-Richardson Maryland, Virginia, and North Carolina Almanac for the Year 1917* (Richmond: Warrock-Richardson Publishing Co., 1918), pp. 77–79.

Chapter 7

1. Hooker, ed., *History of the Progressive Party* by Pinchot, pp. 182–83; New Orleans *Daily Picayune,* November 6, 1912.

2. New York *Times,* December 11 (TR's quotes), 12, 1912; New Orleans *Daily Picayune,* December 11, 1912; Harbaugh, *Power and Responsibility,* pp. 453–54; Garraty, *Right Hand Man,* p. 290.

3. *Progressive Bulletin,* December 7, 1912.

4. "Minutes of the Progressive National Committee, 1912–1916" (typescript, copy in Harvard College Library), passim.

5. *World Almanac and Encyclopaedia, 1915* (New York: Press Publishing Co., 1915), passim; Memphis *Commercial Appeal,* September 14, 1914; San Antonio *Daily Express,* August 12, 1914; Charleston (S.C.) *News and Courier,* November 2, 1914; New Orleans *Daily Picayune,* November 2, 1914; Raleigh *News and Observer,* November 6, 1914.

6. J. M. Parker to Walter F. Brown, August 6, 1913, J. M. Parker to A. J. Beveridge, July 1, 1913, September 9, 1913, Parker Papers; "Speech Made by B. F. Fridge at a Meeting of the Progressive Party Held at Newport, R. I., June 30, 1913," Fridge Papers.

7. *Arkansas Gazette,* March 8, June 25, 1913 (Murphy quotes); New York *Times,* July 5, 12, 23, 1913.

8. *Arkansas Gazette,* July 1, 1913; *Progressive Bulletin,* July 1913; Powell Clayton to H. L. Remmel, May 7, 1913, Remmel Papers; Weston A. Goodspeed, ed., *Arkansas: The Province and the State* (Madison, Wis.: Western Historical Association, 1904), pp. 373–74.

9. *Who's Who in Little Rock, 1921,* p. 103; *Arkansas Gazette,* July 2, 1913.

10. *Arkansas Gazette,* July 22, 23, 27, 1913.

11. Richmond *Virginian,* November 4, 1913; New York *Times,* November 5, 1913; *Progressive Bulletin,* August 1913; Dabney, *Virginia,* p. 463 (Election quote).

12. New Orleans *Daily Picayune,* November 16, 1913 (Beveridge quote); New York *Times,* December 17, 1913; J. M. Parker to G. W. Perkins, September 23, 1913, O. K. Davis to J. M. Parker, December 10, 1913, Parker Papers; Bowers, *Beveridge,* pp. 445–46; *Official Report of the Proceedings of the Sixteenth Republican National Convention Held in Chicago, Illinois, June 7, 8, 9, and 10, 1916* (New York: Republican National Committee, 1916), p. 7.

13. Nashville *Banner,* April 15, 1914; Jacksonville *Florida Times-Union,* April 16, 1914; Columbia *State,* May 30, 1914; Boyce, ed., *Unwanted Boy,* p. 153; B. W. Hooper to Mrs. S. Holman, July 3, 1914, Hooper Papers (Hooper quote); Memphis *Commercial Appeal,* April 23, 1914.

14. Memphis *Commercial Appeal,* June 17, 24 (Hooper quote), 29, August 10, 1914; Moore and Foster, *Tennessee,* IV, 835–36, III, 262–63; Paul M. Fink, "Samuel Cole Williams," East Tennessee Historical Society *Publications* 20 (1948): 3–8 (Williams quote); Pollyana Creekmore, "A Bibliography of the Writings of Samuel Cole Williams," East Tennessee Historical Society *Publications* 20 (1948): 14–15.

15. *Hinds County Gazette*, November 3, 1914; New Orleans *Times-Picayune*, June 10 (Fridge quote), November 4, 1914; Memphis *Commercial Appeal*, November 4, 1914; *Progressive Bulletin*, June 1913.

16. Jacksonville *Florida Times-Union*, June 3, July 16, November 2, 1914; *Report of the Secretary of State, 1916* (Tallahassee: State of Florida, 1917), passim; Tebeau, *History of Florida*, p. 340; Cash, *Democratic Party in Florida*, p. 122.

17. Jacksonville *Florida Times-Union*, March 10, August 26, October 7, 1914.

18. Ibid., April 20, 1914.

19. Memphis *Commercial Appeal*, June 9 (Conference quotes), August 22, 1914; Knoxville *Journal and Tribune*, June 9, 1914; New York *Times*, July 9, 1914; F. L. Snedeker to B. W. Hooper, August 27, 1914, Hooper Papers.

20. *Arkansas Gazette*, June 18, 1914; Hempstead, *Historical Review of Arkansas*, II, 628–30.

21. *Arkansas Gazette*, June 18, 1914; *Progressive Bulletin*, February 1913; Mayer, *Republican Party*, pp. 338–39; Herndon, *Centennial History of Arkansas*, p. 384.

22. New Orleans *Times-Picayune*, June 1, 19 (Parker quote), 1914; Davis, *Released for Publication*, pp. 424–26; George B. Tindall, *The Emergence of the New South, 1913–1945* (Baton Rouge: Louisiana State University Press, 1967), pp. 10–11; Taussig, *Tariff History*, p. 425; Pringle, *Roosevelt*, p. 403.

23. New Orleans *Times-Picayune*, June 19, July 8, 1914; Memphis *Commercial Appeal*, June 19, 1914; Charleston (S.C.) *News and Courier*, June 22, 1914.

24. J. M. Parker to A. J. Beveridge, October 8, 1914, Parker Papers; New Orleans *Times-Picayune*, July 8, 14, 1914; Memphis *Commercial Appeal*, July 6, 1914; Richmond *Times-Dispatch*, July 6, 1914; TR to Pearl Wight, September 7, 1914, TR Papers.

25. *World Almanac, 1915*, pp. 807–08; Richmond *Times-Dispatch*, May 11, 17, 23, 1914; Jacksonville *Florida Times-Union*, July 10, 1914.

26. TR to P. S. Stephenson, October 26, 1914, TR Papers; Richmond *Times-Dispatch*, May 11, 17, 23, June 17, July 10, September 18, 23, 1914; Jacksonville *Florida Times-Union*, July 10, 1914; *Arkansas Gazette*, November 4, 1914; Norfolk *Ledger-Dispatch*, July 8, 1953.

27. Charleston (S.C.) *News and Courier*, August 9, September 10, November 1, 4, 1914; *World Almanac, 1915*, p. 799.

28. *Arkansas Gazette*, May 24, June 15, 16, July 14, 1914; W. H. Taft to H. L. Remmel, October 30, 1913, Remmel Papers; D. B. Gaines, *Racial Possibilities as Indicated by the Negroes of Arkansas* (Little Rock: Philander Smith College, 1898), pp. 79–80.

29. *Arkansas Gazette*, July 14, 15 (Negroes quote), 30, August 26, September 14, 15, 16, November 4, 1914; Memphis *Commercial Appeal*, September 15, 16, 1914; Birmingham *Age-Herald*, September 14, 1914; Herndon, *Centennial History of Arkansas*, p. 384.

30. Birmingham *Age-Herald*, July 8, 15, 21, 22, 1914; *Arkansas Gazette*, July 23, 1914; Memphis *Commercial Appeal*, July 23, 1914; Montgomery *Colored Alabamian*, July 24, 1914; *Who's Who in Colored America, 1930–1931–1932* (Brooklyn, N.Y.: Who's Who in Colored America Corp., 1933), p. 299; J. H. Moorman and E. L. Barrett, eds., *Leaders of the Colored Race in Alabama* (Mobile: News Publishing Co., 1928), p. 96.

31. Birmingham *Age-Herald,* August 6, 7, 1914; *Biographical Directory of the American Congress, 1774–1961,* p. 1082.

32. Birmingham *Age-Herald,* August 28, 1914; Gadsden *Times,* April 20, 1949, September 9, 1952; New York *Times,* November 4, 1914; *World Almanac, 1915,* p. 760; Mrs. Helen F. Blackshear, Montgomery, Alabama, to the author, October 22, 1976; Helen F. Blackshear, *Mother Was a Rebel* (Montgomery: Privately printed, 1973), pp. 59–68.

33. Birmingham *Age-Herald,* October 5, 20, November 1, 4, 1914; Memphis *Commercial Appeal,* November 4, 1914; *Who's Who in Alabama, 1939–40* (Birmingham: Who's Who Publishing Co., 1940), I, 243; *World Almanac, 1915,* p. 729.

34. San Antonio *Daily Express,* August 12, 1914; *Arkansas Gazette,* August 12, 1914; Dallas *Morning News,* May 15, August 12, 1914; Casdorph, *Republican Party in Texas,* pp. 108–10 (Convention quote); Winkler, *Platforms of Political Parties in Texas,* p. 606 (Platform quotes).

35. San Antonio *Daily Express,* November 4, 1914; Dallas *Morning News,* November 1 (Etheridge quote), 3, 4, 1914; *The Texas Almanac, 1961–1962* (Dallas: Dallas *Morning News,* 1962), p. 472.

36. Raleigh *News and Observer,* July 5 (Douglas quote), 9, 18, 19 (Walser quote), August 17, 18, 19, 21, 1914; Raleigh *News-Dispatch,* August 3, 1914.

37. Raleigh *News and Observer,* August 21, 1914; Charlotte *Daily Observer,* August 21, 1914; Greensboro *Daily News,* June 30, 1928, June 17, 1933; Asheville *Citizen,* October 26, 1955.

38. Raleigh *News and Observer,* November 4, 5, 6, 1914; *Arkansas Gazette,* November 4, 1914.

39. Atlanta *Constitution,* August 12, 1914; Atlanta *Independent,* June 27, 1914; Jacksonville *Florida Times-Union,* March 28, 1914.

40. Charleston (S.C.) *News and Courier,* August 20, 1914; Tindall, *Emergence of the New South,* p. 64; Dudley Glass, *Progressive Georgians* (Atlanta: H. M. and A. H. Howard, 1937), p. 32; Atlanta *Constitution,* September 30, October 4 (Platform quote), 1914; Atlanta *Journal,* October 3, 1914.

41. Atlanta *Constitution,* September 7, November 3, 5, 8, 1914; TR to C. W. McClure, November 17, 1914, TR Papers; Woodward, *Tom Watson,* pp. 410–13; *World Almanac, 1915,* p. 766.

42. New Orleans *Times-Picayune,* September 3, 7, 8, 9, 1914; Charleston *News and Courier,* September 8, 1914; Birmingham *Age-Herald,* September 9, 1914; Atlanta *Independent,* October 16, 1914; Memphis *Commercial Appeal,* September 8, 1914; *Biographical Directory of the American Congress, 1774–1961,* p. 1271.

43. New Orleans *Times-Picayune,* November 2, 3, 4, 1914; *Arkansas Gazette,* November 4, 1914.

44. Memphis *Commercial Appeal,* September 24, October 4 (Littleton quote), November 1 (Benson quote), 3, 4, 1914; Nashville *Tennessean,* November 4, 1914; *Arkansas Gazette,* November 4, 1914; Issac, *Prohibition and Politics,* p. 239; *World Almanac, 1915,* pp. 801–02.

Chapter 8

1. Karlin, *Dixon of Montana,* pp. 208–12; Gable, "The Bull Moose Years," pp. 614–31.

2. New Orleans *Times-Picayune,* June 6, 7, 8, 12, 1915; TR to Pearl Wight, January 15, 1915, TR to F. W. Bache, February 3, 1915, TR to J. M. Parker, March 31, June 16, 1915, TR to R. W. Child, March 29, 1915, TR Papers; Schott, "Parker and the Bull Moose Party," pp. 161–63.

3. Jacksonville *Florida Times-Union,* February 10, May 30, 1916.

4. Ibid., May 2, 1916 (Quote); Cash, *Democratic Party in Florida,* p. 124; Francis P. Fleming, *Memoirs of Florida* (Atlanta: Southern Historical Association, 1902), pp. 410–11; J. H. Reese, *Florida Flashlights* (Miami: Hefty Press, 1917), p. 97.

5. Raleigh *News and Observer,* March 3, April 9, 1916; Charlotte *Daily Observer,* March 3, 1916.

6. Raleigh *News and Observer,* March 23, April 25, May 30, June 4, 8, 1916; New Orleans *Times-Picayune,* March 26, 1916; *Biographical Directory of the American Congress, 1774–1961,* p. 1788.

7. Raleigh *News and Observer,* March 26, April 5, June 6 (Butler quote), 8, 12 (Delegation quote), 1916; New York *Times,* June 6, 1916; TR to A. T. Pritchard, April 3, 1916, TR Papers; James N. Williamson, Jr., to J. M. Parker, June 16, 1916, Parker Papers.

8. Charlottesville *Daily Progress,* May 31, 1916; Richmond *Virginian,* May 30, 1916; Richmond *Times-Dispatch,* May 30, 31, 1916; Merlo J. Pusey, *Charles Evans Hughes* (New York: Macmillan, 1951), I, 317–30; Dexter Perkins, *Charles Evans Hughes and American Democratic Statesmanship* (Boston: Little Brown, 1965), pp. 50–70 (Hughes quote).

9. Charlottesville *Daily Progress,* March 31 (Platform quote), April 4, 1916; Richmond *Times-Dispatch,* May 28, 1916; *World Almanac and Encyclopaedia, 1917* (New York: Press Publishing Co., 1917), p. 817.

10. Atlanta *Journal,* March 10, 1916; Raleigh *News and Observer,* March 10, 1916.

11. Charleston (S.C.) *News and Courier,* April 13, 1916; Jacksonville *Florida Times-Union,* April 13, June 3, 1916; Atlanta *Constitution,* April 13, June 2, 4, 1916; Maurice C. Thomas and Mrs. Grant Williams, eds., *Report of the Proceedings of the Seventy-first Annual Session of the Georgia Bar Association . . . 1954* (Macon: Georgia Bar Association, 1954), p. 147; *World Almanac, 1917,* p. 784.

12. Jacksonville *Florida Times-Union,* April 2, 16, 17, 1916; TR to H. B. Anderson, June 23, 1916, TR Papers.

13. New Orleans *Times-Picayune,* March 29, 30, April 2, 1916; Phillips, "Administration of Governor Parker," p. 29; Schott, "Parker and the Bull Moose Party," pp. 148–56.

14. New Orleans *Times-Picayune,* April 6, 7, 15 (Parker quote), 18, 19, 1916; Chattanooga *Daily Times,* April 23, 1916; Ladisias Lazaro to Claremont Vidrine, February 2, 1916, Ladisias Lazaro Papers, Department of Archives and Manuscripts, Louisiana State University; TR to J. M. Parker, May 4, 1916, TR Papers.

15. New Orleans *Times-Picayune,* March 24, April 28 (Cohen convention quotes), May 27, 1916; *Arkansas Gazette,* May 29, 1916; Jacksonville *Florida Times-Union,* April 28, 1916.

16. New Orleans *Times Picayune,* May 16, 1916 (Convention quotes); *Arkansas Gazette,* May 16, 1916.

17. *Arkansas Gazette,* April 17, 21 (Convention quotes), 1916; Washington *Bee,*

March 23, 1916; Richmond *Planet,* June 3, 17, 1916; Montgomery *Colored Alabamian,* January 29, 1916.

18. *Arkansas Gazette,* April 4, 5, 17, 21, 27 (1st, 2nd, 3rd quotes), 28, June 12, 19, 1916; Herndon, *Centennial History of Arkansas,* III, 906; Dallas T. Herndon, *Annals of Arkansas* (Hopkinsville, Ky.: Historical Record Association, 1947), p. 254; Earl W. Benson to H. L. Remmel, October 23, 1916, C. D. Hilles to H. L. Remmel, October 23, 1916, Remmel Papers.

19. Charleston (S.C.) *News and Courier,* April 30 (1st quote), May 3, June 8, 1916; *Atlanta Constitution,* May 3, 1916 (2nd quote); Richmond *Times-Dispatch,* June 5, 1916.

20. New Orleans *Times-Picayune,* May 3, 1916 (Convention quotes); *Hinds County Gazette,* May 3, 1916; *Arkansas Gazette,* May 31, 1916; TR to S. D. Redmond, May 10, 1916, TR Papers.

21. Birmingham *Age-Herald,* May 7, 1916; Chattanooga *Daily Times,* May 5, 1916; Frank H. Hitchcock to B. W. Hooper, March 1, 1916, E. W. Essary to B. W. Hooper, March 6, 1916, William I. Dunn to B. W. Hooper, March 7, 1916, Hooper Papers.

22. Nashville *Tennessean,* May 4, 1916; Chattanooga *Daily Times,* May 4, 5, 8, 1916; *Arkansas Gazette,* May 5, 1916; B. W. Hooper to R. R. Church, February 16, 1916, J. O. Thompson to B. W. Hooper, May 9, 1916, Charles W. Fairbanks to B. W. Hooper, May 6, 1916, Hooper Papers; Herbert Parsons to J. C. Napier, November 11, 1916, Napier Papers.

23. Richmond *Times-Dispatch,* April 8, May 12, 13 (Convention quote), 28, 1916; H. L. Anderson to J. M. Parker, May 24, 1916, Parker Papers.

24. Atlanta *Constitution,* May 13, June 6 (McClure quote), 15, 1916; TR to W. S. Edwards, May 18, 1916, TR Papers; C. W. McClure, A. T. Hamilton and James L. Sibley to J. M. Parker, July 7, 1916, J. M. Parker to H. G. Hastings, June 16, 1916, H. G. Hastings to J. M. Parker, June 17, 1916, Parker Papers.

25. Birmingham *Age-Herald,* May 10, 18, June 6, 1916.

26. Birmingham *Age-Herald,* May 20 (Negroes quotes), 21 (Convention quotes), 1916; Atlanta *Constitution,* May 21, 1916; Birmingham *Voice of the People,* June 17, 1916; Montgomery *Colored Alabamian,* February 12, 19, 1916; New Orleans *Times-Picayune,* May 20, 1916; *Alabama Blue Book and Register* (Montgomery: State of Alabama, 1929), p. 132.

27. Dallas *Morning News,* May 23, 24 (TR quote), 1916; *Arkansas Gazette,* May 24, 1916; Casdorph, *Republican Party in Texas,* pp. 111–16; TR to Sloan Simpson, April 12, 1916, TR Papers; see also, Billie J. Ellis, "Cecil A. Lyon, the Practical Politician" (Senior Honors Essay, The University of Texas, 1973).

28. Dallas *Morning News,* May 23, 1916 (Convention quotes); San Antonio *Daily Express,* May 23, 1916; Chattanooga *Daily Times,* June 4, 1916 (Borden quote); Winkler, *Platforms of Political Parties in Texas,* pp. 614–16.

29. Dallas *Morning News,* May 23, 1916 (Convention quotes); San Antonio *Daily Express,* May 23, 1916; *Arkansas Gazette,* May 21, 24, 1916; New Orleans *Times-Picayune,* May 30, 1916; Winkler, *Platforms of Political Parties in Texas,* pp. 616–17; Casdorph, *Republican Party in Texas,* pp. 111–43 (Hostrasser quote); *Proceedings of the 1916 Republican National Convention,* pp. 181–82.

30. Charleston (S.C.) *News and Courier,* May 27, June 7, 1916; *World Almanac, 1917,* p. 811.

31. TR to F. V. Brown, May 10, 1916, TR to H. B. Anderson, May 11, 1916, TR to W. J. Oliver, April 17, 1916, TR Papers; Morison, ed., *Letters of Theodore Roosevelt*, VIII, 1038; Chattanooga *Daily Times*, June 4, 11 (Committee quote), 15 (Dagley quote), 1916; Memphis *Commercial Appeal*, June 4, 1916; J. C. Ford to B. W. Hooper, June 28, 1916, Hooper Papers.

32. New York *Times*, June 6, 1916 (Johnson quote); New Orleans *Times-Picayune*, June 6, 1916; John A. Garraty, "TR on the Telephone," *American Heritage* 3:1 (December 1957): 100; Mowry, *TR and the Progressive Movement*, pp. 344–49.

33. New York *Times*, June 1–8, 1916; Atlanta *Constitution*, June 2 (Johnson quote), 3, 1916; Washington *Bee*, June 17, 1916; Birmingham *Age-Herald*, June 5, 1916; New Orleans *Times-Picayune*, June 3, 5, 1916; *Arkansas Gazette*, May 31, 1916.

34. New York *Times*, June 6–8, 1916; Washington *Bee*, June 22, 1916; Schlesinger, ed., *American Presidential Elections*, III, 2249 (Platform quote); *Proceedings of the 1916 Republican National Convention*, pp. 1–183 (Harding quote); Butler, *Across the Busy Years*, I, 257–58.

35. New York *Times*, June 8, 1916; Mowry, *TR and the Progressive Movement*, p. 349; Eric F. Goldman, *Charles J. Bonaparte: Patrician Reformer, His Early Career* (Baltimore: Johns Hopkins University Press, 1943), pp. 11–13; Joseph B. Bishop, *Charles Joseph Bonaparte* (New York: Scribners, 1922), pp. 188–89; TR to W. P. Jackson, June 8, 1916, TR Papers.

36. New York *Times*, June 9, 10, 1916; Butler, *Across the Busy Years*, I, 256–64; Garraty, *Right Hand Man*, p. 339.

37. Southern totals in the convention were: Alabama 16, Arkansas 15, Florida 8, Georgia 17, Louisiana 12, Mississippi 12, North Carolina 21, South Carolina 11, Tennessee 21, Texas 26, Virginia 15. Candidates receiving southern votes were: Hughes 53½, Roosevelt 23, Root 11½, Burton 14½, Cummins 2, Weeks 30, Fairbanks 11½, du Pont 5, Sherman 5, Taft 14, Borah 1, McCall 1, Willis 1. Sources: New York *Times*, June 10, 1916; *Proceedings of the 1916 Republican National Convention*, pp. 106–80 (Convention quotes); Milton R. Merrill, "Reed Smoot: Apostle in Politics" (Ph.D. dissertation, Columbia University, 1950), pp. 194–216.

38. New York *Times*, June 9, 10, 1916.

39. Ibid., June 10, 1916; *Proceedings of the 1916 Republican National Convention*, pp. 183–89; John A. Garraty, *Henry Cabot Lodge: A Biography* (New York: Knopf, 1953), pp. 322–23; Garraty, "TR on the Telephone," pp. 105–07; Pusey, *Hughes*, I, 326–28; Butler, *Across the Busy Years*, I, 263–66.

40. New York *Times*, June 11, 1916; *Proceedings of the 1916 Republican National Convention*, pp. 190–219.

41. New York *Times*, June 11, 1916 (Convention quotes); New Orleans *Times-Picayune*, June 11, 1916; H. L. Stoddard, *As I Knew Them* (New York: Harper and Brothers, 1927), p. 437.

42. New York *Times*, June 11, 1916 (Convention quotes); Moos, *The Republicans*, p. 292 (Photograph quote); TR to Progressive National Convention (n.d.), TR Papers.

Chapter 9

1. New York *Times,* June 11, 1916; New Orleans *Times-Picayune,* June 11, 1916; Harold L. Ickes, "Who Killed the Progressive Party?" *American Historical Review,* 36:2 (October 1941): 330; Stoddard, *As I Knew Them,* p. 437.

2. J. M. Parker to J. C. Houk, June 16, 1916, J. M. Parker to J. O. Thompson et al., June 20, 1916, Parker Papers; New York *Times,* June 27, 1916; New Orleans *Times-Picayune,* June 27, 1917; Schott, "Parker and the Bull Moose Party," pp. 176–78.

3. TR to T. H. Wannamaker, June 24, 1916, TR Papers; New York *Times,* August 4, October 8, 10, 15, 1916; New Orleans *Times-Picayune,* October 15, 1916; V. G. Hinshaw to J. M. Parker, July 6, 1916, Woodrow Wilson to J. M. Parker, November 16, 1916, Parker Papers.

4. New Orleans *Times-Picayune,* August 3, 1916; Dallas *Morning News,* August 9, 1916; San Antonio *Daily Express,* August 9, 1916; J. C. Ford to B. W. Hooper, June 28, 1916, Hooper Papers; Austin *American,* August 9, 1950.

5. New York *Times,* June 11, 1916; A. J. Beveridge, "The Launching and Wrecking of the Progressive Party" (typescript), A. J. Beveridge Papers, Manuscripts Division, Library of Congress, Washington, D.C.; Pusey, *Hughes,* I, 355.

6. New York *Times,* October 15, November 8, 1916; *Arkansas Gazette,* November 7, 8, 1916; *World Almanac, 1917,* passim; Robinson, *Presidential Vote,* passim.

7. Tindall, *Emergence of the New South,* pp. 168–69; Elbert W. Tatum, *The Changed Political Thought of the Negro, 1915 1945* (New York: Exposition Press, 1951), p. 94; Alexander Heard, *A Two Party South?* (Chapel Hill: University of North Carolina Press, 1961), p. 226.

Bibliography

Manuscript Sources

Albert J. Beveridge Papers, Manuscripts Division, Library of Congress, Washington, D.C.

Joseph M. Dixon Papers, University of Montana Library, Missoula.

Benjamin F. Fridge Papers, Mitchell Memorial Library, Mississippi State University, Mississippi State.

William E. Glasscock Papers, West Virginia and Regional History Collection, West Virginia University Library, Morgantown.

Charles D. Hilles Papers, Sterling Library, Yale University, New Haven, Connecticut.

Ben W. Hooper Papers, University of Tennessee Library, Knoxville.

Frank Knox Papers, Manuscripts Division, Library of Congress, Washington, D.C.

Ladisias Lazaro Papers, Department of Archives and Manuscripts, Louisiana State University, Baton Rouge.

Whitefield McKinlay Papers, Carter G. Woodson Collection, Manuscripts Division, Library of Congress, Washington, D.C.

John M. Morehead Papers, Perkins Library, Duke University, Durham, North Carolina.

James C. Napier Papers, Fisk University Library, Nashville, Tennessee.

John M. Parker Papers, Southern Historical Collection, University of North Carolina Library, Chapel Hill.

Richmond Pearson Papers, Southern Historical Collection, University of North Carolina Library, Chapel Hill.

George W. Perkins Papers, Butler Library, Columbia University, New York, New York.

Harmon L. Remmel Papers, Series 1, University of Arkansas Library, Fayetteville.

Theodore Roosevelt Papers, Manuscripts Division, Library of Congress, Washington, D.C.

Oscar D. Street Papers, William Stanley Hoole Special Collections Library, Amelia Gayle Gorgas Library, University of Alabama, University, Alabama.

William Howard Taft Papers, Manuscripts Division, Library of Congress, Washington, D.C.

Booker T. Washington Papers, Manuscripts Division, Library of Congress, Washington, D.C.

Newspapers

Asheville *Citizen,* 1955.
Atlanta *Constitution,* 1912, 1914, 1916.
Atlanta *Independent,* 1912, 1914.
Atlanta *Journal,* 1909, 1914, 1916.
Austin *American,* 1950.
Austin *Statesman,* 1911, 1912, 1924.
Baltimore *Afro-American Ledger,* 1911.
Baltimore *Sun,* 1912.

Birmingham *Age-Herald,* 1912, 1914, 1916.
Birmingham *News,* 1912.
Birmingham *Voice of the People,* 1916.
Charleston (W.Va.) *Daily Mail,* 1912.
Charleston (S.C.) *News and Courier,* 1912, 1914, 1916.
Charleston (S.C.) *Evening Post,* 1912.
Charlotte *Daily Observer,* 1912, 1914, 1916.
Charlottesville *Daily Progress,* 1916.
Chattanooga *Daily Times,* 1916.
Chicago *Daily Tribune,* 1908, 1912, 1914.
Cincinnati *Enquirer,* 1912.
Columbia *State,* 1894, 1912.
Dallas *Morning News,* 1892, 1911, 1912, 1914, 1916, 1942.
Gadsden *Times,* 1949.
Galveston *Daily News,* 1892, 1912.
Greensboro *Daily News,* 1928.
Hinds County Gazette, 1912, 1914.
Jackson *Clarion Ledger,* 1912, 1914.
Jacksonville *Florida Times-Union,* 1898, 1904, 1912, 1914, 1916, 1945 (Known as *Florida Times-Union and Citizen* from September 9, 1897 until January 20, 1903).
Knoxville *Journal and Tribune,* 1912, 1914, 1936, 1945.
Knoxville *News-Sentinel,* 1912.
Little Rock *Arkansas Gazette,* 1911, 1912, 1913, 1914, 1916.
Memphis *Commercial Appeal,* 1912, 1914.
Memphis *Press-Scimitar,* 1942.
Miami *Daily Metropolis,* 1912.
Montgomery *Colored Alabamian,* 1912, 1914, 1916.
Nashville *American,* 1912.
Nashville *Banner,* 1911, 1912, 1914.
Nashville *Tennessean,* 1916.
New Orleans *Daily Picayune,* 1909, 1911, 1912, 1913, 1914, 1915, 1916, 1939 (Changed to *Times-Picayune,* May 1, 1914).
New York *Times,* 1909, 1912, 1913, 1914, 1916.
Norfolk *Journal and Guide,* 1912.
Norfolk *Ledger-Dispatch,* 1953.
Orlando *Evening Star,* 1946.
Orlando *Sentinel,* 1937.
Raleigh *News and Observer,* 1912, 1914, 1916.
Raleigh *News-Dispatch,* 1916.
Richmond *Planet,* 1912, 1914, 1916.
Richmond *Times-Dispatch,* 1914, 1916.
Richmond *Virginian,* 1909, 1912, 1914, 1916.
San Antonio *Daily Express,* 1902, 1908, 1909, 1912, 1914, 1916.
Savannah *Press,* 1923, 1939.
Tampa *Morning Tribune,* 1912.
Uniontown (Ala.) *Negro Leader,* 1912.
Washington *Bee,* 1912, 1914, 1916.

Party Documents and Publications

A Stolen Nomination for the Presidency: The Facts of the Chicago Convention of 1912. New York: Progressive National Committee, 1912.

"The First Convention of the Progressive Party Held at Chicago, August 5, 6, 7, 1912." Typescript, Theodore Roosevelt Papers, Manuscripts Division, Library of Congress, Washington, D.C.

History and Facts of the Regular Reorganized Republican Party of Florida. N.p.: The Reorganized Republican Party of Florida, 1927.

"Minutes of the Progressive National Committee, 1912–1916." Typescript, Harvard University Library, Cambridge, Massachusetts.

Official Report of the Proceedings of the Fourteenth Republican National Convention Held in Chicago, Illinois, June 16, 17, 18, and 19, 1908. Columbus, Ohio: Republican National Committee, 1908.

Official Report of the Proceedings of the Fifteenth Republican National Convention Held in Chicago, Illinois, June 18, 19, 20, 21, and 22, 1912. New York: Republican National Committee, 1912.

"Official Report of the Proceedings of the Progressive National Committee Held in Room 1102 of the Congress Hotel, August 3, 1912, Senator Joseph M. Dixon in the Chair." Typescript, Theodore Roosevelt Papers, Manuscripts Division, Library of Congress, Washington, D.C.

Official Report of the Proceedings of the Sixteenth Republican National Convention Held in Chicago, Illinois, June 7, 8, 9, and 10, 1916. New York: Republican National Committee, 1916.

Proceedings of the Republican National Convention Held at Chicago, Illinois, Thursday, Friday, Saturday, Monday, and Tuesday, June 2d, 3d, 4th, 6th, and 7th, 1880. Chicago: Republican National Committee, 1880.

Proceedings of the Thirteenth Republican National Convention Held in the City of Chicago, Illinois, June 21, 22, 23, 1904. Minneapolis: Republican National Committee, 1904.

Progressive Bulletin. New York: Progressive National Committee, December 1912–March 1913.

Roll of Delegates and Alternates to the First National Convention: The Coliseum, Chicago, Illinois, August 5, 6, and 7, 1912. New York: Progressive National Committee, 1912.

Federal and State Publications

Alabama Blue Book and Register. Montgomery: State of Alabama, 1929.

Alabama Official and Statistical Register. Montgomery: Alabama State Department of Archives and History, 1903.

Annual Report of the Secretary of State, 1912. Baton Rouge: State of Louisiana, 1913.

Areas Administered by the National Park Service and Related Properties as of January 1, 1972. Washington, D.C.: U.S. Department of the Interior, 1972.

Biennial Report of the Secretary of State, 1911–1913. Little Rock: State of Arkansas, 1913.

Biennial Report of the Secretary of State, 1913–1915. Memphis: State of Mississippi, 1915.

Biographical Directory of the American Congress, 1774–1961. Washington, D.C.: U.S. Congress, 1961.

Congressional Record, 61st Congress. Washington, D.C.: U.S. Congress, 1909.

Official Congressional Directory, 55th Congress. Washington, D.C.: U.S. Congress, 1897.

Official Congressional Directory, 62nd Congress. Washington, D.C.: U.S. Congress, 1913.

Official Congressional Directory, 63rd Congress. Washington, D.C.: U.S. Congress, 1913.

Official and Statistical Register of the State of Mississippi. Jackson: State of Mississippi, 1912.

Report of the Secretary of State, 1912. Tallahassee: State of Florida, 1913.

Report of the Secretary of State, 1916. Tallahassee: State of Florida, 1917,

Yearbook of Agriculture, 1911. Washington, D.C.: U.S. Department of Agriculture, 1912.

Secondary Materials

Books

Alexander, Charles C. *The Ku Klux Klan in the Southwest.* Lexington: University of Kentucky Press, 1965.

Armes, Ethel M. *The Story of Iron and Coal in Alabama.* Birmingham: Birmingham Chamber of Commerce, 1910.

Atwell, William H. *Autobiography.* Dallas: Warlick-Law Printing Co., 1935.

Bagby, Wesley M. *The Road to Normalcy: The Presidential Election and Campaign of 1920.* Baltimore: Johns Hopkins University Press, 1962.

Bain, Richard C. and Judith H. Parris. *Convention Decisions and Voting Records.* Washington, D.C.: Brookings Institution, 1973.

Baker, Richard C. *The Tariff under Roosevelt and Taft.* Hastings, Nebr.: Democrat Printing Co., 1941.

Barck, Oscar T., Jr., and Nelson M. Blake. *Since 1900: A History of the United States in Our Times.* New York: Macmillan, 1968.

Barr, Alwyn. *Reconstruction to Reform: Texas Politics, 1876–1906.* Austin: The University of Texas Press, 1971.

Bates, J. Leonard. *The United States, 1898–1928: Progressivism and a Society in Transition.* New York: McGraw-Hill, 1976.

Bettersworth, John K. *Mississippi: A History.* Austin, Tex.: The Steck Co., 1959.

Billington, Monroe. *The Political South in the Twentieth Century.* New York: Scribners, 1975.

Bishop, Joseph B. *Charles Joseph Bonaparte.* New York: Scribners, 1922.

Blackman, William F. *History of Orange County, Florida.* DeLand, Fla.: E. O. Painter Printing Co., 1927.

Blackshear, Helen F. *Mother Was a Rebel.* Montgomery, Ala.: Privately printed, 1973.

Blum, John M. *The Republican Roosevelt.* Cambridge: Harvard University Press, 1962.

Boris, Joseph J., ed. *Who's Who in Colored America: A Biographical Dictionary of Notable Living Persons of Negro Descent in America.* 2 vols. New York: Who's Who in Colored America Publishing Co., 1927.

Bowers, Claude G. *Beveridge and the Progressive Era.* New York: The Literary Guild, 1932.

Boyce, Everett R., ed. *The Unwanted Boy: The Autobiography of Governor Ben W. Hooper.* Knoxville: University of Tennessee Press, 1963.

Brawley, Benjamin. *A Social History of the Negro Problem in the United States and a Study of the Republic of Liberia.* New York: reprint, Collier Books, 1970.

Bruce, Philip A., ed. *History of Virginia.* 6 vols. New York: Macmillan, 1926.

Buni, Andrew. *The Negro in Virginia Politics, 1902–1965.* Charlottesville: University of Virginia Press, 1967.

Butler, Nicholas Murray. *Across the Busy Years.* 2 vols. New York: Scribners, 1939.

Candler, Allen D. and Clement A. Evans. *Georgia: Comprising Sketches of Counties, Towns, Events, Institutions, and Persons, Arranged in Cyclopaedic Form.* 3 vols. Atlanta: State Historical Association, 1906.

Casdorph, Paul D. *A History of the Republican Party in Texas, 1865–1965.* Austin: Pemberton Press, 1966.

Cash, Wilbur J. *The Mind of the South.* New York: Knopf, 1941.

Cash, William T. *History of the Democratic Party in Florida, Including Biographical Sketches of Prominent Florida Democrats.* Tallahassee: Florida Democratic Historical Association, 1936.

Chambers, Henry E. *A History of Louisiana.* 3 vols. New York: American Historical Society, Inc., 1925.

Charleston, South Carolina, City Directory, 1913. Charleston: Walker, Evans, and Cogswell, 1913.

City of Atlanta, 1892–1893. Atlanta: Inter-City Publishing Company, 1893.

Clark, Thomas D. and Albert D. Kirwan. *The South since Appomattox.* New York: Oxford University Press, 1967.

Clayton, Powell. *The Aftermath of the Civil War in Arkansas.* New York: Neale Publishing Co., 1915.

Coletta, Paolo. *The Presidency of William Howard Taft.* Lawrence: University Press of Kansas, 1973.

Coulter, E. Merton. *Georgia: A Short History.* Chapel Hill: University of North Carolina Press, 1947.

———. *William G. Brownlow: Fighting Parson of the Southern Highlands.* Chapel Hill: University of North Carolina Press, 1937.

Cutler, Harry G. *History of Florida: Past and Present, Historical and Biographical.* 3 vols. Chicago: Lewis Publishing Co., 1923.

Dabney, Virginius. *Virginia: The New Dominion.* Garden City, N.Y.: Doubleday, 1971.

Davis, Edwin A. *Louisiana: The Pelican State.* Baton Rouge: Louisiana State University Press, 1969.

Davis, Oscar K. *Released for Publication: Some Inside Political History of Theodore Roosevelt and His Times, 1898–1919.* New York: Houghton Mifflin, 1925.

Deacon, William M. *Reference Biography of Louisiana Bench and Bar.* New Orleans: Cox Printing and Publishing Co., 1922.

Dedication: McClennan-Banks Hospital, Inc. of Charleston County, South Carolina, 1959. Copy in South Carolina Historical Society, Charleston.

Degler, Carl N. *The Other South.* New York: Harper and Row, 1973.

De Santis, Vincent P. *Republicans Face the Southern Question: The New Departure Years, 1877–1897.* Baltimore: Johns Hopkins University Press, 1959.

Dittmer, John. *Black Georgia in the Progressive Era, 1900–1920.* Urbana: University of Illinois Press, 1977.

Dufour, Charles L. *Ten Flags in the Wind: The Story of Louisiana.* New York: Harper and Row, 1967.

Durden, Robert F. *The Climax of Populism: The Election of 1896.* Lexington: University of Kentucky Press, 1966.

Edmonds, Helen G. *The Negro and Fusion Politics in North Carolina, 1894–1901.* Chapel Hill: University of North Carolina Press, 1951.

Ezell, John S. *The South since 1865.* New York: Macmillan, 1963.

Fausold, Martin L. *Gifford Pinchot: Bull Moose Progressive.* Syracuse: Syracuse University Press, 1961.

Felton, Rebecca L. *My Memoirs of Georgia Politics.* Atlanta: Index Publishing Co., 1911.

Fleming, Francis P. *Memoirs of Florida.* 2 vols. Atlanta: Southern Historical Association, 1902.

Fleming, G. J. and C. E. Burckell, eds. *Who's Who in Colored America.* Yonkers, N.Y.: Who's Who in Colored America Corp., 1950.

Fletcher, John G. *Arkansas.* Chapel Hill: University of North Carolina Press, 1947.

Folmsbee, Stanley J., Robert E. Corlew, and Enoch L. Mitchell. *History of Tennessee.* 4 vols. New York: Lewis Historical Publishing Co., 1960.

Fortier, Alcée. *Louisiana: Comprising Sketches of Counties, Towns, Events, Institutions, and Persons, Arranged in Cyclopaedic Form.* 2 vols. Atlanta: Southern Historical Association, 1903.

Gaines, D. B. *Racial Possibilities as Indicated by the Negroes of Arkansas.* Little Rock: Philander Smith College, 1898.

Gardner, Joseph L. *Departing Glory: Theodore Roosevelt as Ex-President.* New York: Scribners, 1973.

Garlington, J. C. *Men of the Times: Sketches of Living Notables.* Spartanburg, S.C.: Garlington Publishing Co., 1902.

Garraty, John A. *Henry Cabot Lodge: A Biography.* New York: Knopf, 1953.

———. *Right Hand Man: The Life of George W. Perkins.* New York: Harper and Row, 1960.

Garrett, Franklin M. *Atlanta Scrapbook of Obituaries, 1923–1932.* Copy in Georgia Department of Archives, Atlanta.

Gatewood, Willard B. *Theodore Roosevelt and the Art of Controversy: Episodes of the White House Years.* Baton Rouge: Louisiana State University Press, 1970.

Glass, Dudley. *Progressive Georgians.* Atlanta: H. M. and A. H. Howard, 1937.

Goldman, Eric F. *Charles J. Bonaparte: Patrician Reformer, His Early Career.* Baltimore: Johns Hopkins University Press, 1943.

Goodspeed, Weston A., ed. *Arkansas: The Province and the State.* Madison, Wis.: Western Historical Association, 1904.

Gore, Eldon H. *From Florida Sand to the City Beautiful: A Historical Record of Orlando, Florida.* Orlando: J. M. Cox, 1957.

Gould, Lewis L. *Progressives and Prohibitionists: Texas Democrats in the Wilson Era.* Austin: The University of Texas Press, 1973.

Graham, Otis L., Jr. *An Encore for Reform: The Old Progressives and the New Deal.* New York: Oxford University Press, 1967.

Grantham, Dewey W. *Hoke Smith and the Politics of the New South.* Baton Rouge: Louisiana State University Press, 1958.

Guess, William F. *South Carolina: Annals of Pride and Protest.* New York: Harper and Row, 1960.

Hackney, Sheldon. *Populism to Progressivism in Alabama.* Princeton: Princeton University Press, 1969.

Hagedorn, Hermann, ed. *The Works of Theodore Roosevelt.* 20 vols. New York: The National Edition, Scribners, 1926.

Hair, William Ivy. *Bourbonism and Agrarian Protest: Louisiana Politics, 1877–1900.* Baton Rouge: Louisiana State University Press, 1969.

Hale, Will T. and Dixon L. Merritt. *A History of Tennessee and Tennesseans: The Leaders and Representative Men in Commerce, Industry, and Modern Activities.* 8 vols. Chicago: Lewis Publishing Co., 1913.

Hamer, P. M. *Tennessee: A History.* 4 vols. Washington, D.C.: American Historical Association, 1933.

Hanna, Kathryn A. *Florida: Land of Change.* Chapel Hill: University of North Carolina Press, 1948.

Harbaugh, William H. *Power and Responsibility: The Life and Times of Theodore Roosevelt.* New York: Farrar, Straus, and Cudahy, 1961.

———, ed. *The Writings of Theodore Roosevelt.* New York: Bobbs-Merrill, 1967.

Hart, Weldon and James A. Clark. *The Tactful Texan: A Biography of Governor Will Hobby.* New York: Random House, 1958.

Heard, Alexander. *A Two Party South?* Chapel Hill: University of North Carolina Press, 1961.

Hechler, Kenneth W. *Insurgency: Personalities and Politics of the Taft Era.* New York: reprint, Russell and Russell, 1964.

Hemphill, J. C. *Men of Mark in South Carolina.* Washington, D.C.: Men of Mark Publishing Co., 1907.

Hempstead, Fay. *Historical Review of Arkansas.* 3 vols. Chicago: Lewis Publishing Co., 1911.

Herndon, Dallas T. *Annals of Arkansas.* Hopkinsville, Kentucky: Historical Record Association, 1947.

———. *Centennial History of Arkansas.* Little Rock and Chicago: S. J. Clarke Publishing Co., 1922.

Hirshson, Stanley P. *Farewell to the Bloody Shirt: Northern Republicans and the Southern Negro.* Bloomington: Indiana University Press, 1962.

History of North Carolina. New York and Chicago: Lewis Publishing Co., 1919.

History of North Carolina: Brief Biographies of Leading People for Ready Reference Purposes. Asheville: Evening News Publishing Co., 1906.

Holmes, William F. *The White Chief: James Kimble Vardaman.* Baton Rouge: Louisiana State University Press, 1970.

Hooker, Helene M., ed. *History of the Progressive Party, 1912–1916,* by Amos R. E. Pinchot. New York: New York University Press, 1958.

In Memory of Edward B. Downie. Unsigned Pamphlet. Copy in Little Rock Public Library.

Issac, Paul E. *Prohibition and Politics: Turbulent Decades in Tennessee, 1885–1920*. Knoxville: University of Tennessee Press, 1965.

Jacobson, Charles. *The Life Story of Jeff Davis: The Stormy Petrel of Arkansas Politics*. Little Rock: Parke-Harper Publishing Co., 1925.

Jessup, Philip C. *Elihu Root*. 2 vols. New York: Dodd, Meade and Co., 1938.

Karlin, Jules. *Joseph M. Dixon of Montana: Senator and Bull Moose Manager*. Missoula: University of Montana Press, 1974.

Kendall, John S. *History of New Orleans*. 3 vols. Chicago: Lewis Publishing Co., 1922.

Kirby, Jack Temple. *Darkness at the Dawning: Race and Reform in the Progressive South*. Philadelphia: J. B. Lippincott, 1972.

Kirwan, Albert D. *Revolt of the Rednecks: Mississippi Politics, 1875–1925*. New York: reprint, Harper and Row, 1965.

Kousser, J. Morgan. *The Shaping of Southern Politics: Suffrage Restrictions and the Establishment of the One-Party South*. New Haven: Yale University Press, 1975.

La Follette, Bella C. and Folla La Follette. *Robert M. La Follette, 1855–1925*. 2 vols. New York: Macmillan, 1953.

La Follette, Robert M. *Autobiography: A Narrative of Political Experiences*. Madison: reprint, University of Wisconsin Press, 1963.

Larsen, William. *Montague of Virginia: The Making of a Southern Progressive*. Baton Rouge: Louisiana State University Press, 1965.

Lefler, Hugh T. *History of North Carolina*. 4 vols. New York: Lewis Historical Publishing Co., 1956.

_____ and Allen R. Newsome. *North Carolina: The History of a Southern State*. Chapel Hill: University of North Carolina Press, 1963.

Lewinson, Paul. *Race, Class, and Party: A History of Negro Suffrage and White Politics in the South*. New York: Oxford, 1932.

Lewis, William D. *The Life of Theodore Roosevelt*. Philadelphia: John C. Winston Co., 1919.

Link, Arthur S. *Wilson: The Road to the White House*. Princeton: Princeton University Press, 1947.

_____ and William B. Catton. *American Epoch: A History of the United States since the 1890s*. New York: Knopf, 1967.

Loewen, James W. and Charles Sallis. *Mississippi: Conflict and Change*. New York: Pantheon, 1974.

Logan, Rayford W. *The Betrayal of the Negro from Rutherford B. Hayes to Woodrow Wilson*. New York: reprint, Collier Books, 1965.

Lowitt, Richard. *George W. Norris: The Making of a Progressive*. Syracuse: Syracuse University Press, 1963.

McKay, Seth S. *Texas Politics, 1906–1944: With Special Reference to the German Counties*. Lubbock: Texas Tech Press, 1952.

Malone, Dumas and Allen Johnson, eds. *The Dictionary of American Biography*. 20 vols. New York: Scribners, 1958.

Marcus, Robert D. *The Grand Old Party: Political Structure in the Gilded Age, 1880–1896*. New York: Oxford University Press, 1971.

Martin, Ralph G. *Ballots and Bandwagons.* New York: Rand McNally, 1964.

Mason, Alpheus T. *Bureaucracy Convicts Itself: The Ballinger-Pinchot Controversy of 1910.* New York: Viking Press, 1941.

Mather, Frank L. *Who's Who of the Colored Race, 1915.* 2 vols. New York: Who's Who in Colored America Corp., 1915.

Maxwell, Robert S., ed. *Great Lives Observed: La Follette.* Englewood Cliffs, N.J.: Prentice Hall, 1969.

Mayer, George H. *The Republican Party, 1854–1966.* New York: Oxford University Press, 1967.

Merrill, Horace S. and Marion G. Merrill. *The Republican Command, 1897–1913.* Lexington: University of Kentucky Press, 1971.

Moore, Albert B. *History of Alabama.* Tuscaloosa: Alabama Book Store, 1951.

Moore, John T. and Austin P. Foster. *Tennessee: The Volunteer State.* Chicago and Nashville: S. J. Clarke Publishing Co., 1923.

Moorman, J. H. and E. L. Barrett, eds. *Leaders of the Colored Race in Alabama.* Mobile: News Publishing Co., 1928.

Moos, Malcolm. *The Republicans: A History of Their Party.* New York: Random House, 1956.

Morison, Etling, ed. *The Letters of Theodore Roosevelt.* 8 vols. Cambridge: Harvard University Press, 1954.

Morris, Edmund. *The Rise of Theodore Roosevelt.* New York: Coward, McCann, and Geoghegan, 1979.

Mowry, George E. *The California Progressives.* Chicago: reprint, Quadrangle Books, 1963.

———. *The Era of Theodore Roosevelt and the Birth of Modern America, 1900–1912.* New York: Harper and Row, 1958.

———. *Theodore Roosevelt and the Progressive Movement.* New York: reprint, Hill and Wang, 1960.

National Cyclopaedia of American Biography. 153 vols. New York: White, 1892–1971.

Norris, George W. *Fighting Liberal.* New York: Collier Books, 1945.

Nye, Russell B. *Midwestern Progressive Politics: A Historical Study of Its Origins and Development, 1870–1958.* New York: Harper and Row, 1959.

Owen, Thomas M. *History of Alabama and Dictionary of Alabama Biography.* 4 vols. Chicago: S. J. Clarke Publishing Co., 1921.

Paine, Albert B. *Captain Bill McDonald: Texas Ranger.* New York: J. J. Little and Ives Co., 1909.

Payne, George H. *The Birth of the New Party: Or Progressive Democracy.* New York: n.p., 1912.

Pendleton, W. C. *Political History of Appalachian Virginia.* Dayton, Va.: Shenandoah Press, 1927.

Penick, James, Jr. *Progressive Politics and Conservation.* Chicago: University of Chicago Press, 1968.

Perkins, A. E. *Who's Who in Colored Louisiana.* Baton Rouge: A. E. Perkins Co., 1930.

Perkins, Dexter. *Charles Evans Hughes and American Democratic Statesmanship.* Boston: Little, Brown, 1965.

Porter, Kirk H. and Donald B. Johnson. *National Party Platforms, 1840–1968.* Urbana: University of Illinois Press, 1972.

Price, H. D. *The Negro and Southern Politics: A Chapter in Florida History.* New York: New York University Press, 1957.

Pringle, Henry F. *The Life and Times of William Howard Taft.* 2 vols. New York: Farrar and Rinehart, 1939.

––––––. *Theodore Roosevelt: A Biography.* New York: reprint, Harcourt, Brace, and World, 1956.

Proceedings of the Thirty-ninth Annual Session of the Bar Association of Arkansas Held at Hot Springs, May 1 and 2, 1936. Little Rock: Bar Association of Arkansas, 1936.

Pusey, Merlo J. *Charles Evans Hughes.* 2 vols. New York: Macmillan, 1951.

Rankin, Robert S. *The Government and Administration of North Carolina.* New York: Crowell, 1955.

Reese, J. H. *Florida Flashlights.* Miami: Hefty Press, 1917.

Report of the Louisiana Bar Association, 1918. New Orleans: Louisiana Bar Association, 1919.

Resek, Carl, ed. *The Progressives.* New York: Bobbs-Merrill, 1967.

Rice, Lawrence D. *The Negro in Texas, 1874–1900.* Baton Rouge: Louisiana State University Press, 1971.

Richardson, Elmo R. *The Politics of Conservation: Crusades and Controversies, 1897–1913.* Berkeley: University of California Press, 1962.

Richardson, Rupert N. *Texas: The Lone Star State.* Englewood Cliffs, N.J.: Prentice Hall, 1958.

Robertson, James I., Jr. *The Stonewall Brigade.* Baton Rouge: Louisiana State University Press, 1963.

Robinson, Edgar E. *The Presidential Vote, 1896–1932.* Stanford: Stanford University Press, 1934.

Robison, Daniel M. *Bob Taylor and the Agrarian Revolt in Tennessee.* Chapel Hill: University of North Carolina Press, 1935.

Roseboom, Eugene. *A History of Presidential Elections.* New York: Macmillan, 1959.

Rosewater, Victor. *Backstage in 1912: The Inside Story of the Republican Convention.* Philadelphia: Dorrance, 1932.

Rowland, Dunbar. *Encyclopaedia of Mississippi History.* 2 vols. Madison, Wis.: S. A. Bryant, 1907.

Russell, Thomas H. *The Political Battle of 1912.* New York: n.p., 1912.

Schlesinger, Arthur M., ed. *History of American Presidential Elections.* 4 vols. New York: Chelsea House, 1971.

Schuyler, Robert L., ed. *Dictionary of American Biography, Supplement.* 5 vols. New York: Scribners, 1958.

Sellers, James B. *The Prohibition Movement in Alabama, 1702–1943.* Chapel Hill: University of North Carolina Press, 1943.

Shadgett, Olive H. *The Republican Party in Georgia from Reconstruction through 1900.* Athens: University of Georgia Press, 1964.

Sherman, Richard B. *The Republican Party and Black America from McKinley to Hoover, 1896–1933.* Charlottesville: University of Virginia Press, 1973.

Smith, Samuel D. *The Negro in Congress.* Chapel Hill: University of North Carolina Press, 1940.

Standard History of Georgia and Georgians, A. 6 vols. Chicago: Lewis Publishing Co., 1917.

Stephens, A. Ray. *The Taft Ranch: A Principality.* Austin: The University of Texas Press, 1964.

Stoddard, H. L. *As I Knew Them.* New York: Harper and Brothers, 1927.

Tatum, Elbert W. *The Changed Political Thought of the Negro, 1915–1945.* New York: Exposition Press, 1951.

Taussig, F. W. *The Tariff History of the United States.* New York: reprint, Capricorn Books, 1964.

Tebeau, Carleton W. *A History of Florida.* Coral Gables: University of Miami Press, 1971.

Terral, Rufus. *Newell Sanders: A Biography.* Kingsport, Tenn.: Kingsport Press, 1935.

Texas Almanac, 1961–1962, The. Dallas: Dallas Morning News, 1962.

Texas Almanac, 1964–1965, The. Dallas: Dallas Morning News, 1965.

Thomas, David Y. *Arkansas and Its People.* 4 vols. New York: American Historical Society, 1930.

Thomas, Maurice C. and Mrs. Grant Williams, eds. *Report of the Proceedings of the Seventy-first Annual Session of the Georgia Bar Association . . . 1954.* Macon: Georgia Bar Association, 1954.

Tindall, George B. *The Emergence of the New South, 1913–1945.* Baton Rouge: Louisiana State University Press, 1967.

————. *The Persistent Tradition in New South Politics.* Baton Rouge: Louisiana State University Press, 1975.

Tribute To Harry King Cochran. N.p., n.d. Copy in Arkansas History Commission, Little Rock.

Troup, Cornelius V. *Distinguished Negro Georgians.* Dallas, Tex.: Royal Publishing Co., 1962.

Tyler, Lyon G. *Men of Mark in Virginia.* 5 vols. Washington, D.C.: Men of Mark Publishing Co., 1906.

Wallace, David D. *South Carolina: A Short History, 1520–1948.* Chapel Hill: University of North Carolina Press, 1951.

Walters, Everett. *Joseph Benson Foraker: Uncompromising Republican.* Columbus: Ohio History Press, 1948.

Walton, Hanes, Jr. *The Negro in Third Party Politics.* Philadelphia: Dorrance, 1969.

Warner, Hoyt L. *Progressivism in Ohio, 1897–1917.* Columbus: Ohio State University Press, 1964.

Warrock-Richardson Maryland, Virginia, and North Carolina Almanac for the Year 1917. Richmond: Warrock-Richardson Publishing Co., 1918.

Watson, Margaret. *Greenwood County Sketches.* Greenwood, S.C.: Attic Press, 1970.

Webb, Walter P., ed. *The Handbook of Texas.* 2 vols. Austin: Texas State Historical Association, 1952.

Wharton, Vernon L. *The Negro in Mississippi, 1865–1890.* New York: reprint, Harper and Row, 1965.

Wheaton, Augusta A. *The Negro from 1863 to 1963.* New York: Vantage Press, 1963.

White, William Allen. *Autobiography.* New York: Macmillan, 1946.

_____. *A Puritan in Babylon: The Story of Calvin Coolidge.* New York: Macmillan, 1938.

Who Was Who in America, 1897–1942. Chicago: A. N. Marquis Co., 1942.

Who Was Who in America, 1949–1950. Chicago: A. N. Marquis Co., 1950.

Who Was Who in America, 1951–1953. Chicago: A. N. Marquis Co., 1953.

Who Was Who in America, 1961–1968. Chicago: A. N. Marquis Co., 1968.

Who's Who in Alabama, 1939–1940. Birmingham: Who's Who Publishing Co., 1940.

Who's Who in America, 1912–1913. Chicago: A. N. Marquis Co., 1912.

Who's Who in America, 1930–1931. Chicago: A. N. Marquis Co., 1930.

Who's Who in America, 1936–1937. Chicago: A. N. Marquis Co., 1936.

Who's Who in America, 1938–1939. Chicago: A. N. Marquis Co., 1938.

Who's Who in Colored America, 1930–1931–1932. Brooklyn, N.Y.: Who's Who in Colored America Corp., 1933.

Who's Who in Little Rock, 1921. Little Rock: Who's Who Publishing Co., 1921.

Who's Who in the South, 1926–1927. Chicago: A. N. Marquis Co., 1927.

Wilensky, Norman M. *Conservatives in the Progressive Era: The Taft Republicans of 1912.* Gainesville: University of Florida Press, 1965.

Wilson, Charles H. *God! Make Me a Man: A Biographical Sketch of Dr. Sidney Dillon Redmond.* Boston: Meador Publishing Co., 1925.

Winkler, Ernest W. *Platforms of Political Parties in Texas.* Austin: The University of Texas, 1916.

Woodward, C. Vann. *Origins of the New South, 1877–1913.* Baton Rouge: Louisiana State University Press, 1951.

_____. *The Strange Career of Jim Crow.* New York: reprint, Oxford University Press, 1974.

_____. *Tom Watson: Agrarian Rebel.* New York: reprint, Oxford University Press, 1963.

World Almanac and Encyclopaedia, 1913. New York: Press Publishing Co., 1913.

World Almanac and Encyclopaedia, 1914. New York: Press Publishing Co., 1914.

World Almanac and Encyclopaedia, 1915. New York: Press Publishing Co., 1915.

Zucker, Norman L. *George W. Norris: Gentle Knight of American Democracy.* Urbana: University of Illinois Press, 1966.

Articles and Periodicals

Casdorph, Paul D. "The Bogus Delegation to the 1860 Republican National Convention." *Southwestern Historical Quarterly* 65:4 (April 1962): 480–86.

_____. "Governor William E. Glasscock and Theodore Roosevelt's 1912 Bull Moose Candidacy." *West Virginia History* 28:1 (October 1966): 8–15.

_____. "Norris Wright Cuney and Texas Republican Politics, 1883–1896." *Southwestern Historical Quarterly* 68:4 (April 1965): 455–64.

_____. "The 1912 Republican Presidential Campaign in Mississippi." *Journal of Mississippi History* 33:1 (February 1971): 1–19.

Clayton, Bruce L. "An Intellectual in Politics: William Garrott Brown and the Idea of a Two Party South." *North Carolina Historical Review* 62:3 (July 1965): 319–34.

Colliers Magazine, April 6, 13, May 4, 25, June 1, 1912.

Creekmore, Pollyana. "A Bibliography of the Writings of Samuel Cole Williams." East Tennessee Historical Society *Publications* 20 (1948): 9–15.

Dillard, Tom. "To the Back of the Elephant: Racial Conflict in the Arkansas Republican Party." *Arkansas Historical Quarterly* 33:1 (Spring 1974): 3–15.

Fink, Paul M. "Samuel Cole Williams." East Tennessee Historical Society *Publications* 20 (1948): 3–8.

Fishel, Leslie H., Jr. "The Negro in Northern Politics, 1870–1900." *Mississippi Valley Historical Review* 42:3 (December 1955): 466–89.

Garraty, John A. "TR on the Telephone." *American Heritage* 3:1 (December 1957): 99–108.

Gatewood, Willard B. "Theodore Roosevelt and Arkansas, 1901–1912." *Arkansas Historical Quarterly* 22:1 (Spring 1973): 3–24.

Gould, Lewis L. "New Perspectives on the Republican Party, 1877–1913." *American Historical Review* 74:4 (October 1972): 1074–82.

―――. "Theodore Roosevelt, William Howard Taft, and the Disputed Delegates in 1912: Texas as a Test Case." *Southwestern Historical Quarterly* 80:1 (July 1976): 33–56.

Grantham, Dewey. "Dinner at the White House: Theodore Roosevelt, Booker T. Washington, and the South." *Tennessee Historical Quarterly* 17:2 (July 1958): 112–30.

Green, George N. "Republicans, Bull Moose, and Negroes in Florida, 1912." *Florida Historical Quarterly* 43:2 (October 1964): 153–64.

Hahn, Harlan. "The Republican Party Convention of 1912 and the Role of Herbert S. Hadley in National Politics." *Missouri Historical Review* 59:4 (July 1965): 407–23.

Ickes, Harold L. "Who Killed the Progressive Party?" *American Historical Review* 36:2 (January 1941): 306–37.

Lacy, Eric R. "Tennessee Teetotalism: Social Forces and the Politics of Progressivism." *Tennessee Historical Quarterly* 24:3 (Fall 1965): 219–40.

Ledbetter, Cal, Jr. "Jeff Davis and the Politics of Combat." *Arkansas Historical Quarterly* 33:1 (Spring 1974): 16–37.

Link, Arthur S. "Correspondence Relating to the Progressive Party's 'Lily White' Policy in 1912." *Journal of Southern History* 12:4 (November 1944): 480–90.

―――. "The Progressive Movement in the South, 1870–1914." *North Carolina Historical Review* 23:2 (April 1946): 172–95.

―――. "Theodore Roosevelt and the South in 1912." *North Carolina Historical Review* 23:3 (July 1946): 313–24.

McKinney, Gordon B. "Southern Mountain Republicans and the Negro, 1865–1900." *Journal of Southern History* 61:4 (November 1975): 493–516.

Nation, The. June 10,1880.

Patterson, Michael S. "The Fall of a Bishop: James Cannon, Jr. versus Carter Glass, 1909–1934." *Journal of Southern History* 39:4 (November 1973): 493–518.

Pringle, Henry F. "Theodore Roosevelt and the South." *Virginia Quarterly Review* 9:1 (January 1933): 1–25.

Queener, Verton M. "The East Tennessee Republicans as a Minority Party, 1870–1896." East Tennessee Historical Society *Publications* 15 (1943): 49–73.

———. "The East Tennessee Republican Party, 1900–1914." East Tennessee Historical Society *Publications* 22 (1950): 94–127.

Russell, Marvin F. "The Rise of a Republican Leader: Harmon L. Remmel." *Arkansas Historical Quarterly* 36:3 (Autumn 1977): 234–57.

Scheiner, Seth M. "President Theodore Roosevelt and the Negro, 1901–1908." *Journal of Negro History* 67:3 (July 1962): 169–82.

Smith, Howard W. "The Progressive Party and the Election of 1912 in Alabama." *Alabama Review* 9:1 (January 1956): 5–21.

Steelman, Joseph F. "Republicanism in North Carolina: John Motley Morehead's Campaign to Revive a Moribund Party, 1908–1910." *North Carolina Historical Review* 62:2 (April 1965): 153–68.

———. "Richmond Pearson, Roosevelt Republicans, and the Campaign of 1912 in North Carolina." *North Carolina Historical Review* 63:2 (Spring 1966): 122–39.

Thornbrough, Emma Lou. "The Brownsville Episode and the Negro Vote." *Mississippi Valley Historical Review* 44:3 (December 1957): 469–93.

Tinsley, James A. "Roosevelt, Foraker, and the Brownsville Affray." *Journal of Negro History* 41:1 (January 1956): 43–65.

Unpublished Sources

Casdorph, Paul D. "Texas Delegations to Republican National Conventions, 1860–1896." M.A. thesis, The University of Texas, 1961.

Crawford, Sidney R. "The Poll Tax." M.A. thesis, University of Arkansas, 1944.

Cripps, Thomas R. "The Lily White Republicans, the Negro, the Party, and the South in the Progressive Era." Ph.D. dissertation, University of Maryland, 1967.

Detzer, David W. "The Politics of the Payne-Aldrich Tariff of 1909." Ph.D. dissertation, University of Connecticut, 1970.

Ellis, Billie J. "Cecil A. Lyon, the Practical Politician." Senior Honors Essay, The University of Texas, 1973.

Evans, Edith S. "The Progressive Party in Tennessee, 1912." M.A. thesis, University of Tennessee, 1933.

Fain, James H. "Political Disfranchisement of the Negro in Arkansas." M.A. thesis, University of Arkansas, 1961.

Gable, John A. "The Bull Moose Years: Theodore Roosevelt and the Progressive Party, 1912–1916." Ph.D. dissertation, Brown University, 1972.

Goodwin, Paul G. "Theodore Roosevelt: The Politics of his Candidacy, 1904, 1912." D.S.S. dissertation, Syracuse University, 1961.

Gould, Alan B. "Secretary of the Interior Walter L. Fisher and the Return to Constructive Conservation: Problems and Policies of the Conservation Movement, 1909–1913." Ph.D. dissertation, West Virginia University, 1969.

Graves, John W. "The Arkansas Negro and Segregation, 1890–1903." M.A. thesis, University of Arkansas, 1967.

Harris, David Allen. "Racists and Reformers: A Study of Progressivism in Alabama, 1896–1911." Ph.D. dissertation, University of North Carolina, 1967.

Hathorn, Guy R. "The Political Career of C. Bascom Slemp." Ph.D. dissertation, Duke University, 1950.

Merrill, Milton R. "Reed Smoot: Apostle in Politics." Ph.D. dissertation, Columbia University, 1950.

Needham, David. "William Howard Taft, the Negro, and the White South." Ph.D. dissertation, University of Georgia, 1970.

Phillips, Benjamin S. "Administration of Governor Parker." M.A. thesis, Louisiana State University, 1933.

Schott, Matthew J. "John M. Parker and the Bull Moose Progressive Party in State and Nation." M.A. thesis, Tulane University, 1960.

Scott, Anne F. "The Southern Progressives in National Politics, 1906–1916." Ph.D. dissertation, Radcliffe College, 1957.

Simpson, Alexander J., Jr. "George L. Sheldon and the Beginnings of the Lily White Movement in Mississippi, 1909–1932." M.A. thesis, Mississippi State University, 1962.

Warner, Robert M. "Chase S. Osborn and the Progressive Movement." Ph.D. dissertation, University of Michigan, 1957.

Index